OLD DOMINION,
NEW COMMONWEALTH

❖

A HISTORY
OF VIRGINIA
1607–2007

Ronald L. Heinemann

John G. Kolp

Anthony S. Parent Jr.

William G. Shade

OLD DOMINION, NEW COMMONWEALTH

A HISTORY OF
VIRGINIA

1607–2007

UNIVERSITY OF VIRGINIA PRESS

CHARLOTTESVILLE AND LONDON

University of Virginia Press
© 2007 by the Rector and Visitors of the University of Virginia
All rights reserved
Printed in the United States of America on acid-free paper

First published 2007

1 3 5 7 9 8 6 4 2

LIBRARY OF CONGRESS CATALOGING-IN-PUBLICATION DATA
Old Dominion, new commonwealth : a history of
Virginia, 1607–2007 / Ronald L. Heinemann . . . [et al.].
p.   cm.
Includes bibliographical references and index.
ISBN 978-0-8139-2609-4 (cloth : alk. paper)
1. Virginia—History.   I. Heinemann, Ronald L.
F226.O53   2007
975.5—dc22   2006032721

Illustration credits follow index

FOR
SANDRA HEINEMANN,
RUTH KOLP,
MARIAN PARENT,
AND
JAKE, TOMA, AND PIERRE

CONTENTS

MAPS

PREFACE

Four centuries of remarkable history. Site of the first permanent English settlement in the New World. Home of the first representative assembly in America. Landing place of the first Africans in the Chesapeake, whose heirs were among the first to be enslaved on the plantations of British North America. Birthplace of the great generation of founders, who led the Revolution and created a brilliant constitutional order, four of whom were among the first five presidents of the new republic. Mother of presidents. Mother of states. The state whose territory was the scene of much of the critical fighting of the Civil War, whose own son won recognition as this country's most renowned military leader. The Commonwealth of Virginia—the Old Dominion—was without peer in the first two-and-a-half centuries of American history.

But its allegiance to the losing and dying side in the Civil War, as well as its continued promotion of racial discrimination, consigned Virginia to mediocrity for the next century, mired there by a commitment to the Lost Cause that stifled economic and political renewal. Not until the defeat of massive resistance to racial desegregation in the 1960s was the state able to emerge from this malaise. Now with the beginning of a fifth century, Virginia is reclaiming its place among the first rank of states through its economic development and a more visible national leadership: a new commonwealth.

Virginia's history has not been thoroughly treated since the histories by Virginius Dabney and Louis Rubin appeared in the 1970s. Since that time, new scholarship, primarily in the fields of social and economic history, has given just attention to long-neglected minorities, average citizens, and women in the Virginia story. Now, as Virginia celebrates its quadricentennial, this volume provides an up-to-date account, accessible to all Virginians interested in their state's history. Accessibility demands brevity, and although this synthesis of available scholarship is broad, it is not meant to be a comprehensive history of the state.

We have emphasized the major themes that play throughout Virginia history—change and continuity, a conservative political order, race and slavery, economic development, and social divisions—and have related that story to national events. A central theme is the transition of Virginia from the dominant mainstream model of British North American settlement and development (up to 1820) to a defensive, tradition-bound, inward-looking, and different version of American development (1820–1960) and back again to a progressively conservative society in the late twentieth century. The history of Virginia is at times a national story and a regional one as the state's influence changed over time.

Each author addresses the events of a century: Anthony Parent of Wake Forest University discusses the pre-Jamestown era and the seventeenth century; John Kolp of the United States Naval Academy, the eighteenth century; William Shade of Lehigh University, the nineteenth century to the Civil War; and Ronald Heinemann of Hampden-Sydney College, the late nineteenth and twentieth centuries. Professor Heinemann assumed primary editorial responsibility with the assistance of Professor Kolp, but all authors shared their knowledge and evaluations. Bibliographical listings for each chapter refer to the books and articles consulted in writing this history, and the General Bibliography lists general sources used throughout the text. The following shortened citations are used:

AHR   *American Historical Review*
JAH   *Journal of American History*
JSH   *Journal of Southern History*
VMHB   *Virginia Magazine of History and Biography*

Our greatest debt is to the many students of Virginia history who have produced an array of scholarly work on which this volume relies. Responsibility for all material rests with us, but it should be noted that discrepancies within the primary and secondary sources about dates, figures, spellings, and quotations often necessitated a choice based on what appears to be the most accurate and verifiable information. Population figures before the first official census in 1790 are rough estimates.

We appreciate the cogent criticism of Liz Varon, Deborah Van Broekhoven, Lewis Gould, Herb Ershkowitz, Maria Troyanovski, James Moore, Larissa Smith, Karen Snead, Peter Wallenstein, Warren Hofstra, Brent Tarter, and Nelson Lankford, who have read all or portions of the book. Chapters on the eighteenth century benefited from access to the resources of the Nimitz Library at the Naval Academy and the University of Iowa Library and from comments by Laura Kamoie and the Naval

Academy History Department Works-in-Progress Seminar. Thanks to Dale Neighbors of the Library of Virginia and Jeffrey Ruggles of the Virginia Historical Society for their assistance in locating and copying illustrations and to Bill Nelson for his excellent maps. Professor Heinemann is grateful to Hampden-Sydney College for summer grant support and to Jane Holland for secretarial assistance. We have benefited greatly from the editorial advice of Susan Lee Foard, who generously forfeited retirement time to review another work in Virginia history.

OLD DOMINION, NEW COMMONWEALTH

A HISTORY OF VIRGINIA 1607–2007

1

BEFORE VIRGINIA

On the morning of 26 April 1607, three small ships carrying 143 Englishmen arrived off the Virginia coast of North America, having spent four months at sea. The men had come to advance the interests of England in its quest for New World wealth against other European competitors. They intended to build a colonial outpost—a military fort and a commercial trading post—like those that Spain and France had tried to establish along the southeastern coast of North America. These Englishmen had heard tales of the ill-fated Roanoke settlement two decades earlier and knew they would encounter native peoples, but they were confident that their superior English culture and technology would easily win the day over the "heathen savages." All hoped for financial success and perhaps a little adventure; as it turned out, their tiny settlement eventually would evolve from colony into a prominent state in an entirely new nation.

The region they colonized featured a variety of land forms, from coastal plain, to rolling hills, to valleys and mountains. Millions of years before, a massive meteor convulsed the Atlantic coastal plain below the Appalachian Mountains near where the Englishmen first made landfall, creating the largest impact crater in what is now the United States. During the last glacial period, beginning about 18,000 years ago, the ice melt running down the mountains began mixing with the rising seawater below, slowly filling the crater and swelling it into a great bay. As the temperatures warmed, a 3,000-year melt (11,000–8,000 BCE) elevated the water level, submerging sixty miles of coastline and filling in not only the bay but also the river channels. The coastal basin became a giant estuary, the largest on the continent. The freshwater running down from the mountains, which had formed millions of years before the bay, mingled with

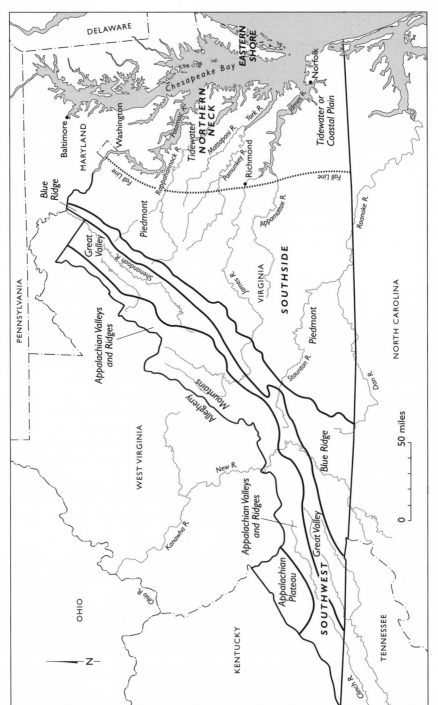

GEOGRAPHICAL REGIONS OF VIRGINIA

the saltwater, forming tidal estuaries that widened with the glacial thaw. The Algonquian speakers called this tidal motion *rappahannock,* and one of the four great rivers in Virginia still carries this name. It and the Potomac, the York, and the James all drain into the bay in a parallel southeasterly direction, creating peninsulas or "necks." Waterfalls and rapids punctuate these rivers at the fall line, separating Tidewater from Piedmont. The soils of the alluvial floodplain are sandy and silt loam, but clay and gravel are found along the streams. From the wet Tidewater soils grow huckleberries, cranberries, and chinquapins. Poplars, pines, cedars, and cypresses rise together with sweet gums, hollies, sweet myrtles, and live oaks.

In the Piedmont above the fall line, where the land rises gently upward to the mountain ridges, the soils are more diverse, ranging from rich black loam to a reddish-brown mixture of dirt and clay. A canopy of deciduous trees graces the Piedmont where twenty species of oaks reign. In their shadows sycamores, silver maples, box elders, and green ashes tussle with black and sweet gums and hickory and beech trees. In their shade wild strawberries and blueberries blossom and bear fruit.

To the west lie the mountain chains of the Appalachians: the Blue Ridge and the Alleghenies divided by the Great Valley of Virginia, which runs northeast to southwest for 360 miles. Its limestone-based soils are among the most fertile in the state. Running northward down the upper half of the Valley is the Shenandoah River, its name an Indian word for "beautiful daughter of the stars." Rivers on the far side of the Alleghenies run westward to the Ohio and Tennessee River basins. The mountain slopes are covered with deciduous and evergreen trees, whose hydrocarbon emissions give the ridges their distinctive blue haze. Throughout Virginia the climate is temperate, ranging from the cooler mountain elevations to the warmer, more humid areas of the Tidewater, with an average rainfall of forty inches a year.

Paleo-Indians entered the region about 12,000 years ago as hunters, fishers, and foragers. With the great melt creating new coastal estuaries and new sources of food, these seminomads of the Archaic Period migrated to the marshlands near the Dismal Swamp. Knowing where to set their weirs in the streams and rivers, the Indians caught herring, striped bass, and sturgeon. They continued to hunt white-tailed deer, as former game like elk and caribou migrated northward in search of a colder climate. About 4,500 years ago as the estuaries began to table off, mixtures of salt and fresh water combined with sea grasses to produce reefs where fish and shellfish became abundant. These reefs became ideal incubators for oysters, which the Indians began harvesting along with clams and mussels. The aboriginal Algonquians called the bay *k'tchisipik* (Chesapeake), the "great shellfish bay."

The Virginia Algonquians of the Early Woodland Period, beginning about 5,000 years ago, comfortably exploited this ecosystem for food and freshwater, which was essential when living alongside the brackish estuaries. Like their ancestors, they were hunters, foragers, and fishers, who knew the best sources and seasons for procuring food. They tracked smaller animals than their ancestors had—beavers, possums, rabbits, raccoons, and squirrels—and trapped turtles and snakes and shot migrating turkeys and ducks with bow and arrow. They harvested shellfish and fished creeks, streams, and rivers for catfish, gar, golden shiner, yellow bullhead, and pumpkinseed.

Unlike their ancestors, they eventually became farmers about a millennium ago by cultivating wild grains, amaranth, gourds, and sunflowers. By 900 CE or so, they had applied their experience with domesticating wild plants to the cultivation of corn, beans, squash, and tobacco. The seed corn apparently came from Mexico, providing convincing evidence of long-distance contact with other aboriginals. By the Late Woodland Period (900–1500 CE), the Virginia Algonquians had founded towns on the alluvial soil of the Tidewater. Because corn depletes the soil of nitrogen, they periodically shifted their farms up or down Virginia's major rivers. After 1400 they increased their supply of oysters, roasting and drying them for later use, adding one more ingredient to their relatively stable subsistence economy.

Indian cultures also developed in the mountains and valleys of western Virginia. The Mississippian people migrated to Virginia from the Tennessee River area around 700 CE, while Ohio Valley groups migrated up the New River. From about 950 CE until the Europeans settlers arrived, a group known as the Earthen Mound Burial Culture lived in the Shenandoah Valley and the northern Piedmont region of Virginia. Their mounds were sacred places where they buried their ancestors. The English may have encountered two tribes that were members of this culture: the Mannahoacs, near the upper Rappahannock River, and the Monacans at the falls of the James River, both of whom spoke a Siouan language, rather than the Iroquoian languages of the Indians living south of the James River or the Algonquian languages of the coastal tribes. By the time the settlers moved into the Piedmont and the Shenandoah Valley, disease had severely reduced the population of these inland tribes.

The need for farmers, foragers, and hunters led to both seasonal and gendered divisions of labor. The Virginia Algonquians divided their year into five seasons: *popanow* (winter), *cattapeuk* (early spring), *cohattayonough* (late spring), *nepinough* (summer), and *taquitock* (fall). During the cold months of popanow, men hunted migrating fowl and women gathered dry reeds and fibrous plants for matting used for building houses. During the spring months of cattapeuk and cohattayonough, men set their traps and weirs for spawning fish. Women gathered sapling and bark suitable for mat making. As men went off to hunt after the spring harvest and during taquitock, the time of the falling leaf, women foraged. Women also took on the responsibility for the crops on fields that men had cleared with slash-and-burn techniques. Women cultivated the corn, harvesting green corn, the year's first crop, during cohattayonough and mature maize during nepinough. Because the corn required a four-month growing season with adequate rainfall, drought brought dire consequences for their main dietary staple. To supplement the corn crop during these uncertain times, women foraged for tuckahoes, starchy edible tubers, in freshwater marshes during the cattapeuk and cohattayonough seasons. During the late fall taquitock season, the men hunted white-tailed deer, which women dressed. All prized its venison, both fresh and dried, for sustenance, its hide for clothing, and its bones for tools. Indians used their environment; they did not abuse it, knowing that their survival as well as their relationships with nature depended upon its preservation.

The Virginia Algonquians occupied 6,000 square miles of coastal plain that they called Tsenacommacah. Their land was bounded by the bay in the east, the fall line in the west, the Potomac River in the north, and the James River basin in the south. Hemmed in by the Appalachian Mountains and by Siouan and Iroquoian enemies and without access to a major artery feeding into the Mississippi or the St. Lawrence River valleys, the Virginia Algonquians began to develop an insular, cohesive culture. This culture can be discerned in religious beliefs, pottery styles, political organization, marriage patterns, burial rites, and housing and palisade construction.

The Virginia Algonquians believed in *mantoac*, a cosmology of deities with a diversity of powers over a sacred universe. Priests engaged in divination, appealing to animistic powers for protection in a natural world fraught with danger. Their propitiations to these deities were ritualized in ceremonies devoted to the harvest, the hunt, and war. At pow-wows they entreated rain deities to favor farmers, forest deities to shield hunters from harm, and river deities to protect travelers. Warriors girded themselves for battle amid chants for victory. Priests aided in judicial procedures, determining truth by reading minds. They also prophesied important events and conjured up natural phenomena to deal with invaders. Only priests and chiefs could enter temples, which were mortuaries for the relics of chiefs, caches of treasures, armories for weapons, and stores of healing herbs. The holiest site in Tsenacommacah was the temple at Uttamussak on the Pamunkey River.

If men could serve as priests, assuming the mantle of spiritual power, women celebrated material culture by crafting ceramics. During the Late

Woodland Period, women artisans shaped, coiled, and decorated pots tempered by shells that they used for everyday household chores. After 1550, however, a shift in ceramic styles suggests a growing cultural and economic integration of the entire Chesapeake region. While pottery glazed with crushed quartz or tempered sand now became the norm, innovators in specific locations developed at least three distinct styles that can be identified by archaeologists today: Potomac Creek, Gaston-Cashie, and Roanoke.

Pottery trade and marriages between Indian groups in the region added to the cultural exchanges and helped cement diplomatic and political alliances that became critical to the development of a large coalition on the eve of English colonization. It was not the presence of European explorers or depopulation from European disease that influenced the move toward consolidation. The Virginia Algonquians combined into a paramount chiefdom—the Powhatans—after 1570 in response to the threats posed by Siouans in the west and Iroquoians in the north. The Massawomecks, an Iroquoian-speaking people, raided Algonquian villages along the Potomac River in their swift birch canoes. Iroquoian Susquehannocks harassed Algonquians living on the northern banks of

ALGONQUIAN INDIAN, BY WENCELAUS HOLLAR

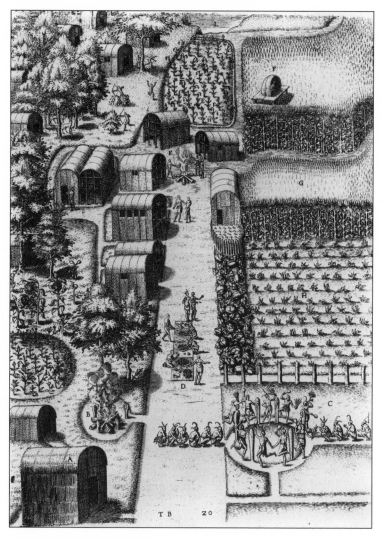

SECOTA INDIAN VILLAGE, BY JOHN WHITE AND THEODOR DE BRY

the Potomac. Siouan Monacans and Mannahoacs regularly raided Algonquian villages in the summer or fall for wives and slaves.

To ward off these hostile attacks, the Powhatans constructed and fortified towns. Using stone hatchets, they shaped and set poles to build palisades, which were closely latticed with branches and small saplings to shield dwellers from both visibility and arrows. The strategic location of these towns, overlooking the river networks for trading and defensive purposes, gives evidence of the consolidation into chiefdoms. Most towns accommodated fewer than one hundred people; but larger sites included Powhatan near the James River falls, Patawomeck near the bend in the Potomac River, and Werowocomoco on the York River.

Powhatan consolidation was also designed to control trade routes that would bring them high-status goods. From their home bases at the fall line of the James River, they guarded traffic on rivers and roads and controlled the copper, puccoon, and shell trades within Tsenacommacah. Indicative of high status, copper was esteemed by Virginia Algonquians. They treasured the reddish-colored metal imported from the Great Lakes and the Appalachians through Siouan-speaking Mannahoacs and Monacans to the west or the Iroquoian-speaking Tuscaroras to the southeast. Monacans had been the chief suppliers of copper to the Powhatans; but when relations soured between them, the Powhatans turned to the Tuscaroras for copper. Jewelers fashioned tubular beads and flat sheets of copper into necklaces, pendants, bracelets, chokers, earrings, and chimes or "tinklers."

Virginia Algonquians also esteemed the mulberry-colored dyes extracted from the puccoon root. They imported puccoon from the Iroquoian-speaking Nottoways and Tuscaroras to the south. The chiefs' wives ceremonially painted their necks and faces with puccoon dye, vaunting their elevated position in society. Women provided to very important visitors readied themselves for their assignations with the reddish dye.

Mollusks were also important trade goods, serving Algonquian society not only as a food source but also as ornaments and currency. Powhatans valued the freshwater pearls harvested in the James River at Weyanoke Point and exchanged *rawranoke* (roanoke) shells as money. Harvesters dredged seacoasts for the tubular conch shells and white and dark blue disks of hard clams, prizing the rarer blue. Artisans crafted these shells into pendants, necklaces, and burial masks. Regular, uninterrupted access to copper, puccoon, and crustaceans remained an important impetus for political confederation.

The development of the paramount chiefdom was the key political development in the Late Woodland Period. A kinship-based society, Algonquian groups organized themselves into chiefdoms governed by a *weroance* (male) or by a *weroansqua* (female) under the umbrella of the paramount chief or *mamanatowic*. In a matrilineal society where descent is passed down on the mother's side of the family, Powhatan women enjoyed higher status than did their counterparts in English society. Men were, however, allowed more than one wife. The weroances were assisted in their governance by a council of elders. Each weroance in turn pledged loyalty and offered counsel to the mamanatowic. Contrary to the usual tributary order, the mamanatowic gave gifts to the weroances for their allegiance. But the weroances and mamanatowic also received tribute from their subjects in the form of foodstuffs, skins, and luxury goods and held these in common storehouses for use by their own families and for religious ceremonies and other communal activities.

Wahunsonacock, born about 1540, inherited three districts on the James River and three districts on the Pamunkey River. Becoming the

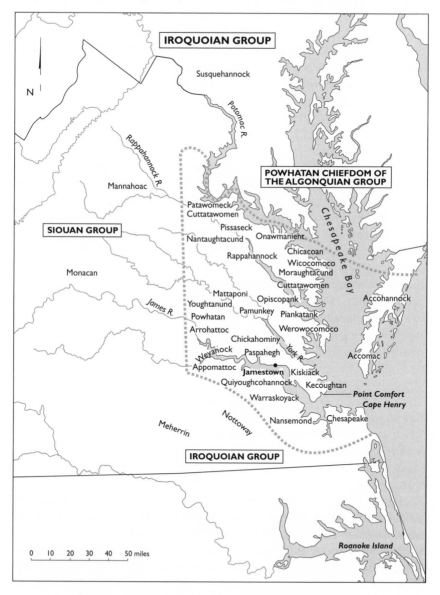

INDIAN TRIBES OF SEVENTEENTH-CENTURY VIRGINIA

mamanatowic about 1572, he took the name Powhatan from his ancestral
home near present-day Richmond on the James River. By the time the
English arrived in 1607, he had expanded his hegemony to include thirty
districts covering 6,000 square miles and 14,000 of the 20,000 Algonquian
speakers in the eastern Tidewater. Only the Chickahominies to the south
and the Patawomecks to the north managed to maintain their autonomy.
The Chickahominies shielded the Powhatans from the Monacans, their
traditional enemy; and the Patawomecks buffered Tsenacommacah from
the Iroquoian-speaking Susquehannocks. The Patawomecks also controlled an antimony mine which produced a widely traded silver-white
substance used like puccoon as decorative body and facial paint that the
Powhatans highly valued. (See map on p. 9.)

The Chesapeakes, who inhabited what are now Virginia Beach and
the Elizabeth River sites of Norfolk and Portsmouth, were the last to fall
to Powhatan expansion. Covetous of the coastal shell trade, Wahunsonacock or Powhatan pressed them to join the paramount chiefdom; but
they refused, causing bad feeling between the two groups. Although Algonquian, they were more closely related to the Roanokes in North Carolina than to the Powhatans. Indeed, in an effort to shore up their defense
in the face of the Powhatan menace, the Roanokes may have loaned them
the remnants of the "Lost Colony." Enmity intensified with a prophecy
that Powhatan received from the oracles of Uttamussak that a nation
from the Chesapeake Bay would emerge and destroy the Powhatan paramount chiefdom. Partly because of this prophecy and partly because of
their economic significance, Powhatan destroyed the Chesapeakes early
in 1607, perhaps terminating the last link to the Roanoke colony. Meanwhile, the English had arrived in the Chesapeake Bay, fulfilling the pro-
phetic warning.

Years before the English arrived, the Spanish had claimed the Chesapeake
Bay as part of a large North American territory they called La Florida.
Their claim was recognized by the papal bulls issued by Pope Alexander
VI from 1493 to 1495 and the Treaty of Tordesillas with Portugal. Lucas
Vasquez de Ayllón, a Spanish administrator in Santo Domingo, first fired
European enthusiasm about the Chesapeake Bay with his tales of the
"Land of Chicora," a vision of a Mediterranean-like climate similar to
Andalucia in southern Spain where grapes and olives could be fruitfully
grown. Ayllón also promoted Chicora as the location of a Pacific passage
to the China trade. Bolstering his claim, he ventured that the Indians
there could easily be subjected by the Spaniards and could supply them
with gems and pearls.

Searching for a new Andalucia and a westward passage to the Pacific, Ayllón sent expeditions under the command of Pedro de Quejo to the Chesapeake Bay in 1521 and again in 1525. Quejo explored the Outer Banks, the barrier islands that run from southern Virginia to North Carolina. He found neither the westward passage to China nor Chicora. Instead, he determined that the barrier islands' sandy soil and the absence of an exploitable Indian population made the area unsuitable for colonization. From the Outer Banks, Quejo explored the southernmost inlet of the Chesapeake Bay, arriving there on 2 July, the feast day of Mary, the mother of Jesus. For this reason he called his sighting the Bahía de Santa Maria. After the last Ayllón voyage in 1526, Spain ignored the Chesapeake for a generation, realizing that both Chicora and a western passage were myths. During the 1540s and 1550s Spain regarded the Outer Banks and its environs as a desert island, not a new Andalucia.

The Spaniards' indifference did not dampen French desires for American colonies. Giovanni da Verrazano, a Florentine, sponsored by King Francis I of France, voyaged in 1523–24 toward the Chesapeake Bay. Looking across the Outer Banks at the Albemarle and Pamlico sounds, he presumed this body of water to be a passage to the Pacific. Promoting his discovery as a western passage, he christened the land Francesca after King Francis. However, France instead chose to explore a northwest passage, encouraged by reports from cod fishermen in the North Atlantic of a great river on the continent there. In 1534 Francis I sponsored Jacques Cartier's voyage to the St. Lawrence River.

For the remainder of the century, the two European powers continued to sail into the South Atlantic region, largely to keep an eye on possible colonization by the other. Small garrisons were established in the Florida and South Carolina areas. To counter a French outpost, the Spanish established St. Augustine in 1565, the first permanent European settlement in the future United States. When their activity attracted the interest of England, the Spanish renewed efforts to colonize their northern frontier. After hearing the description of Tsenacommacah from two Powhatans picked up by an expedition which had taken refuge from a storm in the Chesapeake Bay in 1561, they believed that this colonization could best be accomplished from the Bahía de Santa Maria. One of the Indians, Paquiquineo, was renamed Don Luis de Velasco, after the viceroy of Mexico.

Lucas Vasquez de Ayllón the younger and Pedro Menéndez de Avilés now planned expeditions to the Chesapeake. Ayllón revived interest in his father's Chicora, but his failure to satisfy his investors ended in his disgrace. Menéndez was more successful. Encouraged by what he learned of the Chesapeake Bay from the Indian informants, Menéndez requested that Don Luis and his companion accompany his expedition. After one unsuccessful attempt, a disappointed Don Luis returned to Seville where he was schooled by the Jesuits. In return for his education, he promised to aid them in establishing a mission in Virginia.

With support from Menéndez for another expedition, the missionaries arrived at Bahía de Santa María on 10 September 1570, disembarking along the James River not far from the later Jamestown site. From there they crossed the peninsula to where Kings Creek feeds the York River. Don Luis and other Indians assisted them in building their base camp, which came to be called Ajacán. However, the Jesuit-trained Algonquian soon abandoned his Christian colleagues and returned to his people. By January 1571 the mission, reduced to privation, sought assistance from Don Luis and the Powhatans, but their request resulted in martyrdom; he had the entire group massacred except for one boy, who was spared by the local weroance. The grisly failure of the mission led Spain to abandon the Chesapeake, leaving an opening for the English.

England's penetration of the New World had been delayed by internal disputes highlighted by Henry VIII's breach with the Catholic Church in Rome and the religious strife under his children, Edward VI and Mary I. The ascendancy of Elizabeth I to the throne in 1558 brought relative calm to the realm, but the growing animosity toward Spain encouraged English interests in a variety of maritime activities. Added to this was a certain envy of the successful and expanding long-distance trade of Holland. Finally, new social and economic pressures caused by a booming rural population and the agricultural enclosure movement that forced migration to crowded cities demanded release. Excited by the stories of discovery, the English looked westward.

Those promoting English exploration and settlement of North America had to convince investors and the queen that these expeditions would return a profit and redound to the glory of England. They emphasized the gold and silver that had made Spain into a world power. They pointed to lessons learned from European exploration literature and experiences in Ireland about how to colonize indigenous peoples and establish trading centers and networks. They painted Spanish political, military, and religious activity in the New World in the worst possible light and offered, instead, a positive alternative of English civility and Protestant Christianity: an English empire.

But for the lure of precious metals, these were precisely the arguments advanced by the Hakluyt cousins. The elder Richard Hakluyt, a lawyer resident at London's Middle Temple, encouraged the English to abandon the model of Roman conquest employed in Ireland; he wrote in 1578 that successful colonization could be achieved with peaceful overtures to the Indians. The colonists should treat them humanely and convert them; then they could count them as dutiful subjects. When confronted with a plurality of Indians in the same place, carefully crafted alliances should be made.

Richard Hakluyt the younger received not only his name from his guardian cousin but also his passion for English colonization. He advocated a systematic approach to navigation, exploration, and settlement. Trained as a minister, Hakluyt promoted Christianity as the primary motive for colonization. He pointed to the abuses in Spanish colonization and projected the English as American liberators who would offer civility and true religion to benighted Indians. Once converted, they would become cooperative, and settlement, trade, and an enduring peace would follow suit. If they resisted, they would be conquered. Hakluyt accepted Allyón's Chicora myth of a new Andalucia: the middle latitudes of North America could provide olive oil, wine, silks, and other semitropical products such as rice and sugar that England now procured from Spain. He recognized America's potential as a refuge for the English poor, a post for attacking Spanish shipping, and a supplier of raw materials. Hakluyt's major work, *The Principal Navigations, Voyages, Traffiques, and Discoveries of the English Nation* (1589), chronicled English activity abroad, introducing the English public to the recent expeditions of Frobisher, Gilbert, and Ralegh.

Searching for a northwest passage, Martin Frobisher's Cathay Company made three voyages from 1576 to 1578. His first voyage established a colony at Baffin Bay in the first English effort at American colonization. He encountered Inuits and kidnapped a family of three who died shortly after arrival in England. He was convinced that a successful settlement could be sustained by gold mining, but when the local ore proved to be fool's gold, the settlement collapsed.

Like Frobisher, Sir Humphrey Gilbert looked for a passage to China, but he also sought a place suitable for a farming settlement where England's poor could be suitably employed for their own good and that of the nation. Yet his violent experience in the Irish war of the 1560s tempered his perspective on colonization. As a military man he understood that the logistics in America differed from those in Ireland. The long-distance supply lines and the numerical superiority of the Indians made peaceful overtures to the natives a prudent strategy. Although he received royal patent rights in 1578 to discover lands, his personal efforts came to nothing when he was lost at sea in 1583 on a return voyage from North America.

Walter Ralegh inherited his half brother Gilbert's patent to explore and exploit the North American coast. One of the most notable of the Elizabethans, Ralegh was a Renaissance man with interests in politics, the arts, history, and adventure, who was to die on the chopping block for suspected treason. But he is best remembered for his association with the Lost Colony. Sensitive to the loss of Gilbert, Queen Elizabeth denied Ralegh permission to command the expedition. Instead, Ralegh sent Philip Amadas and Arthur Barlowe to the Outer Banks of the North Carolina coast in 1584.

The Indians encountered on Roanoke Island were the Carolina Algonquians, who, like the Virginia Algonquians, hunted, fished, and foraged under the authority of weroances while living in farming towns along the riverbanks. They grew corn, beans, squash, and tobacco and celebrated both corn and tobacco in their festivals. At first, relations between the Roanokes and the explorers were cordial. Led by Granganimeo, brother of Roanoke weroance Wingina, the Roanokes welcomed the English, perhaps seeing them as useful allies against sporadic Spanish encroachment. As a sign of friendship, two Indians, Manteo of Croatoan and Wanchese of Roanoke, returned to England with the expedition.

Ralegh's delight in the success of the voyage prompted him to name the new land Virginia after his "virgin queen"; Elizabeth returned the favor by granting him a knighthood. With knowledge gained from the 1584 reconnaissance, Ralegh planned a Virginia colony based upon his experiences in Ireland. Believing that the entry to the Chesapeake Bay lay along the Outer Banks, he began to promote English claims to the region north of 36° and the possibility of a westward passage there. Ralegh selected Richard Grenville to command the expedition and Ralph Lane to govern the settlement. Principal among the explorers were the mathematician Thomas Hariot and the painter John White, both of whom may have been on the first voyage. What we know of the people and the land can be found in White's "Map of Virginia" (1585) and Hariot's *A Brief and True Report of the New Found Land of Virginia* (1588). Elizabeth endorsed the second voyage not only in spirit but materially as well, loaning Ralegh her ship *Tiger*, which along with six other ships set sail 9 April 1585 with 600 passengers. One-half were soldiers and sailors, most with military experience in Ireland or the Netherlands. Their efforts were hamstrung at their arrival when the *Tiger* wrecked on the shoals and nearly sank, ruining most of the colonists' food supply.

In early July, Grenville established the Roanoke colony at the north end of the island near Wingina's town; however, it soon became apparent that this would not be a good site for a future port because of shallow waters. Grenville soon departed for England, leaving Lane and 107 men to live off the munificence of the Indians. They built a palisade to serve as a refuge for settlers in case of attack from sea and to secure livestock at night. They began brick making but dug no wells, relying instead on rainfall or assistance from the natives in locating freshwater. The English also made no preparations for their subsistence and continually made demands on the Roanokes to supply them with corn. Under normal conditions the Indians might have complied, but their surpluses were limited because the area was experiencing one of the worst droughts in nearly 800 years. Despite their growing dependency on the Roanokes, Lane and his colleagues treated them as inferiors, not equals, and overreacted when an English silver cup disappeared. Finding the home village of the alleged thieves abandoned, the English retaliated by burning another village and spoiling their corn. This was not the approach to indigenous peoples that Gilbert and others had recommended, but it fit well with the experiences and attitudes of men like Ralegh.

In search of a better harbor with deeper water, Lane sent out scouting expeditions that ventured into the Pamlico and Albemarle sounds and the Chesapeake Bay. Lane personally explored the Chowan and Roanoke rivers. Amadas, Hariot, and White reached the Chesapeake Bay and wintered in what is now Norfolk. Their survey of the bay was covered up on their return to England, so as not to alert the French or Spanish, whose interest in the region was renewed by fears of the English establishing a base for piracy. The New World had become a potential battleground in Spain's quest for European domination.

Initially, the Carolina Algonquians viewed the newcomers as an especially powerful foreign tribe who could bring good or evil to their society. The English possessed large supplies of precious copper that might be obtained through friendly trading. And too, the strange men from across the sea had ships and weapons that might be useful against the Roanokes' traditional enemies. But the Algonquians also had no immunity from European diseases; and within days of Englishmen visiting their towns, the Indians began dying at a very high rate. Indians and English both believed that the power of the English god had been demonstrated in this mysterious killing of people without weapons. Making death and supplying copper demonstrated the power of the English mantoac. But if the Roanokes were at first awestruck by the English presence, they quickly became disenchanted with the newcomers, put off by their demands for gold and corn and by their heavy-handed tactics in the reaction to the stolen chalice.

When the friendly Granganimeo died, Wingina changed his name to Pemisapan, meaning "one who watches over his people," signaling a change of attitude toward the English. Now believing that death and drought were brought on by the English presence, Pemisapan decided to separate his Roanoke people from them. Using the wealth generated from his control of the copper trade, Pemisapan began making allies to drive out the English, but in a skirmish he was killed and beheaded. Shortly afterward, ships of Sir Francis Drake, who had been raiding Spanish ships and harbors, arrived at Roanoke. Seeing the plight of the settlement, Drake provided provisions and offered passage home, an offer that Governor Lane and the demoralized colonists readily accepted.

Ralegh's third expedition in 1587 differed from the earlier ventures in that this group included ninety-four colonists organized in fourteen families. It had the goal of establishing a colony separate from Roanoke in the Chesapeake Bay, an area the new governor, John White, had reconnoitered two years earlier. The vessels left London in March and arrived at Roanoke in July 1587 where the Spanish captain refused to go any farther. What they found disheartened them. The fort erected by Lane had been abandoned and was in disrepair. The fifteen soldiers left to safeguard it were not to be found, save for a single skeleton found on the settlement grounds. If the skeleton served as a bad omen, the birth of the first English child born in America, on 18 August 1587, augured a fortuitous outcome for this new venture. White's grandchild was christened Virginia Dare, her name expressing the hope that a colony of that name would become a reality. Manteo's Croatoans warily offered friendship but cautioned the English that they had no corn to supply them, at which point White returned to England to lobby for further support. War with Spain, however, deterred any immediate efforts at resupply; and White did not return until 1590, only to discover a deserted settlement and the word "Croatoan" carved into a tree. The fate of the Lost Colony is unclear, but it is possible that the colonists abandoned Roanoke and were taken in by either the Chesapeakes or the Chowanocs, both of whom were later annihilated by Powhatan. The failure of Roanoke delayed the exploration of Virginia for another sixteen years.

SOURCES CONSULTED

Philip Curtin, Grace S. Brush, and George W. Fisher, eds. *Discovering the Chesapeake: History of an Ecosystem* (2001); Keith Egloff and Deborah Woodward, *First People: The Early Indians of Virginia* (1992); Frederic Gleach, *Powhatan's World and Colonial Virginia* (1997); Paul Hoffman, *A New Andalucia and a Way to the Orient: The American Southeast during the Sixteenth Century* (1990); Hoffman, *Spain and the Roanoke Voyages* (1987); James Horn, *A Land as God Made It: Jamestown and the Birth of America* (2005); Harry Kelsey, *Sir Francis Drake, the Queen's Pirate* (1998); Karen Ordahl Kupperman, *Roanoke: The Abandoned Colony* (1984); Eugene Lyon, *The Enterprise of Florida: Pedro Menéndez de Avilés and the Spanish Conquest of 1565–1568* (1979); Peter Mancall, ed., *Envisioning America: English Plans for the Colonization of North America, 1580–1640* (1995); Debra Meyers and Melanie Perreault, eds., *Colonial Chesapeake: New Perspectives* (2005); Lee Miller, *Roanoke: Solving the Mystery of England's Lost Colony* (2000); Michael Oberg, *Dominion and Civility: English Imperialism and Native America, 1585–1685* (1999); David B. Quinn, *North America from the Earliest Discovery to First Settlements: The Norse Voyages to 1612* (1977); Helen C.

Rountree, *Pocahontas, Powhatan, Opechancanough: Three Indian Lives Changed by Jamestown* (2005); Rountree, *Powhatan Foreign Relations, 1500–1722* (1993); Rountree, *The Powhatan Indians of Virginia: Their Traditional Culture* (1989); Helen C. Rountree and E. Randolph Turner, *Before and after Jamestown: Virginia's Powhatans and Their Predecessors* (2002); Camilla Townsend, *Pocahontas and the Powhatan Dilemma* (2004); Peter H. Wood, Gregory A. Waselkov, and M. Thomas Hatley, eds., *Powhatan's Mantle: Indians in the Colonial Southeast* (1989).

2

ATLANTIC OUTPOST

1607–1650

The founding of Jamestown in 1607 was no sure thing. The Roanoke failures, competition with other Atlantic powers, opposition from native peoples, a lack of available funds, and problems of enticing prospective settlers to risk their lives in a questionable venture challenged the most enthusiastic promoters. And throughout the early settlement these problems bedeviled this Atlantic outpost, risking its success. In time, luck, leadership, perseverance, and tobacco won the day.

Despite the debacle of the Lost Colony, Richard Hakluyt, who had been a direct link to the Roanoke experiment, kept the dream of Virginia alive. His persistent agitation and promotion led to the chartering of the Virginia Company of London in April 1606 to found a colony to compete with the Spanish, find a western route to the Indies, and proselytize the natives. Authority was placed in the hands of a council, which had full power to supervise the venture. A subsidiary resident council would carry out its orders in the colony. This was a business organization; and the investors, who included high government officials and London merchants, pursued a profit that they hoped would come from locating precious metals, just as the Spanish had done in Mexico and Peru, then from the Indian trade, and finally from finding a passage to the China Sea. If all else failed, the colony could pay for itself with the production of glass and iron, potash for fertilizers, and pitch and tar for naval stores. A second company, the Plymouth Company, was chartered to colonize the northern half of the Virginia region, which extended from the Cape Fear River to Maine, but its efforts would prove unsuccessful.

To attract settlers, the Virginia Company promoted Virginia as a refuge and land of fortune for England's burgeoning population, which had increased 25 percent from 1570 to 1600. The enclosure movement that had forced peasants off ancestral lands to make way for sheep had exacerbated the poverty of the English people, swelling the populations of cities and inciting disorder. They were prime targets for exploration literature. As an added incentive, colonists were guaranteed all English liberties as if they were still at home.

Hakluyt advised the expedition to Virginia not to offend the "naturals" because the colony would depend on their sufferance to survive. This goal could be accomplished by bringing Protestant Christianity, English civility, and happiness to the unfortunate Indians. The council instructed Captain Christopher Newport, who was to command the mission, to seek out ways to govern these natives so that their trade, labor, and gold could be exploited by the company.

Unlike the last Roanoke expedition, which never made it to its intended Chesapeake destination, this one included neither females nor families. Acting on the intelligence gathered by the 1585 Roanoke expedition, the company sent to the Chesapeake Bay a party of 144 adventurers, laborers, artisans, and crew members, all but one of whom survived the voyage. Newport piloted the four-month voyage of the *Susan Constant, Godspeed,* and *Discovery* through the West Indies to the Chesapeake Bay. He had distinguished himself as a privateer for thirteen years in the West Indies and even had scouted the bay sometime early in the 1590s. No stranger to violence, he believed the settlement's survival would depend more on force than on conversion of the natives. A clash of arms was inevitable.

The colonists made landfall near Cape Henry on 26 April 1607. Indians promptly attacked, wounding two. Undeterred, the Englishmen explored the lands and waters of today's Hampton Roads and then sailed up the river where they had made first camp, naming it the James in honor of the king. They explored it to the mouth of the Appomattox River, visiting chiefdoms and surveying the region before returning to their Point Comfort encampment. During their surveillance they met Pochins, Powhatan's brother at Kecoughtan, and Wowinchopunck, weroance of the Paspaheghs, lords of the environ that became known as Jamestown Island, which was actually a peninsula jutting into the James River.

Point Comfort, where the confluence of the James, Nansemond, and Elizabeth rivers enters the Chesapeake, was hardly an ideal location for a fort. Not only was it indefensible and pestilential, but it also lacked natural resources, especially fresh water. The Powhatans could lay siege and starve them out or attack them in their vulnerable habitation; Spanish ships could attack them from the sea, a potential threat the colonists feared for the next twenty years. Jamestown Island, on the other hand, could provide them with a Gibraltar-like defense against Spanish and

Indian attackers. Its upriver location, off the beaten path of the Gulf Stream, made it difficult to find; its islandlike feature offered a natural moat, dissuading Indian attackers; and the depth of water there allowed oceangoing ships to moor, facilitating supply and troop deployment. Yet it, too, suffered from an absence of fresh water and was plagued by marshy ground that bred mosquitoes. Nonetheless, Jamestown was selected; and the crew turned to clearing land, constructing sketchy fortifications, and cutting a timber cargo for the return voyage.

The new world they were about to inhabit inspired them with fear and wonder. It was, on the one hand, a primeval wilderness, a land of vast dark forests and hostile savage natives totally unfamiliar to the settlers. And yet it was a new Eden, so virgin, so unspoiled, and full of fish and game and birds beyond counting. George Percy described its "faire meddowes and goodly tall Trees, with such Fresh-waters running through the woods, as I was almost ravished at the first sight thereof. . . . Going a little further we came into a little plat of ground full of fine and beautifull Strawberries, foure times bigger and better than ours in England."

The fledgling settlement's only chance for survival rested with its ability to trade with the Powhatans, who were anxious about a new European encampment in their midst. The memory of the Ajacán mission and Roanoke colony certainly colored their reaction to the English newcomers. To be sure, they remembered that in 1603 English sojourners had attacked the Rappahannocks, killing some and kidnapping others. The absence of women and children among the English contributed to the Powhatans' apprehension, for clearly this was a war party. Yet these Tassantassas (squatters) were rich in copper, beads, and iron tomahawks. Their presence on the wasteland of James Island did not trouble the Powhatans as much as their arrogance in building a fort without permission. They determined to keep a close watch on the Tassantassas, whom they immediately recognized were desperate for food.

The English were likewise anxious in their dealings with the Indians, fearing the worst. They refused to lay down their arms or to stay overnight in Indian camps, rejecting their hospitality. When Wowinchopunck visited their encampment on 18 May with a fresh-killed deer, the English stood armed and ready for danger. They also made the Indians aware of European technical advances; awestruck Indians witnessed an arrowhead shatter when it struck an English shield. Later, tempers flared over the alleged theft of an iron hatchet, and the party broke up.

A few days later, perturbed by the building of a fort and affronted by the English response to his hospitality, Wowinchopunck attacked with 200 warriors gathered from regional chiefdoms. English cannon repelled the assault, terrifying the Indians. After the defeat a wary Powhatan sensed the danger posed by the visitors and agreed to trade corn to them.

By mid-June, concerned for their safety, the English completed James Fort, a three-sided earthen bulwark capable of withstanding Indian stone arrows and Spanish warships. The dwellings inside the fort were temporary four-pole structures supporting both the roof and lean-to walls. Satisfied that the camp was secure, Newport returned to England for supplies in late June.

The adventurers arrived in the Chesapeake during a prolonged drought (1606–12) that, combined with their lack of preparedness, jeopardized their chances for survival. They were undisciplined in their consumption of stores and lazy in replenishing them. Not only did they have trouble finding food—few of them knew how to hunt or fish—but they also had difficulty locating clean water. Like the settlers at Roanoke, they did not dig wells for the first two years. Instead, they took water from the river that was both brackish and polluted by their waste, and as a result they suffered from dysentery and typhoid. When Newport returned six months later, only 38 of the original 104 settlers left behind were still alive.

What the English traded for corn was their copper and beads, especially blue ones that were much desired by the Powhatans. Even with the conquest of the Chesapeakes, blue beads made from shells were rare in Tsenacommacah. The English copper was much better quality than their present supply, being a deeper red and more durable. Hence the Powhatans found in the English trade a way of realizing both wealth and status, and a market developed between the two. Powhatan's ability to monopolize the English supply enabled him to secure loyalty by paying tribute downward to weroances. Nevertheless, what he coveted most were their iron objects: axes, knives, hatchets, hoes, but especially their guns. His desire for trade and weapons likely saved the vulnerable English from an attack that could have eliminated them.

Nevertheless, tensions arising from differing perspectives on gift-giving and making alliances strained the relations between the Indians and the English from the outset. The two groups valued gifts differently. Whereas Europeans paid tribute to betters, the Powhatans reversed the process of tribute by giving gifts to underlings. The Powhatans used marriage as a method of alliance within the chiefdom, a practice the English gentry might find understandable, but not commoners. Other cultural differences relating to concepts of work—the English thought hunting was a sport and a sign of leisure—inherited status and leadership versus consensual decision making, and property ownership further increased the friction between the two groups.

Newport was expected to return to Jamestown with the first supply ship by November, but he did not. By then the English were starving. The Powhatans had showed them how to plant corn; but the English did

JOHN SMITH   POCAHONTAS

not save any corn for seed, rations, or gifts. Nor did the adventurers for-
age, apparently not realizing that the Powhatans supplemented their di-
ets with tuckahoes and other wild foods. Arrogant colonists demanded
Indian corn for beads and pieces of metal. The Powhatans, whose har-
vests were being affected by the drought, gave them gifts of corn, but
the English believed this gesture was a sign of divine intervention rather
than a tribute of goodwill.

During this first starvation crisis, Captain John Smith emerged as
the leader of the colony. A short, stocky soldier of fortune from Lincoln-
shire, Smith had fought Spaniards and Turks across Europe. He had been
captured and enslaved in Turkey until he killed his master and escaped
to Russia before returning to England. Having survived internal bickering that had led to his temporary arrest on the voyage over, Smith saved
the colony by imposing discipline among the colonists and negotiating
with the Powhatans to supply them with corn. The drought conditions
made the price dear: the Powhatans demanded iron hatchets, copper,
and beads for their scarce staple.

During his trading ventures Smith discovered that the autonomous
Chickahominies were highly interested in English goods as well. They
sold him seven hogsheads of corn for iron tools and beads. These hold-
outs from the paramount chiefdom had brokered Monacan copper to
the Powhatans and believed that a relationship with these new trading
partners could bolster their independence from the Powhatans.

Troubled by this burgeoning alliance, the paramount chief authorized Smith's capture as he scouted the woodlands shared by the Chickahominies and the Powhatans. Opechancanough, weroance of the Pamunkeys and Powhatan's brother, caught Smith but killed his two companions. Smith was escorted through several towns, including that of the Rappahannocks, en route to the Pamunkey capital where Opechancanough entertained Smith as an honored guest, showering him with gifts. Feted with venison and bread, Smith feared that his hosts were cannibals who were fattening him up for the slaughter. To avoid such a fate, the wily Englishman delivered numerous speeches and fascinated the Indians with the "magic" of writing on paper. The priests of Uttamussak divined Smith's intentions as honorable.

Opechancanough then sent Smith to Powhatan's capital at Werowocomoco on the north side of the York River, where, according to Smith, his life was spared by the intervention of Pocahontas, Powhatan's favorite daughter. Smith's account of this event in his 1624 memoirs is replete with sexual fantasy, lacks collaboration, and is considered myth. The ceremony that Smith described may have been an adoption ceremony that he did not understand or was, perhaps, a mock execution to demonstrate Powhatan's power over the English. If he had intended to kill Smith, it is unlikely that the eleven-year-old Pocahontas would have defied her father's wishes and intervened. She might, however, have participated in a ritual that inducted Smith into the tribe.

Powhatan, an aging man of "goodly looks, tall stature, and cleane lymbes," entertained Smith as a very important guest and interrogated him about the English intentions. Smith dissembled, explaining that their ships were simply seeking refuge in the bay after being attacked and damaged by the Spanish and were waiting for "Father" Newport to return before leaving. Aware of the enmity between the Powhatans and the Siouans to their west, Smith, by his own account, offered an explanation for their continued presence and the need for directions: "We are seeking the great salt water beyond the great mountains so that we can avenge the murder of the King's child by the Monacan." Despite his doubts about Smith's intentions, Powhatan offered to adopt him. Making him a weroance and giving him the town of Capahosic would enable Powhatan to keep an eye on the Tassantassas.

After almost a month of captivity, Smith returned on 2 January 1608 to Jamestown Island where he was nearly hanged for causing the deaths of his two men. He was saved by the timely arrival of Newport with a new contingent of about 100 colonists, including artisans, laborers, and gentlemen but no farmers whose skills would be necessary for Jamestown's survival. Their arrival was followed by a devastating fire that consumed many of the buildings and supplies within the fort, once again leaving them at the mercy of the Indians. During Newport's absence several changes had occurred in the governance of the colony. Edward Wingfield, accused of harboring private stores during the food crisis, had been replaced as president of the colony by John Ratcliffe; and councilor George Kendall had been executed for supposedly spying for the Spanish, who were interested in England's colonization effort.

Newport and Powhatan conducted extensive negotiations. The Indian tried to discern the long-term intentions of the English while acquiring their hatchets and copper, and Newport sought information about the location of gold. As a sign of friendship, they exchanged gifts and young boys. Over the objections of a skeptical Smith, Newport and his settlers spent most of their time searching for gold along the riverbanks of the James.

Once Newport departed in April 1608 with his shipload of "gilded durt," Smith resumed his explorations of the region. Reconnoitering the rivers and roads, locating Powhatan towns, and sounding the depth of the Chesapeake Bay, he mapped Virginia, ever searching for gold and the water passage to the West. He visited the Eastern Shore, the great falls of the Potomac River, the headwaters of the bay, where he met the Susquehannocks, and the Rappahannock River, where he contacted the Mannahoacs. But there was no gold and no western passage.

When Smith returned to Jamestown, he found that the situation there had worsened. Food was scarce; and Ratcliffe, like Wingfield before him, had monopolized the supply. Smith was elected to replace him. As president of the colony, he continued his forceful leadership of Jamestown, organizing work gangs, instilling military discipline with drill in the use of firearms, and constructing more housing. Newport's return to the colony in September, accompanied by Virginia's first two women, led to renewed efforts to subject Powhatan to English rule. In an elaborate ceremony Newport crowned the paramount chief as a prince of the king of England, but the wily Powhatan refused to bend his knee and used the coronation to enhance his own prestige. The gifts of crown, cloak, and bed became symbols of his authority over the English, not the reverse.

With the departure of Newport in December, this time on ships laden with clapboard, pitch and tar, and glass, the English and Indians embarked upon a struggle over the colony's existence. Once again the English had not grown enough corn to get them through the winter, forcing Smith to send out expeditions to secure a supply. Powhatan demanded guns in return for corn. The two continued to profess friendship for one another, but both now concluded that their survival depended upon the elimination of the other. The sparring was over. Powhatan reportedly told Smith, "Many do inform me, your coming is not for trade, but to invade my people and possess my country." The English now posed a greater threat than his Indian enemies. Smith avoided one assassination attempt through a warning from Pocahontas. To escape another ambush, he grabbed Opechancanough by his hair lock and pointed his pistol at his chest in order to disarm his warriors. By threatening other tribes with harsh penalties, Smith secured enough corn for the colony. To ensure the supply would last until spring, he imposed draconian rules: "He that will not worke, shall not eate." Having observed what the Indians did when their food ran low, he dispersed the colonists to different camps along the river to feed off oysters and fish. All the while, armed skirmishes with the Powhatans continued, often accompanied by desecration of Indian cultural sites and artifacts.

In July 1609 a lone ship arrived with news of the colony's reorganization. Having failed to get quick returns from a colony now teetering on the brink of failure, the backers of the Virginia Company gained a new charter in 1609. It facilitated the raising of additional capital through creation of a joint-stock corporation and reorganized the colony's government, consolidating direction from London and placing complete power in Virginia in the hands of a governor. Shares were sold for £12 10s. each. Shareholders willing to sail for Virginia were awarded an additional share. The charter expanded the boundaries of the colony another 200 miles north and south of Point Comfort and an undetermined distance westward. The officers of the company also determined to send larger groups of colonists to Jamestown.

The new governor was Thomas West, Baron De La Warr, an experienced military officer; but he was unable to accompany the 400 new settlers, the "third supply," who arrived in Jamestown in August 1609. Their arrival set off another attempt to dislodge Smith from power; but it was a severe wound from a gunpowder explosion, perhaps not accidental, that forced him to give up his position and return to England in October, never to return to the colony that he had been so instrumental in saving.

Weakened by an arduous journey and without the leadership of Smith, the new settlers, much like their predecessors, succumbed to dwindling food supplies, starvation, and disease. Unable to come to terms with the English, Powhatan contributed to this new "starving time" from October 1609 to June 1610 by blockading the rivers, making it difficult for them to reach Indian towns. No longer acting as Samaritans, the Indians started killing Englishmen seeking corn. One expedition was found murdered, their mouths stuffed full of bread. John Ratcliffe, leading another group of supplicants, was skinned alive and burned at the stake. Evacuating Werowocomoco, the Powhatans retreated into the woods, carrying their stores of corn with them, trying to force the English to leave Tsenacommacah.

Their strategy almost succeeded. One group of colonists seized corn from the Patawomecks, beheaded two Indians, and mutinied, setting sail for England. Settlers robbing the storehouse were executed. Reduced to cannibalism, the remaining English were ready to evacuate when Lord De La Warr's second fleet arrived, making landfall in June 1610. They found a town and fort in ruins and 100 emaciated settlers, 60 at Jamestown and 40 others scattered about. Reinvigorated by the arrival of 150 new colonists, who included 10 women and children, the English rebuilt their settlement under the forceful leadership of De La Warr's second-in-command, Thomas Gates, who imposed new labor and military practices.

Confronting an obdurate Powhatan, De La Warr and Gates determined to escalate the war with the Indians and began establishing fortified settlements along the James River. The colony made its first aggressive move against the Kecoughtans, even though this tribe had been friendly with the colony from the very beginning. Gates orchestrated the attack while the unsuspecting Pochins and his warriors were engaged in the late spring hunt. As the women and children scattered into the woods, the hungry raiders seized their food reserves as spoils of war. Pochins never tried to retake the town. On 10 August 1610 the militia under George Percy attacked Paspahegh, home of Wowinchopunck. They killed several of his warriors, seized his corn, and took his wife and children captive before coldheartedly slaughtering them. They later killed him in battle. Similar attacks were made against the Chickahominies and Warraskoyacks. All Indians, regardless of past friendships, were now deemed enemies; consideration of Christian conversion was temporarily shelved.

More supply ships arrived with new settlers throughout 1611, benefiting from Samuel Argall's discovery in 1609 of a shorter, more direct route from England that bypassed the Spanish Caribbean. Now the trip could be made in seven to nine weeks instead of four months. The availability of more supply ships on which the colonists were so dependent improved their chances for survival.

Sir Thomas Dale, appointed marshal of Virginia responsible for military discipline, arrived in May 1611 with 300 settlers. With De La Warr and Gates back in England, Dale, who had compiled a distinguished military record in the Netherlands and Ireland, instituted a more rigorous set of rules that included penalties for noncompliance: death for running away to the Indians, stealing from the common store, or returning to England without permission. He restored the fort and introduced specialization of labor for food production. To extend the colony's control of the area and alleviate crowding in Jamestown, Dale, under company instructions, founded a new city. Fifty-five miles northwest of the capital, Henricus was more defensible and less pestilential than Jamestown. The English laid out three streets and built a fort, houses, and a church. Between 1613 and 1619 the colonists moved southward from Henricus to the mouth of the Appomattox River and palisaded the Bermuda Hundred, named after the Atlantic island where the 1609 supply ship had shipwrecked. The area soon became the most populated in the colony.

Under Dale's leadership the settlers seem to have finally learned their lesson. Trying to become less dependent on the Powhatans, they began planting corn, bringing in a tolerable crop in 1612. By 1614 they had introduced the vegetables of an English garden: peas, onions, turnips, cabbage, cauliflower, and carrots. They had set Jamestown's three streets in a triangular grid, with market and chapel on the grounds. The houses were covered in the Algonquian style, sheltered with bark rather than clapboard and enclosed with mats rather than plaster. In hopes of stimulating greater immigration while scuttling talk of abandoning the colony, Dale wrote to Sir Thomas Smythe, "I have seen the best countries in Europe, but I protest unto you, before the Living God, put them all together, this country will be equivalent unto them if it be inhabitant with good people." By 1616 there were 351 settlers who remained from the nearly 1,500 who had crossed the Atlantic to Virginia. The company had turned to a lottery to raise funds with which to sustain the colony.

Despite Jamestown's new vitality, the Indians continued to wage a war of attrition, engaging in guerilla warfare in which their bows and arrows were more accurate and quicker than the English flint-lighted muskets. They began building an arsenal of captured English swords and axes but still had no access to pistols and muskets. Hostilities came to an end, however, through a stroke of luck. In March 1613 Captain Argall, while trading with the rival Patawomecks, learned of a visit by Pocahontas and conceived a plan to kidnap her and hold her hostage in return for some English prisoners. With the assistance of the Patawomecks, he lured Pocahontas aboard the *Treasurer,* abducted her, and took her to Jamestown as his prisoner. Powhatan offered the English 500 bushels of corn and permanent amity in return for his daughter, but Dale rejected the ransom, and peace remained elusive until the marriage of Pocahontas and John Rolfe on 5 April 1614 ended the first Anglo-Powhatan war.

After her first encounter with John Smith, Pocahontas had often visited James Fort, serving as an intermediary and translator. She would have understood the intermarriage of the English and the Indians within the context of strategic alliance; but during her captivity she had also grown fond of English freedom and John Rolfe, whose wife had died shortly after their arrival in Virginia and who was clearly drawn to the young, vivacious princess. He also was likely impressed by her conversion to Christianity during her imprisonment. Powhatan, who was losing influence among the other tribes, also saw the strategic possibilities of the marriage and approved. Only about seventeen years old, Pocahontas changed her name to Rebecca and married Rolfe in a Christian ceremony. In 1616 Pocahontas and their infant son accompanied Rolfe to England, where they were wined and dined and she was paraded about as an exotic princess from America. She also sat for a formal portrait in full Elizabethan dress and met with John Smith; but just before returning to America, she died and was buried at Gravesend in 1617.

Before their trip to England, Rolfe, in search of a marketable commodity, had begun experimenting with a milder Caribbean strain of tobacco that European smokers preferred over the more acrid Powhatan ceremonial tobacco. Perhaps learning Indian tobacco husbandry from Pocahontas—fertilizing by slash-and-burn, planting on inclines that drained into creek or stream beds, cultivating the seeds in mounds, topping the plants, and curing or drying the leaf—Rolfe achieved a breakthrough. By 1616 his tobacco gardens were thriving, enabling him to cask 20,000 pounds in 1617 and twice that in 1618.

Tobacco's marketability in England set off a mania for planting that would transform the colony from a pseudomilitary outpost into an agricultural community of families and political institutions that would become a key player in the developing trade patterns of the Atlantic world. The English dispersed throughout the James River region, planting tobacco on Indian lands. With their eyes on riches, the settlers justified taking this property on grounds of cultural superiority. They believed Indians lacked a concept of private property—most Indian groups held land communally—underutilized the land, were irreligious or heathen, and, although intelligent, were a culturally deprived people with benighted souls whom the English could civilize and Christianize and teach the appropriate use of land.

Initially the Virginia Company retained ownership of the land, parceling out hundreds of acres as provincial units (the hundreds) to recipients who in turn paid an annual quitrent or tax to the company. However, a major reorganization in 1618 led by Sir Edwin Sandys converted Virginia to the Bermuda model where proprietors held private title to the land. The new land distribution and ownership methods established the basis for future tobacco plantations. The "Greate Charter" of 1618, as these land reforms came to be known, institutionalized the headright system, created the previous year, that gave fifty acres to a settler for paying his own way over and for every person he brought into the colony; and it imposed quitrents on the land to be paid to the company. One hundred acres per share were given to stockholders and to every settler who had been at Jamestown for more than two years. Landownership and the headright system became the primary incentives for attracting new settlers. But they also created the system of indentured servitude, whereby workers would sign an indenture or contract agreeing to serve four to seven years in the employ of the person paying their way to the New World. The system was a windfall for the labor importers, who received both rights to land and labor for the price of a ticket to Virginia. This became the major source of labor in seventeenth-century Virginia; but because the indentured servants eventually lost any rights to land after their contract was fulfilled, many would become part of a growing landless class.

Over 3,750 new colonists arrived in Virginia from 1618 to 1621. Included was a shipload of 90 "younge, handsome and honestly educated maydes," recruited to find husbands, who would have to pay the cost of passage for their chosen wives. Also included among the new arrivals were three separate boatloads of hundreds of poor children, generally boys, ranging in age from eight to sixteen, forcibly consigned to Virginia by the City of London between 1617 and 1622. Calling them vagabonds, the Privy Council reasoned that they could better themselves by purchasing land after their service. After the frightful mortality of the first group, the colony's Quarter Court asked that the children be at least thirteen years old.

Another arrival of note in 1619 was a group of "20 and Odd Negroes" on a Dutch frigate, which had taken them from a Portuguese vessel. These first Africans were likely Kimbundu-speaking Christians from Ndongo, Angola, where 4,000 had been captured in 1618. Although probably considered slaves by their captors, they apparently were accorded the status of indentureship in the Virginia colony "in the service of several planters." Census takers recorded 23 Africans in 1625. The number slowly increased during the next two decades as new merchants captured the African trade from the English Guinea Company, which, according to its founder Richard Jobson, did not engage in the slave trade. Governor William Berkeley reported that there were but 300 blacks in 1649, many of whom were free.

An important attraction for liberty-loving Englishmen to come to Virginia in the 1620s was the creation of a representative assembly authorized by the new charter. Twenty-two elected delegates or burgesses convened with the new governor, Sir George Yeardley, and his advisory Council of State on 30 July 1619 in the wooden Jamestown church to discuss company rules and enact laws of governance that prohibited gambling, drunkenness, swearing, and idleness. Although not intended as a miniature Parliament, the General Assembly became the first elected representative body in the New World, establishing the principle of self-government that would be a hallmark of the American experiment. Until 1670, all freemen were eligible to vote. Affirming its independence a few years later, the assembly told the governor that he could not "lay any taxes or impositions upon the colony, their lands or commodities, other than by authority of the General Assembly." Nonetheless, acts of the burgesses required the approval of the governor and the council, which sat with them.

Sandys's reorganization also aimed at strengthening the colony by diversifying its economy. He encouraged the production of silk and wine and iron smelting; but the worms died, as did the ironworkers, and the vintners turned to raising tobacco because it was more profitable. And no reorganization could counter the continuing high mortality rate due to disease, malnutrition, and hostilities. In 1624 only 1,300 of the 8,000 colonists who had migrated to Virginia were still alive. Of those who survived, men outnumbered women by seven to one, and the overwhelming number of them were tenants. Epidemics were even more rampant among the Indians, who proved susceptible to the diseases brought by the English.

As the English expanded beyond Jamestown to their surrounding fortified towns, their dispersal made them vulnerable to attack. As long as Pocahontas and her father, Powhatan, lived, a tenuous peace held between the English and the Indians. But she died in 1617 and he the following year. At the same time the "superior" English forgot the lesson of the "starving time" even though they were carving out farms on the fertile ground of Indian gardens. They forgot the necessity of growing corn for sustenance, choosing to plant every available acre in tobacco, even the streets of Jamestown. As a result the settlers resorted to old tactics, forcing the Indians, under a veiled threat of violence, to trade corn for beads and copper. Growing weary of the English demand for corn, Opechancanough, the new paramount chief, complained to Governor Yeardley in 1619 to end this coercion. The newly installed General Assembly dealt with Opechancanough's complaint by restricting the Indian trade to licensed and bonded merchants. Two years later the assembly tried to lessen land pressure, raise tobacco prices, and deal with the corn issue with new legislation. By restricting the planting of tobacco to 100 plants per hand, the assembly hoped that the reduction would increase the output of corn and improve relations with the Powhatans. But before the new policy could have its intended effect, Opechancanough led the Indians in a massive attack to wipe out the English settlement: a preemptive war to defend his homeland from the acquisitive colonists.

Although Opechancanough had deceptively maintained a spirit of friendship with the English, even professing a desire to be Christianized, he used the murder of war hero and mystic Nemattanew as a pretext to rally his people against the Tassantassas. Two weeks after the murder, on the four-year anniversary of Chief Powhatan's death, the Powhatans surprised the English in the Great Assault of 22 March 1622, massacring at least 347 settlers, almost one-third of the colony. Attacking from Jamestown to the fall line on both sides of the river, the Indians practically wiped out the new settlements at Henricus, Bermuda Hundred, Martin's Hundred, and Berkeley Hundred, where the first Thanksgiving service had been held in 1619; after the massacre, settlers did not return to these sites. Jamestown was saved by a warning from two Indian converts to Christianity. At this point Opechancanough made the tactical error of ending his assaults, assuming the English would, in Indian fashion, withdraw from battle and return to England. He was sadly mistaken.

After the Great Assault the English retaliated with a policy of "perpetual warre without peace or truce" against the Powhatans. They rationalized that the unprovoked attack had given them legal justification to kill Indians and seize their land under international law. Before the attack the English had felt a responsibility to engage in the civilizing mission of Christian conversion and English civility. After the attack, however, the English believed the Indians had forfeited that possibility.

During the summer and autumn following the Great Assault, the English killed more Indians than they had in all previous engagements.

INDIAN UPRISING OF 1622, BY THEODOR DE BRY

Under company orders, Governor Francis Wyatt and his soldiers de-stroyed Indian fishing weirs, ruined their cornfields, and burned their towns. The following spring, Captain William Tucker used subterfuge to subdue the Indians. Under a flag of truce, the colonists first incapacitated their hosts with tainted libations and then opened fire on them, killing several dozen and scalping some of the dead. Thereafter, Governor Wyatt launched annual raids on Indian towns, destroying their cornfields and forcing their residents to flee into the woods. In July 1624, Wyatt followed up his earlier successes by routing an army of 800 Pamunkeys with 60 English troops. While 16 settlers were killed, the Indians suffered severe casualties and lost their most important cornfields, crippling their ability to feed their families during the coming winter season. This crushing de-feat of Opechancanough's best warriors foreshadowed the demise of the Powhatan chiefdom.

Sporadic raiding by both parties continued for another eight years, as the English expanded their landholdings. Yet the war and new immi-gration were affecting the colonists' ability to feed themselves; another significant "starving time" had occurred during the winter of 1622–23. The need for Indian corn and the desire to cease hostilities prompted the English in 1632 to negotiate a peace treaty with the Chickahominies and the Pamunkeys that ended the second Anglo-Powhatan war, but it did not lead to more amicable relations.

By this time the colony was under new direction: that of the king. Indian troubles, high mortality, bankruptcy (the company had paid no dividends), and dissension among the stockholders had exhausted the pa-tience of King James. In 1624 he had the Virginia Company's charter re-voked. There had been no El Dorado. Bad luck, incompetent leadership, and poorly prepared colonists had risked England's New World mission; but at least it was still alive. In May 1625 James's son, Charles I, proclaimed Virginia a crown colony under the direction of his appointees.

Charles's problems with Parliament over the next twenty years would leave the colony nearly free to pursue its own development and governance. Ironically, in view of his disdain for legislatures, in 1639 he legitimized the General Assembly, which up to that time had no consti-tutional authority, and agreed that no taxes could be levied on Virgin-ians without the consent of the assembly. Burgesses had the power to tax, form parish and county lines, regulate church and militia affairs, and revise existing law.

In 1643 the House of Burgesses won the right to sit independently of the king's councilors, who now constituted an "upper house." Though appointed by the king, the ten to eighteen councilors were usually more concerned with protecting their own interests than those of the crown and were in frequent conflict with the governor, who sat with them. The

Council of State also served as the Quarter Court (later known as the General Court) that met four times a year, adjudicating both civil and criminal cases, approving petitions, and issuing licenses. The governor presided over the council and introduced bills in the assembly. His duties included signing land patents, calling elections, and issuing judicial orders, edicts, and proclamations.

At a lower level, county courts manned by governor-appointed justices of the peace were created in 1634 to administer local justice and manage county affairs such as tax collecting, militia service, road building, and tavern regulation. They became the keepers of records, notably of land transactions, tax receipts, and estate settlements. Augmented by sheriffs, clerks, and militia lieutenants, the justices became the basis of a ruling elite, perpetuating the patriarchal system common to the society they had just left, albeit with much less formality and ritual.

Another agent of governance was the Church of England, which promoted Anglican cultural hegemony and moral and social order through its parish churches, whose jurisdictional boundaries generally corresponded with those of the counties. There was no separation of church and state. Virginians were required by law to attend church and provide financial support for religious purposes. The House of Burgesses specified the duties of the ministers, who were not to "give themselves to excesse in drinking, or ryott, spending their tyme idellye by day and night, playing at dice, cards or any other unlawful game."

The governing body of the parish was the vestry, a self-perpetuating body of twelve prominent men, who managed all ecclesiastical affairs as well as many local civil activities. The parish vestry selected the minister, collected and managed the tithes or taxes that supported the minister and maintained glebes, churches, and chapels, served as overseers of poor relief, and disciplined moral transgressors, especially "fornicators." Planters of substantial means served for life on the vestry, which often was a stepping-stone to a political career as a county official or a burgess.

Beginning in 1662 and every four years thereafter, vestrymen oversaw processioning, an English feudal practice of inspecting property lines. The vestry chose knowledgeable inspectors to walk the boundaries of estates in order to commemorate specific persons to specific places. Taking place between Easter and Whitsunday, this quadrennial event became ritualized into a festival. The lack of towns and market fairs made processioning festivals and court days more significant in Virginia. The importance of the vestry and parish in the religious and civil lives of rural Virginians cannot be overemphasized; in fact, the parish performed so many critical functions that by the eighteenth century its budget and tax rates were often two or three times larger than those of the county government.

Although vestrymen served for life, finding and keeping responsible clergymen for long periods of time was no easy task. At midcentury one-third of the parishes had no regular clergy. A number of factors contributed to this problem. Because Virginia had no episcopacy, the colony's clergy were ordained by the bishop of London, who had jurisdiction over the colonial Church of England. During the period of intense immigration from the 1640s to 1670, when the population swelled more than threefold to 35,000, the bishop could not find enough qualified clerics to appoint, ensuring little denominational oversight or enforcement of church attendance. With never more than a handful of clergy resident in the colony for the rest of the century, the practice of circuit riding arose to cover parishes as large as 270 square miles.

During the company period the Anglican Church did not provide a unified ecclesiastical vision or avidly pursue conversions, which left an opening for other Protestant sects. Under Charles I and Archbishop William Laud, the Anglican Church attempted to reassert its authority in England, much to the chagrin of other Protestants, especially the Puritans. Laud's policies stimulated the great emigration of Puritans and other dissenters to the colonies in the 1630s. In Virginia they settled in Nansemond, lower Norfolk, and Isle of Wight counties, where their numbers ranged from 15 to 25 percent of the taxpayers, challenging the dominance of the Anglicans.

Parish and county service were avenues of opportunity for new investors who had come to Virginia seeking the chance to break into the English commercial system. These men were often merchants or from middling gentry families, either younger sons shortchanged by primogeniture or sons of yeoman families. Locked out of the more lucrative trade of the East Indies by established London merchants and spurred by the excitement of the tobacco market, they opted for Virginia. Some of these merchants traveled to the colony where they cornered both the market and the government. William Claiborne, Samuel Mathews, and William Tucker were examples of these emerging elites who obtained seats on the Council of State. Organizing their interests into syndicates, they began gaining title to or patenting the land acquired from the hundreds, formerly under company dominion, and the new lands seized from the Indians.

Governor John Harvey, who had strengthened the Jamestown fortifications and improved local defenses, butted heads with the Council of State on the land issue. Conscious of the 1632 treaty with the Indians and the conflicts that might be generated through expansion, he restricted settlement of new lands. Fearing this policy portended an effort to seize their lands and return them to the stockholders of the defunct Virginia Company, the councilors petitioned the crown for redress, resting their claim on the Great Charter of 1618, which had institutionalized the land system. In response to their petition, King Charles I in 1634 appointed William Laud to head the Lords Commissioners of Foreign Plantations, who administered colonies. The Laud Commission reaffirmed the head-right system, and the council "thrust" Harvey from office, but not before he had knocked out the teeth of one of the councilors.

With Harvey's exit, John West became the new governor and proceeded to open the door for expansion. In addition to the patenting of former Indian lands, the councilors and their associates in 1635 began to amass tens of thousands of acres that formerly were company lands by breaking up the hundreds into private estates. These tracts included the Berkeley Hundred (8,000 acres), Martin's Hundred (80,000 acres), Martin's Brandon Hundred (4,500 acres), and Southampton Hundred (200,000 acres).

Labor for these estates continued to be provided by indentured servants, who were migrating into the colony by the thousands in the 1630s and 1640s. A majority of them, driven by poverty or seeking fortune, came from the cities of London and Bristol and from rural central and southern England. Most of them were young single males who would outnumber female immigrants two or three to one; many of them died unmarried and childless. A further restraint on the birthrate was the stipulation that female servants could not marry until their service was completed, which often did not occur until they were in their midtwenties or older. These factors meant that immigration, not natural increase, would be responsible for most of Virginia's population growth throughout the seventeenth century. The combination of low population density and large farms inhibited town development, producing an isolation that was far different from English life.

Although women were outnumbered and experienced extremely harsh conditions in work and childbirth during the early years of the colony, their lives improved as Virginia began to take on the appearances of English society. Once a woman married, becoming a "goodwife," she had reason to be apprehensive because of the common law of coverture. An unmarried, divorced, or widowed woman possessed a legal personality as *feme sole* and was solely responsible for her affairs. On the other hand, a married woman was under the cover of her husband's authority as *feme covert* and had few property rights. Land she brought to the marriage became her husband's to manage as he saw fit, although he normally could not sell her inherited property unless he got her permission to do so.

Although women on average died ten years earlier than men in Virginia, a widow did materially better than a widower, often surviving more than one husband. When her husband died, she received a one-third interest in their entire estate; and this could not be taken by surviving children until her death. Even if a husband purposely tried to limit his wife's share in his will, courts normally sided with her, awarding the one-third share for life. Husbands often left custodial control to their wives, making them executors in an effort to protect their children from unscrupulous new husbands.

Propertied widows had bargaining power with suitors, often insisting on a prenuptial agreement called jointure that ensured the integrity of their children's estates. The county courts arbitrated these jointure contracts in the interest of equity, protecting spouses and children. These agreements varied from wives controlling their assets during marriage to wives putting their assets into trust during the marriage. Even though husbands controlled these trusts, the property reverted to their wives after death or divorce. Wives could stipulate the disposition of their jointure in their wills. Temperance Yeardley, the widow of Governor George Yeardley, managed their extensive estate after his death in 1627. Exercising the prerogative of jointure when she married war hero Francis West that same year, Temperance retained the lion's share of her estate for her three children and limited Francis's inheritance to £1,000. When Temperance died seven months after her wedding day, Francis unsuccessfully tried to break the will, claiming she had a deathbed change of heart.

If propertied widows had rank and status in seventeenth-century Virginia, all women were proscribed in their civil rights. Although the burgesses did not explicitly exclude women from franchise until 1699, they did not vote before that date. They could neither serve in the militia nor hold public offices. They could not act as jurors, but they could give testimony. Single women exercised property rights through owning titles and signing contracts and wills, while wives could be assigned legal responsibilities by husbands in their absence. Seventeenth-century observers ridiculed assertive women as unruly and disorderly and held them responsible for social discord. Their outbursts were taken as manifestations of domestic disharmony and challenges to patriarchal authority. Consequently, in 1662 the assembly made "brabbling" (quarrelsome) speech among women a crime, punishable by fines or the humiliation of a public ducking.

To meet increasing labor needs, planters preferred youth entering the colony without contracts, like those sent over by the City of London, because they could be signed up for longer terms of service. According to a 1643 statute, those over twenty served four years; those twelve to nineteen, five years; and those under twelve, seven years. The assembly revised the law in 1666 so that those over nineteen served five years and those under nineteen served until they were twenty-four. The longer duration of service encouraged the purchase of younger servants whose ages were adjudged in court. For this reason Virginia became a market for kidnapped English children. Before 1640 English authorities had winked at hawks abducting children from London streets who were destined for Virginia or Barbados. In 1645 Parliament criminalized kidnapping, a term which came into use about that time; but during the Restoration prosecution waned and did not revive until the 1680s.

For the few Africans who had arrived after 1619, their status was ambiguous. They likely had been brought to Virginia as persons to be sold into slavery, but no such condition of lifetime servitude was recognized in English or Virginia law at that time. Listed in the records as "Negroes" without surnames, this description alone, while discriminating, did not reflect enslavement. Although England had a long history of bound labor, by the time of the colonial expansion, its law provided no mechanism for enslaving anyone. The choice for slavery required the creation of a coercive state, which flew in the face of English attitudes about individual liberty.

However, the adjudication of court cases involving Africans suggests a shift in treatment from indentureship to a more permanent servitude. In the first case where the term *Negro* is used to distinguish Africans from others, John Philip, a "Negro," was allowed to testify against an Englishman in 1624 because he was a Christian. Without a law to the contrary, it appears that baptized blacks could count on the same rights as other Christians coming to the colony, rights that could be denied to non-Christians of African descent. They could also count on the customary status of indentured laborers, exchanging their transportation costs for seven years of labor. "Antonio a Negro," who was probably a Christian, served out his indentureship before becoming Anthony Johnson, a slave-owning freeholder of a 250-acre estate named Angola after his homeland. Johnson was one of a small number of free blacks who owned land on the Eastern Shore, acted as defendants and plaintiffs in court cases against whites, and eventually had servants and slaves of their own.

"Negroes" were further differentiated from others in Virginia in the Hugh Johnson case of 1630. The court sentenced the white Johnson to be whipped before an assembly of blacks because he had copulated with a "Negro." Performing public penance in front of an assembly was consistent with English custom. What distinguished this case from others was the racial nature of the crime and the penalty. The sex was interracial, and the court specifically intended that he be publicly humiliated before Africans.

The assembly and courts in the 1640s signaled the further discrimination of Africans by laws and judgments. Gradually, distinctions between whites and blacks began to correlate with freedom and slavery. In 1640 the assembly legislated that any blacks who were not freeholders, that is, almost all Africans, were prohibited from bearing arms. Denying Africans the intrinsically English right to bear arms made them defenseless and easier to enslave. After 1640, jurists began to assume that indentured blacks kept that status for life, meting out to them more brutish and degrading punishments than those given to whites for the same offense.

Interracial escapes from service, not unusual given the makeup of the labor force, particularly chagrined authorities. In 1640 John Punch and Emanuel, both of African descent, escaped with whites but received harsher punishments than their coconspirators. The courts punished Punch's cohorts with three additional years of service but consigned Punch to lifelong slavery. Emanuel and six white servants schemed to escape to New Amsterdam. Once their plot was discovered, the whites were each given an additional year; but Emanuel, who was already enslaved, was burned on the cheek with the letter R for runaway and forced to work in shackles for a year, more if his master deemed it necessary.

The assembly in 1643 explicitly legalized racial discrimination by taxing all black women as field laborers and exempting all white women as household dependents. The assembly reaffirmed the tax law in 1668, specifying that African women, regardless of status, should not be accorded the same stature as English women. This policy degraded free families with African or mixed-ancestry wives, discouraging their property accumulation and contributing to their economic plight. Faced with increasing discrimination, many free blacks emigrated from the colony to Maryland, whose settlement had begun in 1634.

Virginia's borders had been restricted by the granting of proprietary charters for Maryland in 1632 and "Carolana" in 1629. Maryland's grant included land from the south bank of the Potomac River northward and a portion of the Eastern Shore peninsula north of where Virginia settlements were located. Maryland's ownership of the Potomac led to periodic disputes with Virginia over navigation and fishing rights. Settlement to the south was delayed until 1663 when a new charter was granted for a Carolina colony that eventually was divided into two colonies. Virginia's border with North Carolina was agreed upon in 1728.

Population growth and rampant land acquisition rekindled Indian resistance in the 1640s. In a last desperate attempt to drive out the English, the aged Opechancanough led the Second Great Assault against the English in 1644, killing 500, about 8 percent of the settlers. Once again the English called on the right of war in international law as they pursued the Pamunkeys with abandon. After they captured the reputedly 100-year-old Opechancanough, a soldier unceremoniously shot him in the back while he was in custody.

The treaty of 1646 with the new Pamunkey chief Necotowance required an annual tribute to the governor of twenty beaver skins and removed the Indians from their lands between the James and York rivers, further opening that area to settlement. The Pamunkeys and the Chick-ahominies were restricted to 5,000 acres in the Pamunkey Neck. Over the next twenty years, English settlers flooded the peninsulas between the James and Rappahannock rivers, acquiring land through trickery and cheating, especially during the Commonwealth era when Governor Berkeley was politically ineffective. The General Assembly attempted to protect the tributary Indians, reaffirming the Pamunkey Neck reserve in 1658 and prohibiting land sales in 1662. With the Restoration in 1660, Governor Berkeley checked further settler encroachment. By 1669, diminished by war and disease, the nineteen tributary tribes could muster only 725 bowmen out of a population of 2,900.

By 1650 Virginia was a stable crown colony with political institutions and land titles following English custom. The colonial government had become more decentralized through the county system of governance, with commissioners, justices of the peace, and sheriffs commanding authority in local matters. The combined effect was to make the emerging great planters, who held many of these offices, paramount in local governance. By then Jamestown had taken on the bustle of an imperial outpost. The poor lived in wattle-and-daub houses with thatch roofs, the middling sort in houses with frames of wood, and the wealthy in newly constructed brick homes. Jamestown boasted artisans engaged in several trades as coopers, masons, carpenters, sawyers, blacksmiths, and ship-wrights. Demonstrating their expectation of permanence, the colonists bricked their churches. The end of the Indian threat, increased immigration from England, and political stability signified the success of the Jamestown experiment, now forty years old; but the cost had been high in terms of lives lost and an aboriginal civilization destroyed.

SOURCES CONSULTED

Philip L. Barbour, ed., *The Jamestown Voyages under the First Charter, 1606–1609* (1969); Warren Billings, *Sir William Berkeley and the Forging of Colonial Virginia* (2004); Edward L. Bond, *Damned Souls in a Tobacco Colony: Religion in Seventeenth-Century Virginia* (2000); T. H. Breen and Stephen Innes, *"Myne Owne Ground": Race and Freedom on Virginia's Eastern Shore, 1640–1676* (1980); Robert Brenner, *Merchants and Revolution: Commercial Change, Political Conflict, and London's Overseas Traders, 1550–1653* (1993); Holly Brewer, *By Birth or Consent: Children, Law, and the Anglo-American Revolution in Authority* (2005); J. Frederick Fausz, "An 'Abundance of Blood Shed on Both Sides': England's First Indian War, 1609–1614," *VMHB* (Jan. 1990); David W. Galenson, *Traders, Planters, and Slaves: Market Behavior in Early English America* (1986); James Hagemann, *The Heritage of Virginia: The Story of Place Names in the Old Dominion* (2d rev. ed., 1988); April Lee Hatfield, *Atlantic Virginia: Intercolonial Relations in the Seventeenth Century* (2004);

James Horn, *Adapting to a New World: English Society in the Seventeenth-Century Chesapeake* (1994); Horn, *A Land as God Made It: Jamestown and the Birth of America* (2005); John Gilman Kolp, *Gentlemen and Freeholders: Electoral Politics in Colonial Virginia* (1998); Martha W. McCartney, *A Study of the Africans and African Americans on Jamestown Island and at Green Spring, 1619–1803* (2003); John J. Mc-Cusker and Russell R. Menard, *The Economy of British America, 1607–1789* (1985); Edmund S. Morgan, *American Slavery, American Freedom: The Ordeal of Colonial Virginia* (1975); John K. Nelson, *A Blessed Company: Parishes, Parsons, and Parishioners in Anglican Virginia, 1690–1776* (2001); Mary Beth Norton, *Founding Mothers and Fathers: Gendered Power and the Forming of American Society* (1996); Michael Oberg, *Dominion and Civility: English Imperialism and Native America, 1585–1685* (1999); John Ruston Pagan, *Anne Orthwood's Bastard: Sex and Law in Early Virginia* (2002); Anthony S. Parent Jr., *Foul Means: The Formation of a Slave Society in Virginia, 1660–1740* (2003); Helen C. Rountree, *Pocahontas, Powhatan, Opechancanough: Three Indian Lives Changed by Jamestown* (2005); Helen C. Rountree and E. Randolph Turner, *Before and after Jamestown: Virginia's Powhatans and Their Predecessors* (2002); Terri L. Snyder, *Brabbling Women, Disorderly Speech, and the Law in Early Virginia* (2003); Linda Sturtz, *Within Her Power: Propertied Women in Colonial Virginia* (2002); Brent Tarter, "Reflections on the Church of England in Colonial Virginia," *VMHB* (2004); John Thornton, *Africa and Africans in the Making of the Atlantic World, 1400–1800* (2d ed., 1998); Camilla Townsend, *Pocahontas and the Powhatan Dilemma* (2004); Alden T. Vaughan, *The Roots of American Racism: Essays on the Colonial Experience* (1995).

3

IMPERIAL OUTPOST

1650–1690

The second half of the seventeenth century witnessed a radical transformation in the Virginia colony. Patterns of political behavior and land tenure, labor and gender relations, and racial and class distinctions were established that endured for another three centuries. Power was becoming concentrated in the hands of large landholders, and enslaved Africans would replace indentured Europeans as the primary source of labor. Social stratification was increasing. Events in the mother country—the civil war, the Cromwellian Interregnum, the Restoration, and finally the "Glorious Revolution"—would complicate the relationship of the outpost to the metropolis. Several rebellions, notably Nathaniel Bacon's in 1676, challenged the emerging new order; but the results confirmed the planters' authority.

In 1642 William Berkeley arrived in Jamestown as the new royal governor, beginning a momentous thirty-five-year career that had a greater influence on the development of the Virginia colony than that of any other colonial figure. Born in 1605 into a prominent Somerset family, Berkeley received an undergraduate education at Oxford and training in the law at the Middle Temple; but his primary interests were in the arts and politics, which gained him an appointment to the court of Charles I in 1632. His loyalty to the Stuarts never wavered thereafter. The new governor ingratiated himself with all classes, encouraged crop diversification by planting flax, cotton, and rice, experimented like Sandys before him with silk production, and supported the efforts of Abraham Wood and John Lederer in exploring the Blue Ridge and Allegheny Mountains. When Opechancanough attacked the colony in 1644, Berkeley personally

WILLIAM BERKELEY

led expeditions against the Indians and then instituted policies aimed at preventing further hostilities between the two groups.

Berkeley gave the large planters great authority in local matters in exchange for his control of external affairs. As part of this negotiation, Berkeley in 1643 divided the General Assembly into a bicameral House of Burgesses and Council of State. Although the house began to resemble a "little parliament," the burgesses, unlike their English contemporaries, chose their presiding officer and clerk. Demonstrating the significance of this bicameral division, Thomas Stegge stepped down from the Council of State to take the Speaker's position. Berkeley also instituted the office of attorney general to advocate for the governor in the Quarter Court.

When civil war broke out in England between the king and Puritan parliamentarians shortly after Berkeley's arrival in Virginia, he immediately aligned himself with the crown and convinced the assembly to condemn the Puritan rebels. Yet not wanting to alienate Parliament as the struggle went on, Virginia officially remained neutral during the war.

Such neutrality did not extend to the religious scene. Although Virginia Anglicans were steeped in the religious traditions using the Book of Common Prayer and King James's Bible, they were tolerant of dissenters.

Berkeley, on the other hand, was suspicious of the Puritans in Virginia because of their role in the English Civil War. Following crown instructions, Berkeley made the colony aware that it had an established church and insisted on an oath of allegiance to the church. He introduced legislation in the assembly banning Catholics from holding offices and priests from entering the colony. This action coincided with the 1643 expulsion of three Puritan clergymen who had arrived from Massachusetts to minister to parishioners in Isle of Wight and Nansemond.

Fearful that the English religious strife could spread to the colony, the assembly in 1647 repealed the oath of allegiance and the banishment of dissenting clergy. Nevertheless, it accused Puritans of belonging to the sect responsible for the schism in England, inducing many of them to emigrate to Maryland and New England. Several left from the Eastern Shore and the Southside following fellow Puritan William Stone to Maryland, where he became governor in 1648. Those who remained became more closely connected to fellow Puritans in New England.

Because the war threatened to disrupt Virginia's tobacco sales, Berkeley used his influence to encourage greater trade with the Dutch; but if this trade was crucial to Virginia's commerce, it was detrimental to English merchants. Berkeley's promotion of free trade opened the door to the Netherlands merchant marine and encouraged intercolonial commerce as well, especially with New England and the West Indies. This development pitted the planters, who preferred the competitive rates of the Netherlands trade, against London merchants, represented in Virginia by William Claiborne and Samuel Mathews.

In 1643 Berkeley accorded the Dutch merchants favored status in the Virginia market, comparable to that of the English. This policy ran counter to Parliament's 1647 law that encouraged English adventurers and discouraged Dutch merchants. The London faction of Claiborne, Mathews, Stegge, and Richard Bennett had lobbied against the Dutch trade; but Berkeley challenged Parliament's authority on the matter, arguing that the Great Charter had given Virginians the right to trade with any nation at peace with the realm. His advocacy came to naught with King Charles's defeat in the English Civil War.

Oliver Cromwell's victory over Charles and the subsequent execution of the king in 1649 produced a bitter denunciation by the assembly of the "traitorous proceedings" and a proclamation recognizing Charles's son, Charles II, as the new king. The new regime could not tolerate such defiance; and it restricted trade with the colony and then, through the Treaty of Jamestown in 1652, forced Virginia to recognize the Puritan Commonwealth. In return, Virginia also became a commonwealth, organized for the good or "common welfare" of its citizens, who would continue to enjoy the "freedoms and priviledges as belong to the free borne people of England." Berkeley, who for a time threatened war with Cromwell's military representatives, surrendered and retired to his Green Spring estate. The House of Burgesses, which effectively governed the colony until the restoration of the monarchy in 1660, elected Richard Bennett to replace him.

The king's defeat led many of his followers to seek exile in Virginia, which was known for its loyalty to the crown during the war. These royalist cavaliers included members of the Washington, Randolph, Carter, and Lee families, who would be so influential in the subsequent history of the colony and state. But their numbers were not large, as most royalists remained in England or migrated to the Continent. Contrary to the cavalier myth that most Virginians were descended from the English aristocracy, most of the immigrants to Virginia in the seventeenth century were indentured servants or "middling" people such as merchants or artisans.

Aside from the removal of Berkeley, life in Virginia was little changed during the Cromwellian Protectorate. Indifferent to what was happening in Virginia once loyalty had been established, Cromwell left the colony alone. Most officeholders remained in their positions, assembly prerogatives remained, royalists kept their property, and Anglicans were permitted to use their prayer book, but persecution of Puritans ceased. Consequently, they were able to shore up their standing in Virginia until the Restoration in 1660 when they began emigrating from the Old Dominion once again.

The brief period of religious toleration encouraged the immigration of Quakers to Virginia during the 1650s. Their sense of inner light led them to disavow the need for a clergy, making their gospel attractive to backcountry residents who had no access to a resident ministry. They gained further popularity because their message muting hierarchical relations allowed women to participate in their meetings. They traveled through Indian country as guests and guides, appealing directly to the Indians by recognizing their spiritual equality. Disturbed by the Friends' rejection of an established church, the assembly passed statutes in 1660 and 1663 aimed at keeping these itinerants out of the colony, calling the Quakers a secretive sect. During the English-French war in 1691, the assembly, still suspicious of their pacifist position, forbade Quakers to congregate.

Cromwellians were more concerned with Virginia's trade with foreign nations than with religious freedom. In 1651 they passed the Navigation Act, which required shipping to and from the colonies to be carried in English vessels. This new policy, popular among English merchants, reversed Berkeley's efforts and excluded the Dutch from Virginia. English seizure of Dutch ships in carrying out this policy led to the First Anglo-Dutch War. Although the Dutch trade was seriously disrupted, it was not eliminated altogether. The war ended with the Treaty of Westminster in 1654, partly because the lord protector, Cromwell, found war with the Calvinist Netherlands anathema, feeling that there was enough commerce worldwide for both Protestant nations. The illegal commerce with the Dutch continued.

If challenged by the Commonwealth on foreign trade with the Navigation Act, the assembly's autonomy became more pronounced in local governance. Under new Commonwealth rules, the House of Burgesses elected the governor every two years, which severely compromised the office, much to the delight of the burgesses. Edward Digges followed Richard Bennett, and Samuel Mathews Jr. followed Digges. Emboldened by their new power, the burgesses became more independent of the Protectorate, quietly supporting Charles II's claim to power. While the colony feigned neutrality, protecting its principal investment in the tobacco trade, Berkeley and others plotted a coup d'état in Virginia in 1654. Although the conspiracy was uncovered, the plotters denied any wrongdoing and escaped punishment.

After Mathews died in 1660, two years after the death of Cromwell, the Council of State, sensing a turn of events in England, chose Berkeley to be governor pro tempore, a selection confirmed by the assembly. He quickly moved to establish Jamestown as Virginia's only port of call, to diversify the economy, and to promote trade. He restored relations with the Dutch with a comprehensive treaty that opened trade and provided a remedy in each other's courts for debt collection and the return of runaway servants. The years out of power had left Berkeley embittered toward his political enemies and wary of any future rebellious activity.

Within two months of Berkeley's return to power, Charles II became the new king of England. He immediately recognized Berkeley as Virginia's rightful governor, who had been improperly deposed during the Commonwealth era. Tradition has it that Charles gave Virginia its nickname "the Old Dominion" out of affection for its loyalty to the crown, but it is likely that the name stemmed from Virginia's position as England's oldest American colony.

Ironically, it was the return of the monarchy that led to greater restrictions on Virginia's commerce. The king and Parliament enacted a new Navigation Act in 1660 that once again excluded the Dutch from the tobacco trade. Berkeley had just developed commercial treaties with Governor Peter Stuyvesant of New Amsterdam and felt that this regulation, like the earlier act, was deleterious to Virginia's economy. Planters would now pay more for shipping on English vessels and receive lower prices for surplus tobacco sold on the Continent.

Berkeley made his case in *A Discourse and View of Virginia* published in 1662. He promoted Virginia as a fertile country capable of supporting

a mixed economy; tobacco had become the prime commodity only because of massive immigration and cheap labor. He feared that the Navigation Acts would put Virginia's monoculture at the mercy of London
merchants, whereas the colony could attain greater prosperity with an
open, free, and diversified economy. But in the mercantilist world of the
seventeenth century, nations attempted to monopolize trade at the expense of the competition; and the colonial producers of raw materials
paid the price for that monopoly. When he traveled to England to protest
the legislation, Berkeley was told to go home. A third Navigation Act
in 1663 required imports to the colony to proceed through England and
thence to Virginia in English ships, raising the prices of imported goods.
The result was a major depression in the late 1660s that reduced the price
of tobacco and threw small farmers and tenants off the land. The king
obstructed attempts to cut production to stimulate prices, for he collected a tax on all the tobacco shipped to England.

During the Second Anglo-Dutch War, which began in 1665, James,
duke of York, seized New Amsterdam. Bracing for a retaliatory attack,
Governor Berkeley raised revenue for defense by getting the assembly to
increase taxes and sell land that belonged to the king of the Patawomecks.
The colony hastily threw up fortifications, including a rampart at Old
Point Comfort, a site which the colony had recognized as indefensible
from the sea during its first decade. A Dutch war fleet attacked the colony
in June 1667, seized prizes, and sailed away without causing any damage.
The war ended shortly afterward with the Peace of Breda in July 1667.

Charles's declaration of war on the Dutch on 14 March 1672 found
Virginia, as previously, unprepared. The frontiers were virtually defenseless from Indians, and the Chesapeake Bay was open to a naval assault. Its
forts were in ill repair or abandoned, its militia units had not regularly
mustered, and its armories were poorly stocked. With the advent of war,
the colony refurbished its forts; but Berkeley worried that the colony was
more vulnerable to the masses of indebted, indentured, and enslaved,
who had no stake in the colony's welfare. In July 1673 the Dutch war fleet
entered the bay just as a tobacco convoy had assembled. The English convoy lost four merchant ships in a fierce battle but managed to retreat to
safe harbors up the James and Elizabeth rivers. The Netherlanders burned
four stragglers but lost their opportunity for a major prize because they
feared chasing the convoy upriver. Holland and England ceased hostilities in this third war with the Treaty of Westminster in February 1674.

By this time a planter elite had secured control of the colony through
a great land grab. After the Indian wars the English had usurped Tsenacommacah's roads and territory, moving quickly to establish farms and
plantations on the Powhatans' lands along the James, York, and Rappahannock rivers. Their fertile soils allowed for the growth of the highly

prized sweet-scented tobacco, which commanded the transatlantic trade with England. Its success left little consideration for land conservation or greater economic diversification.

The Southside—that area of the Piedmont south of the James River—and the Eastern Shore had less fertile soils and so grew the less desirable Orinoco tobacco. Planters here sold their tobacco in the intercolonial market. They developed a more diversified economy and ancillary trades for these markets, including grains, naval stores, livestock (cattle and hogs), and meats, finding buyers in Barbados and other Caribbean markets and in New Netherlands and New England. Clearly Virginia had become an integral part of an Atlantic world that would become even more consolidated with the development of the slave trade.

The emerging planter class continued to find its wellspring in the younger sons of England's middling gentry, drawn to Virginia by the expectations of wealth-producing plantations. Unrestrained by the strictures of feudalism or family, these newcomers were highly ambitious men on the make. Their land grab was made possible by the headright system. Taking out fifty-acre patents on indentures, they secured almost a million acres from 1650 to 1665, making windfall profits fifty to one hundred times the cost of their investment by renting or selling land to ex-servants. Many of these newcomers instantly became part of the provincial gentry by marrying wealthy widows. They created large estates by patenting land and building plantations with indentured and enslaved labor and diversifying their commercial activities.

The more aggressive planters organized the tobacco consignment trade as agents of London syndicates bent on controlling the tobacco market. As business associates of the London merchants, they were able to secure credit and obtain manufactured goods and other merchandise from English firms. Acting in the dual role of planters and merchants, these men parlayed their earnings into landholdings situated on the major rivers. They managed the hinterland from their riverside wharves and warehouses, dominating the commerce within a twenty-five-mile radius. Taking control of the local economy, they purchased tobacco from smaller planters and sold them English goods. They speculated in land, breaking it into smaller farms, which they either leased or sold to small planters, including the class of freed servants. By 1680 this planter gentry had obtained substantial wealth and power.

A separate land grab took place in the Northern Neck Proprietary, an expanse of land that Charles II gave to loyal supporters as he fled England in 1649. Not unlike the Maryland proprietary, the grant was a "baronial" estate of a million acres between the Potomac and Rappahannock rivers. When the Stuarts were restored to power, Charles revived the proprietary. By then Thomas Culpeper, second Baron Culpeper of Thoresway, had amassed six of the seven shares of the estate. These shares were combined when the fifth Baron Fairfax of Cameron, holder of the other share, married Culpeper's daughter, Catharine, making their son Thomas, sixth Baron Fairfax of Cameron, sole proprietor. Proprietary agents busied themselves by collecting quitrents from tenants and disbursing multiple grants to themselves and large tracts to friends for speculative sale. By this means William Fitzhugh and later proprietary agent Robert "King" Carter amassed vast stretches of land in the Northern Neck, whose early history has been described as a story of "grab, grab, grab."

Ensuring their elite status, large planters also held profitable appointments, posts, and seats in the colonial government. The most prominent planters were appointed by the governor to serve on the Council of State and held appointments as secretary, collector of customs, and surveyor general. The emerging gentry were elected to the House of Burgesses and held multiple posts as constables and surveyors of the highways. Both the great and middling planters held major appointments as justices of the peace, sheriffs, and vestrymen, through which they secured more land and greater power, often by fraud and malfeasance.

Representative of the great planters were the Byrd and Carter families. William Byrd, the son of a London goldsmith, arrived in America in 1669. He inherited 1,800 acres from his uncle near the fall line on the James River and parlayed his good fortune into a profitable trading business, a seat in the House of Burgesses, appointment to the Council of State, and expanded landholdings. At his death in 1704, he left his son William 26,000 acres and 200 slaves. William Byrd II also was active in politics, serving on the council for thirty-five years, but he is best remembered as a Renaissance man. He built the beautiful colonial mansion at Westover where he had a library of 3,500 volumes, founded the city of Richmond, wrote poetry, surveyed the line between Virginia and North Carolina, and kept one of the most informative, if not scandalous, diaries of the colonial period. When he died in 1744, he left an estate of almost 180,000 acres.

John Carter came to Virginia in 1649 after service to his deposed king. He held seats in the house and on the council during the interregnum. His second son, Robert, starting with a modest inheritance of 1,000 acres, combined his political connections and a sharp eye for land development to create one of the largest estates of the colonial period: 333,000 acres scattered over many plantations in a dozen counties, on which there were over 700 slaves, 100 horses, and 2,000 cattle and pigs. He served in the burgesses, as Speaker of the House, as colonial treasurer, and as a member of the council from 1700 to 1732. He was, indeed, a "king."

The middling planters of more modest means often managed their accounts through the colony's gentry, but they could deal directly with English freighters. Using their lands and laborers as equity, they purchased goods on credit from the larger merchant-planters and in turn sold these to farmers and tenants nearby. The small planters were often former servants who had become proprietors through hard work and thrift. They could sell their tobacco to larger planters in the neighborhood or, by the midcentury, if they had riverside access, deal directly with English factors who established their stores along the rivers and traded merchandise for tobacco. From 1630 to 1670 the amount of tobacco produced in the Chesapeake region rose from 400,000 pounds to 15 million pounds per annum.

The availability of thousands of acres of land for tobacco planting demanded a concurrent expansion of the labor force. The number of indentured servants in Virginia exploded, and the entire Tidewater region was quickly settled. They constituted one-half of the workforce at midcentury. Planters preferred Englishmen as laborers; but when they became harder to attract, they turned reluctantly to Englishwomen and then, more reluctantly, to Irishmen. Indentured servants were not slaves, but their status as semiproperty was clear. Their contracts could be purchased by other masters or extended for bad behavior, they could be forced to work and punished for running away, and there was little legal protection for their welfare. A clergyman denounced "tyrannical masters" for treating their servants like "galley slaves, compelling them unmercifully beyond their strength." Most worked as field hands; but a few became tailors, seamstresses, or domestics. On most plantations the male or female servant probably slept on a cot in the kitchen or in one of the small outbuildings and generally worked alongside the master performing the endless tasks of tobacco production. Although fewer servants now died during their indenture and working and living conditions had improved for most, opportunities to own or even rent land in the Tidewater after their servitude were becoming rare.

Controlling the sexual choices and behavior of laborers strengthened the patriarchy. Servants were unable to marry until after they satisfied their terms, and the enslaved were not allowed the sacrament of matrimony. The statutes of 1643, 1658, and 1662 confirmed the master's authority in giving consent to his servants' marrying. Servants were not allowed to marry until age twenty-four without their master's consent. Violations usually entailed an additional year of service. In 1696 legislators fined ministers 500 pounds of tobacco for blessing the banns of a marriage without proper consent.

Because of the disproportionate ratio of men to women and laws forbidding bound laborers to marry, out-of-wedlock births were commonplace. County magistrates, concerned more with an employer's lost labor resulting from maternity and childcare than with the sexual exploitation of women, usually found in favor of contractors over indentured servants.

Parents were liable for bastards to both the master and the parish. If they were unable to pay the customary fine, which was almost always the case with servants, they were required to serve additional years. The assembly legislated in 1658 that the responsible father serve a year for the mother's master or indemnify him 1,500 pounds of tobacco, approximately the cost of rearing that child. The mother was charged a ton of tobacco or had two years added to her contract. These servants also could expect public censure according to English common law, facing the shame of public penance or the corporeal pain of flogging.

Following the English apprenticeship practice, parish churchwardens often relieved poor parents of their children and bound them out to learn domestic and agricultural skills. The boys served until twenty-one, and the girls until eighteen. Virginia's 1646 statutes on the poor adopted English laws on custody, abrogating parental rights, unlike Massachusetts, which embraced parental custody and gave money to families. In Virginia fatherless and destitute families often found themselves at the mercy of the churchwardens. Rather than becoming a financial handicap to the parish, they and their bound children were added to the parish workforce.

Before 1665, landholders either leased or sold lands accumulated from the headright system to freed servants eager to enter the booming tobacco trade. Some former servants who lived out their terms were able to become landowners themselves by purchasing land with their savings from work as laborers or tenants. However, unlike the company period when freed servants were able to lay claim to fifty acres once they had terminated their contracts, during the crown period the colony did not give former servants rights to land. At the end of their service, they could customarily count on their masters to give them freedom dues of corn and clothes, but not the rights to land.

The opportunity for landownership declined dramatically during the 1660s as tobacco prices dropped and land prices increased. After 1665, former servants had difficulty buying land, and immigrants began choosing other destinations, especially the proprietary colonies of Maryland, Carolina, and Pennsylvania. Given the diminishing opportunity in Virginia, many poor Englishmen chose to stay at home to work in new industries developing out of the tobacco, sugar, and textiles markets.

By the 1660s in England, the birthrate had fallen, partly because of the earlier emigration, and the death rate had risen, partly because of the plague. Over the next twenty years, the number of youth fifteen to twenty-four years old in the workforce had declined by one-sixth. At the same time the English economy was rapidly expanding as a result of the new network of colonial trade and the twenty-year building boom following the Great Fire of London in 1661. An unprecedented demand for labor arose. Regarding the laboring poor as the key to the English economy, Restoration-era policy makers began discouraging emigration as harmful to the creation of national wealth. By the 1680s Chief Justice Francis Pemberton was prosecuting merchants for spiriting Englishmen to Virginia.

By this time perhaps 80 percent of Virginians were or had been indentured servants. As many as one-quarter of the freed servants were landless, forced to hire out their labor or move to the backcountry, where they were vulnerable to Indian attack. Poverty was more apparent among their numbers, and social tensions increased. The presence of this growing landless class was of great concern to the planters, who began searching for a more tractable and permanent labor force to replace the indentured servants who were no longer coming.

By 1700 Virginia's largest planters had turned to African slavery as the primary source of labor. Their reasons for doing so are complex. Was it purely economic necessity, that is, the market forces of supply and demand, that pushed planters to slavery? Clearly a declining pool of poor laborers in the British Isles and new and healthier opportunities for servants in places like Pennsylvania made it harder to find young people willing to come to the Chesapeake. At the same time the expansion of Virginia's white population by natural increase created more households and encouraged the settlement of the Piedmont region, which increased the need for even more laborers. White planters also had before them a successful model of plantation agriculture that depended exclusively on African slaves: the sugar plantations of the West Indies. If Dutch and later British ships could easily bring the needed laborers to Virginia at a reasonable price, why not accept slavery as a logical substitute for indentured labor?

But why enslave only Africans? Englishmen had fought battles with the "barbarians" of Ireland in the sixteenth century and "heathen" natives of North America in the seventeenth century and could have easily moved to enslave both populations. And war would have easily justified such actions as English custom did allow for those captured in battle to be sold into slavery. Some Indians were enslaved after Bacon's Rebellion in the 1670s as were native groups in New England and South Carolina at about the same time; but because they did not adapt well to slavery and their numbers were relatively small, large tobacco planters never fully embraced the bondage of this group.

Literary evidence from the Shakespearean era indicates that Englishmen adhered to a deep-seated racism that viewed anything black as dirty and evil and anyone from the African continent as savage and heathen. Seventeenth-century Englishmen were predisposed toward a hierarchy of skin coloration that placed persons of African descent at the bottom of the heap. This predisposition to think of Africans as inferior to lighter-skinned persons was manifested in the racial laws passed by the House of Burgesses between the 1640s and 1660s, before their labor was needed. Racism clearly crossed the Atlantic from England and now was strengthened by the materialistic ambitions of a developing planter elite.

Recognizing their risk in a society turning toward color as a marker of class status, people with African ancestry sued to preserve their free status, relying on their paternity and Christian conversion as shields against enslavement. Elizabeth Key in 1655 successfully claimed free status because she was a Christian, she had been party to a contract, and her father was an Englishman. Because the English associated their Protestantism with their liberty, suits challenging enslavement based on this fundamental principle provided them with a moral dilemma. Manuel and Fernando were African-descended men who sued for freedom based on their Christianity. Their Hispanic names suggest that they were Creoles who had emigrated from a Spanish colony. Manuel won his freedom from slavery in 1665, the court finding that he should serve only as long as any other Christian. Two years later a Norfolk court judged Fernando a slave for life, but he appealed to the General Court. Although its judgment is not extant, the assembly that year resolved the uncertainty concerning Christianity and slavery by passing a law explicitly stating that baptism did not affect enslaved status. After 1670 most Africans entering Virginia would be enslaved under the cover of international law as non-Christian war captives.

To address the paternity issue, the assembly in 1662 stipulated that children born bond or free would take the condition of their mother, thus giving planters authority over the children of enslaved women. Paternity then would not matter if the mother was enslaved; furthermore, no man would be held answerable for her pregnancy. In that same year the assembly doubled the fine for a "Christian" (white) who engaged in interracial fornication. This act was principally directed against white women, for their offspring, following the condition of the mother, would increase the free nonwhite population, even if she were indentured. To avoid that eventuality, lawmakers felt compelled to try to curb the sexual choices of European women.

Despite the law, white women continued to bear mixed-raced babies, so in 1691 the assembly increased the penalty for interracial sex. A free white woman could pay a fine of £15 sterling within a month of bearing a child of mixed ancestry, or she would be sold as a servant for five years. A servant who could not pay the fine would be sold for five years after completing her service; her child was bound out for thirty years. Trying to preserve the racial character of the free population, authorities increasingly viewed interracial marriage as threatening to the social order and so outlawed it in 1691, labeled the offspring of such unions as "spurious," and banished from the colony anyone disobeying the statute. That same year the legislature required that manumitted slaves be transported out of the colony. All of these laws were consolidated into a slave code in 1705 which denied blacks the civil rights accorded whites. Virginia had become a slave society ready to utilize African slave labor to meet its economic needs. Ironically, the institution of black slavery may have intensified a greater appreciation of liberty among the white slaveholding class and a stronger sense of equality among all whites at the expense of blacks.

The demand for slave labor did not manifest itself immediately. There were approximately 2,000 slaves in Virginia in 1670 out of a population of 35,000. The decline in indenture immigration occurred at the time of depression, which lessened the need for more labor. However, the tobacco culture revived in the 1670s, and planters sought new sources, looking longingly toward Africa. Their desires coincided with those of the crown to grab a portion of the African trade. In 1660 Charles chartered a royal company to compete with the Netherlands—the Royal Adventurers into Africa—licensing them to trade for Africa's natural commodities, not human chattels. The company in 1663 slightly changed its name to the Royal Adventurers Trading to Africa but considerably changed its mission to engage in the slave trade. The new charter granted it a monopoly to supply British colonies with 3,000 Africans annually, but the great demand for enslaved labor in the British West Indies, especially in Barbados and Jamaica, left only a few hundred for the Virginia market. In 1670 Governor Berkeley estimated that only two or three slavers from Barbados had arrived in Virginia after the reorganization of the company.

The crown attempted to increase its share of the slave trade by privatizing the Adventurers into a joint-stock company in 1672. The new Royal African Company retained monopoly status, excluding English-owned ships that were not part of the company. That exclusivity was dropped in 1678 when the crown gave the company the authority to license separate traders. Virginia's new demand for enslaved labor was initially met by Royal African captains avoiding regulations and independent traders trying to break into the market, who smuggled slaves from the West Indies to the Chesapeake's numerous inlets, points, and bays. Rarely before 1680, Colonel Edmund Jennings reported, did a slave ship come directly from Africa. More likely its last port of call was Bridgetown, Barbados.

The improved tobacco market and depressed sugar prices changed this pattern. Faced with mounting debts, Barbadian planters began shipping excess labor northward, and soon they were accompanying their slaves to Virginia. They could instantly establish plantations there with the headright acreage accrued with the transportation of the enslaved

property. Before long, Royal African Company ships and separate traders operating under its license began bypassing Barbados, sailing directly
from Africa to Virginia.

By this time Virginia planters had changed their economic strategy,
shifting purchases from indentured to enslaved laborers. The slave trade
offered a remedy to the haphazard servant trade. Now planters could invest in a permanent labor force, not only owning the laborers for life but
their progeny into perpetuity as well. Slaves also had fewer legal protections and could be more easily exploited. Stafford planter William Fitzhugh quickly transformed his plantations from indentured to enslaved
labor during the 1680s, purchasing Africans from merchants operating
with royal licenses. He bragged in 1686 that his twenty-nine Africans
were young and fertile and would replenish that "stock forever."

Despite the influx of African laborers, the Royal African Company
could not meet the Virginia demand during the 1680s. It refused to change
its monopoly policy, allowing only its licensees to deliver slaves to Virginia. Nevertheless, planters continued to import slaves; by 1700, 6,000
to 10,000 slaves lived in Virginia, half of whom had been born in Africa.
More significantly, they had become one-half of the bound labor force.
In the older sweet-scented tobacco counties, enslaved laborers amounted
to 40 percent of the population and were the mass of tobacco workers.
African labor had become essential to Virginia.

These Africans, having endured a harrowing Middle Passage across
the Atlantic, were more culturally alienated than the earlier generation
of African Creoles from the West Indies who had had some experience
with a foreign culture before coming north. Without a common identity
or language, the new arrivals struggled to assimilate, only reluctantly
giving up their African roots. They congregated in the countryside to cel-
ebrate their customs in feasts and burial rituals. Their burial goods might
include tobacco pipes with African stylized motifs bearing patterns from
the Akans (Ghana), Tivs, Igbos, and Ejaghans (Nigeria). They met on
Saturday evenings and Sundays when laborers were customarily given
time off. Following West African practices, which the enslaved blended
from their various cultures, these rites, which Morgan Godwyn called
"Idolatrous Dances and Revels," included the ring shout and took place
at night. These weekend gatherings, especially the nocturnal festivities,
frightened the settlers, who believed that the slaves were using this time
to plot insurrection. They were highly suspicious of the funerary ritual
of the second burial, which occurred weeks, even months, after a death
to allow for preparation and attendance.

Such fears were translated into laws controlling the slaves' behavior. In 1680 the colony outlawed funerals for Africans. The Surry County
court required the enslaved to carry passes when away from their plan-

tations and to wear blue clothing as a badge of their status. If that color was unavailable, then they had to wear clothes made of coarse linen or canvas material rather than the fine linen that they preferred. The assembly in 1680 specified that a fugitive slave be whipped with twenty lashes in each county on his way back to his master's county. Owners of a slave killed resisting capture would be compensated by the county with 4,000 pounds of tobacco.

Despite harsher laws, a rebellious spirit among some slaves could not be crushed. In 1687 an African plot to rise up in the Northern Neck, destroy the English, and carry the rebellion throughout the colony prompted the governor to issue a proclamation to enforce the laws banning black assembly. In that same year John Nickson, a white servant on Ralph Wormeley II's Middlesex County plantation, organized servants and slaves in a plot to secure powder, bullets, and guns before making their escape by force of arms. The authorities, learning of the conspiracy, jailed Nickson before they could act. Two years later Mingoe and Lawrence, both enslaved and likely members of Nickson's conspiracy, escaped from the Wormeley plantation and became outliers. Gathering others under their command, they raided plantations in Rappahannock and Middlesex counties, where they seized livestock and firearms. After their capture the court sentenced Mingoe to be flogged with thirty-nine lashes and sent Lawrence, who had been carrying a gun, to Williamsburg to appear before the General Court. Although the disposition of his case is unknown, he was probably hung.

White indentured servants like Nickson had good reasons to feel rebellious. Those on the land felt the pinch of low tobacco prices; those released from service had no resources to sustain a decent existence and complained that they were reduced to hiring themselves out into virtual slavery. The first sign of organized protest came in 1663 when nine veterans of Cromwell's army organized bound laborers in Gloucester to march on Governor Berkeley's house in Green Spring and demand their freedom. Should he refuse their demand, they were prepared to overthrow him and seize the colony in a coup d'état. Thomas Birkenhead, a fellow servant, betrayed the conspirators; and some of them were arrested as they rendezvoused for their march. In the aftermath of the insurrection scare, the General Assembly passed laws that required servants to carry passes when away from their masters' plantations, rewarded Birkenhead with his freedom and 5,000 pounds of tobacco, and memorialized the event on 14 September as an annual thanksgiving day. Continued unrest and fear of servile revolt induced the assembly in 1670 to deny entry to transported felons.

This fear was realized shortly afterward in 1676 with Bacon's Rebellion. This significant event in Virginia history was brought on by the confluence of renewed Indian raids, government policy that hindered planters from taking Indian land, land competition between elite groups, and a growing number of discontented impoverished laborers seeking changes in their condition. What began as an effort to stop Indian attacks and reform Governor Berkeley's land policy turned into a serious effort to overthrow the colonial government.

An encounter in July 1675 between a Doeg Indian trading party from Maryland and Thomas Matthews, a major planter in Stafford County, ended in a skirmish leaving several Doegs and Matthews's overseer dead. When Berkeley did not respond vigorously with military action, several northern Virginia planters led militias in deadly attacks against the Doegs and Susquehannocks in the Potomac and Rappahannock river basins. Susquehannocks retaliated with raids of their own, killing thirty-six settlers in one assault in Stafford in January 1676. Encouraged by these successes, other Indian groups began pillaging settlements. Panicked frontiersmen demanded a forceful response from the governor; but Berkeley, not wanting a full-fledged Indian war, delayed any action. At his suggestion the assembly approved a defensive posture, building forts at key locations and authorizing search missions but prohibiting them from engaging the enemy until further orders came from the governor. An angry populace petitioned for action; but the aging and petulant Berkeley rebuffed their entreaties, even forbidding additional petitions. What the anti-Berkeley faction needed was a leader.

Nathaniel Bacon provided that leadership. Twenty-nine years of age, he was the well-educated son of an English lord who had wasted away his inheritance before being sent to Virginia in 1674 for a fresh start. He settled on a small plantation in eastern Henrico County and within six months was appointed to the Council of State, perhaps because William Berkeley was a cousin by marriage. In April 1676 Bacon and a group of young planter friends, motivated by land hunger and fears of a combined Indian attack, challenged Berkeley's leadership, especially his Indian policy. Other small farmers, especially the freed servants who were denied access to the greater landownership enjoyed by the previous generation, were rankled by the policy opposing their designs on Indian lands. They coveted the Pamunkey reserve in the Pamunkey Neck, denied them in statutes of 1654, 1656, and 1662. The planters hoped that by defeating the Indians, perhaps even driving them away, their lands would become available for additional tobacco cultivation.

Against the warnings of Berkeley, who rejected his request for a commission, Bacon, who had lost a servant to an Indian attack, agreed to lead the war against the Indians. While he was on this mission, Berkeley declared him a rebel and called for the election of a new assembly, the first in fourteen years, to deal with the Indian problem; he even expanded the electorate to include freemen as well as freeholders. Bacon's successful Indian campaign gained him election to the Burgesses, but upon arriving in Jamestown to take his seat, he was arrested and brought before the governor, who reportedly exclaimed, "Now I behold the greatest rebel that ever was in Virginia." Amazingly, Berkeley pardoned a contrite Bacon and restored him to the council. The new assembly, minus Bacon, who returned home to be with his sick wife, then proceeded to enact changes that guaranteed the vote to freemen, proscribed unlawful assemblies, liberalized local office holding, reformed county government, extended the time for debtors to pay their debts, and authorized aggressive warfare against the Indians. Some have interpreted "Bacon's Laws," clearly aimed at addressing political grievances and equalizing class differences, as the forerunner to the Revolutionary protest a century later.

Near the end of the session, Bacon, accompanied by 500 militia, marched back to Jamestown and demanded exoneration along with his pardon and commissions to fight the Indians. In a dramatic personal encounter, Berkeley rejected the requests and called Bacon a rebel and a traitor. Bacon then swore, "God damne my Blood, I came for a commission, and commission I shall have before I goe." He then prepared his soldiers to fire on the statehouse, at which point the terrified burgesses persuaded the governor to concede. With commission in hand, the young rebel went off to subdue the Indians.

During the summer relations between Berkeley and Bacon deteriorated. Proclaimed a traitor once again, Bacon marched on Jamestown and forced the governor, who had little support among his planter friends, to flee to the Eastern Shore. Bacon was now the ruler of Virginia. In a "Declaration to the People" and a "Manifesto," he justified his actions while condemning the governor for failing to address the Indian attacks. He also won pledges of loyalty from subordinates should the king send a force against him. Once again he went after Indians, this time defeating the Pamunkeys.

While Bacon was away, Berkeley returned to the capital in September, pardoned its defenders, and waited for Bacon to attack him. Before marching on Jamestown, the young rebel broadened the rebellion by promising bondservants land and freedom if they would support his cause; many blacks joined the effort. He then besieged Jamestown, forcing the governor to depart for Accomack once more. Bacon then burned the town to the ground. Thereafter, his men grew tired of inaction and began pillaging loyalist plantations. Then suddenly Bacon died of dysentery on 26 October; he was buried in a secret grave.

Lacking Bacon's leadership abilities, his successors were overwhelmed by Berkeley's forces, and the rebellion came to an end. The vengeful governor proceeded to court-martial and hang every conspirator he could get his hands on, causing King Charles reputedly to remark, "That old fool has hanged more men in that naked country than I have done here for the murder of my father." The king, who had ordered a 1,000-man expedition to retake the colony when he learned of the rebellion, moved to restore order to his "Old Dominion." The discredited Berkeley was ordered home, but for a short time he defiantly refused to give up his authority to the new governor, Sir Herbert Jeffreys; he died two months after returning to England. A royal investigation of the rebellion put most of the blame on Berkeley and recommended stronger crown authority to check the independence of the colony. The assembly repealed some of "Bacon's Laws" and authorized payment for the English troops sent to quell the uprising.

Bacon's Rebellion was not a fight for liberty but a struggle for power and land among competing planter groups. The winners were the older gentry, not the recently arrived parvenu planters like Bacon or the indentured class. Bacon was himself an equivocal revolutionary, unsure of what he was doing, except for suppressing Indians. The obstinate Berkeley was unsympathetic to the rebels' anger over Indian attacks, partly because he believed it reflected their appetite for Indian lands. Although the rebellion failed, it served as a warning to subsequent royal governors that the wishes of the colonists were not to be trifled with.

Indians suffered the greatest losses during the rebellion, further contributing to their decimation; but in the aftermath the Pamunkeys at least had their lands restored. In the Middle Plantation Treaty of 1677, signed for the Indians by the weroansqua Cockacoeske and her son, Indian land was secured by English patent law, and settlement was prohibited within three miles of the tribal holdings. The Indians were to pay ceremonial tribute of three arrows to the crown and twenty beaver pelts to the governor. Because the land was now patented, the English could purchase it, unlike earlier restrictions; and the Pamunkeys began to sell it. But the deals were voided after the Indians were only given partial payment. Indians also unsuccessfully petitioned the assembly for the right to sell land that was off-limits to settlement. A second treaty signed in 1683 included Meherrins and Monocans.

By the 1690s the English were still trying to seize the reserved Indian land, pointing to the Indians' demise as justification. Planters had attempted to swindle the Chickahominies out of their land in the late 1680s by removing them from Pamunkey Neck to the Dragon Swamp. The council voided the deal and repatriated the Chickahominies. Nevertheless, the council petitioned the crown in May 1688 to open land to settlement in Pamunkey Neck and Blackwater Swamp because the Indians were not able to fully use the land with their reduced numbers. William Blathwayt of the Lords of Trade refused their request. In 1696 the General Assembly petitioned Governor Edmund Andros to open these

lands because of the Indian decline. By that time Indians, who were selling most of the patented land, could muster only 362 bowmen, including
100 from the tribes of the Eastern Shore. The Indian population of eastern Virginia numbered less than 2,000, an 85 percent decline from the
first contact with the English at Jamestown.

Virginia Indians continued to have conflicts with settlers and were
involved with the competing parties in the wars of empire in the eighteenth century. Nevertheless, having lost their struggle for their homeland by the end of the seventeenth century, Indians were no longer major
players in the history of the commonwealth. Three centuries later their
population had only reached the numbers at the time of the Jamestown
landing; but there were eight active tribal governments, two of whom,
the Mattaponis and Pamunkeys, still comply with the requirements of
the 1677 treaty that obligates them to pay tribute to the state, now offered to the governor in the form of turkeys or deer.

King Charles blamed Bacon's Rebellion on an independent governor
and assembly who had not been sympathetic to the desires of the crown
or the problems of the colonists. Continued acts of defiance by an assembly still dominated by friends of Berkeley forced the king's hand. As part
of his plan to centralize control over the empire, he moved to restore
crown authority in Virginia by dispatching a close adviser, Thomas,
Lord Culpeper, as the new governor in 1680 with instructions for reining
in the assembly. Culpeper informed the burgesses that henceforth they
would meet at the pleasure of the king and would consider only bills
that the king, through the governor, presented to it. Although such royal
orders were rarely enforced, the assembly was now on notice regarding
its independent, anticrown behavior. Culpeper also requested a tax on
tobacco to pay for the cost of colonial government. Burgesses objected
to the loss of spending control to the governor, but they reluctantly approved the legislation.

The king's efforts to reassert authority did not prevent another more
modest rebellion in 1682 caused by low tobacco prices. Attributing the
prices to overproduction, planters petitioned the crown for a cessation
of tobacco sales, which they hoped would artificially create a demand,
allowing the price to rise. Charles was not sympathetic to their request
because he received taxes from the sale of tobacco; the more tobacco produced, the more money he received. Before the crown could answer their
petition, some planters began destroying their crops. Even goodwives
picked up hoes in defiance, a breakdown in cultural decorum, for only
wenches were supposed to work with hoes. Robert Beverley, the clerk of
the House of Burgesses, who had refused to turn over its journals to the
royal commission after Bacon's Rebellion, egged on the rebellion. A great
planter with holdings of over 50,000 acres and forty-two enslaved Africans

by the time of his death in 1689, Beverley stood to gain a windfall profit on unregistered tobacco that he had seized and shipped to England in the winter of 1682. The rebels were the poorer planters, many of whom were ex-servants like those who had joined Bacon's Rebellion just five years earlier. That spring they cut fledgling plants on over 200 plantations at a time when it was too late to reseed the beds. Acting governor Sir Henry Chicheley called out the militia to restore order; two of the rebels were hanged; and a general pardon was issued. Although the Council of State considered evidence of crimes against the state in Beverley's actions, he was only chastised after demonstrating contrition. The assembly made plant cutting a treasonous offense in 1684.

In 1683 Culpeper, for violating his orders to remain in Virginia, was replaced by Francis Howard, fifth Baron Howard of Effingham, who chose to live in Virginia and vigorously prosecute the king's charge to reduce assembly power. His imperious tenure was marked by bitter contests with the burgesses, who reluctantly conceded some of their independence. In 1684 Effingham won repeal of the legislature's right to hear appeals of lawsuits and annulled laws passed that were not to his liking. The burgesses rebuffed demands that they give up their taxing power; but Effingham continued to veto their bills; removed Beverley, Thomas Ludwell, and other critics from their offices; and repeatedly sent the assembly home when it proved obdurate, as was often the case during his governorship. The assembly did, however, successfully resist the crown's efforts to establish a town system out of fear that it would undermine the tobacco monoculture. Effingham also increased his authority over the militia and the church; and when he sailed for home in 1689, he left behind a Virginia that was clearly less independent of England's supervision than it had been during the Berkeley years.

In 1688 Charles's brother, who came to the throne three years earlier as King James II, was deposed for his authoritarian and Catholic tendencies by parliamentary Anglicans under the leadership of James's Protestant daughter Mary and her Dutch husband, Prince William of Orange. This "Glorious Revolution" caused great anxiety in the colony. Rumors spread that Maryland Catholics, joined by vengeful Indians, would invade the province as part of a religious war. But the accession of William and Mary to the throne and Parliament's adoption of an act of religious toleration and a Bill of Rights soothed raw nerves. A religious war in France did lead to the settlement of 500 Protestant French Huguenots in Manakin Town west of Richmond in 1700.

Although King William and Queen Mary seemed favorably disposed toward the Old Dominion, they continued the Stuarts' efforts to consolidate the realm. They pursued greater intercolonial coordination through a postal system, a vice-admiralty court system for the colonies, and a new Board of Trade. They sought to control colonial trade and facilitate defensive arrangements in the likelihood of wars with Indians and the French. To achieve these goals, strong loyal governors and compliant assemblies were required; but the monarchs' Atlantic vision had difficulty competing with local concerns for profits and rights.

Virginia's planter leaders maintained their parochial outlook. Although embarrassed by slow growth in the colony and economic instability, they were unwilling to tamper with the tobacco culture that undergirded their political power. After a three-year tour of the colonies ending in 1695, Edward Randolph, the commissioner of customs, found bribery and faulty certificates in the land offices and fraud in the tobacco trade. Responding to Randolph's report, which criticized the concentration of land in the hands of a few, the crown in 1696 instituted the Board of Trade, whose most influential member would be the philosopher John Locke. Locke queried Commissary James Blair, the bishop of London's ecclesiastical representative in Virginia, about the problems with Virginia's economy. Blair described a fraudulent land system that retarded both tobacco production and the peopling of the colony. The next year Blair, Henry Hartwell, and Edward Chilton reported in *The Present State of Virginia* that fraud was rife in land policy and had hindered tobacco cultivation through land hoarding. In response, Locke in 1698 directed the Board of Trade to reform Virginia's land policy; but this move was too late. The gentry had already established themselves as a permanent powerful landholding elite capable of obstructing crown policy.

Locke and Blair also teamed up to urge the compulsory Christianization of "Negroes" and Indians, seemingly in violation of Locke's well-known defense of religious toleration. Although he may have believed that exposure to the Gospel would improve their intellectual capacity, Locke and Virginians were in agreement that conversion would not affect their status as slaves. Nonetheless, planters resisted Christianization efforts for another generation.

By the end of the seventeenth century, Virginia was a well-established and flourishing English colony of nearly 60,000 inhabitants. A declining death rate allowed the population to reproduce itself just as indenture immigration lessened. It was, in James Horn's estimation, "a simplified version of English society, but also a highly aberrant one." Settlers to Virginia had come, not as visionaries or victims of religious persecution seeking to create a new "city upon a hill," but as Englishmen intent on gaining fortunes in a community much like the one they had left. Customs, law, and political and religious institutions represented local adjustments to traditional English practices. A hierarchy of place—a patriarchy—was now growing more permanent through control of land and tobacco production in the hands of a small elite. Government officials owned 60 percent of all landholdings over 2,000 acres. At the other extreme, tenancy was very high, perhaps including a third of all small farmers. But as English as Virginia was, it was also "aberrant" in its growing slave labor system, the absence of a town culture, and its economic dependence on a single commodity. Furthermore, both the distance from the mother country and an environment of isolation encouraged a more independent outlook that would tolerate little interference with individual pursuits of happiness. Virginians had transformed English law and custom into a powerful sense of justice and rights that became the basis for questioning political legitimacy in the eighteenth century.

SOURCES CONSULTED

Warren M. Billings, *Sir William Berkeley and the Forging of Colonial Virginia* (2004); Edward L. Bond, *Damned Souls in a Tobacco Colony: Religion in Seventeenth-Century Virginia* (2000); Robert Brenner, *Merchants and Revolution: Commercial Change, Political Conflict, and London's Overseas Traders, 1550–1653* (1993); Kathleen M. Brown, *Good Wives, Nasty Wenches, and Anxious Patriarchs: Gender, Race, and Colonial Virginia* (1996); David W. Galenson, *Traders, Planters, and Slaves: Market Behavior in Early English America* (1986); April Hatfield, *Atlantic Virginia: Intercolonial Relations in the Seventeenth Century* (2004); James Horn, *Adapting to a New World: English Society in the Seventeenth-Century Chesapeake* (1994); Allan Kulikoff, *Tobacco and Slaves: The Development of Southern Cultures in the Chesapeake, 1680–1800* (1986); John J. McCusker and Russell R. Menard, *The Economy of British America, 1607–1789* (1985); Edmund S. Morgan, *American Slavery, American Freedom: The Ordeal of Colonial Virginia* (1975); Philip D. Morgan, *Slave Counterpoint: Black Culture in the Eighteenth-Century Chesapeake and Low Country* (1998); John Ruston Pagan, *Anne Orthwood's Bastard: Sex and Law in Early Virginia* (2002); Anthony S. Parent Jr. *Foul Means: The Formation of a Slave Society in Virginia, 1660–1740* (2003); Carla Gardina Pestana, *The English Atlantic in an Age of Revolution, 1640–1661* (2004); Jacob M. Price, *Tobacco in Atlantic Trade: The Chesapeake, London, and Glasgow, 1675–1775* (1995); Darrett B. Rutman and Anita H. Rutman, *A Place in Time: Middlesex County, Virginia, 1650–1750* (1984); Alden T. Vaughan, *The Roots of American Racism: Essays on the Colonial Experience* (1995); Wilcomb E. Washburn, *The Governor and the Rebel: A History of Bacon's Rebellion in Virginia* (1954).

4

A PLANTER'S PATRIARCHY

1690–1775

On 5 July 1726 William Byrd II wrote to the earl of Orrery, "Like one of the Patriarchs, I have my Flocks and my Herds, my Bond-men and Bond-women, and every Sort of trade amongst my own Servants, so that I live in a kind of independence [of] everyone but Providence." As he reflected on his life at his Westover plantation along the James River, Byrd seemed much like an Old Testament patriarch who was master of all he sur-veyed: the vast acres, fields, woods, streams, and all the people who lived therein literally belonged to him. Whether white or black, free or unfree, male or female, family or tenant, all of the men, women, and children who inhabited Westover were technically his to command. English tradi-tion, Virginia law, and local custom upheld this nearly absolute power; and few would have openly challenged Byrd's position of authority on his plantation, in his neighborhood, his parish, his county, or in the colony at large. He was indeed a patriarch.

Byrd is representative of a small group of families that by about 1700 had achieved substantial political, social, and economic power at both the local and provincial levels. Although in many ways the Byrds, Carters, Lees, Beverleys, Randolphs, Washingtons, Masons, Cabells, and others would retain this hegemony through the Revolutionary era, the opera-tion of and challenges to this patriarchal system can be most clearly seen from the 1690s to the 1760s. Here a variety of patriarchies would be es-tablished in which a certain group of adult white men held sway over all aspects of colonial society from the legislative chambers in Williamsburg to the houses and fields of rural Virginia. Central to this society would be the mature tobacco economy and the chattel slavery that sustained it. Racial patriarchy would be found both in the benevolent and harsh treat-ment of black slaves and in the laws and customs that developed around this unique labor system. A patriarchy of gender would place white

WILLIAM BYRD II, BY HANS HYSSING

WESTOVER, CHARLES CITY COUNTY, HOME OF WILLIAM BYRD II

women within a narrowly defined set of duties and expected behaviors. Beyond the farmsteads and plantations, a political patriarchy would develop that saw prominent planters achieve success in county and parish offices and then move on to serve in the House of Burgesses or council.

Yet this planter patriarchy was never as uniform or as all-powerful as sometimes imagined. Mismanagement of tobacco cultivation brought financial and social ruin to the best of families. Inattention to the local freeholders meant defeat in House of Burgesses elections; rivalry between local families fostered decades of discord, not harmony. Passive resistance from the slave quarters gave agency to those who were assumed to have none; the property white women brought to marriages both bolstered and undermined male economic and political status; and the Baptists and other religious nonconformists challenged the established church and the gentry who ran its vestries. Eighteenth-century Virginia may have had its share of patriarchs, but they ruled "Uneasy Kingdoms."

Virginia's patriarchal society was intimately connected to the cultivation of tobacco, and the production of the noxious weed dictated the economic and cultural rhythms of the Old Dominion. Although many planters had begun to diversify into corn and other grains during the eighteenth century, tobacco still represented three-quarters of the exports from the Chesapeake in the 1770s. A "tobacco mentality" dominated much of the Tidewater and Piedmont, and the plant touched every Virginian in some way.

A single tobacco crop took more than a year to produce. On large plantations slaves performed nearly all of the work; on small farms the planter and his family plus a few servants and/or slaves executed the required tasks. The production cycle usually began a few weeks after Christmas when the best seeds collected from the previous year were planted in specially prepared beds rich in livestock manure. By March workers were in the main fields preparing the individual hills in which the seedlings would be placed. A very large planter like Landon Carter saw to the preparation of more than 200,000 hills on his Richmond County lands. Between April and early June, the transplant process occurred; children (slave or free) often pulled up the seedlings and carried them to the fields, but adults usually performed the more delicate task of inserting the plants in the individual hills.

As the tobacco grew, each plant required attention from the workers. When the stalk contained eight to twelve leaves, the plant was topped to prevent flowering; but this topping soon encouraged the growth of additional "sucker" leaves that then had to be removed by hand. Constant hoeing kept unwanted weeds at bay and the workforce continually busy. In September workers cut the plants at the base and hung them on drying racks usually located in specially designed tobacco barns. Each planter had his own, often secret, method of deciding when to cut, carefully examining the color, texture, and moisture content of the leaves. The curing was often augmented by building fires that helped dry the leaves but also ran the risk of burning down the entire barn. When the planter determined that the tobacco had cured properly, the leaves were stripped from the stalks and laid in large piles to await packing. The final task for the planter and his workforce was "prizing" or packing the tobacco leaves in huge barrels called hogsheads. Layer upon layer of tobacco was laid in the barrels and pressed until the hogshead weighed approximately 1,000 pounds.

Before the hogsheads could be shipped to the British Isles, they had to be taken to public warehouses and there examined by inspectors looking for "trash" tobacco that was often produced by small farmers on marginal lands or from the use of "sucker" leaves that had not been removed from the maturing plant. Officials burned any low-quality tobacco they found and, for everything that passed inspection, issued tobacco notes that often circulated like cash. By March the tobacco ships began to arrive in the Chesapeake; and the huge hogsheads were loaded for shipment to mercantile companies in London, Bristol, or Glasgow. Fifteen months had elapsed since the tobacco cycle began, and the next cycle was already three months under way.

As the ships pulled away from the public and private docks along the James, Rappahannock, York, and Potomac rivers or eased out of the inlets of the Chesapeake Bay, their cargo was on consignment to British merchants who then resold the hogsheads to English or French tobacco dealers. Most merchants also acted as purchasing agents—having taken over this role from the planters—buying fine china, furniture, linens, silk, hats, shoes, paint, glass, or whatever else the large planters needed and shipping it back to Virginia. Actual cash money or specie rarely changed hands as the merchants simply kept a running list of debits and credits for each planter they represented. Only rarely did small farmers deal directly with the major mercantile houses, and in the seventeenth and early eighteenth centuries they usually sold their tobacco to a larger planter in their neighborhood who then combined it with his hogsheads for shipment to Britain. By the third decade of the eighteenth century, this system began to change as factors representing Scottish firms moved to Williamsburg, Norfolk, and Alexandria or into the settlements of the growing Piedmont region and set up small stores where they traded tobacco for finished goods from Britain. Here, too, the small planter operated like his larger neighbor by maintaining a running account of debits and credits.

The consignment and factor systems of the tobacco economy depended upon continuing demand for the product in Europe, sustained production in the colonies, and a reasonable return on investment for the planters. The initial tobacco frenzy had lasted until about 1680 when demand leveled off for the next forty years bringing stagnation and uncertainty to Virginia and the Chesapeake. But in the early eighteenth century, the French became addicted to the weed; and demand again began to climb steadily until the Revolution. The period of stagnation also brought depressed prices; but these, too, began to rise about 1720 and increased steadily but not dramatically for the rest of the colonial period. These positive long-term trends of the eighteenth century encouraged Tidewater planters to maintain or expand their acreage under cultivation and fostered land speculation and population explosion in the Piedmont region where the colonial government created twenty-five new counties between 1728 and 1761. Nevertheless, short-term fluctuations remained worrisome as planters and merchants, creditors and debtors, speculated about the future. What was a planter to think as the average price per pound of tobacco dropped from 0.8 pence in 1740 to 0.45 pence in 1747 and then rose to 1.16 pence in 1750?

The tobacco planters and farmers of Virginia adhered to the concept of a hierarchical society that they or their ancestors had brought with them from England. Most held to the general idea of a Great Chain of Being: at the top were God and his heavenly host; next came kings (and sometimes queens) who were divinely sanctioned to rule, then a hereditary aristocracy who were followed in descending order by wealthy landed gentry, small independent farmers, tenant farmers, servants, and finally vagabonds, transients, criminals, and the mentally ill. People entered these classes at birth and expected to end their days with the same status as their parents. A hierarchy within families mirrored the Great Chain: husband as head, then the wife, children, and finally servants. Aspirations to rise above one's station in life were considered a sin. God had created this world, and he expected man to live appropriately within it. Most Virginia men and women readily acknowledged that this was the proper ordering of society.

Yet Virginia was not Europe. The landscape, crops, animals, and the mixture of peoples here challenged these traditional definitions of a proper society. Few aristocrats immigrated to America, and kings and queens remained far away in Europe. Slavery was narrowly defined in English law but was now being widely established in many British colonies, especially Virginia. Indigenous peoples had to be fit into English law and custom, but how? What economic and legal power does a wife have if her husband is absent for months at a time on business or if he dies and no adult male relatives are nearby? These and many more unique issues would haunt Virginians during the early years of settlement; and many, but not all, of the problems would be resolved by pushing and bending English law and custom to fit the new conditions in the new environment. Old World hierarchy and Old World households were transplanted, but they gained a Virginia twist here.

The basic unit of societal organization in Virginia was the household, and in most respects it operated much like those in England. Living arrangements in the seventeenth century had often been chaotic as unmarried men lived together, death ended most marriages after only a few years, and infant mortality remained high. By the eighteenth century, however, the traditional English household became the norm as mortality rates declined due to better housing and improved and reliable nutrition. The husband headed the household and represented it to the outside world. He was liable for all the debts owed to local or overseas creditors, and he paid all the taxes to the county or parish. He was also responsible for the behavior of every member of the household, including his own immediate family, other relatives who lived there, employees, servants, and slaves. If an unruly servant or wife continued to plague the community with inappropriate behavior, the head of the family might find himself in court along with the offending member of his household. Tasked with the economic well-being of the household, the male head of household spent long days tending to the tobacco crop and on the smallest farms did most of the fieldwork himself, perhaps with the help of a servant or slave.

The planter's wife was the secondary authority figure in the household, acting as a kind of junior partner in the management of both the family and the plantation. During the seventeenth century when there were twice as many men as women, single women and widows had enjoyed increased power to negotiate marriage contracts and manage their own property; but as the sex ratio evened out and both men and women lived longer, traditional English definitions of the husband-wife relationship returned. The use of the prenuptial jointure contract dwindled, and most wives had no property rights independent of their husbands'. Although law and custom allowed husbands to grant power of attorney to their wives when they were away on business, and a number of men did, as a general rule the legal and practical power of married women declined in Virginia during the eighteenth century.

The only group of women with substantial independence and power were widows, who could buy and sell land, execute contracts, will their property to whomever they pleased, and represent themselves in court. Although the male head of household was clearly the norm, the economic importance of widows cannot be overlooked. In Accomack County, for example, women represented 10 to 15 percent of the landowners and controlled nearly 20 percent of the county's acreage during the eighteenth century. Despite these contributions, English Protestant traditions and customs still imagined women as weaker than men in body and mind; and therefore, even the wealthiest widows sometimes had trouble getting servants, male neighbors, or business associates to take them seriously. For these reasons, most widows sought remarriage as a simpler way to have someone to manage and protect estates that they hoped one day to pass on to their children.

A wife's job was to run the home. Normally, her major responsibilities included the cooking, cleaning, and sewing as well as the supervision of the children, stepchildren, and any domestic servants or slaves. On large plantations her duties were primarily managerial, seeing to it that others performed the needed tasks; on small farms, she did much of the household labor herself, possibly assisted by a single servant or house slave. The wife of a small planter also might be in the fields helping at critical times when every hand was needed for planting or cutting. Whether a wife had one or twenty slaves, it was her responsibility to keep them working at their assigned tasks and to discipline any and all as needed. And the law stood behind her. Servants and slaves had to obey; severe punishment for insubordination was thought appropriate except in extreme cases of abuse by masters or mistresses.

Children occupied the next rung in the household hierarchy. The father concerned himself with economic issues of food and shelter and the long-term goal of providing an appropriate inheritance; the mother cared for the children with little assistance from the father. Children entered the family every two to three years until the mother reached menopause, so a typical couple had four to six children at home during most of their marriage. Sons of small farmers worked in the fields beside their fathers until they married; daughters helped with kitchen and household chores as soon as they were able. When children married and left the family unit, they were usually given the use of some of their parent's land or slaves but rarely got clear title to either until the father died. Although the law ensured that a widow received adequate resources after her husband's death, adult children were not so protected; and unruly or ungrateful sons and daughters frequently were left out of wills.

Servants and slaves were next in the plantation hierarchy. The former had dominated the field and domestic workforces of the seventeenth century; the latter occupied these positions in the eighteenth century. In some places the transition from indentured servants to African slave labor was remarkably quick; and in other areas of Virginia, slavery arrived more gradually. By 1710 the governor reported that virtually no indentured servants had arrived in the past few years. Although African labor would soon dominate the farms and plantations of Virginia, the eighteenth century also witnessed the importation of another group of unfree workers: convicts. As a result of the Transportation Act of 1718, perhaps as many as 20,000 criminals, both men and women, were transported from the British Isles to Virginia where they worked off their punishment as field, domestic, or artisan servants.

By 1720 or so, the entire colony of Virginia had been transformed from a society with slaves to a slave society. For the first hundred years of settlement, Virginia had been a place where slavery existed alongside other forms of labor as a variety of economic interests and practices competed for prominence. In a slave society, however, slavery stood at the center of the economy, and all social, political, and religious institutions supported the master-slave relationship. Although the large planters began the transformation in the late seventeenth century, by 1720 small planters had joined the ranks of slaveholders and had begun to share in the ideology that supported the institution.

Virginia planters created a slave society by importing nearly 90,000 Africans between 1690 and 1770; in peak years over 3,000 came ashore. A high percentage of them came from the Bight of Biafra, Angola, and Senegambia. In the seventeenth century ships had arrived with a mixed cargo of goods and a few slaves from the West Indies; by the 1720s special slave ships sailed directly from the coast of Africa to specific destinations in the Chesapeake. In 1727, for example, a ship with 140 slaves pulled up at Robert "King" Carter's Corotoman plantation along the Rappahannock in Lancaster County; and for the next three weeks, Carter helped sell the cargo to his friends and neighbors while taking a percentage of the receipts for himself. These importations and sales continued at a feverish pace throughout the Tidewater until about 1740 when imports declined gradually as the native-born slave population began to replace itself by natural increase. Now large planters could count on generation after generation of laborers produced in their own slave quarters. Black slaves had been only 7 percent of Virginia's population in 1680, had increased to 30 percent in 1720, and stood at 187,000 or 42 percent by 1770. Virginia had the largest slave population in North America and was indeed a slave society.

These tens of thousands of African slaves lived in a world controlled and defined by their owners. The slave could be whipped or beaten at will, or his toes or fingers cut off for chronic disobedience; he could be sold to a distant planter at a moment's notice or sexually exploited by any member of the master's family. The slaves had no freedom. Yet within the very narrow limitations of their lives, slaves developed family life, kinship associations, and cultural practices that helped them get through each day and make sense of their existence. The shape and texture of the slave existence often depended upon the size of the slave community, the ratio of men to women, the mixture of African and native born, the type of work done, and the level of interaction with whites.

Large slave communities, like those found on the major Tidewater plantations, offered the possibility of some form of stable family life. Half of the adults may have lived in some form of marriage or union, and most of the children resided with their parents and may have had grandparents and aunts and uncles nearby. Even those families that had been split apart often continued to live in the same neighborhoods, and it was usually possible for husbands and wives or parents and children to see each other on a regular basis. The somewhat more stable family life also meant that marriage-like unions formed early, slave women produced large families, and plantation populations grew rapidly enough that few new slaves entered the community directly from Africa. Although these communities contained some vague elements of the African past in the form of spiritual and magical practices, they reflected much of the white society around them as well. Most of these slaves spoke some form of English, wore Anglo-American clothing, and had grown up around the tobacco culture like their white counterparts. Although only a small number of Virginia slaves were Christian before the Revolution, black children were being routinely baptized in some parishes by the 1760s; and many slave communities had begun to incorporate some kind of one-God idea into their traditional worldview.

The more settled Tidewater plantations also offered some opportunities for adult male slaves to acquire skills that often gave them access to better housing and food and a more privileged position within their communities. Conversely, the greater the diversity of skills among the male slaves, the more likely that the monotony and drudgery of fieldwork would be placed exclusively on the adult women. In each case, however, male and female children learned artisan, field, or domestic skills from a parent much like the white children with whom they often played. While the year-round and never-ending tobacco cycle left little free time for anything but the master's work, many slaves did manage to raise chickens or tend a small garden on their Sunday day off. The slave household could consume these fruits of their own labors or sell them to other families on their home or nearby plantations.

Piedmont slave communities tended to be somewhat different. Because most of the slave imports after 1740 went to these newly settled regions, slave groupings here tended to be predominantly young and male and often included a remarkable collage of African cultural influences and languages. The English language would have been new to many of these slaves, but they probably learned the basics quickly as they were more likely than their Tidewater cousins to work side-by-side with the small farmers who owned them. Here, too, the material conditions of life were simple and plain. Clothing was coarse and housing crude, but the slaves' close association with their white owners and white servants often meant better nutrition. With few elderly slaves on the farm and few slave women, the opportunities for family life or kinship associations remained limited. By the end of the eighteenth century, however, Piedmont slave communities began to resemble those of the Tidewater as the sex ratio evened out, locally born children began to form families, and no new slaves arrived directly from Africa.

The communities to which these slaves and their masters belonged were entirely rural. Unlike New England where the town or village was the focal point of community life, Virginia contained almost no towns; and thus the sense and operation of community played out very differently. Connections between isolated plantations or farmsteads often began with kinship networks. In the older, settled Tidewater areas, the average white family might be related to five other families nearby; and a household head might interact with thirty or more relatives on a regular basis. Beyond kinship connections, networks of friends visited the plantation routinely and also witnessed wills, stood security for posted bonds, acted as godparents, or provided testimony in legal disputes. Although their economic and political responsibilities meant that men had broader networks of friends and contacts, women formed bonds by assisting friends during childbirth and illness. These kinship and friendship networks merged to form neighborhoods that might include all those households in an area between two streams or along a particular road.

Small planters and their families rarely ventured beyond the neighborhood, but when they did, it was normally for judicial proceedings and market days at county seats or religious services at the closest church or chapel. Some counties contained only a single parish and, thus officially, a single parish church; many others had two parishes or a mother church that served the entire parish and smaller chapels located in precincts of the parish, as in Lancaster County. The two large neighborhoods on either side of the wide Corotoman River came to think of themselves as separate parishes with separate churches—Christ Church and St. Mary's White Chapel—even though legally they were only precincts of a single parish. Thus on Sunday mornings at either church, several smaller rural neighborhoods came together not only to worship but to exchange business documents, discuss tobacco prices, argue over the quality of horses, catch up on local gossip, and share news of the wider world. By the eighteenth century a majority of the white residents seem to have attended services on a regular basis, and every church and chapel served as an information center for the community, for notices and announcements were posted on the church door and read by the parson from the pulpit.

These complex circles of association involved all Virginians in some way. Servants, slaves, women, children, and poor whites operated within the smallest circles and only rarely interacted with the larger county community; small planters who owned their own land had a wider association that occasionally put them in touch with tobacco inspectors, churchwardens, vestrymen, sheriffs, and justices of the peace. Only the largest planters and their families had much contact outside the county as they visited with their wealthy cousins throughout the Chesapeake and gentlemen journeyed to Williamsburg, Annapolis, Philadelphia, or even London. Routine matters fueled these associational networks month in and month out, but every three years or so the community connected for yet another purpose: politics.

While the interconnectedness of rural Virginia life makes it difficult to separate the social, economic, and religious aspects from the political, House of Burgesses elections demonstrate how different layers of county society related to the world of legislators, governors, ministers, and even kings. Each of Britain's North American colonies had some type of legislative assembly elected by the people. By the early eighteenth century,

CHRIST CHURCH, LANCASTER COUNTY, 1732

Virginia had defined "the people"—its political citizens—as adult white male freeholders at least twenty-one years old; a freeholder was someone who owned land outright or a tenant with a life lease. In 1736 a final amendment to the law specified that a freehold contain at least 25 acres of improved land or 100 acres of unimproved land in the possession of the voter for at least a year. Persons living in the incorporated towns of Jamestown, Williamsburg, and Norfolk had to own a lot and house of specified size to qualify. Although few if any women voted in earlier years, in 1699 they were specifically excluded; disenfranchisement of free blacks, mulattoes, and Indians occurred in 1723. Like the laws of England and the other colonies, the Virginia franchise sought to limit the political community to those with a stake in society: those who had a long-term economic connection and commitment to the community in which they lived.

Although the dream of owning land and thus having a stake in society drew many Englishmen to Virginia during the colonial period, such dreams did not always become a reality. By the 1750s only about one-half of the adult white males owned enough land to qualify to vote, and perhaps another 20 percent met the requirements as tenants by holding life leases on property. The remaining 30 percent of the adult white male population along with all women and free blacks were excluded from direct participation in the political life of the Old Dominion. Although this electorate seems much restricted by modern standards, Virginia was more democratic than the mother country, where no more than 15 percent of the adult males could vote, and on a par with Pennsylvania and some New England colonies. Within Virginia opportunities to vote varied enormously, with only 35 to 45 percent of the white males qualified in Fairfax, Loudoun, and Fauquier counties but as many as 70 to 85 percent in Lancaster, Berkeley, Halifax, and Lunenburg counties. As the Revolution approached these numbers decreased, and Virginia became less democratic; a booming population and fewer opportunities to own land put more and more white men outside the political community.

Those that did belong to the political community participated in a process that seems at odds with the hierarchical and patriarchal society in which they lived: they got to select freely and openly the men who would represent them in Williamsburg. Yet here, too, the layered society held its ground. In most counties those who ran for election and especially those elected were the same wealthy, prominent elite gentry who owned the largest plantations and served as parish vestrymen and county justices of the peace. This was the case in most of the older Tidewater counties and often occurred in the Piedmont and Valley counties as they reached maturity. Numerous Carters, Lees, Randolphs, and Cabells, as well as George Washington, Patrick Henry, and Thomas Jefferson, all won election to the house. Planters with a strong economic base in land and slaves had the time and interest to devote to local and provincial politics; smaller farmers who worked alongside their slaves in the fields could ill afford to be away for weeks or months at a time. Traditional English civic virtue also encouraged gentlemen of breeding, education, and wealth to shoulder the responsibilities of public office as a duty owed to the lower orders of society who in turn treated them with deference and respect.

But if members of the planter elite monopolized elections to the House of Burgesses, how did local voters distinguish between one gentlemen and another? The process began when the governor dissolved the sitting House of Burgesses and issued writs for new elections. Although English precedent dictated elections at least every seven years, other factors triggered more frequent elections: the death of a monarch, arrival of a new governor, or the governor's displeasure with the actions of the current assembly. With the exception of Jamestown, Williamsburg, Norfolk, and the College of William and Mary, which each elected a single burgess to the assembly, Virginia's counties each sent two representatives to the capital.

The process of selecting the two burgesses varied substantially from county to county and from region to region. Although a candidate's wealth and experience in parish and county offices all pushed him to the forefront in the minds of the freeholders, geography often played a critical role. In general, freeholders favored local men, men they knew, men from their parish or neighborhood whom they greeted at church on Sunday and saw at the nearby ordinary or tobacco warehouse. And a freeholder's daily social and economic sphere had much to do with his perspective on politics. Small farmers saw no farther than the boundaries of their familiar neighborhoods and usually voted for local gentlemen who could address very local issues, but larger planters interacted with other planters from across the county and tended to favor candidates with broad interests in the general welfare of the whole county. Sometimes, too, voting reflected different perspectives on local issues; a proposal to build a new church or split a county or parish usually gained strong support from those most affected, but such plans might also raise the taxes of everyone in the parish or county. Finally, freeholders also equated the plantation management skills of potential candidates with their general ability to manage public affairs. Virginia's layered rural society certainly had a political dimension that usually mirrored the local social and economic hierarchy; but unless gentlemen remained acceptable to ordinary men, in most cases they were not entrusted with legislative office.

Those elected to the House of Burgesses journeyed out of the county a few weeks each year to join the larger political community in Williamsburg. Here they interacted with other burgesses, with members of the governor's council who held crown appointments, often for life, and with the governor himself. Although Williamsburg was just a small provincial town of a few thousand, it was the big time for most burgesses; and there was serious business at hand. The Virginia House of Burgesses had begun in 1619 as a stop-gap measure to help the failing colony avoid ruin, but over the next 150 years it evolved into an assertive legislative assembly with greater authority than the royal governors appointed by the king. As the burgesses pursued their quest for power, they came into direct conflict with both the council and a series of governors and lieutenant governors. Sometimes these conflicts spilled over into elections for the assembly and thus further enhanced the notion that the voters had an important and serious duty to perform. Such struggles also elevated the status of the political patriarchs coming out of each county, for they truly held the future of the colony in their hands. By the 1720s governors finally realized that they could neither dominate nor bully the house and council and chose instead to work with them to solve the colony's problems; this cordial relationship would stand until the final decade of the colonial period.

The House of Burgesses' drive for power had sputtered by the 1680s and seemed on its deathbed following the Glorious Revolution of 1688 when members of the council and several governors pushed the house aside and fought among themselves for control of the colonial government. Central to this struggle was the Reverend James Blair, who became one of the most powerful men in the colony by virtue of his leadership of the Church of England in Virginia and the College of William and Mary, which gained its charter in 1693. Having lost his Scottish parish for his refusal to endorse Catholic succession to the throne, Blair won his colonial appointment as commissary for the bishop of London through friendships with Protestant bishops who had been restored to authority by the Glorious Revolution. He proceeded to reform the church in Virginia, attempting to expand his power over clerics and laity alike. His unwavering desire to create and sustain the college put him at odds with councilors and governors and resulted in the downfall of several of the latter.

The period began on a positive note with the appointment of Francis Nicholson as governor in 1690. He courted the goodwill of council members and other leaders in Jamestown, supported Blair's efforts to establish a college, reorganized the militia, and in general supported whatever legislation the council or house proposed. However, in 1692 he became the governor of Maryland. His successor was Sir Edmund Andros, who had been governor of New York and of the short-lived Dominion of New England. He had a reputation as a strong advocate of crown author-

JAMES BLAIR, BY JOHN HARGRAVE

ity; and within a year tensions between him and local political leaders began to build over plans to establish new towns, the crown's desire for tighter control over tobacco shipments, and the governor's need to send money to New York to support the war with France. Andros's undoing came at the hands of Blair, who became a member of the council in 1694. Convinced that the governor had thwarted funding for the college, Blair began working for his removal. Through friendship with John Locke who served on the newly established Board of Trade, Blair built a strong case against Andros, who finally resigned in ill health in 1698.

Andros's replacement was none other than Francis Nicholson. When the statehouse at Jamestown burned for a third time in 1698, Nicholson moved the capital to Middle Plantation where the new college now re-sided and where Nicholson could once again practice the town design skills he had used in Annapolis a few years earlier. The governor laid out a grid pattern of streets for the town, now called Williamsburg, and made plans for a capitol and a substantial residence for the governor. While the Capitol would be completed by 1705, the governor's house was not fin-ished until 1720.

Although Nicholson received much praise for his efforts to establish the new capital, his instructions from the Board of Trade to reform the

FIRST CAPITOL AT WILLIAMSBURG, BUILT 1705,
RECONSTRUCTED AND DEDICATED IN 1934

land grant system, revise the laws of the colony, and redefine the powers of the council soon soured the governor's relations with Virginia leaders. Nicholson did end the practice of issuing headrights for imported slaves, but he accomplished little else toward land reform, and much western land ended up in the hands of the Virginia elite. His biggest problem came when he challenged the powers and privileges of the council. He began by insisting that large land patents come through him and not the council. Next he took away the group's power to appoint county sheriffs and had the secretary of the colony appoint county clerks without the council's input. At the same time he ended plural office holding by forcing old and new councilors alike to give up lucrative posts as naval officers, collectors, auditors, and other positions related to the custom system.

By 1702 the Council of State was in open revolt, and in the House of Burgesses' elections that year, both sides worked for the selection of their candidates, a battle that Nicholson seems to have won. This defeat did not deter six members of the council from petitioning Queen Anne to have the governor removed. Nicholson also aggravated a former ally, the irascible Blair, by failing to revise religious laws and establish separate ecclesiastical courts as the commissary desired. Blair sailed for England to maneuver his political connections against the governor, whose character, Blair claimed, made him unworthy to rule. Although Nicholson mounted a last-minute defense against his detractors, it came too late; and the queen dismissed him in early 1705. His replacement, Lieutenant Governor Edward Nott, died after serving a year; and the French captured the next appointee as he traveled to Virginia. The council then assumed control and ran the colony for the next four years without either a House of Burgesses or a governor. Twelve elite patriarchs now ruled Virginia, and for the moment the council was the most powerful body in the colony.

In 1710 the earl of Orkney, the new governor of Virginia, sent Alexander Spotswood as lieutenant governor to serve in his stead; lieutenant governors would now occupy the executive mansion until 1768. Although the councilors had relished their near-absolute power, their four-year rule saw tobacco prices fall, a major crop failure, and a general economic depression brought on by the continuing Continental wars. Everyone including the council was ready for a change. Spotswood proved a master politician in his first few years in office by tackling head-on the colony's defense, relationships with Native Americans, and the tobacco problem. He saw Indian problems as something more than a military issue and moved to strengthen diplomatic and economic ties with various tribes. In addition, Spotswood confronted the growing piracy problem by sending a naval expedition to the North Carolina Outer Banks where royal sailors killed the infamous pirate Blackbeard.

For the more complex tobacco problem, Spotswood hit upon a scheme that would raise prices and increase his own political power at the same time. In 1713 he introduced legislation proposing a series of tobacco warehouses and inspectors who would ensure that tobacco of less quantity but higher quality would reach the European market. Both large and small planters initially balked at the plan; but when Spotswood announced that twenty-nine of the fifty-one burgesses would receive appointments to the lucrative inspector posts, the bill passed both houses. Although tobacco prices did not immediately increase, Spotswood's new patronage network seemed to guarantee his success, until Queen Anne's death and the Carolina Yamasee War in 1715 forced him to call new elections. The ensuing election campaign, perhaps the most competitive thus far in Virginia history, resulted in the overwhelming defeat of incumbents, including all but one of the tobacco inspectors. Although the governor's patronage scheme was now in shambles, the new House of Burgesses was too inexperienced to strike back at him through legislative channels. The council was a different matter, however; and when Spotswood tried to streamline the collection of quitrents, which would increase crown revenues but likely decrease the commissions of men like Receiver General William Byrd II and Attorney General Philip Ludwell, they used their political pull in London to get the Privy Council to disallow both the tobacco inspection act and the governor's Indian trading company.

Spotswood responded to this affront as he had done several times in the past by calling for new elections. Again he miscalculated; nearly all of his enemies retained their seats. Not surprisingly, Spotswood soon sent the new house home while he weighed his options for the future. First, he tried to get the Privy Council to replace a number of councilors including William Byrd II; he was partially successful, but Byrd remained. Second, he decided to strengthen his royal prerogatives by insisting that as governor he could appoint new parish ministers without consulting the local vestry; this scheme backfired. Finally, he announced that he intended to become a Virginian and live there the rest of his days. This approach brought better results. The council and governor agreed to work out their future differences at home and not in England, and the 1720 elections saw Spotswood increase his strength in the house to a significant minority. He also improved his popularity among the elite by initiating a new land settlement plan in the west to create a buffer against the French by offering lucrative land grants to prospective settlers. The council granted tens of thousands of acres to prominent Virginians including themselves; the governor got 86,000 acres and named the new county Spotsylvania.

Spotswood's new cozy relationship with the political patriarchs of Virginia came too late. In 1722 Hugh Drysdale arrived from England as the new lieutenant governor. Spotswood's ten-year squabble with the council was well known in Britain, and officials there may have decided a change was in order. Unlike many of their fellow councilors, neither William Byrd II nor the Reverend James Blair had reconciled with the governor; and both were in London at the time. If Blair was behind the change, and there is some evidence that he was, then Spotswood was the third governor in a row to have his career ended by the unforgiving, single-minded cleric. And since Drysdale apparently owed his office to Blair, the new governor remained very conciliatory toward him and the other councilors during his brief four-year term. When Drysdale died in 1726, he was remembered fondly as the first governor in fifty years to have gotten along completely with the Virginia elite.

Drysdale's successor, Lieutenant Governor William Gooch, would follow in his footsteps. Although the new elections Gooch called for early 1728 had no overriding issue at stake, it had been five years since the last contest; and a more assertive House of Burgesses under the leadership of Speaker John Holloway now encouraged more new men to seek legislative office. The resulting contest saw competition in 70 percent of the elections; 35 percent of the incumbents lost their seats.

The newly invigorated house spent much of the next decade debating a tobacco inspection plan that would become the hallmark of the Gooch administration. The governor's proposal had many of the same features as the highly controversial plan Spotswood put forward fifteen years earlier, but Gooch's political suavity and willingness to work with the Burgesses eventually would bring him success. As before, the plan called for public tobacco warehouses and inspectors and the elimination of poor-quality tobacco, but it also standardized the size of the hogsheads used to ship tobacco and authorized warehouse receipts as legal tender. Immediate opposition from large and small planters forced Gooch to add a "place bill" that reduced the governor's own political patronage by forbidding burgesses and sheriffs from holding the lucrative inspector posts. This and other lobbying by Gooch brought the burgesses around, and the plan passed both houses in 1730 and was approved by the Board of Trade.

Small planters still did not like the tobacco inspection plan, for it increased their transportation costs by forcing them to move their hogsheads to the warehouses, and it appeared to favor the larger planters who often produced the higher-quality tobacco. This dissatisfaction turned to violence in 1732 when rioters burned warehouses in Lancaster, Northumberland, Prince William, and King George counties. The burgesses were horrified and quickly authorized rewards for the names of arsonists; Gooch called out the militia and arrested some of the leaders. Threats of violence continued for the next year or so, and the freeholders and leaseholders of several Tidewater counties sent petitions to the Burgesses asking for repeal. When the house ignored the petitions and renewed the act in 1734, frustrations again mounted. Things came to a head in 1735 when Gooch had to call new elections. Voters now had their say. Competitive elections raged throughout Virginia; and 45 percent of the incumbents suffered defeat, especially those who had supported the tobacco law. In Richmond County 90 percent of the eligible voters turned out and sent one incumbent packing; even the normally docile electorates of York and Warwick counties rose up and unseated, respectively, Speaker John Randolph and long-serving William Harwood. The small farmers had gotten their way; and in the opening session of the new assembly, the house did

TOBACCO PROCESSING IN MID-EIGHTEENTH CENTURY

their bidding and voted to repeal the tobacco act. The council, however, rejected the repeal. The tobacco inspection issue would continue to simmer below the surface; but in 1738 the new Speaker, John Robinson, easily got the law renewed against only modest opposition. Three years later it passed once more with no dispute.

Gooch could now turn his attention to a mounting problem beyond Virginia shores: the ever-expanding circle of European war. At this particular moment Spain, not France, was the enemy; and the point of contention for Britain and its colonies was trade competition in the Caribbean. In 1740 former lieutenant governor Spotswood urged the colonies, including Virginia, to raise an expeditionary force and join the proposed siege of the Spanish stronghold at Cartagena in modern Colombia. Spotswood's death a few months later put Gooch in the spotlight, and he soon left Virginia to command the "American" unit. The siege was a disaster. Injury and disease took a large toll; Gooch was wounded in the leg and permanently crippled. By 1744 France had joined the war effort, and for the next few years the governor and burgesses directed their attention toward the French in Canada and their Indian allies in New York and Pennsylvania.

Although the house reluctantly voted funds for some of these war efforts, local issues soon took center stage when the Capitol in Williamsburg burned in 1747. The need to rebuild soon turned into a debate over whether the capital should be moved to a more central location in the expanding colony. Naturally, burgesses in the Piedmont and Northern Neck wanted it moved farther west while those near Williamsburg saw no reason for change. The house voted for the move; but the councilors, who all lived nearby, blocked the measure twice. Elections in 1748 brought some new faces but did not change the sentiment of the house; and it again tried to move the capital, this time to Hanover County. The council held its ground, and finally the house agreed to rebuild in Williamsburg with the caveat that the capital could be moved at some point in the future. With the rebuilding under way, Gooch decided it was time to retire after twenty-two years in office; he sailed for England in August 1749, leaving the colony in the hands of the council president, now interim governor, Thomas Lee.

Gooch left behind a mature colonial society that seemed on the verge of greatness. The Tidewater and parts of the Piedmont had been settled for decades by large and small planters who all embraced a slave-based tobacco economy. The stately homes of the gentry, the modest wooden houses of the middling farmers, and the brick churches and courthouses that dotted the countryside all presented a picture of stability, prosperity, order, and confidence. A vibrant Atlantic trading system brought both luxury goods and everyday necessities to many Virginia households; and decent housing, rural living, and adequate foodstuffs meant long and healthy life spans for most whites. A locally elected House of Burgesses now controlled most of the colony's internal affairs while Virginians received all the benefits of membership in the British Empire and only occasionally had to put up with interference from officials in London. This indeed seemed like a perfect planter's patriarchy.

Yet bubbling below the surface of this idyllic midcentury world were internal and external factors that would challenge this patriarchal regime. Some of the challenges came from abroad but were triggered by local conditions and developments. Land speculation and settlement in the West brought Frenchmen and Englishmen into direct contact, sparking renewed conflict and eventually a world war fought primarily in America. War, overproduction, and limited increase in demand hit tobacco markets just at the point when the rhythms of Virginia society had become psychologically, as well as economically, wedded to the plant.

The uncertainties in the tobacco economy may have had the most profound impact on patriarchal authority and the confidence that patriarchs had in themselves. The modest but steady increase in prices from the 1720s onward not only had encouraged the expansion of tobacco lands into the Piedmont but had led long-established planters to take on greater indebtedness to British merchants so that they could put marginal lands into production, increase their slave holdings, and diversify into other economic activities. The Virginia gentry also used their tobacco credits to increase the quality of their lives; the most fashionable manufactured goods from England could now be found in homes like William Byrd's Westover and Robert Carter III's Nomini Hall. Middling planters also joined the consumer revolution with the help of Scottish factors who gladly exchanged small quantities of tobacco (or the promise of future tobacco) for goods similar to those found in the homes of the elite. By the 1750s white Virginians of all social levels had become full members of an Atlantic "empire of goods."

When this empire became less predictable after midcentury, as the up-and-down swings in the economy came at closer and closer intervals, planters had trouble recovering from each downturn before the next one arrived. The Seven Years' War did not help matters. Disrupted shipping lanes hindered the flow of goods, and British financiers became more cautious with investments. Improved markets in the late 1760s spurred further optimism that again fell apart in 1772. As each new recession came and went, the relationship between Virginia planters and British merchants began to change. Where once the merchants had been considered friends and economic compatriots as they extended nearly unlimited credit, they now became suspicious adversaries when they called in accounts or refused to honor bills of exchange that acted like personal checks. By 1775 Virginia planters owed £1.4 million to British merchants, a figure that probably had tripled since 1750; Virginians held 46 percent of all British debt in the thirteen mainland colonies. Thomas Jefferson and George Washington each owed more than £1,000; fifty-five members of the House of Burgesses also owed more than £500 each.

This increasing indebtedness and its fiscal impact began to take its toll on the planters, and their letters and diaries reflect a growing psychological uneasiness. Virginians stewed about the loss of personal independence that seemed at the heart of their patriarchal culture. Being an independent gentleman, as William Byrd II noted in 1726, meant having full control over family, slaves, servants, and lands; the only dependency was to God. The word *dependent* had negative connotations: wives, children, servants, and bondspeople were dependents; gentlemen planters were not. But by the 1760s Virginia planters saw themselves as dependents, and the economy provided little hope that things would get better. Debt equaled dependency; and the more they reflected on the notion, the more the planters seemed to realize that they had always been dependents and that they had never been the independent patriarchs they once imagined.

Tobacco markets, debt, and dependency set the tone for the decades of the 1760s and 1770s. Planters began to think of every disagreeable event in their lives as part of some larger crisis afflicting the entire society. Even the occurrence of highly competitive elections and the occasional defeat of an incumbent planter came to be seen as a creeping malaise infecting the body politic. Just as tobacco prices declined, so too did the civic virtue of their youth; and in its place, they imagined, had developed a corrupting public culture like that of the mother country. Theodorick Bland Sr. was shocked in 1765 that a friend in Dinwiddie County had been "swilling the planters with bumbo"—a cheap rum punch—to solicit votes. And in his 1770 drama *The Candidates,* Robert Munford portrayed men like Sir John Toddy, Mr. Strutabout, and Mr. Smallhopes who would do and promise anything to get elected, the kinds of candidates who were challenging traditional gentlemen like Mr. Worthy and Mr. Would'be. The patriarchal ideal of disinterested civic virtue, according to these planters, was fast receding from view.

While some saw challenges in the electoral arena as disturbing, others found discomfort in recent religious developments. On the eve of the Revolution, growing numbers of evangelical dissenters—non-Anglicans who were primarily Separate Baptists and New Light Presbyterians—were beginning to worry the planter patriarchy and to challenge the long-established Anglican Church of Virginia. Some found the increasing numbers alarming. Jefferson believed dissenters outnumbered Anglicans in 1775, although his estimate is probably a wild exaggeration. There were nine Separate Baptist congregations in Virginia in 1769 and fifty-four congregations just five years later. The growth of non-Anglican groups threatened the established order in two ways. First, the movement represented individuals and families who had forsaken the Book of Common Prayer for false or misguided religious ideas; second, these dissenters challenged the role of the parish in the everyday life of Virginians and the authority of the gentry-controlled parish vestries.

Dissenters had been a small presence in Virginia throughout the colonial period and until the 1740s represented little or no threat to the establishment. At the beginning of the eighteenth century, authorities had even encouraged French and German Protestant settlements in places like Germanna in Spotsylvania County by offering a seven-year exemption from parish taxes. The vestry in King George County helped sustain a small dissenter congregation for a few years, and the Anglican minister in Hanover County went out of his way in 1734 to help some local Lutherans. In the older, settled regions of Virginia, these early non-Anglican groups played by the rules, paying their parish levies as required by law, getting an official license for their ministers, having their members married in the Anglican Church, and keeping their religious ideas within the confines of their chapel or meetinghouse.

Some strains on the established system began to be felt in the 1730s as Scotch-Irish, Germans, and other Europeans moved into the northern end of the Shenandoah Valley and spread south and eastward. In some places they came to be the majority; and thus Presbyterians, Baptists, and Lutherans dominated some newly created county courts and parish vestries. As late as 1740, however, the slowly growing dissent ruffled few among the established order and presented no cause for alarm.

The nature and character of dissent changed in the 1740s, and so did the response by traditional authorities. A Great Awakening had hit the British Atlantic world in the 1730s, bringing with it an evangelical message of "new birth" and dividing old New England Puritan congregations and Presbyterian assemblies into New Lights and Old Lights. The movement infected Anglicanism as ministers like George Whitefield first aroused churches in England and then traveled to the colonies in the late 1730s and early 1740s to spread his message of salvation to standing-room-only crowds from Pennsylvania to Georgia. While some Anglicans and Presbyterians in Virginia responded to this enthusiastic message, the biggest response came from middling and lower-class whites who would come to be called Separate Baptists. They did not play by the rules. Rather than keeping to themselves as earlier dissenters had, these evangelicals insisted on spreading their message to everyone, including devout Anglicans and black slaves. While the Lutherans and Presbyterians had educated ministers specifically trained for duty in their churches, the Separate Baptists believed that anyone who was truly converted could spread the gospel; an illiterate blacksmith called by God was to be preferred over an English-educated Anglican cleric. These evangelicals also saw no need to obtain the customary licenses required by law and wandered from county to county as itinerant preachers speaking for hours in fields, homes, or taverns.

It is possible that many of these middling and tenant farmers found the emotionless, ritualistic Anglican service unfulfilling, or some may have chaffed against their assigned place at the bottom of the traditional county social order. Whatever led them to gravitate toward the evangelical message, the Separate Baptists promoted the equality of all souls before God and welcomed and baptized slaves into their congregations, treating them as "brothers" and "sisters" but also insisting that they adhere to the strict moral code of the evangelicals. The Baptists railed against the gambling, horse racing, card playing, dancing, swearing, drinking, and Sabbath-breaking that seemed to be the mainstay of traditional gentry culture. To Virginia elites this was indeed a world turned upside down.

This overtly antihierarchical, antiauthoritarian, and antigentry message provoked official and unofficial responses from Virginia leaders. In general, the newly settled areas of the Southside and Valley, where non-Anglicans were often a significant minority, witnessed only minor confrontations between traditional authorities and the New Lights; however, major conflict occurred in the older Tidewater and Piedmont regions. In 1750 the council began to tighten restrictions on issuing meetinghouse licenses for Presbyterian groups in Hanover and nearby counties. The House of Burgesses also nullified the Hanover County elections of 1752 because of promises both winning candidates had made to dissenters regarding the creation of new parishes. Occasionally, when colonial authorities seemed to be ignoring the evangelical threat, the local gentry took matters into their own hands. In 1771 an Anglican minister disrupted a dissenter service by beating the preacher at the pulpit and dragging him outside where the sheriff of Caroline County, in the presence of several other gentlemen, gave him twenty lashes with a horsewhip. Such violence in the late colonial period indicates that some members of the traditional elite saw religious dissent as an attack on their patriarchal world.

Slavery posed another challenge to the planter patriarchy. The vast majority of farmers and planters were dependent upon slave labor for their very existence, and the presence of a growing black population made them nervous. In 1750 Virginia's slaves numbered 100,000; doubling to 200,000 by 1775, they amounted to more than 40 percent of the total population. Slavery was much less pronounced in the western Piedmont and the Valley; but in many older Tidewater counties, blacks outnumbered whites. Although violence by slaves against whites was extremely rare, an occasional organized uprising—like those of 1710, 1713, 1722, and especially 1730—and a murder now and then sent tremors throughout the white population and would be remembered for decades. After each of these major rebellions and dozens of smaller events, white patrols increased their vigilance by making regular visits to the slave quarters; but after a month or two such surveillance would become intermittent at best. Rumors from the 1730s onward of attempts by renegade slaves to set up permanent maroon communities in the Dismal Swamp on the North Carolina border or in the western mountains continued to fuel fears of massive black-armed insurrections like those that had occurred in Jamaica from 1725 to 1740. Patriarchs feared black slaves but could think of no way to live without them.

Runaway slaves added to the frustrations of the patriarchal class as each escapee represented a direct affront to the power and authority of the master. As long as the slave remained at large, the master could no longer claim to have complete control of "his people"; a recaptured slave put the patriarchal regime back in order. Conversely, slaves increased their own independence and freedom of action the longer they remained away from their master. Slaves ran away for a variety of reasons. Those newly arrived from Africa often tried to escape in a desperate attempt to return home but were nearly always recaptured quickly as they had no knowledge of the countryside and no one to help them as they fled. Slaves who had been in Virginia a number of years or those who were born here often escaped to be with wives or other kin on nearby plantations or farms. Some also chaffed against the workload or against a particularly tough master or overseer. Slaves who did take flight often remained at large for many weeks by relying on a widespread network of kin and friends, and occasionally even members of the white community.

Runaways illustrated an important reality of the Virginia patriarchal society: slaves had a good deal more control over their daily lives than masters were willing to admit. They could hide out for weeks under the master's nose with the aid of kinship networks on their own and adjacent plantations. Slaves also developed ways to regulate their own work patterns. Planters continually complained about slaves loafing and sleeping on the job; and some like Landon Carter tried almost everything, including a variety of punishments, to root out such habits, but to no avail. What the planters called laziness was, in fact, a combination of slower work patterns brought from Africa and behaviors learned on the tobacco farms of the Chesapeake. Because most Virginia planters organized their workforce into gangs who toiled at jobs day in and day out and were then moved to another task, there was no incentive to get the work done quickly. Household slaves learned the same habits; and they, too, slowed down their workdays as much as possible, again to the great frustration of their masters and mistresses.

In the decades before the Revolution, the final challenges to patriarchal authority came from the planter's own children and wives. Viewed separately, these challenges appear minor; but when combined with the other threats to their supremacy, independent action by women and children seemed the ultimate slap at the traditional patriarchal regime. Some of the rebelliousness among family members can be traced outside Virginia to new Enlightenment ideas about personal relationships and child rearing and to the sentimental novel that was now all the rage among literate English men and women on both sides of the Atlantic. The new novel in particular suggested that young adults and especially young women might be better served in life by discovering their own true essence and then remaking themselves in that new image. True love between men and women must be pursued at all costs; and a kinder, gentler approach to parenting was in order. In part this development was also a natural outgrowth of a society with decreased mortality where parents and children lived longer and healthier lives together and where slave labor kept family members out of the fields and together in the home. With more hours each day and more years together as families, a more affectionate, caring relationship developed. Following the stern dictates of the family patriarch was no longer the only model for a proper family or a proper society.

This paternalistic way of governing families and plantations represented a change from the divinely sanctioned, kingly rule of male patriarchs to one in which guidance, encouragement, and thoughtful persuasion shepherded wives, children, and slaves along in life. Yet for male heads of families who had reached adulthood in the 1730s or 1740s and were reaching old age in the 1760s, the clash of old and new ideas—the movement from patriarchal to paternal—presented a significant challenge that left women in an ambivalent position. Planters' wives and other married women faded from public view as the eighteenth century wore on, suggesting that the patriarchal notion of submissive womanhood had been fully realized. Fewer wives were granted power of attorney to handle the family business affairs in the husband's absence, and fewer acted as executors when their husbands died; women who used unruly, quarrelsome language—"brabbling" speech—to confront male authorities in public disappear from the court records; and the amount of land controlled by women declined in the Tidewater and probably elsewhere. The lower mortality rates and longer marriages that helped promote the new affectionate, paternalistic household by 1750 also pushed the majority of Virginia white women into exclusively domestic roles that kept them out of the tobacco fields and out of the county courthouses.

Yet a look into the private lives of Virginia families reveals that adult women had not been completely driven into submission inside the home. The property women brought to marriages both supported the patriarchal ideal and gave some wives a small amount of leverage in local politics. For large and small planters alike, women's property provided an economic boost to family financial prospects. A wife's 50 or 100 acres might be all the couple had as they started life together, or this land might increase the couple's holdings to 200 or 300 acres. Members of the elite might find a wife with thousands of acres as George Washington did when he married the young widow Martha Dandridge Custis in 1759. Most wives probably saw nothing unusual or extraordinary about the use of their property to enfranchise their husbands, but some women in a few counties took a keen interest in local politics and may have tried to influence the voting behavior of husbands and other male relatives. Candidates' wives were also very much involved in county politics, often entertaining voters in their homes or serving liquor at the courthouse on election day. Finally, male diaries and letters from this period give ample testimony to female independence in marriage, especially when husbands tried to interfere with child rearing or the management and discipline of house slaves or any other area thought to be the sole preserve of the planter's wife.

The patriarchal world of the gentlemen planter and the middling farmer had been severely shaken by the downturns in the tobacco economy, the increasing indebtedness to British merchants, the boldness of the evangelicals, the growth of the slave population, and the domestic rebellions of wives and servants. Such challenges can test the character of any society, but Virginia had a solid base upon which these crises could be weathered. Its booming population, now at half a million on the eve of the Revolution, had settled most of the Piedmont region and was spilling over the Blue Ridge into the Valley and beyond; a stable political system with an experienced House of Burgesses now ran the colony with little interference from crown authorities in Britain; and a diversifying economy with less dependency on tobacco held out promise for better years to come. The problems and the promises of Virginia might have slowly sorted themselves out in a dozen different ways, but larger forces operating throughout North America and Europe took hold of the Old Dominion and moved it in new and startling directions no one could have imagined in 1760.

SOURCES CONSULTED

Richard R. Beeman, *Varieties of Political Experience in Eighteenth-Century America* (2004); Ira Berlin, *Many Thousand Gone: The First Two Centuries of Slavery in North America* (1998); Warren Billings, *A Little Parliament: The Virginia General Assembly in the Seventeenth Century* (2004); Warren M. Billings, John E. Selby, and Thad W. Tate, *Colonial Virginia: A History* (1986); T. H. Breen, *Marketplace of Revolution: How Consumer Politics Shaped American Independence* (2004); Breen, *Tobacco Culture: The Mentality of the Great Tidewater Planters on the Eve of Revolution* (1985); A. Roger Ekirch, *Bound for America: The Transportation of British Convicts to the Colonies, 1718–1775* (1987); Jack P. Greene, *The Quest for Power: The Lower Houses of Assembly in the Southern Royal Colonies, 1689–1776* (1963); Greene, *Historical Statistics of the United States, Colonial Times to 1970*, pt. 2 (1975); Peter Hoffer, *Law and the People in Colonial America*, rev. ed. (1998); Warren Hofstra, *The Planting of New Virginia: Settlement and Landscape in the Shenandoah Valley* (2004); Jay B. Hubbell and Douglass Adair, "Robert Munford's *The Candidates*," *William and Mary Quarterly*, 3d ser. (April 1948); Rhys Isaac, *Landon Carter's Uneasy Kingdom: Revolution and Rebellion on a Virginia Plantation* (2004); Isaac, *The Transformation of Virginia, 1740–1790* (1982); John G. Kolp, *Gentlemen and Freeholders: Electoral Politics in Colonial Virginia* (1998); John G. Kolp and Terri L. Snyder, "Women and the Political Culture of Eighteenth-Century Virginia: Gender, Property Law, and Voting Rights," in *The Many Legalities of Early America*, ed. Christopher L. Tomlins and Bruce H. Mann (2001); Allan Kulikoff, *Tobacco and Slaves: The Development of Southern Cultures in the Chesapeake, 1680–1800* (1986); Kris E. Lane, *Pillaging the Empire: Piracy in the Americas, 1500–1750* (1998); John McCusker and Russell Menard, *The Economy of British America, 1607–1789* (1991); Philip D. Morgan, *Slave Counterpoint: Black Culture in the Eighteenth-Century Chesapeake and Lowcountry* (1998); John K. Nelson, *A Blessed Company: Parishes, Parsons, and Parishioners in Anglican Virginia, 1690–1776* (2001); Anthony S. Parent Jr., *Foul Means: The Formation of a Slave Society in Virginia, 1660–1740* (2003); Bruce Ragsdale, *A Planter's Republic: The Search for Economic Independence in Revolutionary Virginia* (1996); A. G. Roeber, *Faithful Magistrates: Creators of Virginia Legal Culture* (1981); Darrett B. Rutman and Anita H. Rutman, *A Place in Time: Middlesex County, Virginia, 1650–1750* (1984); Terri L. Snyder, *Brabbling Women: Disorderly Speech and the Law in Early Virginia* (2003); Mechal Sobel, *The World They Made Together: Black and White Values in Eighteenth-Century Virginia* (1987); Linda Sturtz, *Within Her Power: Propertied Women in Colonial Virginia* (2002); Charles Sydnor, *American Revolutionaries in the Making: Political Practices in Washington's Virginia* (1952); Brent Tarter, "Reflections on the Church of England in Colonial Virginia," *VMHB* (2004); Marion Tinling, ed., *The Correspondence of the Three William Byrds of Westover, Virginia* (1977).

5

AN EMPIRE IN CRISIS

1750–1775

Until the late 1740s warfare in Virginia was either localized action against Native Americans or at the most a distant sidelight to the major wars of Europe. Colonists, including Virginians, fought and died in these earlier wars as part of a number of grand European struggles to determine who sat on the throne of Spain or Austria or the principality of Hanover. But now the struggle had little to do with which dynasties ruled Europe but rather focused on who controlled North America. It would take two wars to determine the fate of the continent: in the first Virginians and other colonists joined with their mother country to strengthen the British Empire by expelling the French from all but a few islands off the coast of Newfoundland; in the second Virginia and its twelve sister colonies fought with the help of France to leave that empire and create an independent United States.

The causes of the first North American conflict, the French and Indian War, can be traced to the competing claims over ownership and possession of the Ohio Valley. The western boundaries of the colonies of Virginia, Maryland, and Pennsylvania remained vague, and each province could reasonably point to some early colonial charter that gave it legitimate claim to the region. Various Indian groups had lived and hunted in these forests for centuries and believed they retained certain rights to the territory. However, in 1744 the Six Nations of the Iroquois signed a treaty at Lancaster, Pennsylvania, giving up rights to the Valley of Virginia and beyond; and Virginia immediately assumed that the Ohio Valley was now part of the Old Dominion. Yet France also claimed this area as part of its vast North American possessions stretching from the St. Lawrence River through the Great Lakes and down the Mississippi River to New

Orleans. Each claim seemed legitimate; but except for the Indians, no one yet possessed the land. The French had forts along Lake Erie but had not moved south to the Ohio. Few Virginians had moved into this region; but the gradual settlement of the land immediately over the Blue Ridge, what came to be called the Great Valley of Virginia or the Shenandoah Valley, had been under way for several decades and provided a springboard for populating the Ohio country.

Settlement of the Shenandoah Valley began in the 1730s as a result of British and Virginia policies designed to create a buffer between the more settled regions of the colony and French and Indian lands farther west. Governor Spotswood was most responsible for promoting expansion into the area with his 1716 expedition across the Piedmont and the mountains into the Valley. To dramatize his adventure and encourage further settlement, Spotswood created his order of the Knights of the Golden Horseshoe for the intrepid adventurers who had traveled with him and had the House of Burgesses create two large western counties, Spotsylvania and Brunswick, and exempt settlers from paying quitrents on landholdings west of the fall line. The Board of Trade had begun formulating its own policy for the broad management of the American frontier, and Spotswood's ideas fit perfectly into its plans.

Coincidental with these settlement schemes, a number of immigrant groups were looking for a place to settle, encouraged by large land grants tendered by London and Williamsburg. Although members of established Tidewater and Piedmont families did migrate west, the vast majority of settlers in the Valley were of German and Scotch-Irish background. Pushed out of the Rhineland by a series of wars early in the century and nudged out of Ulster Ireland by high rents, short leases, and increased poverty, these non-Anglican Protestants journeyed through New York or Philadelphia and eventually found their way to the Valley, using what came to be known as the Great Wagon Road. Often attracted to the area by an entrepreneurial member of their own ethnic group, like the German Jost Hite, who got 140,000 acres in the early 1730s, they settled on scattered farmsteads among their own kind to raise livestock and grain. The closely knit German communities in the middle Valley were known for their careful and industrious farming habits, distinctive barns, log homes, and Lutheran churches. The Scotch-Irish, who settled to the south of the Germans in the vicinities of Staunton, Lexington, and Roanoke, were a combative, adventurous lot who continued to move south and west in populating the American frontier; they were jealous of their liberty, both political and religious, especially their Presbyterianism. Not to be outdone, settlers of English descent purchased land in the northern end of the Valley from the Fairfax proprietary, the huge land grant that stretched along the Northern Neck from the Chesapeake Bay to the Alleghenies. Like Virginians to the east, prominent members of these groups became county justices of the peace and occasionally parish vestrymen; but with no tobacco plantations and limited slavery, their diverse Valley society had little in common with the older sections of the Old Dominion.

The shift in official interest from the Shenandoah to the Ohio came in 1747 when council president Thomas Lee and a group of other investors, including Lawrence Washington (George's half brother), members of the Fairfax family, Robert Wormeley Carter, and others from the Northern Neck, formed a speculative venture called the Ohio Company to acquire and eventually resell land in the West. For the next two years, the group worked through Governor Gooch and then the Board of Trade to obtain the needed land. Their petition requested 500,000 acres, 200,000 acres to be awarded immediately and another 300,000 as soon as they built a fort and settled a hundred families on the land. The board saw the request as an important step in thwarting French encroachment and approved the petition in 1749. Shortly thereafter, the Ohio Company got the initial 200,000 acres. George Mason, George Washington, and the newly arrived lieutenant governor Robert Dinwiddie later joined the group. Protecting these investments would soon become a matter of official policy.

The Ohio Company scheme set off a series of actions and reactions by officials in New France and Virginia that would lead to undeclared war in America and then a declared war in Europe. The first of the company land grants had barely been asserted when the French got wind of it and immediately moved to discourage settlement in the region. These moves, in turn, prompted Governor Dinwiddie to write a series of letters to the Privy Council, which in August 1753 issued instructions to Virginia and the other colonies to take whatever action they deemed necessary to protect His Majesty's possessions in North America but to avoid offensive action that might provoke open warfare. Bolstered by the promise of armaments and his own interpretation of the Privy Council instructions, Dinwiddie constructed his own set of policies to deal with the French.

His first move was diplomatic, not military. In late 1753 the governor asked George Washington, a twenty-one-year-old militia major with frontier surveying experience, to carry a letter to the French commander of a newly constructed fort just south of Lake Erie. The tall, robust, and energetic Washington jumped at the chance to enter public service and to view in person the lands of the Ohio Company. He journeyed north with help of a Dutchman who spoke some French and a guide named Christopher Gist who had already surveyed the area. They arrived at Fort Le-Boeuf in early December and formally presented Dinwiddie's letter protesting the erection of this and other French forts in an area which clearly belonged to the king of Great Britain; the French commander summarily

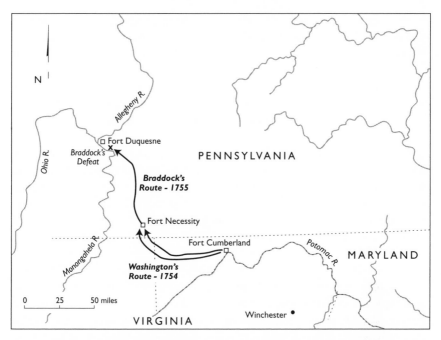

EARLY CAMPAIGNS OF THE FRENCH AND INDIAN WAR, 1754–55

rejected this claim. Diplomacy had clearly not worked; and so Dinwiddie, with the consent of the council, decided it was time to execute his instructions from the crown and forcibly remove the French from the Ohio Valley.

Again Washington was chosen for the task, with a promotion to lieutenant colonel. A troop of 200 men would be raised, further military commissions issued to traders and Ohio Company officials already in the region, and construction of a fort at the forks of the Ohio undertaken immediately. With plans under way, Dinwiddie went to the House of Burgesses for the necessary funding, which it reluctantly gave while insisting that it retain some oversight regarding expenditures. In the meantime, the French dispatched a large force into the region, ran off the small English garrison, and constructed Fort Duquesne (on the site of modern Pittsburgh). When Washington received news of the encounter, he advanced toward the fort and confronted a small French detachment, half of whom were killed in the subsequent clash.

Knowing that the French would likely retaliate, Washington led his troops back to his main encampment and hurriedly finished the seven-foot-high stockade that he called Fort Necessity. An experienced commander might have abandoned the poorly situated, poorly constructed fort and moved his men to safety farther south; but Washington decided to hold his ground. On 3 July 1754 a 1,000-man French and Indian army attacked Fort Necessity and killed or wounded nearly a third of the Anglo-Virginia forces. Late that night the French offered terms of surrender that allowed Washington to return to Virginia with his ragged army intact.

Washington's blunders might have remained a footnote to history had not officials in Britain, France, and even Austria decided to make something out of the engagements. When British officials received word of Washington's defeat, they decided that the bungling colonials could not be trusted with their own defense and in late 1754 sent two regiments of British regulars to America under General Edward Braddock. The French, having gotten wind of the British plans, then sent eight regiments to New France in the spring of 1755. Braddock arrived in Virginia in February 1755, assembled an enormous supply train to support his army of 2,200 men, and marched straight into the wilderness to take Fort Duquesne. Disaster struck on the afternoon of 9 July 1755. As Braddock's army moved through the thick woods just a few miles short of his objective, a force of 300 French and Canadians and over 600 Indians ambushed and routed the British regulars. Braddock was mortally wounded, and nearly a third of his army was either wounded or killed, while French and Indian losses numbered just a few dozen. Washington, who served as Braddock's aide-de-camp and lost two horses in the battle, would take with him a number of lessons from this military disaster, not the least of which was the conclusion that discipline was essential to winning a battle. (See map on p. 95.)

Braddock's death and defeat shifted the major British war efforts to the north, but it did not remove Virginians from the savagery of warfare. An official declaration of war came in 1756, expanding the British government's task into a worldwide conflict that soon spread to Central Europe, the Mediterranean, and India. Armies and navies had to be dispatched to all of these theaters while the war continued in America. Things did not go well for the English and the colonists for the next two years. Despite the efforts of a series of British commanders, the French and their crucial Indian allies took a number of outposts in upstate New York, including in a siege and "massacre" at Fort William Henry in 1757.

In Virginia, too, the frontier erupted into violence and terror. Many decades of relatively peaceful relations with Indians had completely broken down by mid-1755 as nearly all native groups had gone over to the French. At the time of Braddock's expedition, raiding parties hit settlements in Frederick, Augusta, and Hampshire counties and then moved south into long-settled areas of Halifax. Several hundred Virginians were killed or captured, and many more clogged the backcountry roads as they fled east. In the fall the raiding parties struck near Fort Cumberland in Maryland and other locations along the Potomac and again in Augusta

County. The backcountry was in chaos, and the government in Williamsburg seemed only vaguely responsive.

The initial Indian raids had spurred Dinwiddie and the Burgesses into limited action with minimal results. In August 1755 Washington was appointed colonel and commander of a new Virginia Regiment to be made up of 1,200 volunteers or draftees from existing militia units. The only incentive to enlistment was relief from paying county and parish taxes, although some recruiting officers apparently gave out a modest signing bonus of two pistoles (£1 17s.). Neither incentive worked very well. The regiment was often at no more than half strength, and those who could be enticed or forced into service were hardly typical Virginians; 60 percent had been born outside the Old Dominion, and most of these were recent immigrants. Although Virginia remained an overwhelmingly agricultural society, only a third of the recruits came from that background; instead Virginia's soldiers were landless men who had performed a variety of unskilled and semiskilled jobs before enlisting. Few of the elite or middling planters or tenant farmers heeded the call to military duty.

Virginia's military efforts in the war reflected the localized nature of colonial society. Men whose homes, farms, and businesses came under direct attack or imminent threat usually could be counted on to put up a heroic fight to protect their families and property. And militia units rallied to local defense in threatened communities up and down the Virginia frontier. Yet most Virginians who had families and owned property were hesitant to journey more than a few miles from home in defense of others. Middling planters in the Piedmont or Tidewater could find no reason to leave their cozy hearths to defend unknown and unrelated men on the distant western frontier, especially since many of these new settlers were non-Anglican Scotch-Irish and Germans. Furthermore, some of the frontier land under attack belonged to the Ohio Company, and most Virginians, including a majority of the House of Burgesses, had trouble committing money and blood to rescue the investments of a handful of wealthy planters. As a result, many burgesses dragged their feet at nearly every request for funds, county justices of the peace showed great reluctance to draft their neighbors, and Virginians in general exhibited a lukewarm attitude toward the war. Poor white men particularly resented the forced conscription that hauled them away just like black slaves were treated.

Such attitudes made the task of creating a disciplined army all the more difficult. Virginia had two types of troops at this stage: militia units that were called into service from particular counties for brief periods of time for specific activities and provincial troops who had been specifically recruited or conscripted into units that resembled the regular British army but were commanded by officers appointed by Virginia's governor. Trying to figure out a way to train and discipline both types of units became a major problem for Washington, one that would follow him into the War of Independence. In late 1755, however, the problem seemed to be a total breakdown of discipline among all units; things were so bad that Washington threatened to resign if something was not done immediately. The house responded by leaving the militia alone but totally revising military law regarding provincial troops, bringing it in line with the existing laws regarding British regulars. The death penalty could now be imposed for treason, mutiny, desertion, insubordination, and striking a superior officer; refusing to obey an order could bring 1,000 lashes. Washington much favored the new laws for they allowed him to create the kind of disciplined fighting force he so admired in the British army. Further progress occurred in 1757, when the British ministry agreed to pay for recruiting costs and the house authorized a £10 enlistment bounty which put the Virginia Regiment on an all-volunteer basis for the rest of the war. Thereafter, the Virginia Regiment drilled, bivouacked, and in general looked like a European army. Relative stability in the officer and noncommissioned officer ranks and a growing loyalty and camaraderie among men serving extended periods of time together fostered a military organization as good as any in the colonies.

As the House of Burgesses revised the military laws in the fall of 1755, Virginia's political leaders also debated the military posture of the colony. Governor Dinwiddie clearly supported a strong offensive response to French and Indian incursions in the West as evidenced by Washington's attempts at Fort Necessity. And even though that and the Braddock expedition had resulted in failure, Dinwiddie remained determined to confront the French in their own backyard as well as to protect the Ohio Company's investments, including his own. Preferring a more defensive posture, the house allocated funds for the construction of a chain of forts along the frontier from Hampshire County in the north to Halifax County on the North Carolina border. Over the next few years, the Virginia Regiment and others erected eighty-one forts of varying sizes and construction; and although none could have repelled a large, concerted attack, they provided psychological comfort to settlers, easing some of the panic on the frontier.

The house also allocated funds for the construction of Fort Loudoun on the southwest border for the Cherokee and Catawba Indians, a feeble attempt to maintain good relations with at least a few native groups. Ohio Indians had gone over to the French in droves by 1755, responding primarily to more savvy diplomatic efforts on the part of the French, to the perception that Virginia settlers would soon be swarming over their lands, and to the abrasive and dismissive posture of Braddock and other officials. Large sums of money and promises of shelter for their families kept the Cherokee and Catawba allied to Virginia. The alliance also allowed Dinwiddie to mount another offensive in the spring of 1756, when he sent a segment of the Virginia Regiment and 130 Cherokee warriors to attack Shawnee villages in Ohio. But once again hurried planning, inadequate supplies, and winter weather doomed the venture. This would be the last offensive action of Dinwiddie's career; the Virginia Regiment then shifted to the defensive posture of building forts and responding to sporadic Indian raids.

The war in Virginia and elsewhere took a decisive turn in late 1757. An important factor was the new administration in Britain under the leadership of William Pitt, who decided to pursue the war with renewed vigor. The mother country would now shoulder many of the costs that had earlier fallen to the colonial assemblies. Virginia politicians were delighted and soon authorized the funding of a second regiment to be commanded by William Byrd III. The British navy had also begun to take its toll with the capture of hundreds of French ships; by late 1757 New France was running out of supplies for its own citizens and soldiers, and little was left over for their Indian allies. Pitt also mounted a new offensive that captured Fort Duquesne in 1758.

The year 1759 brought additional victories for Britain, including the battle for Quebec in September. Nevertheless, although French and Canadian troops no longer posed a threat to Virginia, France's Indian allies and other native groups remained a constant worry to those living on the frontier. Of particular concern were the Cherokee on the southwestern border. They were still technically allies of Virginia, but the relationship had started to unravel by 1759. The Cherokee had willingly participated in the expedition against Fort Duquesne but felt slighted at the limited rewards they received for their efforts. Further, when the French Shawnee attacked Bedford, Halifax, and Augusta counties, settlers indiscriminately retaliated against any Indian they could find, including the Cherokee. Virginia's new governor, Francis Fauquier, tried to calm the crisis by sending William Byrd III to negotiate; but the governor of South Carolina undermined his efforts. When the South Carolinians executed a number of Indian hostages, the entire frontier from Virginia to Georgia erupted into two years of violence known as the Cherokee War. In 1760 the Virginia garrison at Fort Loudoun fell to the Cherokee, who retaliated for the earlier executions of their warriors by killing a number of the Virginia soldiers who surrendered under a flag of truce. Despite these deaths, Virginia officials continued to press for a diplomatic end to the hostilities but were again thwarted by the more aggressive military efforts of South Carolina. Finally, in 1761 an expedition concluded a treaty of peace with the Cherokee, and the violence subsided.

By this time the war shifted to distant battlefields in India, Europe, and the Caribbean where Britain achieved a decisive and permanent victory over France. Diplomats concluded tentative peace terms in mid-1762; and then, after several more months of negotiations that satisfied France, Spain, and others as well as the British Parliament, a final treaty was signed in early 1763. The Treaty of Paris—or what contemporaries called the Definitive Treaty of Peace—gave Great Britain all of North America east of the Mississippi except for the port of New Orleans, which went to Spain. Although British colonists got free and open access to the Mississippi, the western half of North America was now officially Spanish, including the former French territory of Louisiana. With the exception of the tiny islands of St. Pierre and Miquelon in the Gulf of St. Lawrence, France had been eliminated from North America. It was a decisive and impressive victory for the British Empire.

For colonial Americans in general and Virginians in particular, the consequences of this "Great War for Empire" would be immense. The latter stages of the war and the final treaty suggested that a new era of peace, harmony, and prosperity had descended upon Virginia and its sister colonies. The hated empire of French Catholicism—the antithesis of everything English—had been driven from North America, and the future looked rosy. Virginia's militia, draftees, and volunteers had fought side by side with British regulars to expel the dreaded French and their Indian allies. George Washington had made a name as a commanding officer and had become one of the most experienced soldiers in the colonies. The world had been made safe for liberty-loving Englishmen in America.

Yet despite much close cooperation during the war and a renewed sense of British nationalism on both sides of the Atlantic, the two partners in victory came away from the conflict with a very different sense of the contributions made by each party. The British ministry and many in Parliament saw themselves as the saviors of America. British planning and military strategy had driven French armies from North America. The colonies had been reluctant partners at best. Requests for colonial troops were never met in full, and in several years some colonies ignored orders from London. Those troops that were provided never met English expectations; official and unofficial letters from British officers continually berated American soldiers as lazy, brash, undisciplined, unprofessional cowards who would desert at a moment's notice. The colonial fighting man was more hindrance than help in battle. Furthermore, a number of American merchants had been openly unpatriotic, continuing to trade with French and Spanish islands in the West Indies despite an official ban on such activity. Britons also had reimbursed the colonies for many of their military expenditures; by war's end the British national debt had nearly doubled and stood at a whopping £132 million.

Virginia and the other colonies viewed the war quite differently. They saw themselves as equal if not superior partners in the glorious victory. At least 20,000 Americans had served in the war; and while some colonies, like Massachusetts, provided far more than their share of troops, Virginia fulfilled 100 percent of its quota in 1760 and 1761, 80 percent in 1759, and 66 percent in 1762. Perhaps 15 percent of adult white male Virginians served at one time or another in the conflict. And Americans told themselves that they were better fighters than the British regulars, as evidenced by Braddock's defeat in 1755. British generals had planned the various campaigns in America, but units like the Virginia Regiment had made a major contribution to the victories at Fort Duquesne and elsewhere. Colonists also had died fighting for the empire, including hundreds of Virginians. Parliament's reimbursement to the colonies represented only 40 percent of the total military costs; the rest came from the treasuries of individual colonies. By 1763 Virginia's war debt stood at £120,000; Massachusetts's was a phenomenal £818,000. Colonial Americans had sacrificed much for their empire.

Englishmen and Anglo-Americans also had different visions of this newly expanded British Empire. Now that Britain owned the eastern half of North America, all Indian groups living in this region became subjects of the English king. Not only did former French allies like the Western Delaware, Shawnee, Seneca, and Miami now owe allegiance to George III, but the crown had an obligation to protect its new subjects. The expanding frontier regions of New York, Pennsylvania, the Carolinas, and Virginia had to be carefully managed so that neither red men nor white men suffered unduly. The Proclamation Line of 1763 halting all settlement west of the Appalachian Mountains was an initial attempt by English officials to protect their new Indian subjects, slow down the haphazard settlement of the West, and keep the peace between colonists and natives.

The Proclamation Line infuriated Virginians, for they had an entirely different view of what the policy for the postwar West should be. To begin with, frontier inhabitants had come away from the war with an absolute hatred of Indians. Hundreds of settlers had been killed by raiding parties during the conflict, and many more had been forced to abandon their farms and flee east. Now that the French had been defeated, their Indian allies deserved neither forgiveness nor protection. Natives were not loyal subjects of the crown but heathen savages outside the bounds of English law. Virginians also fretted over the status of western lands they had owned before the war. Virginia's original colonial charter made it fairly clear that the Old Dominion not only included present-day West Virginia and Kentucky but also lands north of the Ohio River stretching to the upper Mississippi. Were the future wealth and prosperity of Virginia to be set aside by the stroke of the pen in England?

The settlement of western lands and the status of the Native Americans who inhabited these territories were only two of the matters that caused disagreements and misunderstandings between the colonies and the mother country over the next decade. Such confrontations had occurred time and time again over the past 150 years; and in each case a new colonial governor, a new king, or a new minister in Britain adjusted his position or the colonial elite reversed its policy, thereby averting a permanent crisis. Virginians were loyal subjects of the crown who only wished for the perpetual peace and happiness of the great British Empire; Englishmen took pride in their colonial possessions and appreciated the tobacco, rice, wheat, fish, and naval stores that flowed into the British Isles. Yet despite the best of intentions by politicians in London, Boston, Philadelphia, New York, Williamsburg, and elsewhere, this particular set of disagreements and misunderstandings did not go away; and in April 1775 Englishmen and Anglo-Americans began shooting at each other.

The discord had much to do with notions of the traditional rights of Englishmen, which included trial by jury, free elections, frequent legislative sessions, the right to petition the crown, prohibitions against excessive bail and fines, and legislative consent to all taxes. By 1750 or so, two political bodies claimed to manage and protect these rights within the empire: the British Parliament and the assemblies of the individual colonies. For the Old Dominion the issue pitted the British House of Commons against the Virginia House of Burgesses. Both bodies had ancient and theoretical claims to sovereignty in these matters, but over the eighteenth century both strengthened their actual powers to assert such authority.

While each of the thirteen American colonies had its own particular road to war and independence, all were reacting to a set of practical British ideas and policies supported by the king, most members of Parliament, and a number of different ministerial administrations. Central to these ideas were the Navigation Acts passed in the seventeenth century and designed to regulate trade among British colonies and the mother country. Because these acts and their modifications had been on the books for nearly a century, they were credited with helping to create much of the wealth and prosperity of the empire. As the French and Indian War came to a conclusion, policy makers were determined to enforce and strengthen these all-important trade regulations. There was also the sense in England that the American colonies had been entirely too cavalier toward these acts, ignoring regulations when they felt like it, smuggling illegal goods as they saw fit, and trading with whomever they liked including enemies of the empire in time of war. After 1763 determination to stop such activity was renewed. But of greatest importance was the increased need to raise more revenue to help pay for a much enlarged British Empire and to lower the enormous national debt. At war's end the king's ministers concluded that the older, established American colonies should begin to shoulder more of this financial burden. Taken together, these ideas did not represent some radical change in policy, nor did they seem overly burdensome or out of line to anyone in England; this was simply the most logical and efficient way to run an empire. Colonial Americans did not agree.

While Virginia's path to war and independence can be easily traced after 1763, earlier events provide important clues to what would occur. The first confrontation, in 1749, followed a full-scale revision to the colony's laws. The house had spent two legislative sessions carefully reviewing one hundred years of statutes. It revised some, reaffirmed many more, and in general tried to bring uniformity and consistency to the laws governing the Old Dominion. When the new law code was sent to England for approval, a normal process that for many decades had become almost a formality, the recently energized Board of Trade decided to review the code with great care. In 1751, after nearly two years of scrutiny, the board sent back a detailed reply disallowing or questioning nearly a quarter of the statutes. The key bone of contention was that many of these laws did not contain a suspending clause delaying their implementation until they had been approved in England. The frustrated burgesses, who had only expected a quiet approval of the new code, now had to reinstate old laws and remove new ones that had been on the books for several years. They sent a petition to the king and asked the Board of Trade to reconsider its decision but got little response from either quarter. Crown officials had made it clear that from now on every law and every detail of colonial activity would be closely monitored. Virginia legislators, on the other hand, saw the whole affair as a direct challenge to the independent lawmaking power of the House of Burgesses. As they attempted to push against these claims of authority from England, they were aided by the thinking and writing of individuals like Richard Bland of Prince George County, known as "The Antiquary" for his vast knowledge of legal and constitutional history. Called by Jefferson "the most learned and logical man" of his generation, Bland, through newspaper articles, public letters, pamphlets, and his thirty-four years as a burgess, became the voice of self-government for the colony. Bland argued that these laws could not be overturned by king or Parliament because they related to the internal affairs of the colony, which were the sole preserve of Virginia's own representative body.

A second challenge to legislative power occurred at nearly the same time. Shortly after assuming the governorship in 1751, Robert Dinwiddie decided to supplement his own modest salary as lieutenant governor and bring some order to the land-granting process by instituting a fee of one pistole (18s. 6d.) on all new land patents approved. The burgesses and other prominent Virginians were furious, for many of them had patents awaiting the governor's approval. More importantly, however, as Richard Bland argued in *A Fragment on the Pistole Fee* (1753), this was indeed a tax, and taxes, no matter how small, could only be imposed through the consent of the governed; the governor had no legal right to collect such a fee. The matter eventually went to the Privy Council, which upheld the governor's right to collect such a fee but placed enough restrictions on its use that it became an ineffective mechanism for either revenue collection or land policy management. In a way, both sides won, although the affair again challenged the authority of the House of Burgesses to raise money and to control the internal affairs of the colony and briefly soured more than two decades of friendly relations between Virginia politicians and royal governors.

During the French and Indian War, a third dispute arose that also challenged the legislative independence of the house and resurrected the sticky issue of suspending clauses. Several years of low tobacco yields and high prices encouraged the Burgesses in 1755 and again in 1758 to pass Two-Penny Acts suspending the payment of taxes in tobacco and temporarily allowing taxpayers to fulfill their obligations at a rate of two pence per pound of tobacco. Because this rate was well below market value, Anglican clergymen throughout Virginia, who were normally paid in tobacco, felt they were being forced to take a significant pay cut. In 1758 they sent the Reverend John Camm, professor at the College of William and Mary and rector in York County, to England to have both laws invalidated back to their original date of passage. The Privy Council disallowed the laws but not retroactively, so presumably the clergy's two years of low salaries stood. But the House of Burgesses and the governor both received harsh words from England reminding them that such laws must have suspending clauses, which would prevent them from going into effect immediately.

Although the reprimand from the Privy Council irritated the burgesses, the Two-Penny Acts had accomplished their purpose, keeping clerical and other public salaries stable during a tobacco shortage. The clergy did not give up, however, and over the next five years in what became known as the *Parsons' Cause,* a number of them sued in local court for recovery of back wages; most were unsuccessful, including

PATRICK HENRY ARGUING THE *PARSON'S CAUSE*, BY GEORGE COOKE

Camm. The Reverend James Maury of Hanover County managed to win his case; but in a follow-up trial in 1763, the young lawyer Patrick Henry convinced the jury to award the clergyman only a single penny in compensation. Henry's inflammatory rhetoric attacking the king as a tyrant gained him much notoriety, propelling the red-headed firebrand onto a larger stage where he would use his oratorical powers to great effect. This and similar cases worsened already deteriorating relations between the Virginia gentry and their English-based clergy.

None of these issues stretching from the late 1740s to the early 1760s caused Virginians to think about rebellion and independence; but they did put the political elite into a frame of mind that exacerbated the next salvo from the British ministry, which encouraged custom officials, colonial governors, and naval commanders to strictly enforce existing trade and custom regulations. Additional pieces of the program included the Currency and American Duties Acts of 1764 and the Quartering and Stamp Acts of 1765. All of these were intended to produce a more efficient and more financially sound empire.

Some of these measures had little impact on Virginia, but the Stamp Act was an entirely different matter and drew forceful reactions from nearly every colony. At least part of the reason for the strong negative response was that American colonists had ample information about the act long before it took effect. Initial discussion of establishing stamp duties in America similar to those already collected in England began in late 1763, and a preliminary bill was prepared by March 1764. However, the king's chief minister, George Grenville, decided to postpone the legislation until input had been received from the American colonies, although he included a vague reference to a future stamp act in the Sugar Act passed that spring.

With this early warning and reports from Edward Montague, Virginia's agent in London, colonial leaders immediately set about to resist the legislation. During the summer of 1764, the house's standing committee of correspondence stated its opposition to this "iron hand of power" designed to "oppress America." When the house met in the fall, it prepared with the consent of the council several lengthy addresses to the king and Parliament that firmly but politely affirmed the legislators' belief that they, not Parliament, had the right to tax and manage the internal affairs of the colony. Similar documents arrived from other colonies. The Grenville administration became more determined than ever to institute the tax and to demonstrate that Parliament was the ultimate authority in the empire. Both sides had laid down the gauntlet. Despite some mild opposition in the House of Commons, the bill easily passed; and the king signed it on 22 March 1765.

The Stamp Act, like its counterpart in England, required that a stamp with a specific value be bought and affixed to all paper used for newspapers and certain legal and shipping documents; pamphlets, playing cards, dice, calendars, liquor licenses, and a number of other items also needed a stamp. While more things required stamps in America than in Britain, the specific fees were generally smaller in the colonies than those levied in the mother country. Revenue generated from the tax would be used in America to support British troops protecting the frontiers; and those collecting the tax would be Americans, not career customs officials shipped over from Britain. Initially no one in Britain, not even Benjamin Franklin, who had just arrived from the colonies, imagined there would be much opposition to the tax. Agents would be appointed, and the act would go into effect on 1 November 1765.

Within a month of its passage, news reached the colonies of the final form of the Stamp Act; and for much of May there was little reaction. The first protest came from Virginia where on 30 May the recently elected Patrick Henry rallied the House of Burgesses, with only one-third of the members present, to pass five resolutions against the act. Four of the resolutions simply restated in one form or another the long-held principle of no taxation without representation; but a fifth and more radical resolve, that the House of Burgesses had the exclusive right of taxation, passed by one vote before it was rescinded by a second vote the next day. Two even more radical proposals were strongly opposed and defeated by a group of older, experienced members who, resenting the brash attitude of Henry and his freshmen colleagues, thought the resolutions went too far. Veteran burgesses like Peyton Randolph and John Robinson had spent many years practicing patient imperial politics and believed working through channels ensured the best treatment for Virginia; Patrick Henry and others like him had less experience with English officials and saw little reason for patience or subtleties.

Exactly who wrote the Virginia Resolves and exactly what Henry said or did not say in the debate are unclear, although myth and some evidence point toward a heated exchange between several veteran members of the house and the hotheaded lawyer from Hanover County. Henry apparently hinted that just as Caesar had his Brutus and Charles I his Cromwell, so, too, would George III need his assassin. When a number of burgesses shouted "treason," Henry may have responded, "If this be treason, make the most of it"; but according to the most reliable account, he backed down, expressing his loyalty to the king and asking forgiveness for his outburst. What is important about Henry's words and actions is what politicians in other colonies thought he said and what they thought the House of Burgesses did in late May 1765.

Governor Francis Fauquier did all he could to squelch the impact of the resolves; on 1 June he dissolved the house and sent the burgesses home for the summer. He also kept the resolves out of the Virginia Gazette; but newspapers throughout the colonies picked up the resolves; and many printed all seven of them, including the proposal passed one day and rejected the next and the two that never passed. Thus politicians in other colonies assumed that Virginia not only had protested the passage of the Stamp Act but also had taken a most radical position denying Parliament's authority in almost all matters. These apparent bold actions by Virginia inspired other colonial assemblies. By year's end Rhode Island had adopted all of the proposed resolves, while seven other colonies approved resolutions similar to those actually passed by the House of Burgesses. Massachusetts suggested that the colonies assemble to discuss the matter, and in October 1765 representatives from nine colonies met in a Stamp Act Congress in New York. Although the Virginia Resolves had initiated the protest, no Virginia delegates attended the congress because Governor Fauquier refused to call the house into session where it was sure to select representatives to the congress.

Although the governor prevented any further official action by the colony of Virginia, Richard Henry Lee and others kept the issue alive over the summer and helped stir local protests in a number of counties in the Northern Neck. A protest parade in Westmoreland County honored the English radical John Wilkes and hanged effigies of George Grenville and Virginian George Mercer, who had been appointed stamp agent for Virginia. Justices of the peace in Westmoreland also informed Williamsburg that they would refuse to use stamped paper for legal documents after 1 November, and thus the county court would be permanently closed. Other counties followed suit, and it soon became clear that nearly all public business would cease when the act went into effect. When stamp agent Mercer finally arrived at Hampton at the end of October, he was hounded from the port and fled to Williamsburg where another crowd followed him about town until the governor rescued him. Mercer soon resigned his position and headed back to England, leaving the colony without any means to enforce the act. Shipping halted briefly, but soon commercial pressures forced Virginia ports to do some business without the required stamped paper. Angry crowds turned away a few ships that did manage to obtain the proper documents; one ship's captain was tarred and feathered in Norfolk. The colony's only newspaper, the *Virginia Gazette*, ceased publication rather than comply, and when two rival *Gazettes* reopened in the spring without stamped paper, both assumed a distinctively antigovernment position. With county courts closed, ports doing limited business, and the House of Burgesses on a very long recess, Virginia came to a virtual standstill.

Virginia was not alone in its protests; and by December 1765 news of widespread colonial reaction to the Stamp Act had reached Grenville's replacement, the new Rockingham ministry. Boston, New York, and Newport led the way with demonstrations, harassment of stamp agents, and full-scale riots that resulted in the destruction of public and private property. With the exception of one stamp agent in Georgia, all others resigned their commissions under threat. The Stamp Act was dead. Not only was no revenue being collected, but merchants in a number of American ports stopped importing British goods in protest. Forcing Americans to obey the act at gunpoint was out of the question, so the British ministry looked for a way to repeal it without appearing to cave in to unruly colonists. Their solution, after much discussion and debate, was to repeal the act on the grounds that it was hurting British trade and then to pass a Declaratory Act firmly stating that Parliament did indeed have a right to legislate for the colonies in all matters. Both acts became law in March 1766. Britain backed down but saved face; Virginians offered prayers of thanksgiving and toasted their good fortune.

The exuberance over the repeal of the Stamp Act had barely faded when a crisis erupted within the Virginia political elite after John Robinson, Speaker of the house and treasurer of the colony, died on 11 May 1766. He had held both offices for twenty-eight years and during that time had helped build the house into the robust, assertive body that had defied and frustrated governors in the controversies over the pistole fee, the Two-Penny Acts, and the *Parsons' Cause,* and most recently the Stamp Act. Under Robinson's leadership it had supported the recent war against France, but it had done so reluctantly and on its own terms. By 1760 a royal governor could accomplish very little without the cooperation of the house and leaders like Robinson. Yet, although the recent Stamp Act crisis had demonstrated the confidence and growing power of the house, it had not been Robinson and his generation of leaders who had mounted the offensive; instead leadership came primarily from Patrick Henry, Richard Henry Lee, and a group of younger men who favored heated rhetoric over backroom persuasion. The younger group also had been fighting against the Robinson faction for several years and had tried unsuccessfully to force an investigation into substantial shortfalls in the treasury accounts. With Robinson's death, everything came out in the open: nearly £100,000 was missing from the treasury, and apparently Robinson had loaned that money illegally to his friends and associates. The scandal forced the older leadership to divide the two offices, electing young Robert Carter Nicholas to the treasury and the older Peyton Randolph to the Speaker's post. A less unified leadership now faced the next imperial crisis.

Although William Pitt had argued against the Stamp Act and remained sympathetic to American arguments, he had to face the reality of financing and managing the empire when he became earl of Chatham and prime minister in July 1766. The task of raising some type of revenue in the colonies fell to his chancellor of the exchequer, Charles Townshend, who undertook a systematic study of colonial trade and finances and then presented his plan to the House of Commons in early 1767. His scheme placed a modest import duty on a number of items such as tea, wine, glass, lead, painter's colors, and quality paper. Mindful of the Stamp Act protests, he sought to tax relatively minor products that Americans could only buy from England. Townshend also created a customs commission that would reside in Boston, hoping that collections would be improved and disputes settled more quickly. This proposal would initiate a long-range plan for generating and managing colonial revenue and affirm the principle of parliamentary supremacy. To George III, Chatham, and most English politicians, it was a modest and reasonable plan that only asked Americans to share the financial burden of supporting the British Empire.

American colonists saw nothing modest or reasonable in the Townshend Acts and reacted swiftly and decisively. Other colonies took the lead this time, and Virginia mostly followed. Philosophically, the colonial position had not changed: taxes could be authorized only by the direct representatives of the people, and Parliament did not represent colonial Americans. John Dickinson in his influential and widely circulated *Letters from a Farmer in Pennsylvania* restated this position and suggested that Americans boycott English goods until the duties were lifted. In early 1768 Samuel Adams got the Massachusetts assembly to compose a circular letter arguing against the right to tax and warning of the dangerous precedent set when parliamentary taxes paid colonial salaries. Virginia followed suit; and with no royal governor in the colony after Fauquier's death in early 1768, the House of Burgesses boldly created its own circular letter supporting Massachusetts's position. When Norborne Berkeley, fourth Baron de Botetourt, became governor late in 1768, he tried to charm the burgesses into submission; but when they met in spring 1769, they passed another set of resolutions condemning the most recent set of British actions, which were directed mainly at Boston and Massachusetts. Despite Botetourt's overt friendliness toward Virginians, he knew his duty and followed his instructions from England by dissolving the assembly in early June.

The governor's hope that he had curtailed any further action by Virginia politicians was in vain. The burgesses had anticipated the dissolution, and instead of leaving town, they immediately adjourned to Raleigh Tavern where they elected a moderator and proceeded to act in extralegal session. Their main order of business was creation of a nonimportation association, primarily developed by George Mason and introduced by George Washington, whereby signatories agreed not to import a lengthy list of British goods including those being taxed under the Townshend Acts. Although the association resembled those created by colonies to the north, Virginians were not only thinking about challenging the Townshend Acts as directly as they could, but they also had in mind a revitalization of their own society. By forcing themselves to shun British luxury goods and buy products made in Virginia and the other colonies, the burgesses hoped to lessen their mounting private debt to English merchants and return to a world of virtuous independent gentlemen that they imagined was fast fading from view. Despite such determination and lofty goals, the association had a limited impact. Only a handful of Virginia merchants signed the agreement, and although many planters did so, imports barely decreased; it seems clear that many continued to buy British goods. Nonimportation throughout the colonies did have the desired effect, however; and in April 1770 Parliament, under pressure from British merchants, once again acquiesced and repealed the duties on everything except tea.

For the next three years, the imperial controversy remained fairly quiet although never entirely forgotten. Shortly after the repeal of the Townshend duties, the House of Burgesses sent a petition to the king

complaining of the remaining tax on tea and set up a permanent committee of correspondence to communicate with the assemblies of the other
colonies. Through this committee Virginia did as much as any colony to
keep the issues alive with a constant circulation of news and ideas. As in
the earlier protests, Richard Henry Lee took the lead on the committee,
but he had general support from most of the other burgesses.

Although only a handful of Virginians thought about taxation issues
during these years, planters large and small were continually reminded
of their mounting debt to Britons. The collapse of several English banks
in 1772 and the subsequent tightening of credit throughout the empire
put additional pressure on Virginia planters to pay their debts to English
merchants abroad and to settle accounts with the Scottish factors who
now dotted the Piedmont. Planters knew they had only themselves to
blame for their increasing indebtedness, but they were inclined more and
more to see the English merchant and the government that supported
him as adversaries. All things English now seemed more negative than
positive.

The committees of correspondence and the mild boycott of taxed
tea might have faded into history and an imperial crisis might have been
averted had not the British government decided in 1773 to help the East
India Company, which was on the verge of bankruptcy, dispose of a large
inventory of unsold tea. Three groups in the colonies immediately opposed the disposal scheme: philosophically minded protestors who believed that the plan was a veiled attempt to lure Americans into buying
illegally taxed tea, American tea merchants who were cut out of the tea
sales, and American smugglers who no longer had a monopoly on cheap
tea. Not surprisingly, all three groups were concentrated in the port
cities, and it was there that things got out of hand. Protestors in New
York, Philadelphia, and Charleston forced the tea ships to return to England, and in December 1773 a radical group of Bostonians inspired
by Sam Adams boarded the tea ship vaguely disguised as Indians and
dumped the entire cargo into the harbor. England's reaction to the Boston Tea Party would set Virginia and its sister colonies on the path to war
and independence.

Virginia had remained very much on the sidelines during the initial
stages of the tea controversy, and news of the Tea Party had little impact
on the colony. George Washington, like many American politicians,
condemned the action. The British Parliament was furious and hauled
colonial agent Benjamin Franklin in to explain this wanton destruction
of private property. Whatever support the American colonies had in the
House of Commons disappeared, and the North ministry decided it was
time to hammer Boston and Massachusetts. That town and that colony
appeared to be the cause of all of England's problems, and now it was time

to set an example. A series of acts, usually called the Coercive or Intolerable Acts, sailed through Parliament in early 1774. The Boston Port Act
closed the port until compensation had been made for the infamous tea
cargo and the port was determined to be safe for shipping once again; the
Massachusetts Government Act radically altered a number of aspects of
provincial and local government in the hopes of making them less "democratic"; the Justice Act allowed British officials accused of misconduct in
office to be tried outside the colony rather than by normally hostile local
juries; and finally, a new Quartering Act empowered colonial governors
to use unoccupied public buildings to house British troops. Massachusetts would be brought to heel, and the other colonies would understand
the dire consequences of civil disobedience and flaunting English law.

The American colonies did not react as the British ministry predicted
and instead rose almost in unison to support, not reject, their Boston
brothers. This show of solidarity was greatly enhanced by the passage of
the Quebec Act, which had nothing to do with Boston but instead dealt
with the recently conquered and newly organized province of Quebec.
Although in many ways this was a very enlightened piece of legislation,
American colonists saw the new provincial organization as a harbinger
of things to come. Catholicism could be openly practiced, a French law
code that did not provide for trial by jury would remain in place, and the
colony would operate without an elected assembly. Clearly this was the
future Britain intended for all of its colonies! In addition, and most shocking to Virginia, the act gave the Ohio country and much of the Great
Lakes region to Quebec. When news of the Coercive and Quebec Acts
reached Williamsburg in May 1774, the House of Burgesses, already in
session, began working on a resolution proclaiming a day of prayer and
fasting in support of Boston.

Some of the newer, radical members, including Thomas Jefferson,
Richard Henry Lee, his brother Francis Lightfoot Lee, and Patrick Henry,
spearheaded the resolution, and it passed on 24 May. The new governor,
John Murray, fourth earl of Dunmore, who had arrived in 1771, objected
to the resolution and dissolved the assembly. As in 1769, most of the burgesses remained behind in Williamsburg and again met at Raleigh Tavern where they agreed not to drink East Indian tea and called on the other
colonies to meet in a general congress later in the year. A few days later a
much smaller group decided that the extralegal meeting should continue
and called on the counties to elect special delegates to an August convention. The imperial crisis was once again at the forefront.

When the special convention delegates, mostly recent burgesses, assembled, they voted to begin a complete nonimportation of British goods
on 1 November 1774 and, if necessary, a complete nonexportation on
10 August 1775. If Parliament wanted to play rough, so could Virginia; it

would cut off commerce, the lifeblood of the empire. The delegates also took up the more controversial issue of the use of the local court system in the collection of debts owed British merchants. The annually authorized court fee schedule had expired in April; and thus the radical members argued that the court system should shut down completely, preventing the adjudication of all legal cases including debt suits; others argued the opposite. Although the convention delegates reached no agreement, many local courts began to refuse debt cases; and by year's end English and Scottish merchants had no way to collect the sums owed them.

Most of the other colonies had taken up Virginia's call for a continental congress; and so as a final order of business, the convention elected a group of delegates that was truly representative of the varied opinions in the Old Dominion. Peyton Randolph, Edmund Pendleton, and Benjamin Harrison came from the old, established leadership and were more inclined toward compromise and caution; Richard Henry Lee and Patrick Henry stood for the radical, confrontational wing; and from the middle they sent George Washington and Richard Bland, men of experience and wisdom who were nonetheless ready to meet the British challenge head-on.

Thomas Jefferson had missed the August convention because of illness but had sent along a set of instructions he hoped would be issued to Virginia's delegation to the First Continental Congress. Born on his father's Shadwell plantation in Albemarle County in 1743, the tall, red-headed Jefferson had studied at the College of William and Mary and "took" the law with George Wythe, Virginia's most learned lawyer. After practicing law for several years, he devoted most of his attention to developing his new estate, Monticello, and cultivating his multiplicity of talents in music, architecture, and agronomy. Not an accomplished speaker, Jefferson had a remarkable literary skill that would serve the causes of revolution and nation building.

Jefferson's instructions, published as a pamphlet under the title *A Summary View of the Rights of British America*, were a direct and heated response to the Coercive Acts. Railing against the closing of the port of Boston and the general interference with free trade as well as the suspension of trial by jury, Jefferson also vehemently criticized the Stamp, Sugar, and Townshend Acts and the sending of British troops to the colonies. He echoed the earlier arguments of Richard Bland and others as well as the Stamp Act Resolves: neither Parliament nor king had any right to tax Americans without their consent. But Jefferson went even further than most; and anticipating both his own Declaration of Independence and Thomas Paine's *Common Sense*, he asserted that Parliament had no right to legislate for the colonies on any matter and that kings were the mere servants of the people, and not the reverse. *A Summary View* not only summarized the philosophical journey that Virginians had taken since their initial protest of the pistole fee nearly twenty years earlier, but it prodded members of the Old Dominion to imagine that they had a truly independent and sovereign state within the British Empire. It would take two years for public opinion to catch up with Jefferson's arguments.

Virginians assumed a prominent role in the First Continental Congress, which assembled at Philadelphia in September 1774. Peyton Randolph acted as the presiding officer; and Patrick Henry, George Washington, and Richard Henry Lee all played their familiar roles. Washington worked diligently behind the scenes while Henry argued openly for the most radical stance with his usual inflammatory rhetoric. Richard Henry Lee's role was perhaps the most crucial. Working with John and Sam Adams of Massachusetts and others, he pushed through a Continental Association designed to halt the importation of all British goods and eventually to stop the exportation of American staples to Britain. County and local organizations throughout the colonies would enforce the association. Although Lee expressed his loyalty to George III and wanted the colonies to remain within the British Empire, his arguments essentially stripped Parliament of any power to legislate for America. His opposition to the Coercive Acts got majority support; but when he attacked the Quebec Act, which tolerated Catholicism and eliminated nearly all of Virginia's western lands, and when he proposed new militia training sponsored by Congress, delegates from New York and Pennsylvania as well as more conservative members from Virginia like Pendleton and Harrison united against him. Virginia's delegation had been instrumental in creating an uncompromising stand against Britain, but the debates in Congress also demonstrated that anything beyond a commercial boycott was too radical for some Virginians.

The First Continental Congress adjourned in October 1774 with plans to meet again the following May to reevaluate the British position. Conservative delegates hoped that Britain would understand the unity, firmness, and determination of the colonies and reverse course; radical members like Sam Adams, Richard Henry Lee, and Patrick Henry saw future military action as inevitable. In fact, at a second Virginia convention in Richmond in March 1775, Henry argued defiantly for the raising of provincial troops, uttering his memorable lines: "The war is actually begun! . . . Our brethren are already in the field! Why stand we here idle? . . . I know not what course others may take, but as for me, give me liberty, or give me death!" Most colonists, including most Virginians, were not willing to go that far and felt that Congress had taken a moderate course by boycotting English goods as the colonies had in 1765 and 1769. Only a tiny handful thought about war and independence, while the majority hoped for reconciliation within the British Empire. Yet the past twenty years had seen a gradual shift in the position of many of their leaders. Where once they had only argued for the right to control the taxation of specific items within their own colony, now a number of them denied that Parliament and the king had any jurisdiction over the internal affairs of the Old Dominion. Virginia was moving toward a position of independent sovereignty within the empire, and it seemed more and more unlikely that the British government would go along with such an arrangement. By the time Virginia's delegates journeyed to Philadelphia in May 1775, reconciliation seemed even more impossible; the shooting had already started.

SOURCES CONSULTED

David L. Ammerman, "The Tea Crisis and Its Consequences, through 1775," Robert J. Chaffin, "The Townshend Acts Crisis, 1767–1770," Peter D. G. Thomas, "The Grenville Program, 1763–1765," and "The Stamp Act Crisis and Its Repercussions Including the Quartering Act Controversy," in *The Blackwell Encyclopedia of the American Revolution*, ed. Jack Greene and J. R. Pole (1991); Fred Anderson, *The Crucible of War: The Seven Years' War and the Fate of Empire in British North America, 1754–1766* (2000); Warren M. Billings, John E. Selby, and Thad W. Tate, *Colonial Virginia: A History* (1986); Richard R. Beeman, *Patrick Henry* (1974); "Richard Bland," in *The New Oxford Dictionary of National Biography* 6 (2004); Stephen Conway, "Britain and the Revolutionary Crisis," in *The Oxford History of the British Empire: The Eighteenth Century* (1998); Jack P. Greene, *Negotiated Authorities: Essays in Colonial Political and Constitutional History* (1994); Warren R. Hofstra, "Ethnicity and Community Formation on the Shenandoah Valley Frontier, 1730–1800," in *Diversity and Accommodation: Essays on the Cultural Composition of the Virginia Frontier*, ed. Michael J. Puglisi (1997); Hofstra, "'The Extension of His Majesties Dominions': The Virginia Backcountry and the Reconfiguration of Imperial Frontiers," *JAH* (March 1998); Woody Holton, *Forced Founders: Indians, Debtors, Slaves, and the Making of the American Revolution in Virginia* (1999); Rhys Isaac, *Landon Carter's Uneasy Kingdom: Revolution and Rebellion on a Virginia Plantation* (2004); Thomas Jefferson, "A Summary View of the Rights of British America," in *Major Problems in the Era of the American Revolution, 1760–1791*, ed. Richard Brown (2000); Maldwyn A. Jones, "The Scotch-Irish in British America," in *Strangers within the Realm: Cultural Margins of the First British Empire*, ed. Bernard Bailyn and Philip D. Morgan (1991); Helen Hill Miller, *George Mason: Gentleman Revolutionary* (1975); Dumas Malone, *Jefferson and His Time*, vol. 1 (1948); J. Kent McGaughy, *Richard Henry Lee of Virginia* (2004); John K. Nelson, *A Blessed Company: Parishes, Parsons, and Parishioners in Anglican Virginia, 1690–1776* (2001); James Titus, *The Old Dominion at War* (1991); Matthew C. Ward, *Breaking the Backcountry: The Seven Years' War in Virginia and Pennsylvania, 1754–1765* (2003).

6

FROM BRITISH COLONY
TO AMERICAN STATE

1775–1788

The exchange of gunfire between British regulars and Massachusetts minutemen at Lexington on 19 April 1775 appeared to signal the end of reconciliation, yet the colonies continued to debate the issue of independence for another fourteen months before finally deciding to sever their relationship with Great Britain in July 1776. As the revolution developed, Virginians played a leading role in directing the war, writing the Declaration of Independence that gave purpose and inspiration to the rebellion, waging a local struggle against British and Indian forces, and forging a new state government grounded on rights and privileges. After the war, when the weaknesses of the national government became apparent, Virginians contributed to the writing of a bold, new constitution for the country; and, after a heated ratification debate, the Old Dominion joined the other states in forming "a more perfect union."

News of the First Continental Congress and its actions did not reach England until Christmas 1774 when the ministry and much of Parliament were on holiday. The message was not entirely clear: was America really in open rebellion, or were the protests simply the work of a handful of malcontents in a few colonies? The American complaint about representation seemed genuine to some, but to others it appeared that Americans were just trying to get out of paying taxes and debts. Even colonial governors, including Virginia's Dunmore, had trouble believing and/or conveying the extent of opposition to Parliament. In England the ministry finally decided that a show of military strength would put the Americans back in their places. The king's ministers had been too lenient during the Stamp Act and Townshend protests, leading the Americans to believe they could get away with bullying the government. Now British military commanders and governors would be ordered to get tough.

The orders to Governor-General Thomas Gage forced British soldiers into the countryside around Boston in mid-April 1775 to look for arms and munitions being stockpiled by the extralegal Massachusetts assembly; Lexington and Concord resulted. A day later, on 20 April, before news arrived of the skirmishes in the North, Governor Dunmore ordered the commander and men of HMS *Magdalen* into Williamsburg to remove fifteen half-barrels of gunpowder from the public magazine. Their actions brought the entire population of the city into the streets for a march on the Governor's Palace. Leaders of the Burgesses and city officials quieted the crowd temporarily with assurances from the governor that the powder had only been removed to keep it from falling into the hands of slaves who were rumored to be planning a major revolt. But word spread, and soon militia companies from several counties prepared to converge on Williamsburg. They were deterred from marching by George Washington, Peyton Randolph, and other delegates leaving for the Second Continental Congress, who believed that intercolonial cooperation in Philadelphia would be of greater value than the actions of an unruly mob or undisciplined militia units. However, one congressional delegate and one militia unit chose to ignore the advice and pleas of the colony's leaders and marched to Williamsburg; not surprisingly the unit was from Hanover County, and its leader was Patrick Henry. Halting about fifteen miles from the capital, the group was finally convinced to disperse when a local merchant gave them a £330 note to pay for the powder. Henry then headed to Philadelphia, once more emerging as a folk hero among the middling and small farmers of Virginia.

As the delegates took their seats in Congress, Dunmore received instructions to assemble the House of Burgesses, this time to consider a resolution from Parliament offering to let the colonies raise their own revenue to support military and administrative needs. The colonies would have no choice in the matter; they would have to raise whatever funds Parliament dictated, but they could decide how to raise such funds. Many thought the proposal worthy of consideration; but others like Jefferson and Peyton Randolph wanted none of it, believing it only a ploy to divide the colonies. Another incident at the powder magazine in which a trip-wire shotgun wounded three young men and then Dunmore's refusal to hand over the keys to the powder magazine silenced nearly all those hoping for reconciliation. On 8 June, Dunmore, his family, and his closest aides fled to a British warship. For the next three weeks, the Burgesses continued to meet, passed laws and resolutions, and politely sent them to the governor who was still shipboard. When he refused to sign a bill that would help settle an Indian uprising on the frontier, the house finally decided to act without his approval. Williamsburg soon became an armed camp with official and unofficial militia units loitering about, young men ransacking the palace looking for arms and money, and much drinking at the local taverns. Royal government had been replaced by anarchy.

To bring some order to the developing confusion in Williamsburg, a third convention met in Richmond from mid-July to late August 1775. Still hoping for some kind of reconciliation, the delegates adopted the rules and regulations that had governed the colonial House of Burgesses, including its election procedures. The convention formally defined the membership, length of service, and duties of county committees of safety that would implement the congressionally prescribed boycott, to start on 1 September. As a temporary replacement for the royal governor, an eleven-man Committee of Safety was created to manage affairs after the convention adjourned. With considerably more power over military and economic affairs than any royal governor, the committee, headed by conservative Edmund Pendleton, was designed to meet the immediate needs of wartime and not as a model for permanent government. Yet some, like George Mason, a wealthy fifty-year-old Fairfax County planter, worried about the extraordinary authority being given to a small group of men. Soon and reluctantly, he became one of those men.

The most important task before the convention was the construction of a military establishment to defend the colony from external and internal enemies. To meet these separate but sometimes overlapping needs, it authorized one-year enlistments for fifteen regular companies, one from each of the newly created military districts. These in turn would be formed into two regular regiments of about 500 men each; the local committees of safety would appoint company officers, and the convention would select regimental officers. The latter turned out to be one of the thornier issues as Patrick Henry immediately put his name forward to command a regiment even though he had no military experience. Many delegates favored men like Hugh Mercer who had soldiered in the 1745 Scottish uprising, but Henry narrowly won election as commander of the First Regiment and overall commander of Virginia forces; William Woodford of Caroline County got the Second Regiment. To support these regiments, the convention authorized a "minute" battalion from each of the fifteen districts; they would immediately get twenty days of training and then move into standby mode. The traditional county militia would continue to operate, drilling at least eleven times a year and preparing for home defense as needed. Paying for all of these military forces was an even greater problem, especially with tobacco exports scheduled to end shortly as part of the continental boycott. The convention did what many

GEORGE MASON, BY LOUIS MATHIEU DIDIER GUILLAUME

governments with no revenue source have done before and since; it issued £350,000 in paper money.

Although some form of reconciliation with Britain remained the
hope of most Virginians, the creation of an alternative government for
the colony and the establishment of a military force to fight the mother
country put Virginia on a nonconciliatory path toward independence.
Movement along that road was encouraged by the activities of Dunmore,
who spent the next ten months trying to win back his colony. He began by moving to Norfolk where he had strong support from a loyalist
community made up of English, Scottish, and Virginia-born merchants
closely tied to the trade of the empire. As the year wore on and the British
military and naval presence increased, other residents of Norfolk found
it more convenient to shift their loyalty back to the crown. The port of
Norfolk also provided a useful place to coordinate the activities of British

naval vessels; by August and September several ships under Dunmore's direction had raided plantations in the lower bay looking for supplies and sometimes slaves. On 30 September British soldiers and marines confiscated the presses and supplies of a local anti-British printer, moving them to Dunmore's command ship where he began issuing a loyalist version of the *Virginia Gazette*. In mid-October the governor personally led a raiding party in Princess Anne County where he seized large quantities of arms and munitions after a local patriot militia unit decided to retreat rather than fight. When more British soldiers arrived in Norfolk to assist Dunmore, they were warmly greeted by cheering crowds.

By late October the Committee of Safety in Williamsburg decided that Dunmore's activities in and around Norfolk had become intolerable, and it sent the Second Virginia Regiment under Woodford (and purposely not Henry's First Regiment) to Hampton where it forced a British raiding party to retreat to its support tenders anchored offshore. Dunmore was not to be outdone, however; and on 14 November, British regulars with a small detachment of white and black loyalists routed a sizable patriot militia near Kemp's Landing in Princess Anne County. The governor then insisted that all residents of Norfolk and the surrounding counties take a loyalty oath and wear a red strip of cloth as a symbol of their allegiance; many flocked to Dunmore's banner, but others fled to patriot territory. At the same time, he horrified Virginia planters by offering freedom to any slave who left his patriot master and fought alongside the governor. Hundreds of slaves fled their plantations, and within a few weeks Dunmore was able to construct his Royal Ethiopian Regiment of black soldiers and white officers.

This last step challenged the very existence of the planter patriarchy and their control over the lives of others. It forced the Committee of Safety into further military action. Again doing everything in its power to shun Patrick Henry, the committee took three companies from the First Regiment and gave them to Woodford, who advanced to Great Bridge just south of Norfolk. On 8 December Dunmore marched out to meet the Virginians. In the ensuing battle he was driven back to Norfolk; Woodford followed a few days later and forced Dunmore to retreat to his shipboard command post. On 1 January 1776 the British ships in the harbor began firing on buildings along the wharf, hoping to render the port inoperable for future patriot shipping; instead, the fire spread into town, and residents began to flee. In the confusion that followed, Virginia troops decided to finish the job started by the British, and they looted and burned two-thirds of the town before Woodford ordered them to stop. In early February a fourth convention decided the city might again fall into enemy hands and ordered the remainder of Norfolk burned to the ground.

While Virginians were fighting their own little war with Governor Dunmore during 1775, the Second Continental Congress had moved ahead with its military efforts; and the colonies as a group inched closer to independence. As the British forces retreated from Lexington and Concord in April 1775, thousands of New England militiamen converged on Boston to begin a haphazard siege of the city. The battle of Bunker Hill soon followed; and although technically a defeat for the Americans, the British casualty rate was so high that it was hardly a victory. Several days earlier the Congress had decided to take over this ragtag army and appointed George Washington as the new commander in chief. Washington was an obvious selection for his service in the French and Indian War, his moderate opposition to British policies, and his Virginia roots. A leader was required who could unite the southern colonies with New England. When Washington arrived in Boston in early July, the siege there and the war in general became not just a New England struggle but a continental one. Virginia would soon contribute more to the cause as militia units from Frederick County under Daniel Morgan and Berkeley County under Hugh Stephenson journeyed to Boston. American military efforts also moved from defense to offense. In early May, Ethan Allen from the disputed Green Mountain area of Vermont and Benedict Arnold from Massachusetts took Fort Ticonderoga; later in the summer Congress authorized an invasion of Canada.

Nevertheless, Congress continued to hold onto some hope that Britain would come to its senses and that the empire could be made whole again. In July 1775 Congress issued a *Declaration of Causes and Necessity of Taking Up Arms,* which affirmed the right of Englishmen to resist tyranny but also asserted the desire to restore relations with the mother country. A few days later conservative John Dickinson convinced Congress to send the so-called Olive Branch Petition asking George III to intervene on behalf of his colonial subjects. What many colonists did not yet realize was that the king, his ministers, and Parliament were of one mind. That became clearer in late August when the king refused to receive the petition; instead he declared the colonies to be in open rebellion and called upon loyal Englishmen in America to line up behind their monarch. In October the king told Parliament that the colonies sought independence and the destruction of the empire, neither of which he could tolerate. Two months later Parliament passed the American Prohibitory Act eliminating American commerce from the empire and ordering a blockade of all American ports. When news of the act reached the colonies in January 1776, a growing minority of Americans became convinced that independence was the only answer.

Shortly thereafter, more Americans joined the call for independence as they read and/or discussed a sensational pamphlet entitled *Common*

GEORGE WASHINGTON AT PRINCETON, BY CHARLES WILLSON PEALE

Sense written by a recent English immigrant named Thomas Paine and published in Philadelphia. Only a small excerpt appeared in the *Virginia Gazette,* but over 100,000 copies appeared in print, and a number of these may have circulated among the influential Tidewater elite. *Common Sense* presented a seductive argument. In simple, straightforward language Paine demolished the concept of monarchy and hereditary succession and argued not only that current English politicians were corrupt but that the entire English system of government was rotten to the core. Americans did not need a king; they never had; it was time to dump the British Empire and declare independence. America abounded in natural resources and could easily channel these gifts into building a mighty republican nation. Europe was the past; America was the future.

Virginians soon came to the same conclusion. The first few months of 1776 brought the majority of the Virginia congressional delegation into the independence movement. Jefferson and Richard Henry Lee had moved in that direction by late 1775; Francis Lightfoot Lee, Thomas Nelson, George Wythe, and Benjamin Harrison reached that conclusion by March, if not earlier. Only Carter Braxton hesitated. Public opinion was also moving toward independence in March and April, and elections to the spring convention demonstrated that voters in some counties strongly supported the break from Britain. By the time the fifth convention met in Williamsburg in early May, Virginia's official support for independence was virtually guaranteed; the only decisions to be made were how and when. Interestingly enough, Patrick Henry urged caution, wanting an assurance of French support before proceeding further. The majority of the delegates were less hesitant and finally resolved to ask Congress to make the formal declaration as soon as possible while preserving Virginia's right to construct a government for and by Virginians without outside interference.

On 7 June, Richard Henry Lee presented the Virginia resolution for independence to Congress. After several days of debate, it became clear that a majority of the delegations supported independence, but not all. Some hesitated out of personal conviction; others had not yet received formal instructions from their colonial assemblies. John Adams and others wanted a unanimous declaration, and so they asked Congress to delay the final vote for three weeks. While Adams, Richard Henry Lee, and other radicals lobbied behind closed doors, Congress set a committee of five to work drafting its declaration. On 1 July the first vote on independence was taken, but only nine of the thirteen colonies voted yes. Another round of intense lobbying produced a final vote of twelve to one on 2 July; New York voted against it but changed its mind a week later. The American colonies were now free of the British Empire.

A few days earlier, on 28 June, a Declaration of Independence, written almost entirely by Thomas Jefferson, was presented to Congress and then hotly debated for several days. Congress deleted nearly a quarter of the document, including Jefferson's rather hypocritical clause blaming George III for the slave trade, and made a number of editorial and stylistic changes. On 4 July, Congress voted to accept the revised draft; the delegates formally signed it on 2 August.

The document that Jefferson and Congress constructed in many ways represented the journey that the American colonies and Virginia had taken since 1765. The center section of the Declaration lists eighteen major abuses and a number of minor ones and is based primarily on the notion that the traditional rights of Englishmen had been violated: trial by jury had been suspended, legislative bodies prevented from meeting, standing armies quartered among the people, and taxes instituted without the consent of representatives. Here Americans were taking a conservative position by arguing that the past must be restored; Englishmen living in America must have their ancient rights back. Elsewhere, too, the Declaration sets out in no uncertain terms that as loyal subjects colonists had tried repeatedly to follow English rules and had humbly petitioned their king for redress of grievances. This was the way Englishmen behaved, and only with the greatest reluctance and as a last resort were Americans forced to sever the ties with their beloved mother country. Yet the introduction to the Declaration and parts of the conclusion present new, modern, radical arguments that embody the most advanced thinking of the eighteenth-century European Enlightenment: all men, not just Englishmen, are created equal and have certain inalienable rights that cannot be taken from them by any government or ruler; governments are created by the people themselves, not by the conquests of some ancient king sanctioned by God; and most importantly, all governments, including those headed by monarchs, can be overthrown and replaced when they no longer protect the life, liberty, and happiness of the people who founded them. As an old man, Jefferson looked back with pride at the document he wrote in 1776, but in many ways his own words came to haunt him; neither he nor the Virginians of many generations to come could live up to the creed he had created. This was, indeed, a radical, revolutionary message.

In the meantime, Virginia and several other states began the process of constructing new state constitutions to replace their old colonial charters. In May and early June, the fifth convention spent several weeks debating a declaration of rights to serve as a preamble to the constitution. Mostly the work of George Mason, the Virginia Declaration of Rights addresses the equality of all men, consent of the governed, the right to overthrow a failed government, separation of powers, free election of representatives, speedy trial, freedom of the press, the need

THOMAS JEFFERSON, FROM PAINTING
BY CHARLES WILLSON PEALE

for a militia, and freedom of religion. The constitution, approved on
29 June 1776, created separate executive, legislative, and judicial branches
and forbade any overlap in membership. The legislative branch would
be called the General Assembly and would include two houses: a House
of Delegates elected annually with two representatives per county and
one each from Williamsburg and Norfolk and a Senate of twenty-four
members, a fourth of whom would be elected every year. The executive
branch would include a governor and an eight-member Council of State
elected annually by both houses of the General Assembly. The governor
commanded the state militia, appointed justices of the peace, and issued
commissions and writs but could not veto any legislation; nor could he
dissolve or prorogue the General Assembly. Against the advice of John
Adams, Richard Henry Lee, Patrick Henry, and others, the office of governor would be the weakest part of the new "balanced" government; the
center of power would reside in the legislature. The convention also saw
no reason to change the franchise: adult white males twenty-one years
of age and older could vote in any county in which they had owned 100
acres of unimproved or 25 acres of improved land for at least a year. Prop-

ertyless white males, white women, Indians, free blacks, and slaves remained outside the political system. The planter elite would continue
to rule Virginia as they had in the colonial period. The new constitution
was not submitted to the people for ratification.

The convention selected Patrick Henry as the first governor of the
commonwealth and adopted a state seal and motto: *Sic Semper Tyrannis*—
"Thus always to tyrants." In 1779 Jefferson followed Henry in the gubernatorial chair, serving two terms until 1781 when Thomas Nelson Jr. filled
the post for a brief six-month period. Benjamin Harrison then did three
terms, Henry another two terms, and Edmund Randolph finished out
the Revolutionary era. None served with particular distinction, including Henry who alienated many with his provocative style, dispatch of
troops outside the state, and apparent desire to enhance executive power.
Jefferson held the post out of a sense of duty, not a desire for office, and
created his own enemies and detractors during his controversial second
term. In part the problems each faced resulted from Virginia's inexperi-
ence with republican forms of government and a continuing debate over
the role and power of the executive.

The survival of this infant republic and the planter elite depended
upon the successful operation of the state government just created and
winning the war, neither of which was at all certain from 1776 to 1781. In
early August 1776 Governor Dunmore finally gave up his attempts to regain Virginia and left for New York with a number of supporters and loyalists. His departure freed Virginia from major military conflict for three
years but did not take the state out of the war effort. As battles raged elsewhere, Congress continued to call for substantial troops from Virginia;
and those soldiers fought and died in battles from New York to South
Carolina. By the time Dunmore left the state, Virginia had raised nine
regiments, and the majority of them had headed north to join Washington's army. In September 1776 the First and Third Regiments participated
in the American victory at Harlem Heights and then fought with Washington at White Plains in October. By December five Virginia regiments
were on the banks of the Delaware River and helped the commander in
chief win the stunning victory at Trenton the day after Christmas. In October 1777 Daniel Morgan's battalion of skilled riflemen, handpicked from
Virginia and Pennsylvania regiments, played a crucial role in the victory
at Saratoga, which brought France into the war on the American side.
Virginia organized six more regiments in late 1776; and by the fall of 1777,
all fifteen were with Washington at Valley Forge. The severe winter took
its toll on all units. Sickness, death, desertion, and expired enlistments reduced General Woodford's brigade of four Virginia regiments from over
1,000 men fit for duty in October to just barely 100 by February.

Although Virginia remained solidly in the patriot camp until war's end, distant battles, devastating winters, and three-year enlistments made recruiting difficult. The initial war fever waned after 1776, and Virginia faced a continuing challenge to meet manpower quotas for Continental and state forces. Congress requested 8,100 troops for 1777, but Virginia sent less than 4,000; for the remainder of the war, the Old Dominion's contribution averaged about 3,500 men per year. Local politicians had witnessed the reluctance and sometimes outright refusal of middling farmers to volunteer for the "minute" companies in 1775, and so throughout the war they instituted special drafts with the greatest reluctance. In 1777 the legislature authorized a draft of single men with no children for a period of one year but allowed draftees to pay for substitutes. A $15 enlistment bounty and the use of deserters to fill the quotas still did not produce the desired numbers. A plan to recruit 5,000 militiamen for temporary duty by authorizing six-month enlistments and $10 bounties only caused a decline in long-term recruitment for the Continental army. Many counties refused to hold an official draft for fear of riots. When news of the French alliance reached Virginia in May 1778, the assembly canceled the draft and dramatically increased the incentives for long enlistments; yet $100 bounties, a daily liquor allotment, disability and widow's benefits, and tax exemptions did not prevent recruitment shortages in some areas. By 1780 the assembly was offering a much-inflated $2,000 salary bonus for enlistments. Yet no matter what the state tried, married men with small farms and families had little interest in fighting. Middling farmers and small planters stayed home; a few of them and the planter elite, or their sons, became officers. As had been the case in the French and Indian War, Washington's army came to depend upon the lowest orders of society: single landless men in their early twenties who could not vote became the "hardy Continentals" who won the War of Independence.

The American victory at Saratoga in late 1777 and the British occupation of Philadelphia shortly thereafter produced a stalemate along the Atlantic seaboard, but warfare intensified on the distant western frontier for the next two years. Most of the Indian groups had remained neutral in the early stages of the conflict, believing that this was a civil war between whites. Gradually, however, various groups took sides; and understandably, the vast majority aligned with the British. The British government had drawn the Proclamation Line in 1763 slowing down settlement west of the mountains; British Indian agents, Sir William Johnson and his nephew Guy Johnson in the North and John Stuart in the South, who had developed crucial personal relationships with tribal leaders, remained loyalists during the war. Only the Catawba of South Carolina, the Lower Creeks near Florida, some small New England tribes, the Tuscaroras, and the Oneidas of the Iroquois Confederation sided with the patriots. These groups had perhaps a maximum of 1,000 warriors, while

Britain's allies, including the rest of the Iroquois Confederation, the Delaware, Shawnee, Cherokee, and Creeks, had 13,000 warriors. During the war patriots would pay dearly for their lack of Indian allies; for many decades after the war, the Indians would pay an even higher price for choosing the wrong side.

The attitude of most Virginians had not changed since the end of the French and Indian War: Indians represented a barrier to land speculation and settlement. Renewed conflict in 1774 saw raids and counterraids in the Ohio country. In October, in what came to be called Dunmore's War, Andrew Lewis led Virginia militiamen to a bloody victory over the Shawnee at Point Pleasant on the Ohio River. Defeat of the Ohio Indians gave Virginia title to Kentucky but also ensured that these native groups would be solidly in the British camp during the War of Independence. British officials took advantage of these animosities; one set of encouragements came from Major Henry Hamilton of Fort Detroit whose nickname "Hair Buyer" indicated his reputation for terrorizing the frontier. By 1778 raiding parties were a constant threat to the scattered settlements in Ohio, Kentucky, and southern Illinois; and from Virginia's perspective, something needed to be done to protect its territories and settlers. The Continental army was too busy keeping an eye on the British in New York City and Philadelphia to be of much assistance, so Virginia acted on its own.

Plans for an expedition to the West began as the brainchild of militia officer George Rogers Clark, a native of Albemarle County, who was stationed in Harrodsburg, Kentucky. Clark had gathered intelligence on the British garrisons in Illinois, and in December 1777 the House of Delegates authorized an expedition. On 4 July 1778 Clark and his 175-man party reached Kaskaskia on the Mississippi River and took the town of French inhabitants without a fight. A local priest agreed to go to Vincennes and persuade the French community there to surrender to the Americans, which it did in early August. Clark also took Cahokia near present-day St. Louis but decided not to proceed farther until reinforcements arrived from Williamsburg.

The British soon got word of Clark's activities, and in October 1778 Major Hamilton left Detroit with a small detachment of British regulars; as he journeyed south, he picked up more and more warriors and soon had a formidable force of 500 men. The Franco-American garrison at Vincennes fell to him on 17 December, and he settled there for the winter. Clark decided not to wait for spring and in early February took 130 men across 180 miles of flooded rivers and forests to surprise Vincennes. Although Hamilton thought Clark had a much larger force than he did, the British commander refused to capitulate. Finally, Clark tomahawked several Indian prisoners in front of the fort in full view of Hamilton and his troops; the British surrendered a few days later. Clark and his men remained in the West for several more years, bolstering Virginia's claim to this territory.

Virginians also had to contend with an eastern seaside arena and the constant threat of harassment by the British navy and Tory privateers. The vulnerable Eastern Shore and the Chesapeake Bay itself were easy targets, and for much of the war, little could be done to counter the British. Politicians recognized Virginia's dilemma as early as 1775 and began building ships and a state navy. The state commissioned 77 vessels and officially sanctioned at least 100 privateers; these ships included everything from rowed galleys to larger single- and double-masted oceangoing vessels. Some of these ships attacked and captured significant British vessels; a few even operated off the European coast; many were sunk or captured defending the Old Dominion. The *Liberty,* which served as the flagship of the Virginia navy for part of the war, took part in at least twenty engagements, capturing a British transport and sloop in 1776 and a tender in 1779. Even local militia got involved in naval operations. In 1782 retired army officer John Cropper and twenty-five men from Accomack joined a Maryland naval force intent on stopping six British barges that had been cruising the Bay unmolested; in the heroic but unsuccessful Battle of the Barges, several men died, and Cropper suffered numerous wounds and briefly became a British prisoner.

The continuous presence of British ships in the bay and along the Atlantic coast encouraged a number of residents from the Eastern Shore and Norfolk areas to remain steadfast loyalists throughout the war. Some were merchants who had much to gain financially by trading with Britain; others were smugglers who made handsome profits by bringing in goods forbidden by the nonimportation associations. Still others remained loyal to the mother country out of principle, believing that small losses in personal liberty were more than outweighed by the security provided by membership in the British Empire. Some, too, were outright monarchists who feared that republican forms of government would lead only to chaos and mob rule. A few were recent immigrants, like the Scottish and English merchants of the Norfolk area and the Scottish settlers on the southwestern North Carolina border. The vast majority of the Virginia gentry sided with the patriots; but some notable exceptions included former attorney general John Randolph, former deputy receiver general Richard Corbin, and William Byrd III, who had dissipated his inheritance and in 1777 committed suicide. Several prominent members of the faculty of the College of William and Mary also left for England at the start of the war. Although the General Assembly passed legislation in 1776 and 1779 allowing officials to confiscate the land and slaves of known loyalists, places like the Eastern Shore observed a policy of live and let live. Not until 1781, when British forces moved into the state in large numbers, did overt loyalist sympathies surface once more, forcing patriot officials on the Eastern Shore into more aggressive action. One celebrated case concerned the Reverend John Lyon of St. George Parish and several of his parishioners, who were accused of encouraging draft riots, discouraging the patriot militia from doing their duty, and trading with the enemy. Although a local court found them guilty of treasonous activities, their neighbors did not want them to suffer unduly. Letters and petitions for clemency poured into the governor's office, and eventually all returned quietly to their homes and businesses. Keeping families and communities intact often outweighed the seemingly irreconcilable differences between patriot and loyalist.

Most of the great battles of the Revolution raged on elsewhere, in New York, New Jersey, Pennsylvania, and South Carolina. In early 1780 General Woodford took the Virginia regiments south to help General Benjamin Lincoln defend Charleston against a large force being assembled by British general Henry Clinton. The Virginians arrived in the besieged city on 7 April; but Clinton's forces were too large; and in early May, Lincoln surrendered the entire 5,550-man Southern Army, including 1,300 Virginians, to the British. Two weeks later disaster struck again. Colonel Abraham Buford's 400-man Virginia regiment that had been moving toward Charleston came under attack from Lieutenant Colonel Banastre Tarleton's loyalist cavalry near Waxhaws, South Carolina. The mounted Tories won the day; and when Buford's men laid down their arms and surrendered, Tarleton's men continued the slaughter, leaving only 100 alive. Two months later Virginia troops had another setback when an American army under General Horatio Gates including 100 regular Virginia troops and 700 Virginia militia was driven from the field by General Lord Charles Cornwallis at Camden, South Carolina. The militia ran from the field at the first sight of the advancing British regulars, causing Governor Jefferson great embarrassment when the news got back to Virginia.

Cornwallis's attempt to move north was delayed by two subsequent defeats in South Carolina. In October at King's Mountain, Virginia and Carolina frontiersmen crying "Buford! Buford!" gave the surrendering loyalist soldiers little quarter. Three months later at Cowpens, Daniel Morgan led Continental army units, assisted by Virginia and Georgia militiamen, to a decisive victory over Tarleton's forces. The colonials then won the "race to the Dan River" to escape capture by Cornwallis's larger army.

The year 1781 began with British successes closer to home. On 30 December 1780 former American and now British general Benedict Arnold surprised Virginians by landing near Westover on the James River and marching to Richmond, where he burned most of the city before returning to his base camp near Portsmouth on 19 January. The capital had been moved to Richmond in 1780 to accommodate population growth westward and, ironically, to escape British power in the Tidewater. Jefferson, who had succeeded Henry as governor in 1779, was forced to flee from the city. He was roundly criticized by fellow Virginians and Congress for his flight and the limited resistance put up against Arnold. In April, British general William Phillips moved up the James and on to Petersburg where he defeated a 1,000-man militia force, looted the town, and prepared to move on Richmond. Phillips turned back, however, when he learned that a small Franco-American army under the marquis de Lafayette was headed toward Richmond. Three weeks later Lafayette himself was in retreat as he learned that the much larger army of Cornwallis, fresh from a costly victory at Guilford Courthouse, had arrived in Petersburg. Cornwallis now had the run of much of Virginia and sent Tarleton to Charlottesville where Jefferson and the legislature had moved. Only a last-minute warning by militia captain Jack Jouett Jr., who undertook a midnight ride from Louisa to Charlottesville, saved the governor and a number of officials from capture on 4 June; as officials scattered far and wide, the state had no effective government for several weeks.

The second half of 1781 would go much better. (See map on p. 132.) Although Cornwallis now had an army of over 7,000 men encamped near Williamsburg, American reinforcements soon brought Lafayette's strength to nearly 5,000; and he began moving south toward his adversary. As the two armies jockeyed for position, Cornwallis received orders to move his army to a deepwater port. When he chose Yorktown, Lafayette moved to Williamsburg. In August, Washington learned that a French fleet had sailed for the Chesapeake; and he immediately led a combined Franco-American army of 6,000 from New York to join Lafayette. Fortuitously, French admiral de Grasse's fleet of twenty-eight ships and 2,500 additional troops arrived at the entrance to the bay on 30 August and beat off a British fleet. Washington and General Rochambeau reached Lafayette's camp on 14 September. Two weeks later the Franco-American army of 16,500 moved from Williamsburg to Yorktown, and Washington began positioning his men for an extended European-style siege. The French armies took the left flank, and the American armies took the right; the latter included some Virginia militia and a single unit made up of remnants of all previous Virginia regiments. Additional Virginia militia took up position across the York River at Gloucester Point, hemming in Tarleton and his 700 men. The allied armies dug 2,000 yards of trenches and began bombarding the town; by mid-October they were within 250 yards of Yorktown, Cornwallis was running out of artillery shells, smallpox had broken out, and he had no way to escape. On 19

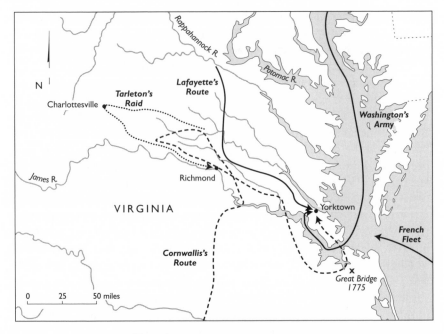

THE YORKTOWN CAMPAIGN, 1781

October 1781 he surrendered. At the official ceremony that afternoon, while a British band played "The World Turned Upside Down," British general Charles O'Hara, filling in for an indisposed Cornwallis, tried to surrender to the French; but they indicated that Washington was the commanding general; and he, in turn, allowed his second in command, General Lincoln, to do the honors. Befitting the protocol of the eighteenth century, Washington hosted a dinner for O'Hara and the French generals. He had come a long way since the debacles nearly thirty years earlier in the woods of Pennsylvania.

Although the Americans, French, and British all knew that the events at Yorktown would alter the outcome of the war, no one knew for certain the final impact of the victory. New York, Charleston, and Savannah were still in British hands; enemy privateers continued to raid the bay and Eastern Shore; and Britain's Indian allies did not change their aggressive tactics. Most of the American army moved north with Washington, while some headed south to join Nathanael Greene; the French stayed in Williamsburg until July 1782, when they left for Boston and from there departed for home. Sea and land battles raged on in the Caribbean, India, Gibraltar, and elsewhere as France and Britain jockeyed for final position. Informal peace negotiations began in Paris in July 1782; a provisional agreement was reached in November; and a formal treaty of peace was signed on 3 September 1783. Britain recognized the independence of the United States and ceded to the new nation all lands south of the Great Lakes and east of the Mississippi River except the Floridas, which went to Spain. The thirty-year war for America was over.

The "United States of America" recognized in the Treaty of Paris was, in fact, a loose confederation of former colonies held together by Articles of Confederation. When Richard Henry Lee introduced the Virginia resolution to declare independence on 7 June 1776, he also asked Congress to construct a "plan of confederation." Congress agreed and selected John Dickinson of Pennsylvania to chair a committee which by mid-July 1776 produced articles for Congress to debate. The Virginia delegation objected to a number of the provisions, including equal representation for all thirteen states, which would give Virginia no more say in Congress than a small state like Delaware or Rhode Island; the small states won this skirmish.

Lee was especially disturbed by Article 13 giving Congress the power to determine the boundaries of those states whose original charters "extend to the South Sea." This provision put Virginia's claims to the Ohio Valley and specifically the lands of the Ohio Company and other speculators in jeopardy. Allying himself with John and Sam Adams and others, Lee worked tirelessly over the next year to undermine or change the western lands clause. The Virginians got their way in the fall of 1777; Congress would not be granted the power to set the boundaries of the "landed" states.

But the issue was not settled, for the ratification of the Articles was held up by the "landless" states, especially Maryland, which deeply resented the potential future wealth and prosperity of those states with vast western territories. Virginia was willing to give up its claims to all of the territory north of the Ohio, but the General Assembly insisted that it would determine the permanent boundaries of the state, not some national government; it was a matter of sovereignty. And that sovereignty was now under intense attack as land companies sanctioned by the governments of Great Britain, Pennsylvania, and Virginia asserted overlapping claims to the West and as "separatist" settlements attempted to establish independent governments in places like Kentucky. The compromise finally reached in 1781 recognized Virginia's historic and sovereign claims to the West as laid out in its earliest colonial charters. Virginia then voluntarily ceded all of its territory north of the Ohio to the United States while retaining complete title to all of the land it claimed south of the Ohio, encompassing what is today Virginia, West Virginia, and Kentucky. In the process Virginia asserted its rights but gave up territory that would have been nearly impossible to manage in the future given the distance and competing claims. Maryland then gave its approval to the Articles; and the ratification process was completed in March 1781, only a few months before the victory at Yorktown. Formal cession of the lands took place in 1784. A few years later Virginia acceded to the separation of Kentucky, and it became a state in 1792.

The final version of the Articles of Confederation gave very limited power to the federal government and left sovereignty in most matters in the hands of the states. Under the Articles there would be just one branch of the federal government, a single unicameral Congress. There would be no upper house or executive or judicial branch; Congress would tend to all of the functions of the new government. Its powers included the right to conduct war, negotiate peace and foreign affairs, partially regulate commerce, and coin money. Congress had no power to enforce the laws it made, and it had no power to tax. There was no national declaration of rights to protect individual liberty; it would be up to the states to define and protect these freedoms. In Virginia, as in the rest of the states, this meant that the state constitution drafted in 1776 and any subsequent laws passed by the General Assembly would regulate the behavior, conduct, and freedoms of its citizens. There would be no national government looking over its shoulder. Left to its own devices, then, Virginia had to sort out the competing claims of a traditional patriarchy, a restive underclass of middling farmers and religious dissenters, and a heady and revolutionary rhetoric that declared the equality of all men.

The most far-reaching and perhaps the most radical issue tackled by the state during these years was the relationship between church and state. Like a majority of the American colonies, Virginia sponsored and supported the Church of England; church attendance was required; and civil authorities collected taxes to sustain the church and its functions. These taxes not only supported strictly religious functions such as ministers' salaries and maintenance of church buildings but a major social welfare system as well. In addition, many believed that civil society, including new republican governments, could only survive if the citizenry was of high moral fiber; and morality could only come in one way: by exposure to and instruction in the Christian religion. For traditional religionists, including most of the Anglican and Presbyterian gentry, the strong connection between church and state should continue in the new state of Virginia and in the new United States.

Others disagreed, especially those Separate Baptists, Methodists, and evangelical Presbyterians who had suffered during the many years that the Anglican Church had been the only official church and now did not want to be required to pay taxes for the support of any church but their own. They believed in the moral value of Christian teachings, but their goal was religious pluralism. In addition, Virginia had its share of Enlightenment rationalists like James Madison and Thomas Jefferson who argued for complete freedom of thought: religion should be an entirely private and voluntary matter.

The movement from religious toleration to religious liberty began with the construction of the Virginia Declaration of Rights in May and June 1776. George Mason's initial draft of Article 16 provided "that all men should enjoy the fullest toleration in the exercise of religion"; but in the view of the young James Madison, these enlightened words did not go far enough. After a number of drafts and debates, Madison got the phrase changed to "all men are equally entitled to the free exercise of religion according to dictates of conscience." The wording was important; it was not just a matter of the majority religion tolerating minority religions but of an equal footing for all religious beliefs. Madison also tried to insert wording that would have come close to disestablishing the Anglican Church, but his colleagues in the convention rejected it. However, non-Anglicans throughout the state rallied to Madison's ideas and forwarded dozens of petitions asking to be relieved "from the long night of ecclesiastical bondage." These petitions forced the assembly into action; and that fall, with wording provided by Mason, Madison, and Jefferson, it nullified all laws requiring church attendance and mandatory support for the Anglican Church. Dissenters were now free to attend and support their own churches and did not have to contribute to the Church of Virginia.

Three years later, in 1779, Jefferson presented his bill for establishing full religious freedom, but others countered with bills to give public financial support to all religions that believed in a specified set of Christian tenets. None of the bills passed, and the public and the legislature remained divided over the proper connection between church and state. By 1784 the debate had solidified around two men and two proposals: Jefferson and his plan of complete religious freedom and disestablishment and Patrick Henry's plan for a public assessment that would support Christian religion in general throughout the state. The loyalist tendencies of some Anglican clergy during the Revolution may have encouraged support for Jefferson's plan. Further debate and further postponement pushed the issue to the 1785–86 legislative session where growing public pressure against the assessment scheme allowed Madison to shepherd Jefferson's 1779 "Statute for Establishing Religious Freedom" through the assembly. Rationalists and dissenters had defeated the traditional religionists. The official connection between church and state in Virginia had been severed; all men and women could now worship or not worship as they pleased, and if they wanted to support a church, they could choose from the full spectrum of religious denominations. Virginia had moved from a state-supported established church, which only tolerated most dissenting Christian religions, to a society with no established church and complete religious liberty. It was the most radical stance taken by any American state.

The Revolutionary rhetoric of liberty and equality not only encouraged Virginians to debate and eventually to act upon the issue of religious freedom, but such talk also inspired discussions of freedom and equality for blacks, white women, and lower-class men. African American slaves had neither equality nor freedom, and Jefferson's stirring words that "all men are created equal" were not a call to give blacks the same rights as whites. Yet slaves surely picked up this rhetoric as they walked the streets of Alexandria or Williamsburg or as they heard their masters discuss such issues. When Dunmore issued his proclamation in 1775 offering freedom to adult male slaves in Virginia who would fight for the British and when General Henry Clinton in 1779 extended the same offer to adult male and female slaves throughout America, African Americans in the Chesapeake responded. Throughout the war the sight of a British warship in the bay always prompted runaways; 300 did so in 1777, nearly 1,000 bolted in 1779, and 17 of George Washington's most important and skilled slaves fled in 1781 when the British raided Mount Vernon. By the time Cornwallis reached his final camp at Yorktown in late 1781, over 4,000 blacks had joined his entourage. Estimates of how many blacks were lost to Virginia during the Revolution range as high as 30,000. It is clear that the conflict shook Virginia's long-established slave society to its core.

Despite the hopes of many blacks and a few whites, slavery in Virginia did not end during the Revolutionary era; and the slave population increased again after the war. But the disruptions of war and the rhetoric of liberty produced some cracks in the slave and racial regimen. White Virginians espoused both a strong commitment to human liberty and an equally strong notion of the sanctity of private property, including slaves. A number of prominent Virginians noted the contradiction and proposed several emancipation plans; but like Jefferson, most could not find a way out of the dilemma. Nonetheless, the war poked and prodded the established order. In 1777, under pressure from Congress to fill its military quotas, Virginia reluctantly authorized the enlistment of free blacks. A year later the Virginia regiments of the Continental army were 13 percent black. The relatively small number of slaves who served for one reason or another were formally given their freedom in 1783. In a bill probably written by Jefferson, the assembly outlawed the importation of slaves in 1778; although the legislation prevented new slaves from entering the state from Africa or the West Indies, it did not restrict sales of slaves within the state or from Virginia to other regions. In 1782 the state took its most radical step toward softening the slave regimen when it authorized private manumission for the first time since 1732. Quakers and Methodists pushed the hardest for this law allowing healthy males twenty-one to forty-five years old and females slaves above eighteen years of age to be freed by a properly executed will or deed. The assembly seems to have been less persuaded by humanitarian arguments than by the notion that white men and women should be able to dispose of their property without interference from the state. This law, however, did provide a mechanism for 10,000 slaves to gain their freedom after the war. Nevertheless, 293,000 slaves still remained in bondage in 1790.

The war also disrupted long-established gender roles, thrusting some women into military and political arenas while forcing others to assume economic responsibilities normally reserved for men. Virginia women could not vote or hold public office; yet like Abigail Adams of Massachusetts, who chided her husband John to "remember the ladies" while he was declaring independence, a few Virginia women took the Revolutionary message to heart. Both Hannah Lee Corbin, older sister of Richard Henry Lee, and Mary Willing Byrd, widow of William Byrd III, resented the fact that as widows and major property owners they had to pay taxes but were not represented actually or virtually in the legislative chambers of Virginia. In 1787 one Virginia woman took action: Ann Holden of Accomack County enfranchised four young men in her neighborhood by giving each of them twenty-five acres so that they would vote for the right candidates in the upcoming elections. Many other women turned their traditional female duties into political statements. Although most of the nonimportation associations initiated just before independence were signed by men, it was the women who had to make the boycott work as they decided what to buy and use in their everyday cooking and household chores. Some Virginia women saw these roles as overtly political, publishing essays in the *Virginia Gazette* in 1773 and 1774 calling upon their fellow "countrywomen" to give up India tea, china, and other luxury goods as a patriotic blow against the evil ministers in Britain. And the role of women was not minor; according to these female writers, their public virtue at this moment in history was critical to the success of the glorious cause. As Ann Terrel of Bedford County noted in 1776, women would practice "another branch of American politics . . . in frugality and industry, at home particularly in manufacturing our own wearing." Homespun clothes became a mark of patriotism; and by 1777 or so, Virginia women and their slaves were making much of the clothing used by families.

The war effort and its repercussions demanded much of Virginia women. Many sent husbands off to war and assumed some if not all of the duties of running their family plantation, farm, or business. And while some families weathered the war despite long absences or even the death of husbands, others struggled to make ends meet. Following the war a number of Virginia women had their property confiscated for back taxes. In these cases women fought back with direct petitions to the assembly, something that had become a rarity in the patriarchal society of the eighteenth century. When loyalist men fleeing Virginia left their wives at the mercy of local magistrates who normally seized Tory holdings, the assembly recognized the difficult predicament of these women and in 1779 passed legislation to protect their interests.

Women in somewhat better circumstances took more direct action to support or encourage the war effort. When Benjamin Franklin's married daughter and other Philadelphia women formed a Ladies Association in 1780 to collect money to buy clothing for the Continental army, Martha Washington contacted Martha Jefferson, who in turn exhorted her friends to establish a similar institution in Virginia. They ran ads in the *Virginia Gazette*, collected money in a number of counties, and forwarded the funds to Mrs. Washington. Finally, most women did everything in their power to encourage manly behavior on the part of their husbands, sweethearts, and lovers. A group of young ladies in Amelia County even gave public notice that they would only have social contact with men who had proved their valor by serving in the army; they would not accept the "addresses" or advances of nonmilitary men. All of these activities and experiences encouraged a number of white women, especially elite women, to imagine a larger public role for themselves and their daughters. However, although Virginia's white women eventually would acquire an expanded role, they would remain tied to their traditional domestic duties: they would become "republican mothers" assigned the special task of nurturing the next generation of "republican men." True liberty and equality were for white men only.

Yet not even all white men were equal. The pre-Revolutionary social order had made a clear distinction between free white men who owned property and those who did not and between substantial property owners and those with limited acres. Property owners and some holders of long-term leases were full members of the colonial polity; they could vote, serve on juries, and hold public office. The other 30 percent or more of adult white male Virginians were socially and economically free, but they were not formal political actors. The new state constitution of 1776 changed none of this; but the disruptions of war, the need for military recruits, the demand for religious liberty by dissenting congregations, the problem of local and overseas debts, and the ever-present Revolutionary rhetoric of liberty all encouraged lower-class white men to question the accepted hierarchal order. When these small farmers came together in volunteer companies in the spring of 1775 in response to the powder magazine incident in Williamsburg, they refused to accept the traditional county militia officers as their appointed leaders and instead elected their own. A few months later these same men balked when local elites, authorized by the assembly, attempted to form "minute" companies across the state in which officers would be appointed, pay would be limited, and anyone owning more than three slaves would be exempted from service. They were further infuriated when the only gentleman they truly trusted, Patrick Henry, was ignored as the duly elected commander of the Virginia Regiment; some threatened to desert, and others became unruly. These same animosities continued to surface throughout the war, forcing the Virginia assembly to abandon any hope of raising a citizen-soldier army. Instead it had to rely on propertyless volunteers who demanded larger and larger enlistment bounties. The war and its aftermath eventually brought pressure upon the established system, and changes in the Virginia political order began to occur early in the nineteenth century.

The substantial funds needed to support a volunteer army of propertyless men were among the financial burdens undertaken by Virginia that had to be dealt with during and after the conflict. And when various tax schemes were proposed and implemented, they not surprisingly fell disproportionately on different segments of the population. During the first few years of the war, the state issued £946,000 in paper currency but took in only a tenth of that sum in revenue. By 1777 the situation seemed dire enough that the legislature began looking for bold and radical proposals to address the revenue shortfall. An extensive debate finally produced a revised tax code that adjusted a number of previous levies while adding a 0.5 percent tax on personal property including slaves, a 10 percent tax on interest income, and a small tax on nonmilitary government salaries. In this case, the tax fell fairly evenly across the population; but it was a bitter pill for the elite who would have to pay the most. But even this apparent fairness began to be questioned as assessors got complaints from large and small farmers alike that their tax obligations had been wrongly assessed. At the same time several legislative bills spearheaded by George Mason attempted to clear up the confusing titles to western lands in the hopes that such lands would provide revenue to the state through direct sales as well as through future taxes. Although Mason tried to be fair to all parties in his bills, the demands of land speculators like the Ohio Company (of which he was a member), the need for bounty lands for veterans, and the hopes of small farmers put different interests at loggerheads, delaying a solution.

Revenue schemes began to coalesce in 1780 when Congress tried to bring runaway inflation under control by making forty Continental dollars equal to one Spanish silver dollar. The assembly eventually approved the action and set about adjusting Virginia's currency to the same ratio; because it had been 150 to 1, this adjustment provided substantial debt relief. This and continuing revisions to the tax code worked, and the amount of paper money in circulation declined rapidly. But because taxes had to be paid in currency, the shrinking money supply made it difficult for small and large farmers to pay their annual levies, forcing county sheriffs to petition the assembly for assistance. In 1781 farmers in western counties, where there was very little paper money, were allowed to pay their taxes in tobacco, hemp, or flour; deerskins were soon added to the list. But even this step did not solve the problem, and in 1783 traditional enemies Patrick Henry and George Mason united on a bill to allow citizens to postpone paying their taxes for six months so that the next tobacco harvest could be completed. Further postponements in spring 1784 finally brought things into equilibrium and stabilized the political waters, at least briefly.

Another important financial problem that affected Virginia more than any other colony was the debts owed British merchants that totaled £4 million, of which Virginians owed nearly half. While the war raged, no one proposed to support the enemy by paying their debts; yet many large planters knew that the debt issue would have to be resolved because they hoped to reestablish trading relations with Britain once the war ended. Early in the war the assembly did allow Virginians to use much inflated paper money to pay their debts to the state treasury where it would be held until the end of hostilities, but only a few took advantage of this scheme. In 1780 this law was repealed, and in 1781 and 1782 the assembly further restricted the payment and collection of British debts. When the preliminary version of the peace treaty and its provisions opening the way for debt collection became known in late 1782, Patrick Henry and his allies rallied against the measure, feeling no obligation to repay any citizens of a country that had destroyed towns and plantations and harbored thousands of Virginia slaves. Others, like Washington, Jefferson, Mason, and the Lees felt that personal honor was at stake and that the operation of civil society depended upon men fulfilling their personal obligations to others. Besides, large planters might have a hard time getting small farmers to repay them if they in turn refused to pay their creditors overseas. Over the next two years, a variety of bills were introduced and debated in the assembly, but nothing was resolved. Yet the two sides of the debate—the pro-creditor forces wanting to repay British debts and the pro-debtor forces hoping to postpone such action for as long as possible—provided a preview of the political alignments that were forming in Virginia and would soon spill into the debate over a new constitution and beyond.

Throughout the 1780s two vaguely defined political groups gradually emerged that eventually would come to be called Federalists and Anti-Federalists. Those on the federal side tended to be more cosmopolitan in their outlook, with contacts and acquaintances beyond Virginia, and whether rich or poor, usually had some direct connection to the world of commerce as investors, shippers, traders, or dockworkers. Many of the educated, wealthy Tidewater elite were among this group and combined traditional agricultural pursuits with newer entrepreneurial business interests. Some had served as senior officers in the Continental army and had developed a broad sense of American nationalism as well as a realistic view of the shortcomings of finances under the Confederation. They believed that paying off debts owed to British merchants was more an issue of personal integrity and national honor than one of finances. And they distrusted the overly democratic state legislatures that appeared incapable of addressing long-term national problems and instead seemed bogged down in petty local issues. The antifederal group, on the other hand, saw the world in very local terms, were more likely to live in the Piedmont where they had less personal or commercial connections with non-Virginians, and remained wedded to agricultural endeavors. They had little interest in seeing that debts were paid to the former enemies in Britain. Many were local officeholders who not only wanted political power to remain in their hands but genuinely believed that their hard-won liberties could be easily taken away by a strong executive in some distant capital. They were Virginians first and Americans second.

By 1784 James Madison had emerged as the central figure among the federalists in Virginia. Having finished three years in Congress, Madison knew all too well the severe problems the Confederation faced in paying its bills without the power to tax and in managing foreign trade without the power to regulate commerce. Within the Virginia assembly Madison worked with George Mason to hold off Patrick Henry and the pro-debtor forces while his replacement in Congress, James Monroe, pushed for amendments to the Articles that would solve the national revenue and trade issues. Monroe got nowhere, so the assembly proposed to meet with Marylanders in early 1785 to resolve their own trade issues concerning navigation of the Chesapeake and the Potomac. Governor Henry, who had little interest in interstate cooperation, mysteriously lost the paperwork for the conference; and so the Maryland delegation showed up in Alexandria, but not the Virginians. Mason and Washington saved face by holding a brief meeting at nearby Mount Vernon where they discussed the need for a nationwide conference and drafted a navigation plan that was carried back to the two state assemblies. In early 1786 the Virginia

JAMES MADISON, FROM PAINTING BY ALONZO CHAPPEL

assembly agreed to send a delegation to this national convention to meet in Annapolis. A group of federalists including Madison, Edmund Randolph, Walter Jones, and St. George Tucker were joined by antifederalists George Mason, David Ross, Meriwether Smith, and William Roland. Delegates from only five states, including Virginia, showed up in Annapolis in September 1786, so the group quickly put together a proposal for yet another meeting, this one to be in Philadelphia the following spring. But Madison, Alexander Hamilton, and others wanted more than just a conference on trade; their proposal to the states now suggested that the convention should undertake a thorough revision of the Articles of Confederation.

Those in the assembly wanting a stronger central government quickly saw the importance of the upcoming Philadelphia convention and got Washington, Madison, Mason, Randolph, George Wythe, and John Blair appointed delegates. Those suspicious of enlarged federal power, Patrick Henry and Richard Henry Lee, declined to go; and so another federalist, James McClurg, was selected. With the exception of Mason, it was a group thoroughly dedicated to a nationalist agenda.

Madison is revered as the "Father of the Constitution," and nothing in the historical record detracts from that epitaph. A man of slight build from Montpelier plantation in Orange County, Madison was only thirty-six years old in 1787, yet he had vast experience in both the Virginia assembly and Congress and had read deeply in the political treatises and pamphlets of the eighteenth century. In April 1787 he produced a memorandum on "The Vices of the Political System of the United States" in which he not only described America's problems but offered a solution. By the time the Philadelphia convention achieved a quorum on 25 May 1787, he had developed a full-blown plan to fix the American political system. Although his plan would be much modified over the next few months, his initial ideas and his carefully constructed comments during the debates set the tone for the entire proceedings.

Madison's experiences in the Virginia assembly had taught him a number of lessons he sought to apply as he constructed a new government for the United States. He believed that the new national government, like Virginia, should have a second legislative branch, a Senate, elected to longer terms. In addition, he had come to see the folly of annual elections and thought that electing representatives every three years without term limits would provide the kind of stability needed to operate a successful government. He also thought Americans had been wrong in eliminating or weakening the executive branch; a strong executive in a republic would not necessarily have the same vices as a strong king in a monarchy. He had other solutions, too, that would allow a stronger government to negotiate with Spain over navigation of the Mississippi and force states to treat each other equitably over border and western land disputes. But his biggest concern was that the people who ran state governments, in Virginia and elsewhere, acted in petty and selfish ways to the detriment of their own states and of the country. Narrow-minded "faction," he would later explain in *Federalist No. 10,* had and would continue to capture state legislatures, encouraging them to look at short-term local interests instead of long-term national problems. A large, powerful republic in which these petty interests would be muted or would cancel each other out was the antidote for America's ills.

Madison's plan of government was introduced in the convention by Virginia's newly elected governor, Edmund Randolph, and came to be known as the Virginia Plan. It called for a bicameral legislature with a lower house elected by the people and an upper house elected by the lower house. Members of the national Congress would select a plural executive from their own number. There would be a separate judicial branch, also selected by the legislature. Finally, a Council of Revision, to include members from the legislative and judicial branches, would review all laws passed and had veto power. The convention eliminated the plural executive and the Council of Revision almost immediately and gave a single executive, called a president, the power to enforce laws and veto legislation.

The two stickiest issues dealt with representation and slavery. As the most populous state, Virginia would benefit from the new plan basing representation on population. But small states, accustomed to having an equal vote with large states under the Articles, refused to accept Madison's plan. After voting down the New Jersey Plan, which would have returned power to the smaller states, the convention compromised on a scheme basing representation in the House on population and that in the Senate on equality among the states.

Some delegates, including George Mason, also wanted to outlaw the slave trade; but those from the lower South would have none of it; a compromise allowed the new government to consider banning the trade in twenty years, but not before. The issue of how to count slaves for purposes of representation in the new Congress also caused a North-South rift but was finally resolved by using a formula Madison had worked out some years before: three-fifths of the slave population of each state would be counted in allotting representation. The Constitution also guaranteed that all states would return runaway slaves to their masters. These final compromises on representation and slavery allowed all thirteen states to participate in the new union, but it left a horrendous legacy to future generations of Virginians.

Once the powers of the president (veto, managing foreign affairs, commander in chief) as well as the manner of his selection (the odd Electoral College) were worked out, thirty-nine delegates signed the final document on 17 September 1787. Mason and Randolph did not. Mason objected to the continuation of the slave trade and believed a bill of rights was essential; Randolph thought the president had too much power. Such objections foreshadowed in many ways the contentious debate over ratification soon to erupt in Virginia and elsewhere. To counter criticism of the new constitution, Madison joined with Alexander Hamilton and John Jay, both of New York, to write a series of essays entitled *The Federalist* that explicated its provisions and supported its adoption. George

Washington had chaired the convention, and his presence and signature on the final document went a long way in persuading Americans in general and Virginians in particular that this was the best way to govern the country. But others, especially Patrick Henry, who stayed at home because he "smelt a rat," saw nothing noble or honorable in the document and vowed to fight against it. And Henry had many on his side. The Virginia delegation had been very much a federalist clique and did not truly represent the sentiments of the Old Dominion. The fight for ratification in Virginia would be an uphill battle.

The struggle began in March 1788 when each of Virginia's counties and boroughs elected delegates to a special Ratification Convention to be held in June. The citizens of Orange County selected Madison, Prince Edward chose Patrick Henry, and Mason decided to run from Stafford County where he held land because his home county of Fairfax appeared overwhelmingly Federalist, as the side supporting the Constitution was now labeled. Washington refused to run; Jefferson was abroad as minister to France. The election outcomes demonstrated the difficult task ahead: while most of the Tidewater, Northern Neck, Shenandoah Valley, and far western counties were strongly Federalist, much of the Piedmont, Southside, and Southwest seemed very Anti-Federalist. (See map on p. 146.) A preliminary count of the 170 delegates suggested a slim Federalist majority, 86 to 80 with 4 unknowns. The Ratification Convention began meeting in early June; and it immediately became clear that Patrick Henry and James Madison would dominate the debate, Henry with his lengthy, emotion-laden harangues, Madison with his quiet, cool, and logical arguments. These men and a handful of others like George Mason and Governor Randolph, who changed his position to favor the document, would speak frequently; 149 delegates would not utter a word.

On 5 June 1788 Patrick Henry gave an impassioned three-hour speech urging his fellow delegates to vote against the new Constitution. As he had already done for several days and would continue to do for several more weeks, Henry argued that this governmental restructuring was both unnecessary and dangerous. In his view the Articles of Confederation that had guided the young nation through a long war and a successful peace had not proved defective. Yes, he admitted, Shays' Rebellion had broken out, but that was in Massachusetts, not Virginia. Most importantly, the new document would be exceedingly dangerous to the liberties of his fellow Virginians: the new president would command a professional army that would soon establish a tyrannical monarchy; the new Senate would make treaties with foreign powers that would compromise the freedom of Virginians; trial by jury and a free press would be trampled; and Virginians would be taxed to death to support the construc-

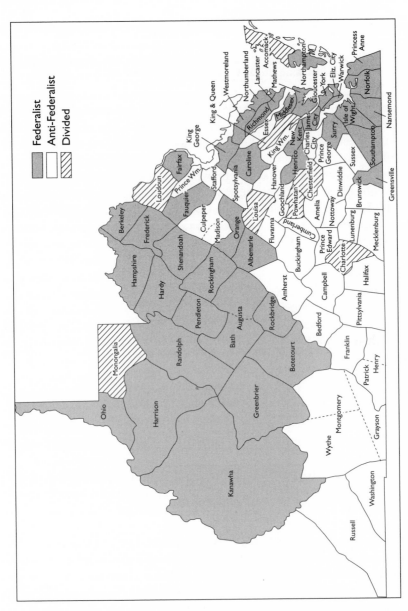

VOTING OF VIRGINIA CONVENTION DELEGATES ON THE RATIFICATION OF THE U.S. CONSTITUTION, 1788.

Reprinted by permission from Richard Beeman, *The Old Dominion and the New Nation, 1788–1801* (Lexington: University Press of Kentucky, 1972).

tion of a huge federal city containing magnificent palaces for the president, senators, and congressmen. To make matters worse, the Virginia state militia, the only true defense against tyranny, would be funded and thus controlled by Congress. This was a government for a "consolidated" America, not for Virginia. A giant tyrannical republic dominated by Northerners would replace thirteen free and independent republics. Liberty-loving Virginians were doomed.

These kinds of speeches went on for days, and each day Madison or sometimes Randolph would patiently point out the historical inaccuracies or the lack of logic in Henry's arguments. But Henry and his followers would not be deterred; in fact, they had decided early on that their best defense was delay. If they could stall a final vote for weeks, perhaps Henry's diatribes, no matter how illogical, would raise doubts in the minds of enough delegates. And if they could not prevent the ratification, then they would try to insist that the Constitution could only go into effect after it had been altered with a lengthy list of amendments. Some of the amendments amounted to a bill of rights, which Mason wanted added to the document before it finally became law; other amendments, supported by Henry, altered the powers of the president and the right to tax; they were designed to gut the Constitution of its most important features and return sovereignty to the states. On 23 June, after three weeks of tiring debates, the rhetoric turned nasty and personal, and Federalists began to fear that some delegates would grow weary and head for home. The next day George Wythe moved that the Constitution be ratified with no prior amendment, but Henry again rose to challenge this proposal. Madison momentarily capitulated and agreed to support the idea of forwarding a set of amendments to the rest of the states before actual ratification. On 25 June 1788 the Convention voted on the amendments issue, and Henry and his colleagues lost 88 to 80; instead, a list of amendments would accompany the ratification document but were not a precondition of its approval. Shortly thereafter a formal roll call was taken on the ratification of the Constitution, and it passed 89 to 79. The Old Dominion became the tenth state to join the new federal union, but with a significant qualification. Virginians reserved the right to withdraw from the new government "whenever the powers granted unto it should be perverted to their injury or oppression."

Patrick Henry's inflammatory and alarmist speeches in June 1788 were intended to scare the delegates into rejecting the Constitution. In the end, his tactics and arguments failed; but the issues and fears he raised concerning state versus national sovereignty and liberty versus security were not new, and they would linger in one form or another until well into the twentieth century.

SOURCES CONSULTED

"The Battle of the Barges," *Virginia Cavalcade* (Autumn 1954); Ira Berlin, *Many Thousand Gone: The First Two Centuries of Slavery in North America* (1998); Warren M. Billings, John E. Selby, and Thad W. Tate, *Colonial Virginia: A History* (1986); Alan V. Briceland, "Virginia: The Cement of the Union," in *The Constitution and the States,* ed. Patrick T. Conley and John P. Kaminski (1988); Thomas E. Buckley, S.J., *Church and State in Revolutionary Virginia, 1776–1787* (1977); Robert M. Calhoon, "The Impact of the Revolution on Church and State," in *The Blackwell Encyclopedia of the American Revolution,* ed. Jack P. Greene and J. R. Pole (1991); Colin G. Calloway, *The American Revolution in Indian Country* (1995); Francis D. Cogliano, *Revolutionary America, 1763–1815* (2000); *The Documentary History of the Ratification of the Constitution,* vols. 9 and 10, *Virginia,* ed. John P. Kaminski and Gaspare J. Saladino (1990); Daniel L. Dreisbach, "Church-State Debate in the Virginia Legislature: From the Declaration of Rights to the Statute for Establishing Religious Freedom," in *Religion and Political Culture in Jefferson's Virginia,* ed. Daniel L. Dreisbach and Garrett Ward Sheldon (2000); Richard S. Dunn, "Black Society in the Chesapeake, 1776–1810," in *Slavery and Freedom in the Age of the American Revolution,* ed. Ira Berlin and Ronald Hoffman (1983); Emory G. Evans, "Private Indebtedness and the Revolution in Virginia, 1776–1796," *William and Mary Quarterly,* 3d ser. (July 1971); David Hackett Fischer, *Washington's Crossing* (2004); Sylvia Frey, *Water from the Rock: Black Resistance in a Revolutionary Age* (1991); *A Guide to the Virginia Military Organizations in the American Revolution, 1774–1787* (1978); Adele Hast, *Loyalism in Revolutionary Virginia* (1979); Woody Holton, *Forced Founders: Indians, Debtors, Slaves, and the Making of the American Revolution in Virginia* (1999); Rhys Isaac, *Landon Carter's Uneasy Kingdom: Revolution and Rebellion on a Virginia Plantation* (2004); Merrill Jensen, *The Articles of Confederation* (1940); Linda K. Kerber, " 'History Can Do It No Justice': Women and the Reinterpretation of the American Revolution," in *Women in the Age of the American Revolution,* ed. Ronald Hoffman and Peter J. Albert (1989); Kerber, *Women of the Republic: Intellect and Ideology in Revolutionary America* (1980); Cynthia A. Kierner, *Beyond the Household: Women's Place in the Early South, 1700–1835* (1998); John G. Kolp and Terri L. Snyder, "Women and the Political Culture of Revolutionary Virginia," Southern Association of Women Historians, 15 June 2000, Richmond; Charles H. Lesser, ed., *The Sinews of Independence: Monthly Strength Reports of the Continental Army* (1976); Pauline Maier, *American Scripture: Making the Declaration of Independence* (1997); James Kirby Martin and Mark Edward Lender, *A Respectable Army: The Military Origins of the Republic, 1763–1789* (1982); Michael A. McDonnell, "Popular Mobilization and Political Culture in Revolutionary Virginia: The Failure of the Minutemen and the Revolution from Below," *JAH* (Dec. 1998); J. Kent McGaughy, *Richard Henry Lee of Virginia* (2004); Charles Patrick Neimeyer, *America Goes to War: A Social History of the Continental Army* (1996); Mary Beth Norton, *Liberty's Daughters: The Revolutionary Experience of American Women, 1750–1800* (1980); Peter S. Onuf,

"From Colony to Territory: Changing Concepts of Statehood in Revolutionary America," *Political Science Quarterly* (Autumn 1982); Onuf, "Toward Federalism: Virginia, Congress, and the Western Lands," *William and Mary Quarterly*, 3d ser. (July 1977); Jack N. Rakove, *Original Meanings: Politics and Ideas in the Making of the Constitution* (1996); Norman K. Risjord, *Chesapeake Politics, 1781–1800* (1978); John E. Selby, *The Revolution in Virginia, 1775–1783* (1988); Craig Symonds, *Battlefield Atlas of the American Revolution* (1986).

7

THE VIRGINIA DYNASTY

1789–1825

Most Americans assume that the ratification of the Constitution guaranteed immediate success and longevity to the United States. In truth, the United States in 1789 was a relatively small emerging nation in the midst of a revolution in the Atlantic world that required the forceful and dignified leadership of George Washington. No state played a greater role in the development of the new republic than Virginia. During the country's first thirty-six years, the Old Dominion provided four of the first five presidents—the Virginia Dynasty—and even when John Adams was president, Thomas Jefferson was vice president. The cabinet and the Supreme Court were both studded with Virginians, including Washington's nephew Bushrod, and the man generally considered to be the greatest of all chief justices, John Marshall. Virginia also dominated the Congress simply by weight of numbers; because its population was so large, it had one-fifth of the members of the House of Representatives in the First Congress. But democratic dynasties do not last forever, and after 1825 Virginia lost its preeminent position in the nation.

During the 1790s Americans created a new constitutional government in the midst of passionate debate and mutual distrust. Almost immediately those who had stood shoulder to shoulder in the Revolution set about squabbling over the powers of the new government and how it should function. Older political elites that dominated the state governments were particularly jealous of their own rights. None was more suspicious of centralized authority than the Virginia patriarchy.

The Federalists—those who had written and supported the Constitution with its formula for a stronger federal government—dominated the 1790s with Washington as president. The Anti-Federalists, who had been powerful in Virginia, decided to accept the new regime, yet their fears and criticisms of the Constitution persisted. Eventually they blended with a portion of the former Federalists to create an opposition to Washington's administration. Favoring limited federal power and a strict interpretation of the Constitution, these Republicans would be led by Thomas Jefferson and one of the most important of the original Federalists, James Madison. Although he held strong reservations about centralized power, Madison remained a true American nationalist to his dying day.

The First Congress had to flesh out the executive branch, create a judicial system, and provide for the promised Bill of Rights. Madison became the most influential congressional leader, assuming a major role in the creation of the five executive departments requested by Washington. In choosing members of his administration, the new president took care not to make it look like a Virginia administration. Washington retained Henry Knox in the War Department, nominated John Jay to be the first chief justice, chose Alexander Hamilton as secretary of the treasury, and asked Jefferson to be secretary of state. The only other Virginian in the cabinet was his protégé Edmund Randolph, whom he selected as attorney general.

Madison's most significant achievement in the First Congress was the adoption of a Bill of Rights, the absence of which had been the most telling Anti-Federalist criticism of the new constitution. However, most states were more worried about the power of the new federal government than they were about protecting the individual rights of free speech and press and trial by jury. Even Virginia Federalists joined Anti-Federalists in supporting twenty amendments designed to limit federal power. Madison addressed the concerns for both rights and power in his proposals, which were based on the Virginia Declaration of Rights. The House and Senate consolidated his suggestions into twelve amendments that were sent to the states for ratification. Ten became the Bill of Rights and were added to the Constitution in 1791.

The most immediate problem facing the new government involved financial policy. The proposals of Secretary of the Treasury Hamilton to refinance the Revolutionary debt, have the national government assume the debts of the states, create a central bank, and impose tariffs to protect manufacturing offended most of the Virginians. Madison in the House and Jefferson in the cabinet opposed Hamilton's recommendations. Funding seemed to reward speculators, and assumption seemed unfair to Virginia, which had already paid most of its debt. The General Assembly passed a resolution declaring assumption unconstitutional, hinting at the possibility of nullification. Jefferson thought both the Bank of the United States and protective tariffs were unconstitutional extensions of power to the federal government that favored commercial development at the expense of farmers. Yet Washington supported Hamilton, forcing Madison and Jefferson to compromise; they traded votes for the funding and assumption schemes in return for locating the new capital on the banks of the Potomac and what they believed to be a fair handling of the Virginia debt.

The clashes over Hamilton's proposals initiated the struggle that eventually led to the party system of the 1790s, with Jeffersonian Republicans facing off against the Federalists, whose Virginia supporters included a recent convert, Patrick Henry. Neither the professional infighter, Madison, nor the aloof Jefferson, who left the cabinet at the end of 1793, believed in the legitimacy of political parties. However, they developed inevitably out of the debates over the powers of the federal government and the differences in both the Congress and the country over the international situation created by the French Revolution.

Americans initially embraced France's rejection of the monarchy as a vindication of their own revolution, but the beheading of the king, France's war with Britain, and "the Reign of Terror" divided sentiment in Virginia as elsewhere. Those who increasingly referred to themselves as the Republicans were termed by their opponents "the party of the French." The supporters of the Washington administration, which had taken a position of neutrality, were termed Federalists and "Anglomen"; they were strong in the cities and the western part of the state.

Ultimately, more substantial divisions occurred over the Jay Treaty with England, which the Republicans thought unduly favored British interests without winning concessions for the United States, including reparations for the thousands of Virginia slaves "confiscated" by the British during the Revolution. A vigorous debate over ratification of the treaty was carried on in Virginia in 1795 in the newspapers and the General Assembly, where Republican voices dominated. Nevertheless, the U.S. Senate narrowly approved the treaty, which won modest commercial concessions from the British and a promise to evacuate forts on American soil; the United States agreed to submit the issue of pre-Revolutionary debts to arbitration. In his Farewell Address of 1796, Washington, whose retirement established a two-term precedent, urged his countrymen "to steer clear of permanent alliances with any portion of the foreign world" and to avoid the "spirit of party," which was infecting domestic debate.

In Richmond political fragmentation was following the pattern set at the national level. In 1788 Virginia legislators moved into a new capitol designed by Jefferson that copied a classical Roman building in Nîmes, France, the Maison Carrée. The constitution of 1776 had created a republic of "gentlemen freeholders" who retained the aristocratic conception of the representative as a man of independent ways as well as independent means. Assembly leaders were descendants of the first families of

Virginia and were among the wealthiest men in the commonwealth. Suspicious of the new government and antifederal at heart, the majority of delegates were generally loath to embrace a democracy that threatened their political power. Although most free adult white males were permitted to vote, deference and apathy kept participation low, ensuring the perpetuation of the patriarchy. Led by Patrick Henry, the assembly selected two notable opponents of the Constitution, William Grayson and Richard Henry Lee, as the first U.S. senators from the commonwealth and denied a prominent Federalist, Edward Carrington, a seat in the assembly. The assemblymen reiterated their opposition to the Constitution in its present form and renewed their call for another convention.

However, party affiliation played a relatively unimportant role in either elections or the business of the assembly, including the legislative selection of governors. As in the other states of the new nation, "parties" remained mere rudiments, traditional connections arising out of the locally powerful county courts and networks of important families that structured state legislative activity during the Jeffersonian era. Legislative sessions were short, and many men served only one term. Members positioned themselves with either the Federalists or the Republicans on matters relating to foreign affairs and federal power, but these designations rarely affected decisions on domestic policy and local matters, such as the sale of glebe lands or laws benefiting slaveholders, where the debates often pitted dissenting, nonslaveholding westerners against the Anglican Tidewater planters. Delegates tended to vote for the particular needs of their constituents, and because those needs were few in an agrarian-based society, most Virginians adopted a laissez-faire, states' rights view of government—"a government that governs best, governs least"—which, in time, favored Republican principles.

An exception to that rule was the demand for defense against Indian attacks. Trouble all along the western borders, fomented by Spanish and British agents and the land hunger of settlers, spilled into the western counties of Virginia in the early 1790s. An incompetent state militia, inadequate state funding, and seemingly indifferent federal authorities compounded the problem. Petitions for help from Governors Beverley Randolph and Henry "Light-Horse Harry" Lee fell on deaf ears until 1794 when a government force under General Anthony Wayne defeated the Indians at Fallen Timbers. Eventual federal assistance in quelling the Indian threat converted many westerners into supporters of Washington's Federalist Party.

Both parties condemned the Whiskey Rebellion of 1794, although neither could refrain from trying to make political capital from the uprising. Federalists blamed the rebellion on the excesses of Democratic-Republican societies, while Republicans complained about abuses of federal authority in putting it down. Congressional imposition of an excise tax on whiskey in 1791 had caused farmers in western Pennsylvania and Virginia, who were converting their grain into distilled spirits in order to get it to market, to refuse to pay the tax. When rioting threatened to spread beyond the region, President Washington ordered Virginia and other state militias to restore order. Governor Lee, whom Washington placed in charge of federalized forces, led the Virginia units into Pennsylvania, but no fighting occurred, few arrests were made, and tax collections resumed. Irate Republicans replaced Lee with Robert Brooke as governor.

Toward midnight on 14 December 1799, George Washington, the commander in chief of the Continental army and the first president of the United States, died at his plantation, Mount Vernon. Four days later he was buried, as he requested, with neither a sermon nor a funeral oration. As the news spread, Americans across the new nation mourned their first citizen. Every town and hamlet held parades and heard countless sermons and orations in his honor. In Congress his friend John Marshall intoned, "Our WASHINGTON is no more! The hero . . . lives now only in his own great actions, and in the hearts of an affectionate and afflicted people."

Washington was, indeed, the "indispensable man" in the founding of the United States. Through his perseverance, sacrifice, and force of character, he kept the colonial army in the field for eight years and so kept the fledgling nation alive. He lent his stature to the writing and ratification of the new Constitution. As the country's first president, he established the precedents of leadership for the American presidency. His name, then and now, is synonymous with character, fortitude, and devotion to duty and country.

Federalist Vice President John Adams of Massachusetts had succeeded Washington in 1797, and in line with the electoral rules established in the Constitution, the Republican Jefferson was elected vice president. At the time the two remained friends, and both believed that they could work with each other. Subsequent hostilities with France, however, turned these two old friends into enemies and further solidified the emerging political parties.

The French seizure of American vessels in the West Indies and their attempts at extortion in the XYZ affair in 1797–98 led to genuine fears of possible war with France and an invasion of the United States. In response, the Federalist Congress passed legislation expanding the army, creating a real navy, and implementing a national tax to pay for these measures. Another part of this effort was the infamous Alien and Sedition Acts, aimed at punishing the activities of alien revolutionaries and suppressing opposition to the government. The Sedition Act led to the prosecution of twenty-three Republican editors and the conviction of ten, including the scurrilous James T. Callender, who was tried and convicted in Richmond.

While some Virginia Federalists like Washington and Marshall, who had been one of the XYZ peace commissioners, were hesitant about this legislation, Jefferson and Madison vigorously opposed it. Acting anonymously, they each drafted resolutions that were introduced by Republican colleagues into the Kentucky and Virginia legislatures, respectively, in 1798. Although they did differ, both the Kentucky and the Virginia Resolutions advanced the view that the Constitution was a compact between the states providing specific powers to the central government and that federal laws exceeding those powers could be ruled unconstitutional by the states and declared null and void within their jurisdictions. The resolutions and Madison's later defense, called in Virginia the "Doctrines of '98," became the basis for the states' rights arguments of the antebellum period and were cited by John C. Calhoun and others in the nullification crisis of 1832–33, although Madison would deny that his intent had been the same as what the South Carolinians wanted.

Polarized into competing parties, the Virginia assembly, with 40 percent of its members dissenting, accepted Madison's resolutions, without a controversial nullification provision, and sent them to the other states to encourage them to vote for candidates who would overthrow the Sedition Act. More radical Republicans, led by John Taylor of Caroline, talked of secession, defensive civil war, and even an alliance of the Old Dominion with France. Federalists thought such talk treasonable. The assembly appropriated funds for an armory in Richmond and a 15,000-man state military force, ostensibly to prevent federal enforcement of the Alien and Sedition Acts and the collection of federal taxes in Virginia. A sense of alarm swelled in the Southern states, but the quiet diplomacy of Adams ended the undeclared war with France (and may have cost him reelection) and prepared the country for the "Revolution of 1800," a peaceful transfer of power to the Republicans.

In the midst of the 1800 campaign, a slave blacksmith who was called "General Gabriel" by his followers led an abortive slave rebellion on the Prosser plantation outside of Richmond. Gabriel conceived a revolutionary scheme of organizing a thousand slaves to attack the city and take control of the government. The plan was leaked to a planter by his slaves, and he informed Governor James Monroe. A terrible storm arose and kept the rebellious slaves from assembling before Monroe managed to mobilize the militia. The insurrection collapsed, and eventually Gabriel was captured in Norfolk and was hanged along with several coconspirators. Rumors that 50,000 slaves had been involved in the plot left white Virginians greatly agitated.

In a close and sharply sectional vote, Jefferson defeated Adams in 1800. The assembly made sure that Adams would not take a Virginia electoral vote, as he had four years before, by introducing a single statewide ticket. Turnout in Virginia, 25 percent of the eligible electorate, was the highest yet for a presidential or congressional election and was higher than it would be for another thirty years. But even after the electoral votes were counted, Jefferson was not elected. The peculiarities of the Electoral College that had produced his vice presidency now created a constitutional crisis. Jefferson and his "running mate," Aaron Burr, received the same number of electoral votes, which forced the choice into the House of Representatives, where many Federalists supported the New Yorker. However, Hamilton and some moderates in his party from the middle states preferred Jefferson to the duplicitous Burr. After an appropriate deal was arranged, the Virginian was duly elected on the thirty-sixth ballot.

Thomas Jefferson, the third president of the United States, was what the eighteenth-century French termed a *philosophe*: a man of the Enlightenment with a remarkable breadth of knowledge. We know Jefferson's political mind from his voluminous letters and the only book he ever published, *Notes on the State of Virginia* (1782), a commentary on the natural history, geography, and political order of the Old Dominion. In the chapter ironically called "Manufactures," he expressed his commitment to the idea that American society should be dominated by small farmers, who were the ideal citizens of a republic: "the chosen people of God." He was never fond of cities and factories, which he believed threatened the purity and civic virtue of rural life.

In "Constitution," one of the longest chapters in the book, the future president addressed the problems with the governmental structure of his beloved Virginia. Here, and continuously throughout his life, Jefferson called for reform. In particular, he believed that the vote should be expanded and that the western portion of the state should be more equally represented. Jefferson believed that legitimate government would exercise few powers over individuals who retained their natural rights, particularly those of free inquiry and religious belief.

A troubled and flawed individual, particularly with regard to slavery, Jefferson was a citizen of the world and perhaps the most sophisticated of American presidents, yet he often said, "Virginia, sir, is my country." No Virginian has made such a significant contribution to both state and nation as he: the Declaration of Independence, the Virginia Statute for Religious Freedom, the Kentucky Resolutions, the Louisiana Purchase, Monticello, and the founding of the University of Virginia.

In his inaugural Jefferson expressed the general principles of his political philosophy: "a wise and frugal government." As Washington had done, he greeted Congress with a warning against both foreign influence and the spirit of faction. He then added his oft-quoted plea for national unity and an end to partisan dispute: "We are all Republicans, we are all Federalists." Yet Jefferson immediately violated this harmonious rhetoric by attacking the Federalist-dominated judiciary. The political purge of the federal courts began with Secretary of State Madison's refusal to deliver the appointments that Adams made in the last days of his administration. Next followed an unsuccessful attempt to impeach Supreme Court justice Samuel Chase, who had strictly enforced the Sedition Act.

Although Jefferson had a low regard for the judiciary and the English common law, the man at whom this hostility seemed aimed was his distant cousin, the Virginia Federalist John Marshall. A Revolutionary War soldier from Fauquier County, Marshall was a pragmatic lawyer with a distinguished résumé of public service as a congressman, diplomat, and secretary of state before Adams in early 1801 appointed him chief justice of the Supreme Court, a position he held longer than any other chief justice. But for Washington, Jefferson, and Madison, no other Virginian exceeded Marshall's contribution to the development of America. He established the Supreme Court as an equal branch of government with the executive and legislative branches, asserted federal supremacy over the states, and encouraged national economic development with his decisions. Seeing Marshall as a major impediment to Republican reform, Jefferson was infuriated by the chief justice's decision in *Marbury v. Madison* (1803) that affirmed the power of the Supreme Court and the principle of judicial review.

Like most Americans, Jefferson believed the nation's destiny was continental. Seizing upon Napoleon's loss of interest in a New World empire, Jefferson purchased the Louisiana Territory in 1803 for $15 million, doubling the size of the country. To explore this vast area and perhaps discover a water route to the Pacific, Jefferson commissioned an expedition commanded by two Virginians, Meriwether Lewis, the president's private secretary, and William Clark, brother of George Rogers Clark. Their expedition traversed the country and returned in 1804–6. Leading the "Corps of Discovery," Lewis and Clark collected information about flora, fauna, and Indians that pleased the amateur naturalist Jefferson and proved of inestimable value to subsequent explorers.

Virginians' interest in the West predated the Lewis and Clark expedition. Continuing the colonial pattern, Virginians migrated westward after the Revolution, lured by opportunity and adventure or driven away by competition with slave labor. Years before the Louisiana mission, thousands of Virginians, in the footsteps of Daniel Boone, had moved through the Cumberland Gap to settle Kentucky and Tennessee, both of which gained statehood in the 1790s. Many native Virginians, notably John Sevier, Henry Clay, and Sam Houston, became leaders in these states.

JOHN MARSHALL, ENGRAVING BY A. B. DURAND
FROM PAINTING BY HENRY INMAN

North of the Ohio River, Virginians were now migrating into the old Northwest Territory, where men like William Henry Harrison, born at the Berkeley plantation on the James River, fought the Indians and established a political base. Over the next half century, Virginia became the primary exporter of black and white labor to the developing frontier.

On all counts—the successful administration of the government, the purchase of Louisiana, the prosecution of the war against the North African pirates—Jefferson's first term was a tremendous success. He was overwhelmingly reelected in 1804, taking 92 percent of the electoral vote while his party won 83 percent of the seats in the House of Representatives. Problems in foreign affairs, however, doomed his second administration.

War between England and France had broken out again in 1803, and the United States became the most important neutral carrier. Shipping boomed as the Americans gained access to areas hitherto closed to them and profited from high prices. However, maritime issues emerged to threaten this prosperity. Both belligerents began seizing American ships and blockading the ports of the other, further restricting trade. The British were also "impressing" or taking sailors from American vessels.

Rather than unleashing the dogs of war, Jefferson turned to economic coercion, convinced that England would give in to such pressure quickly. On 18 December 1807, with Congress's approval, Jefferson imposed an embargo on all American shipping to foreign ports. It backfired. Closing foreign trade brought economic calamity to exporters, including the tobacco planters and wheat growers of Virginia, who joined with New England merchantmen to condemn the administration and its embargo. The shrill and eccentric John Randolph of Roanoke, who had already broken with Jefferson for violating strict republican principles, denounced this coercion. He became the foremost spokesman of a group devoted to an extreme interpretation of states' rights, the "Quids," who challenged the president's leadership and the election of his chosen successor, James Madison.

The cerebral Madison, whose enemies called him "Little Jemmy" and joked about his masculinity because of his short stature, was no more successful than his mentor in settling the differences with England and France. Before he took office in 1809, Congress repealed the embargo and replaced it with the Non-Intercourse Act directed at the belligerents; but initially Madison was duped, first by the British and then by the French, in his efforts to resume trade. The confiscation of American ships continued.

Frustrated by continued British transgressions and the demands of Virginia Republicans for more economic coercion, the president asked for a declaration of war, emphasizing the maritime grievances of impressments, seizures, and blockades. Congress endorsed Madison's request on 18 June 1812 in a partisan vote with most Republicans, including the "war hawks," favoring war. In Virginia, as in Congress, the Federalists and the dissident Quids opposed the war.

Although enthusiasm for engagement was strong, except in New England, the war did not go well. Ill prepared for combat, American forces suffered from incompetent military and presidential leadership. Efforts to take Canada proved disastrous, and a British blockade of the coast cut off most American trade. Only the American navy achieved parity, with victories on Lake Erie and Lake Champlain and the success

JOHN RANDOLPH, BY JOSEPH WOOD

of the USS *Constitution*, "Old Ironsides." The war effort reached its lowest point when the British captured Washington in August 1814 and burned the Capitol, the presidential residence, and most of the public buildings as Madison, his wife, Dolley, and other members of the government decamped in disarray.

Nevertheless, the war-weary British sought an end to the hostilities, and a treaty was signed at Ghent, Belgium, on 24 December 1814 with neither side winning any concessions from the other. A *status quo ante bellum* was achieved. Andrew Jackson's amazing victory at New Orleans two weeks later only made it appear that the Americans had won; yet by challenging the British and holding their own, the upstart young Americans solidified their independence, inspiring a spirit of nationalism that fostered economic and political change in the postwar years.

Virginians played a modest role in the War of 1812. They enthusiastically supported the war, except for some Federalists, who gained seats in the assembly, and John Randolph, who lost his congressional seat. The legislature imposed taxes and sent the militia off to fight. A Petersburg unit marched to Canada and back and looked so impressive on its return that President Madison called Petersburg the "Cockade City of the Union." Although the Chesapeake Bay was controlled by the British navy, Virginia militia forestalled British efforts to take Norfolk in the battle of Craney Island. In retaliation, the British seized Hampton and treated the civilian population brutally. William Henry Harrison, who had achieved fame with a victory over the Indians at Tippecanoe in 1811, defeated a combined British and Indian force in the Battle of the Thames (Ontario) in which Tecumseh was killed, effectively ending Indian power in the Northwest.

In Virginia, as well as in the nation, the war created new political allegiances and renewed debate over the role of the federal government in economic development. Formerly, personal relationships among prominent men had dominated the political process in Virginia. Although identifiable factions with contrasting federal agendas emerged in the 1790s and a frenzy of organizational activity accompanied the "Revolution of 1800," little in the way of a party organization or press existed. Consequently, for most of the Jeffersonian era, the Old Dominion registered the lowest turnouts in the new nation, dropping to 3 percent of the white adult males in the 1820 presidential election.

The initial attempts to fashion party machinery in the commonwealth came in response to the Federalist challenge in the late 1790s. Congressional Republicans who opposed the Adams administration caucused and set up a standing committee to coordinate the activities of the county committees. In 1804 Judge Spencer Roane of Essex County established the *Richmond Enquirer* and installed his cousin Thomas Ritchie, also from Essex County, as editor. Every four years a State Central Committee of Correspondence was chosen that included Ritchie, and this organization brought together several locally powerful elite groups of Republicans in the interest of party unity and continuity. The organization became known as the Richmond or Essex "Junto," and the *Enquirer* was its voice.

After the War of 1812, Roane, chief justice of Virginia's Supreme Court of Appeals, mounted his successful campaign to restore strict construction as the touchstone of republican purity. The essence of Junto ideology lay in the states' rights philosophy expressed in the "Doctrines of '98" as interpreted by antifederalists like Roane, who sought to revive Virginia's reputation among the states and reestablish its moral leadership of the new nation. Though a clique of no more than twenty men, the Junto was the only organization in early Virginia politics, giving it an authority beyond its numbers.

Family influence defined the Junto. All of its members bore some filial relation to one another and to the great families of Virginia. This "connection" involved the Nicholas brothers, the Campbell brothers, the

SPENCER ROANE, BY CEPHAS THOMPSON

THOMAS RITCHIE

Brockenbrough brothers, the Roanes, and the Munfords, father and son. Spencer Roane, Thomas Ritchie, and the Brockenbroughs were all cousins. William Brockenbrough and Andrew Stevenson married sisters, as did Ritchie and Richard Parker, who in doing so became sons-in-law of party stalwart, Richmond mayor, and postmaster Dr. William Foushee. These were men of substance and education who knew instinctively that they had been raised to rule.

The Richmond Junto formed the nucleus of the Republican "center": Tidewater and the Southside. This was "Old Virginia," dominated by large slaveholding tobacco plantations. Opposition came from the politicians of the "periphery": that semicircle of counties from the Eastern Shore to the Northern Neck across the northern Piedmont to the Valley and the Northwest. Here the political and economic culture was more diverse and slavery less important. To challenge the editorial philosophy of Ritchie's *Enquirer,* John Hampden Pleasants, whose father, U.S. Senator James Pleasants, opposed the Junto, assumed editorship of the *Richmond Whig* in 1824.

The Junto's urban base of operations and its affiliation with Virginia's conservative banking system belied the fact that the clique epitomized the traditional system of planter domination. These men embraced the conservative commercial agrarianism associated with John Taylor of Caroline and Jefferson that was more antimercantilist than liberal. They distinctly favored and practiced commercial farming. More diverse economic development, such as manufacturing and transportation networks, especially when supported by government, was to be obstructed. It was this near-reactionary attitude that would hamper the development of the Old Dominion down to the Civil War.

The debate over the means and ends of government was also going on in Washington. The war had revealed major national weaknesses and produced new situations that demanded attention. With President Madison's approval, the Republican War Hawks, notably Henry Clay and John C. Calhoun, pushed for a tariff to protect infant industries and a new charter for the Bank of the United States, which the Republicans had allowed to die in 1811. Rechartering involved a payment to the government that Calhoun, at the time a young nationalist, proposed to use for internal improvements. It seemed very Hamiltonian, this "American System" advanced by Clay of economic development fostered by the federal government. Madison signed the tariff and bank legislation, but he vetoed the internal improvements bill, insisting that federal road building required a constitutional amendment.

Virginians reacted in strange ways to this "Madisonian nationalism." Out of party loyalty, Republicans generally supported the president, while nationalistic Federalists, who were in serious decline, voted against

JAMES MONROE, BY REMBRANDT PEALE

the Bank and the tariff but favored internal improvements. A major shift in political philosophies and loyalties was taking place; Federalists were dying, and Republicans were irreparably splitting into nationalist and states' rights factions.

In the presidential election of 1816, James Monroe became the fourth Virginian to assume the office, the last of the Virginia Dynasty. He was the least talented of the four, but he was a man of substance who had been an AntiFederalist and both a follower and a friend of Jefferson. He had served as governor of the commonwealth twice and as a diplomat in various capacities, as well as secretary of state. His most significant achievements in office were diplomatic, largely the work of his brilliant secretary of state, John Quincy Adams, who settled Canadian border issues with Britain, acquired Florida, and promulgated the Monroe Doctrine of 1823, which warned European powers to keep "hands off" the Americas.

In other areas Monroe followed Madison's lead and supported the Bank and tariff while opposing federal support for internal improvements. In light of the imminent death of the Federalist Party, which ran its last presidential candidate in 1816, Monroe extended a hand to his old foes in hopes of creating a nonparty government. He carried this message on a trip to the Northeast, causing a Boston newspaper to proclaim "An Era of Good Feelings."

At least one historian has described it as an "Era of Ill Feelings" in Virginia. In the assembly Federalists from the periphery generally took the lead on matters concerning economic development, despite sharp criticism from the planter establishment. Charles Fenton Mercer, from Loudoun County in the northern Piedmont, pushed for creation of a state system of internal improvements over Republican opposition. Finally, enough Piedmont Republicans joined Mercer to create a Board of Public Works in 1816 and to initiate a modest program of canal and road building, although most of the money went into a single venture, the James River–Kanawha River canal project.

From the time of the Revolution, Virginians had considered canal systems that would bypass the fall lines of the James and Potomac rivers and link the eastern Tidewater with the western part of the state, perhaps as far as the Ohio River. The James River Company, chartered by the assembly in 1785 at George Washington's urging, achieved a bypass of Richmond a decade later and improved the James for shallow-drafted bateaux westward to Lynchburg. This project cut the transportation time of goods and people between the two cities to five days. The Potomac River Company accomplished a similar feat by 1808, opening travel from the Shenandoah River to Alexandria. Other state-aided companies constructed a channel from the Dismal Swamp to Albemarle Sound and improved the Appomattox River for bateau travel between Petersburg and Farmville.

Under pressure from western farmers, who were not served by these river improvements, the assembly purchased the James River Company in 1820 and pressed for completion of a more substantial James-Kanawha canal system that would permit deeper-drafted vessels to be pulled by horses on a towpath rather than being poled by boatmen. The venture was ill timed and underfunded. Despite much construction, funding dried up in the face of depression, and the project collapsed.

Federalists also lobbied for an expanded banking network, but they were partially stymied by a Republican policy that limited the system to a few large "mother" banks with branches in satellite cities. The assembly chartered the Bank of Virginia in 1804 and provided for Republican domination of its board. After the charter of the First Bank of the United States expired in 1811, the legislature extended the Bank of Virginia's capital and established a second "mother" bank, the Farmers Bank of Virginia, also controlled by Republicans. They pushed through a stringent law prohibiting all private notes and limiting the payment of state taxes to either specie or the notes of the two state banks. They did permit the establishment of additional banks in Winchester and Wheeling in 1817, but Federalists wanted more new banks in the Valley. That same year the recently chartered Second Bank of the United States set up offices in Richmond and Norfolk, further expanding the credit system of the state.

On education Virginians did not follow the advice of Jefferson regarding a public school system. As early as 1779 he had unsuccessfully urged the legislature to create a system of free schools that all white children would attend for three years, after which the able boys would receive additional free instruction at the secondary level. In 1796 the assembly gave counties the option of establishing tax-supported schools, but few availed themselves of the opportunity. In 1810 the legislature created a Literary Fund, reserving collected fines and taxes for education; some of the money went to elementary schools for poor children, but they often went unused because parents did not want to be categorized as paupers.

Advocates of public education could not overcome the sentiments of conservative planters, whose children attended private schools and who were loath to tax themselves to educate the children of others. They argued that no government should interfere with parents' responsibility for educating their children. Even Jefferson resisted common school reform when he believed that it would interfere with the establishment of his university. To overcome eastern Republican opposition, he was forced to rely on Federalist votes to gain a charter for the university in 1819, but he refused to return the favor to Mercer, who wanted a state-funded public education scheme that stressed primary schools. Much of the Literary Fund money went to the university.

Virginia's orthodox Republicans, fearing the centralizing tendencies inherent in Henry Clay's American System and John Marshall's judicial nationalism, initiated a states' rights revival that swept over the South during the 1820s. The Supreme Court, with Marshall at the helm, forced the issue by deciding three landmark cases—*Martin v. Hunter's Lessee* (1816), *McCulloch v. Maryland* (1819), and *Cohens v. Virginia* (1821)—that specifically dealt with the question of federal versus state power. *Martin* and *Cohens,* both of which overturned decisions of Virginia's highest court, constituted the essence of judicial nationalism by asserting the power of the U.S. Supreme Court over both state legislatures and state courts. *McCulloch* denied a state's right to tax a federal institution and upheld the constitutionality of the national bank on the basis of implied powers, a broad interpretation of the Constitution.

The political elite of the Old Dominion rose up against these affronts to their republican purity. After the *McCulloch* decision in March 1819, the *Enquirer* began to criticize the Court. Before the month was out, Ritchie printed a series of attacks signed "Amphictyon" and written by Judge William Brockenbrough, a member of the Junto. Then in June, Spencer

Roane contributed four essays under the general title, "Rights of 'The States,' and of 'The People,'" signed "Hampden," in which he accused Marshall of "federal usurpations" that aimed to "obliterate the state governments, forever, from our political system." Marshall, who often defended his opinions with public essays of his own, accused the Virginia states' rightists of "zealous and persevering hostility" in their efforts "to reinstate that miserable confederation" whose shortcomings were so obvious. Attacking the court was their way of undermining the Union and the Constitution. Jefferson tried to stay out of the public debate, but he wrote Roane on receiving his essays: "I subscribe to every tittle of them. They contain the true principles of the Revolution of 1800, for that was as real a revolution in the principles of our government as that of 1776 was in its form."

Judge Roane proved to be nationalism's severest critic in the Old Dominion. Marshall's Court had been overturning his decisions and challenging the authority of his court. In the "Hampden" essays he insisted that the Constitution "conveyed only a limited grant of powers to the general government, and reserved the residuary powers to the government of the states, and to the people." The judge even more forcefully asserted the "Doctrines of '98" in his vitriolic "Algernon Sydney" essay that attacked the Court's decision in the *Cohens* case. Despite Marshall's able defense of the constitutional authority for federal power, the General Assembly denied the Supreme Court appellate jurisdiction in any case decided by a state court and insisted that the federal court had no right to examine the judgment of "the Commonwealth of Virginia." The roll-call votes in the assembly on these matters showed a clear conflict between the representatives of the center and those from the periphery.

Jefferson and Roane gained support from planter politician John Taylor of Caroline, who had introduced the Virginia Resolutions into the assembly in 1798. In response to the rulings of the Marshall Court, he put forward his defense of states' rights and strict construction in three books. In their discussions of constitutional questions, Taylor and Roane, whose slashing arguments were far more politically effective than Taylor's ponderous prose, both defended slavery and insisted that Marshall's views championing federal power threatened the peculiar institution. The two perspectives became linked in the minds of most Virginians when, in the midst of the battle over the jurisdiction of the Supreme Court, the slavery question broke upon the national scene.

In 1819 Missouri petitioned to enter the Union as a slave state. New York Republican James Tallmadge introduced an amendment to the statehood bill that called upon the prospective state to prohibit the further introduction of slaves and to provide for the gradual emancipation of those born in the new state. Virginians saw the prohibition as a violation

of their rights and a first step in denying slaveholders access to the territories, which eventually would lead to the abolition of slavery, for conditions imposed on new states might be imposed on old ones. Jefferson
likened the proposal to "a fire bell in the night" and perceived in its implications "the knell of the Union."

The Virginia-born congressman from Kentucky, Henry Clay, took
the lead in trying to find a peaceful resolution to the problem. In this
effort he cooperated with President Monroe and Virginia senator James
Barbour. It seemed obvious to Barbour that the Missouri matter should
be joined with the mundane question of statehood for Maine, maintaining the balance between slave and free states. Illinois senator Jesse
Thomas added an amendment that divided the unsettled portion of the
Louisiana Territory lands into slave and free by extending the southern
boundary of the new state and excluding slavery north of that line of
36°30′. These elements constituted the Missouri Compromise, which
passed both chambers after contentious debate.

Using arguments that would intensify over the next four decades,
Southerners adamantly defended the peculiar institution on biblical, racial, and constitutional grounds and condemned the restrictionists as abolitionists and disunionists. The "Doctrines of '98" were revived: Congress
had no such power to interfere on this question. No slave state opposed
the Missouri Compromise as resolutely as the Old Dominion. When the
Southern representatives split their vote on the 36°30′ line with a slim
majority favoring it, the commonwealth's congressmen emphatically rejected compromise. Even the author of the Declaration of Independence
and the architect of the Northwest Ordinance of 1787, which had prohibited slavery in that territory, feared that if the Congress could keep slavery from the territories, it could "declare that the condition of all men
within the United States shall be that of freedom." Thomas Ritchie in the
pages of the *Enquirer* argued repeatedly that the goal of the Northerners
was "extinction of the slave representation feature in the Congress of the
U. States." He dismissed the Northwest Ordinance, denied the possibility
of the citizenship of free blacks, and talked of disunion. John Randolph,
who always managed an apt phrase to summarize his extreme response,
declared, "God has given us the Missouri and the devil shall not take it
from us."

Related to Virginians' fears for slavery were the figures of the 1820
census, which revealed that the Old Dominion was no longer the most
populous state in the nation. Northern states were growing more rapidly than Southern states. And with the departure of President Monroe,
Virginia would likely no longer lead the Union. These facts heightened
their concern about the presidential election of 1824. The campaign typi-
fied the traditional politics of the commonwealth in the Jeffersonian era:

a struggle between the Junto and the moderates. Five potential candidates associated with the administrations of both Madison and Monroe emerged. The *Enquirer* came out rather early in support of the secretary of the treasury, William H. Crawford, a Georgian who had been born in the Old Dominion; a caucus of two-thirds of Virginia's assemblymen overwhelmingly endorsed him.

Yet the response of the eastern planter elite to the various contenders remained distinctly personal and gave no hint of future partisan alignments. There was scattered support for John Quincy Adams and Henry Clay. Nearly all the Virginia elite rejected General Andrew Jackson, whom young John Tyler described as a "mere soldier." Even though Crawford suffered a stroke before the election, he received 56 percent of the Virginia popular vote, but few had bothered to go to the polls. The center supported Crawford while the disorganized periphery rejected the dictation of the Junto and split its votes between Adams and Jackson, who clearly won the national vote. But when the Electoral College did not give a majority to any of the candidates, the election went to the House of Representatives, where the delegations from the states, each casting one vote, chose Adams to be the next president. Clay's support for Adams led to charges from the Jacksonians that a "corrupt bargain" had been struck between these nationalists.

This ended the reign of the Virginia Dynasty and left a dispirited commonwealth facing an unpredictable future. Never again would Virginia influence the course of American history so directly and positively. Trapped in defense of an aristocratic slave society and a parochial political philosophy, its leaders could not develop the liberality, the breadth of vision, the moral sensitivity, and the genius of political compromise so natural to its greatest generation.

SOURCES CONSULTED

Harry Ammon, "The Formation of the Republican Party in Virginia," *JSH* (Aug. 1953); Ammon, *James Monroe: The Quest for National Identity* (1971); Ammon, "The Richmond Junto, 1800–1824," *VMHB* (Oct. 1953); Richard R. Beeman, *The Old Dominion and the New Nation, 1789–1801* (1972); Richard Brookhiser, *Founding Father: Rediscovering George Washington* (1996); James H. Broussard, *The Southern Federalists, 1800–1816* (1978); Richard Brown, "The Missouri Crisis, Slavery, and the Politics of Jacksonianism," *South Atlantic Quarterly* (Winter 1966); James Thomas Flexner, *George Washington*, 4 vols. (1969–73); Douglas R. Egerton, *Charles Fenton Mercer and the Trial of National Conservatism* (1989); Joseph J. Ellis, *The American Sphinx: The Character of Thomas Jefferson* (1997); Joanne B. Freeman, *Affairs of Honor: National Politics in the New Republic* (2001); Joseph H. Harrison Jr., "Oligarchs and Democrats—The Richmond Junto," *VMHB* (April 1970); Annette Gordon-Reed, *Thomas Jefferson and Sally Hemings: An American Controversy* (1997);

Daniel P. Jordan, *Political Leadership in Jefferson's Virginia* (1983); Roger G. Kennedy, *Mr. Jefferson's Lost Cause: Land, Farmers, Slavery, and the Louisiana Purchase* (2003); Ralph Ketcham, *Presidents above Party* (1984); Jon Kukla, *A Wilderness So Immense: The Louisiana Purchase and the Destiny of America* (2003); Leonard W. Levy, *Jefferson and Civil Liberties: The Darker Side* (1963); Charles D. Lowery, *James Barbour: The Biography of a Jeffersonian Republican* (1984); Richard K. Mathews, *If Men Were Angels: James Madison and the Heartless Empire of Reason* (1995); Mathews, *The Radical Politics of Thomas Jefferson: A Revisionist View* (1984); Drew R. McCoy, *The Elusive Republic: Political Economy in Jeffersonian America* (1980); F. Thornton Miller, *Juries and Judges versus the Law: Virginia's Provincial Legal Perspective, 1783–1818* (1994); Miller, "The Richmond Junto: The Secret All-Powerful Club—or Myth," *VMHB* (Jan. 1991); R. Kent Newmyer, *John Marshall and the Heroic Age of the Supreme Court* (2001); Peter S. Onuf, *Jefferson's Empire: The Language of American Nationhood* (2000); Jeffrey L. Pasley, *"The Tyranny of Printers": The Rise of Newspaper Politics in the Early Republic* (2001); Merrill D. Peterson, *Thomas Jefferson and the New Nation* (1971); Jack N. Rakove, *James Madison and the Creation of the American Republic* (1990); Norman K. Risjord, *Chesapeake Politics, 1781–1800* (1978); Risjord, "How the Common Man Voted in Jefferson's Virginia," in *America, the Middle Period: Essays in Honor of Bernard Mayo,* ed. John Boles (1973); Risjord, *The Old Republicans: Southern Conservatism in the Age of Jefferson* (1965); Risjord, "The Virginia Federalists," *JSH* (Nov. 1967); Norman K. Risjord and Gordon DenBoer, "The Evolution of Political Parties in Virginia, 1782–1800," *JAH* (March 1974); A. G. Roeber, *Faithful Magistrates and Republican Lawyers: Creators of Virginia Legal Culture, 1680–1810* (1981); Lisle Rose, *Prologue to Democracy: The Federalists in the South, 1789–1800* (1968); Robert E. Shalhope, *John Taylor of Caroline: Pastoral Republican* (1980); Shalhope, "Thomas Jefferson's Republicanism and Antebellum Southern Thought," *JSH* (Nov. 1976); James Sidbury, *Ploughshares into Swords: Race, Rebellion, and Identity in Gabriel's Virginia, 1730–1810* (1997); James F. Simon, *What Kind of Nation: Thomas Jefferson, John Marshall, and the Epic Struggle to Create a United States* (2002); Daniel Sisson, *The American Revolution of 1800* (1974); Jean Edward Smith, *John Marshall: Definer of a Nation* (1996).

8

DEMOCRATIZING THE OLD DOMINION
1825–1851

The old order lasted in Virginia longer than anywhere else, except perhaps South Carolina. Given the limitations of its leadership, the Old Dominion lumbered into the nineteenth century, practicing politics and governance much as it had in the eighteenth century. By midcentury, however, economic, demographic, and social forces and a new two-party system of Democrats and Whigs would challenge the political order of the commonwealth, democratizing the Old Dominion.

In the wake of the Panic of 1819 and the Missouri debate, the conservative tendencies inherent in Virginia's political culture reasserted themselves in a vigorous defense of states' rights, strict construction, and slave property that tended to set the center of the commonwealth against its periphery. The Republican center in the 1820s was economically stagnant, populated by old white families descended from the early migration of the English, Welsh, and French, their gangs of slaves, and a growing free black population, making Old Virginia demographically and socially similar to the lower South. This part of the state would be the heart of the new Democratic Party. The periphery was more economically dynamic, ethnically and religiously diverse, and socially fluid. It welcomed political and economic change and would become a Whig stronghold by the 1830s.

The Republicans had huge majorities in both houses of the assembly and at any time could have revised the Virginia constitution in line with Jefferson's wishes to make the political order more democratic. The question of revision came up repeatedly; ten times between 1801 and 1813 resolutions to call a convention came before the legislature. Twice the proposal was passed by the House of Delegates and then quashed by a Senate dominated by eastern planters. With the return of peace in 1815, liberal democratic demands for reform reasserted themselves in the expanding periphery. In Norfolk and Richmond artisan republicanism flourished among the mechanics and small manufacturers, iron and textile manufacturers of Wheeling wanted tariff protection, and wheat farmers in the Valley needed better means of transporting their crop to distant markets. But the lack of fair representation in the assembly and the restrictive voting requirements diminished their chances of gaining their objectives. The western counties, benefiting from the rapid migration westward, repeatedly petitioned the assembly, but democratic ideas found little support in the eastern half of the Old Dominion. The assembly established the Board of Public Works in 1816 to promote canal and road building and chartered two western banks, but disgruntled westerners were not appeased.

Critics of the old constitution advanced a comprehensive democratic agenda: expansion of the suffrage, which included only half of Virginia's free white males, to include leaseholders and taxpayers as well as landholders; fair legislative apportionment that would reflect the growing western population; abolition of the governor's council; popular election of the governor; reform of the county court system; and representation based upon white population rather than the "federal numbers" that included three-fifths of the slaves. Reformers were not in total agreement. Chapman Johnson of Augusta County urged equalization of the representation but opposed expansion of the electorate. And not all easterners were opposed. Hoping to build a new political coalition between east and west, Thomas Ritchie favored some of the reforms. But generally the Republican leadership chose to cast their arguments in terms of states' rights and strict construction—"the true Principles of '98"—while the reformers prided themselves on their adherence to true republicanism and appealed to Jefferson, "the father of our political church."

Under increasing pressure, the assembly consented to a popular referendum on a constitutional convention in 1828, which passed 21,896 to 16,646. Over Tidewater objections voters in the Valley and Trans-Allegheny regions won the day. The convention, which convened in Richmond in October 1829, was "the last gathering of the giants." Its members included Madison, Monroe, and Marshall; Congressman John Randolph; Governor William Branch Giles; Senator Littleton Waller Tazewell, a future governor; and Senator John Tyler, a former governor and congressman and future president. Thirty-one of the thirty-nine reformers came from the western half of the state. Over the course of three months, the convention debated the proposals of the reformers; but the eastern slaveholding majority assured the result. Planters feared a broadened suffrage would enable the west to outvote them in the legislature and impose

CONSTITUTIONAL CONVENTION OF 1829–30, BY GEORGE CATLIN

higher taxes on slaves to finance roads and canals. They condemned Jefferson's concept of the equality of men. John Randolph ridiculed the recently deceased Sage of Monticello as an authority only on the construction of a plow.

The Virginia constitution of 1830 represented a triumph of traditionalism that strengthened gentry rule through its recognition of the primacy of the county courts, while avoiding unrestricted white manhood suffrage and just representation. It included a modest expansion of the suffrage and some equalization of representation. In the now smaller House of Delegates, the Piedmont and the Valley gained at the expense of the Tidewater as the result of a pragmatic compromise. The now quite larger Senate used "federal numbers" to determine representation and thus was dominated by the east.

The constitution of 1830 was a product of the conflict between the traditional center and the reform-minded periphery that had characterized the political battles of the Jeffersonian era in the Old Dominion. The behavior of the delegates clearly reflected the sectional split between east and west. The final vote in favor of the revised constitution was 55 to 40. Only six delegates from east of the Blue Ridge voted no, while only one delegate from the west voted yes. Sectional interest rather than ideology determined the outcome as the Piedmont conservatives courted the moderates of the Valley at the expense of the Northwest, where there was talk of seceding from the authority of those "eastern nabobs."

While the delegates debated Virginia's new fundamental law, modern party politics were coming to Virginia. The origin of the slow and complicated process of party formation in the Old Dominion went back to the presidential politics of the previous decade. In 1824 John Quincy Adams had been the second choice of Junto members who had supported Crawford, but his first annual message, which endorsed Clay's American System and called for federal support for education and the arts, quickly alienated the Old Republicans. Many agreed with John Tyler that it was "a direct insult upon Virginia." Subsequently, leading Virginians joined the supporters of Calhoun, Crawford, and Jackson in frustrating the Adams administration and resisting all aspects of the American System: the Bank, bankruptcy legislation, land policy, internal improvements, and the protective tariff. In the process this anti-Adams coalition settled upon Andrew Jackson as its candidate for the presidency in 1828 on a platform stressing his commitment to "Virginia ideas" and the general's vow to return the federal government to republican purity.

The crucial figure in the organization of the emerging Jackson party was New York senator Martin Van Buren, who devised a strategy of drawing "old party lines" around the ideals of states' rights and strict construction. This required the rekindling of the New York–Virginia alliance, which joined "the planters of the South and the plain Republicans of the North." Governor William Branch Giles led the Virginia assembly to reaffirm the "Doctrines of '98" and denounced Adams as "in no sense a Republican either in theory or in practice." The *Enquirer*'s editorials wrapped Jackson in the mantle of Jefferson, portraying the Old Hero as a "politician of the Richmond school."

Jackson's popularity, the memory of the "corrupt bargain" in 1824, and superior party organization enabled "Old Hickory" to win an easy victory in 1828. In Virginia his election represented a triumph for the eastern planter regime. These Old Republicans believed their shift into Jackson's camp, at some cost to their ideological purity, entitled them to a leading role in his administration; but the general's patronage policy alienated many of the commonwealth's conservatives, who thought Jackson showed insufficient deference to the Old Dominion and its leaders. The elements for a future split were already present.

Political debate was interrupted in August 1831, when Nat Turner initiated the most significant slave insurrection in American history. Having learned to read at a young age, Turner studied the Bible and became an inspirational preacher among his fellow slaves, seeing himself as an agent of God. Although not mistreated, he plotted rebellion, perhaps motivated by a runaway father. Believing a strange celestial phenomenon was a sign to begin, he led a band of perhaps seventy slaves on a rampage through Southampton County, killing some sixty whites. Whites retaliated by killing at least twice as many blacks. Turner escaped into the Great Dismal Swamp, but eventually he was captured and executed. His rebellion prompted the House of Delegates to debate the questions of emancipation and colonization in January 1832.

Antebellum slavery had become more diverse, more formalized by law and custom, and more "domesticated" than the slavery of colonial Virginia. By virtue of a Virginia law of 1778 and a national law of 1808, international slave imports had been banned, lessening the African impact and leaving slave sales to the domestic slave trade. Christianity became the religion of the slaves, and the absence of large groups of imports necessitated better treatment for them. Slave codes regulated slave life and treatment in far greater detail, defining slaves as little more than property but imposing obligations on the slaveholders.

By midcentury slaves constituted nearly one-third of Virginia's population, with the overwhelming number of them residing on plantations and farms east of the Blue Ridge in concentrations similar to those of the Black Belt of the Cotton South. In the Southside they were nearly 60 percent of the population. To the west, where 85 percent of the population was white, a more diversified agricultural society had fewer slaves and fewer planters. Although planters—farmers who owned over 20 slaves—dominated the political and economic life of the commonwealth, they were only a small proportion of the 55,000 slaveholders in the state, who themselves were only one-fourth of the heads of families in Virginia. Most slave owners held 1 to 5 slaves; only one Virginian owned more than 300; yet nearly a majority of the slaves lived on the large plantations.

Slave life was hard. Work went from sunup to sundown, twelve months of the year, although it was less onerous during the nonplanting months. On Virginia's tobacco farms slaves usually worked as gang laborers, all doing the same task dictated by the demands of the season, whether it was preparation of the land, planting, tending, or harvesting. Much of the acreage was given over to food production and raising livestock, primarily to feed the slaves. Larger farms offered greater variety of employment for house servants and skilled artisans. The whip was always close at hand, although most planters were careful not to abuse their slaves, knowing that their livelihood depended upon a productive and compliant workforce. Conditions of work and general treatment often reflected the circumstances of the owner: the wealthier planters provided better food, clothing, and shelter than smaller farmers. Monticello's quarters were considerably more substantial than the clapboard-sided, dirt-floor cabins in which most slaves lived. However, relationships may

ADVERTISEMENT AND ILLUSTRATION OF A SLAVE AUCTION

have been more caring on the small farms where owners worked alongside their slaves and ate the same food.

In the 1850s a prime field hand could cost $1,000 or more, and the price was going up. Slavery was not dying; Virginians were willing to pay high prices for labor and land. And on the less productive, worn-out fields of Tidewater, slave sales to the Cotton South made up for declining tobacco production. With the growth of the cotton culture, the domestic slave trade emerged to satisfy the demand for slave labor, and the number of black migrants exploded; it has been estimated that over

300,000 slaves were transported from Virginia to the lower South, either with their owners or through the slave trade. The largest slave-trading firm was Franklin and Armfield, which operated out of Alexandria, buying slaves and shipping them southward by water and by land to New Orleans and Natchez. Yet despite these departures, the slave population in the commonwealth continued to grow, almost entirely through natural increase.

Slave sales put an enormous strain on the family life of the slaves. Marriages were already fragile because they were not recognized by law. Planters condoned slave marriages as a means of controlling the rebellious behavior of young males and enhancing reproductivity, but such bonds were easily dissolved and the families broken up by some economic crisis or the death of the planter. Threat of a sale also was a powerful incentive for a slave to remain submissive. Another hazard to stable families was the sexual accessibility of female slaves to white owners. Slaves were powerless to prevent this abuse, having no legal recourse. Although there were laws against miscegenation, the presence of thousands of mulattoes testified to its existence. Nevertheless, some relations between slaves and their masters were loving, the most enigmatic being that of Thomas Jefferson and Sally Hemings, who was the daughter of Jefferson's father-in-law.

Although treatment of slaves in the Old Dominion was generally less harsh than on the cotton, rice, and sugar plantations of the lower South,

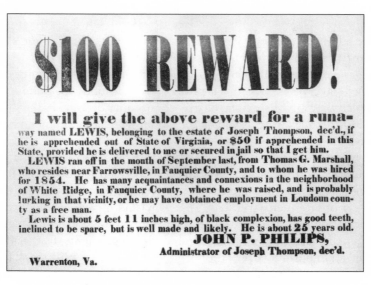

ADVERTISEMENT OF A SLAVE RUNAWAY

many slaves still manifested a spirit of independence and restlessness, slowing down their work, destroying produce and equipment, torching barns, and running away. Virginia's proximity to free states made the latter option a readily available prospect, and patrollers were on constant alert for absent slaves. There were a large number of criminal prosecutions for rebellious behavior in the Old Dominion, where over 300 whites were killed by slaves.

As the Virginia economy diversified, slave labor was used in factories and mines and on canals and railroads, proving its adaptability in a modernizing economy. Hardly any industry did not employ slaves. They made up two-thirds of the workers on the Virginia and Tennessee Railroad and constituted a significant portion of the workforce in the Tredegar Iron Works of Richmond. Tobacco processors in the capital employed thousands of slaves, while smaller businesses and individuals in the city and elsewhere hired or rented slaves. Many of these urban slaves lived on their own and earned their own money, enjoying a degree of freedom unknown on the plantations.

Here they came in contact with free blacks, the progeny of the earliest indentures of the seventeenth century and of those freed by their masters, who were often their fathers. Virginia had one of the largest concentrations of free blacks in the nation. Manumissions had been encouraged by passage of the 1782 statute allowing owners to free their slaves; the law required only that masters support those freed slaves who could not support themselves. The result was an increase in the free black population from 3,000 in 1783 to 30,000 in 1810. Prominent Virginians like George Washington, George Wythe, and John Randolph left wills freeing their slaves; Thomas Jefferson, who was perpetually in debt, did not. Robert Carter III deeded freedom to 450 slaves, the largest private emancipation in American history. Richard Randolph of Prince Edward County, who branded slavery a "monstrous tyranny," left land for bondsmen he freed, on which they established the nearby community of Israel Hill that prospered for decades in relative equality alongside the white neighbors of Farmville.

The revitalization of slavery and the worrisome example of a growing number of free blacks living among slaves led the assembly to pass an 1806 statute that required emancipated slaves to leave the state within one year or face reenslavement. This provision increased the burden of emancipation and reduced the number of manumissions. Although discriminated against by laws that limited their legal rights, free blacks remained an important part of the Virginia economy, owning small farms, working as agricultural laborers, and, in the cities, serving as independent tradesmen—barbers, teamsters, and carpenters—as well as factory workers and domestics. A few of them even owned slaves. In 1850 free blacks and slaves constituted a majority of the populations of Petersburg, Danville, and Charlottesville and 45 percent of Richmond's inhabitants.

Virginia had two of the most famous slave revolts in American history, Gabriel's Rebellion in 1800 and Nat Turner's uprising in 1831, which led to increased limitations on slave activity and the subsequent assembly debate on slavery. But perhaps the greatest legacy of Turner's revolt was its impact on the white mind. In the words of a Virginia planter, there was "the suspicion that a Nat Turner might be in every family; that the same bloody deed might be acted over at any time and in any place; that the materials for it were spread through the land, and were always ready for a like explosion."

The reaction of Governor John Floyd to Turner's insurrection reflects the ambiguity of white Virginians' response to slavery. Privately the governor mulled over various plans for emancipation and confided to his diary that he would "not rest until slavery is abolished in Virginia." But when he had the chance, Floyd shied away from suggesting emancipation in any form. Both the *Enquirer* and the *Whig* encouraged the lawmakers to consider some plan of emancipation, because, as Ritchie put it, "the disease" of slavery "is deep rooted; it is at the heart's core; it is consuming and has all along been consuming our vitals." Petitions poured into the legislature, most requesting that the legislators consider "the speedy adoption of some system for the removal of free negroes from the Commonwealth."

At the instigation of Virginia congressman Charles Fenton Mercer, the assembly had considered this problem in 1816. Later in that year several of his friends founded the American Society for the Colonization of Free People of Color. Mercer became the central figure in what came to be called the American Colonization Society, dedicated to the resettlement of free blacks in Africa. The society acquired land in West Africa for the creation of a black republic named Liberia, whose capital was named Monrovia in honor of President Monroe. Many prominent Virginians joined the organization, including Marshall, Madison, Monroe, and Randolph; the Virginia assembly made several appropriations over the years to support the emigration. Some colonizationists advocated gradual emancipation; but the Virginia society's focus was primarily on the emigration of free blacks, or what was later called "nigger removal." Both Randolph and John Taylor, the "Philosopher of Jeffersonian Democracy," looked upon colonization as a way to strengthen slavery.

Lott Carey of Richmond and Joseph Jenkins Roberts of Petersburg were black Virginians who assumed leadership roles in the colonization movement, Roberts becoming the first president of Liberia. Although several thousand black Virginians departed, their numbers were so small and funds so negligible that colonization proved ineffectual in addressing the question. Whites were reluctant to accept even gradual abolition without deportation, and free blacks were hesitant to depart for what to them was an unknown future.

The House of Delegates debate of 1832 that focused the nation's attention on Virginia revived arguments that had been raised earlier in the Missouri debates and the constitutional convention of 1829–30. Combined with the full discussion in the press, it defined the outlines of the slavery debate for the next three decades. The antislavery men, most of them from the west where slavery was weak, generally advocated gradual emancipation and colonization, while their adversaries from the Tidewater and Southside cautioned against precipitous action.

The opponents of slavery thought the institution undermined "the prosperity and happiness of the whole commonwealth." George Summers, a delegate from Kanawha County in the west, claimed that slavery encouraged idleness and disparaged labor, "and when industry is made dishonorable or unfashionable, virtue is attacked in her strongest citadel." In condemning the sale of slaves, Thomas Jefferson Randolph, grandson of the author of the Declaration, lamented, "How can an honorable mind, a patriot, and a lover of his country, bear to see this ancient dominion . . . converted into one grand menagerie where men are to be reared for market like oxen for the shambles?" The son of another illustrious Virginian, Thomas Marshall, proclaimed the institution "ruinous to the whites; it retards improvements, roots out our industrious population, banishes the yeomanry from the country, and deprives [artisans] of employment."

The defenders of slavery emphasized its economic value to the state and the property rights of the owners. They quoted scripture supporting slavery, denied the natural equality of men, and argued that the institution was "indisputedly requisite in order to preserve the forms of Republican Government." In the view of William Roane, a grandson of Patrick Henry, slavery secured the liberty that provided slave owners the leisure time to serve the public. In the end the House of Delegates rejected gradual emancipation, 73–58, and adopted a halfhearted colonization program that the Senate defeated.

The debate, however, did not stop there. A young professor of political economy at the College of William and Mary, Thomas Roderick Dew, produced a *Review of the Debates in the Virginia Legislature* in response to Marshall. In it he proclaimed slavery "the principal means for impelling forward the civilization of mankind," advanced biblical arguments sanctifying the institution, and predicted economic calamity for the state of Virginia if indolent blacks were freed. "It is the order of nature and of God," he wrote, "that the being of superior power should control and dispose of those who are inferior. It is as much the order of nature that men should enslave each other as that other animals should prey upon each other." The book is notable, however, for its calm, almost conciliatory tone and emphasis on the practical problems that abolition would create. Dew's arguments became the basis of the proslavery position down to the Civil War, which in time silenced any lingering antislavery views in Virginia.

Shortly after the emancipation debates, Virginia and the nation confronted a new crisis that drew the lines of battle between the Republicans who emphasized state sovereignty and the moderate advocates of Madisonian nationalism: the nullification crisis of 1832. Responding to the higher tariffs passed in 1824 and 1828 that Southerners believed favored Northern manufacturers at their expense, John C. Calhoun, now shifting away from his prior nationalism, anonymously published a pamphlet that restated the "Doctrines of '98" with a twist. His *Exposition and Protest* argued the compact theory of government in which a state had the right to nullify a federal law that violated the national government's limited authority specified in the Constitution. Calhoun's process of nullification required a special state convention either to nullify or to affirm the law in question. When Congress passed another high tariff in 1832, South Carolina nullified the tariff, thus obstructing customs officials from collecting the duties in Charleston.

President Jackson was furious and privately threatened to hang Calhoun, his vice president. Though sympathetic to states' rights, he was a devoted nationalist who was loyal to the Union. He proclaimed nullification "incompatible with the existence of the Union" but worked to secure a compromise engineered by Henry Clay that would reduce the tariff over a ten-year period, at which point South Carolina repealed its ordinance of nullification.

Overnight, with the publication of the president's "Proclamation to the People of South Carolina," the honeymoon with Jackson ended for many Virginia Republicans. Although the assembly had previously protested the tariff and had affirmed each state's right "to construe the Compact for itself," it refused to follow South Carolina's lead on nullification in a very close and sharply sectional vote. However, Old Dominion leaders made clear they would not participate in coercing a sister state. Governor Floyd wrote, "If the president uses force, I will oppose him with a military force." Advocates of states' rights were particularly offended by the passages in Jackson's proclamation that denied the compact theory and insisted that the federal government could act directly upon the people. It seemed to the *Enquirer* "dangerously national and unorthodox," expressing doctrines "as obnoxious as nullification itself." However, in his attack on the president's behavior, Ritchie was careful not to distance himself too far from Jackson. He published a pamphlet, *Virginia*

Doctrines Not Nullification, arguing that unilateral action by a single state threatened to substitute the minority will for majority rule. Nullification, he said, was "a revolutionary measure ... an absurd and dangerous heresy" that would never be supported by the Old Dominion, striking as it did "at the very foundation of Republican Government" and threatening "all the horrors of revolution and civil war." The editor of the *Enquirer* had subordinated personal philosophy for political advantage: an alliance with Jackson.

The 1832 election pitting Jackson against Clay represented Ritchie's finest hour. An abortive attempt to run Virginia congressman Philip P. Barbour with Jackson fizzled, and Virginia's twenty-three electoral votes went to Jackson and his running mate, Van Buren, who were now campaigning as Democrats. The New York–Virginia alliance was sound. If the election was a referendum on the American System, as Ritchie defined it, Virginia's voters soundly rejected Clay's formula in favor of the "Doctrines of '98."

To this point, the commonwealth's political system had not changed greatly. Voter turnout increased, but two-thirds of the white adult males still did not participate in the presidential elections; even under the new constitution of 1830 nearly 40 percent could not vote. Most of those who did vote went to the polls in the spring, when members of the assembly were elected yearly and congressmen were chosen in the odd years. But these elections, like the vote on ratification of the new constitution, reflected regional differences and witnessed few intracounty contests involving conflicts over issues. Politics within the Old Dominion remained elitist and very personal into the 1830s.

However, the emergence of new issues disrupted Republican harmony during Jackson's second term and thoroughly reshaped Virginia's political universe. Neither the slavery debate nor the volatile constitutional controversy over nullification had had much impact on the behavior of Virginia voters; but Jackson's 1832 veto of a new charter for the national bank, grounded in the rhetoric of the people versus privilege, was the key factor in formalizing a new party system. The president further promoted the new alignment when he moved to kill the Bank by depositing federal funds in state banks—then called "pet" banks—chosen because of their political stance. In the 1834 assembly elections, Ritchie concentrated on the "Bank War" and portrayed Jackson's opponents as neo-Federalists.

The opposition to both Jackson and the Democrats was an unstable coalition of advocates of states' rights and former Federalists and National Republicans who favored the Bank. They joined on the single practical issue of censuring the president for overstepping his constitutional authority. In 1834, calling themselves "Whigs," a name used by eighteenth-century British opponents of the crown and by the American Revolutionaries, they captured control of the House of Delegates and set about dismantling the Jacksonians' hold on the state government. The new opposition took the state printing contract from Ritchie and removed Peter Daniel from the governor's council, instructed the state's senators to vote to restore the federal deposits, elected Old Republican Littleton Waller Tazewell as governor, and sent Benjamin Watkins Leigh to the U.S. Senate to oppose "King Andrew."

From 1834 to 1838 each yearly election refashioned electoral behavior as old-style local leaders were forced to take public positions on national issues. Turnout for the 1835 spring election of assemblymen and congressmen reached a new high, and most elections took on the outward appearance of two-party contests. Nearly all the candidates could be identified by party. The Democrats regained control of the House of Delegates and ousted several of the Whig congressmen who had won as National Republicans two years earlier. The sweeping victory, however, was achieved with narrower margins than Jackson had obtained in 1832. The Junto was breaking apart.

In May 1837 a financial panic hit the nation, precipitated by bank closings in New York and Philadelphia. Economic conditions temporarily stabilized, but then the country and the commonwealth slid into a major depression that lasted until the mid-1840s. The crisis heightened the saliency of questions concerning money and banking as each of the emerging parties constructed its own interpretation of the economic crisis. Martin Van Buren, elected president over a coalition of Whigs in 1836, had the disadvantage of being in office when the depression broke and being associated with the destructive war upon the Bank of the United States. Most Virginia Democrats defended administrative policies that included creation of an Independent Treasury, a regional depository system without banking functions that operated only with gold and silver coins, not bank notes. Suggested by Virginia congressman William F. Gordon in 1834 and instituted in 1840, the Independent Treasury would further constrict the economy and intensify the depression.

While the fight over the Independent Treasury did draw some entrepreneurial Democrats into Whig ranks, like U.S. senator William Cabell Rives of Albemarle County, it also sent Robert M. T. Hunter and the Calhounites back into the Democratic Party. They were joined by several Conservative Democrats who were also strong advocates of states' rights, such as James M. Mason. Their constitutional views ultimately proved more important than their position on economic policy. In time they would control the Democratic Party of the Old Dominion.

Partisan differences became more sharply defined after the Panic of 1837, often paralleling previous sectional positions. As economic conditions worsened, antibank sentiment within the Democratic Party grew while the Whigs consistently supported state banks. The influence of party affected nearly all of the assembly's business. Questions relating to slavery and black rights, fiscal matters (including taxes on land and slaves), and internal improvements all reflected party conflict. Democrats, primarily from the Tidewater and Southside, tended to be vigorously proslavery, in favor of laissez faire and low taxes, and opposed to state aid to railroads. Whigs from the periphery also defended slavery, albeit a little less vigorously, but were more eager to expand banking facilities, support internal improvements, and reform schools and prisons.

Although the spring elections of 1839 and 1840 affirmed the new electoral alignment, it was the "Log Cabin" campaign of 1840 that signaled the coming-of-age of the Second Party System in the commonwealth. The sedate elitist politics of Jeffersonian Virginia managed by the Richmond Junto and the gentry in the county courts gave way to Walt Whitman's noisy democrat "yawp" and party drill. The campaign's merchandising style celebrated populist politics, and Virginians participated in record numbers.

The Whig National Convention at Harrisburg, Pennsylvania, in early December 1839 was the first to choose the presidential candidate from among possible contenders and the first to form a ticket carefully designed to balance the contending elements of the party coalition. The Whigs chose two native Virginians, William Henry Harrison, who at the time was living in Ohio, and John Tyler, who had broken with Jackson and run for vice president in 1836. Harrison, whose father had signed the Declaration of Independence, was born in Charles City County at Berkeley plantation (by no means a "log cabin") and studied at Hampden-Sydney College; but he left his native state for military and political opportunities in the Northwest. Tyler, on the other hand, was an aristocratic planter who had had a long career in Virginia politics, serving in the House of Delegates, as governor, and as congressman and U.S. senator. Always a strict constructionist and proponent of states' rights, Tyler's Republican roots soon would come back to haunt the Whigs.

Although voters may well have been confused by the variety of claims about hard cider and log cabins as well as the wanton disregard for the truth in press reporting, they did not lack for information in 1840. The number of newspapers in the country and the commonwealth had expanded greatly during the 1830s. Most of the popular press was unabashedly partisan, with editors playing a crucial role as party leaders. They reported on "Monster" rallies and parades "leading to, from, and swirling around" the candidates, who gave "stump" speeches that lasted as long as three or four hours. Portraying themselves as the true heirs of Jefferson, Whig speakers ridiculed the discredited Van Buren administration, while Democrats referred to the "Principles of '98," attacked the "extremes of Federalism" and appealed to the "friends of State Rights."

In 1840 a slight majority of Virginians favored President Van Buren, but Harrison won the election. For the first time in Virginia history, more men voted in a fall presidential election than in the spring assembly elections; four-fifths of those eligible to vote went to the polls. The Whigs retained control of the House of Delegates and also won four seats in Congress. What distinguished the 1840 returns was the competitive balance in all regions and in most of the counties of the commonwealth. Although the Democrats did better in the Southside and Southwest and the Whigs prevailed in the Northwest, the vote was not sectional. Party identification appeared in its modern form for the first time and revealed a shift in the political culture that sanctioned the legitimacy of party strife. (See map on p. 186.)

Both the style and the focus of Virginia politics changed dramatically during these years. The importance of the county courts waned as the legislature assumed a more active role, and partisanship came to dominate the legislative process as well as elections. Candidates for the assembly relied upon recognizable party labels that linked them to national leaders and issues. In his campaign for the House of Delegates in 1845, Samuel McDearmond, a typical Southside Democrat, declared himself "a Polk, Texas, anti-bank, anti-tariff, anti-Distribution Man." Governors, too, were bending to the influence of party. In contrast to the independent executives earlier in the century, those who came after the mid-1830s were party men.

The Whigs and Democrats who served in the Virginia assembly during these years were contemporaries of Lincoln and Lee, born in the nineteenth century after the "Revolution of 1800" and destined to fight the Civil War. "Reputation" was the hard-won key to electoral success, but during these years party fidelity replaced personal association as a major element of reputation. In contested constituencies the same contenders often competed in a series of elections, sometimes handing the seat back and forth in successive years. The modest shifts in county elections for the assembly were correlated with similar shifts in the counties' responses to congressional and presidential elections.

The election of two native Virginia Whigs to the highest offices in the land boded well for the Old Dominion, but death and the partisan politics that followed created havoc. William Henry Harrison died a month after his inauguration, making John Tyler the first vice president to assume the presidency. His many enemies were to call him "His Accidency." Tyler had never been a true Whig, having joined the opposition only out of animosity toward Jackson. His Old Republican principles became clear when he vetoed the entire Whig agenda of Bank, tariff, and

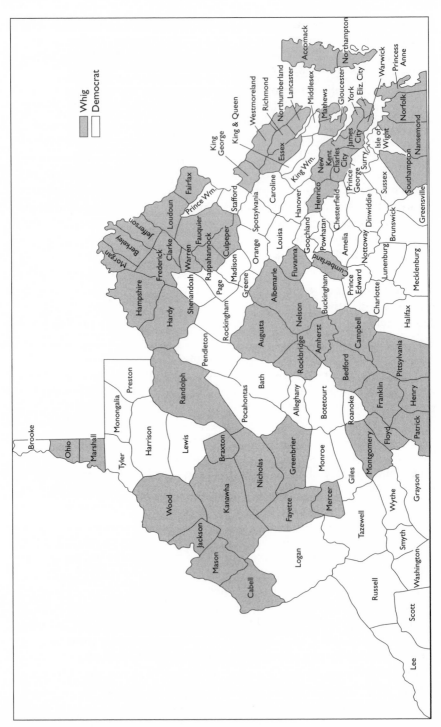

Whig
Democrat

STRENGTH OF THE WHIG PARTY IN THE PRESIDENTIAL ELECTION OF 1840

internal improvements, leaving him a leader without a party for the remainder of his term.

In 1844 both national parties nominated slaveholders as their presidential candidates. Because of Van Buren's opposition to the immediate annexation of Texas, Virginians led the southern move to block his renomination and support James K. Polk of Tennessee, who campaigned on an expansionist Jacksonian platform that demanded "the re-annexation of Texas and the re-occupation of Oregon." Northern critics saw territorial expansion as a subterfuge for expanding slavery. The Whig candidate, Henry Clay, fought aggressively for the policies associated with his name and argued against his opponent's posture on Texas. The results in the Old Dominion maintained the basic paradigm of the Second Party System. The turnout remained high, and the Democrats increased their portion of the vote slightly; Polk proved to be slightly more popular than Clay across the state and nation.

The Democrats' momentum carried over into the Virginia state elections of 1845 when they regained control of the House of Delegates and took all but one of the commonwealth's congressional seats. There was a normal Democratic majority in the Old Dominion during the era of the Second Party System, but it was so small and competition existed in so many constituencies that the Whigs controlled the House of Delegates in 1838–41 and 1844 and generally held between five and ten seats in Congress. The seemingly huge swing to the Democrats in 1845 resulted from many small shifts across the board.

The election of Polk eventually led to a war with Mexico in 1846 that proved to be less popular in the commonwealth than the annexation of Texas that precipitated it. Virginians played a major role in the Mexican War. Winfield Scott of Dinwiddie County, who had performed heroically in the War of 1812, was given command of the American army that captured Mexico City after a remarkable campaign that overcame disease, formidable defenses, and larger forces. Zachary Taylor of Orange County, a veteran of the Black Hawk and Seminole Wars, invaded Mexico from the north and won substantial victories at Monterrey and Buena Vista. Junior officers Robert E. Lee and Thomas Jackson won plaudits for their soldiering. Nicholas Trist, who had married Jefferson's granddaughter and lived at Monticello when he was studying law with Jefferson, was President Polk's envoy to conclude a peace. Despite being recalled, Trist stayed and successfully negotiated the treaty that ended the war and gave the United States a vast empire in California and the Southwest.

In the election of 1848, the politics of slavery seemed to favor the Whigs, who ran war hero General Zachary Taylor, a Virginia-born Louisiana slaveholder, against the Democrats' Lewis Cass of Michigan. The Northerner, however, had married into a prominent western Virginia

WILLIAM HENRY HARRISON, ENGRAVING BY R. W. DODSON
FROM PAINTING BY J. R. LAMBDIN

JOHN TYLER JR., BY WILLIAM HART

family and satisfied the leading Virginia Democrats with his support of popular sovereignty, a procedure that would permit people in the territories to decide the issue of slavery by themselves. Once again, as in 1840 and 1844, Democrats squeaked by with a bare majority of the state's vote; but as in 1840, a Virginia Whig won the presidency.

By the mid-nineteenth century the liberal democratic political culture of the commonwealth contrasted sharply with the aristocratic republicanism that had produced the Virginia Dynasty. Most of the changes had come after Jefferson's death as the result of the emergence of a much more complex and diverse society. In twenty years the proportion of nonslaveholders in the assembly had grown dramatically, and that of large planters sharply declined. Half of the Jeffersonian elite had been planters, but only one-fifth of the midcentury Virginia politicians were. By then the party of Jackson had become a vociferous advocate of slavery and Southern rights. The Whigs' defense of slavery was more ambiguous, and this equivocation, combined with their nationalistic positions on economic issues and social reform, generally made them the minority party in the Old Dominion: visible and vocal, but rarely in control.

Part of the Whigs' dilemma lay in a continuing malapportionment of the assembly. By 1850 the white population of the western half of the state outnumbered that in the east. Yet the Piedmont and the Tidewater still held nearly three-fifths of the seats in the House of Delegates and a larger majority in the state Senate. Conventions at Clarksburg and Lewisburg in 1842 requested another constitutional convention to remedy the inequality, but eastern planters put off action for eight years and only then accepted such a gathering with a guarantee that they would control a majority of the convention seats.

The delegates to the Reform Convention of 1850–51 were far from common men. They were much better off and far better educated than their constituents, and many were personally involved with the peculiar institution. However, most represented neither the landed opulence nor the old family ties that had characterized the planter Republicans who dominated the politics of the Old Dominion in Jefferson's day. The new men mirrored their own economically and socially diverse society. They represented the new class of political leaders often associated with the advance of democracy in yet another way that bothered their detractors: they were partisans—"small lawyers and still smaller politicians"—the product of modern party politics. The members included only three small farmers and two artisans.

The convention was marked by bitter debate over issues that had already been settled, or at least compromised, in nearly all of the other states. The questions before the delegates were much the same as those debated twenty years before: the basis of representation in the assembly;

the extent of the suffrage; the mode of election, term of office, and powers of the governor; and the role of the county courts. The commonwealth's western reformers, aided by their vociferous eastern allies Whig John Minor Botts and Democrat Henry Wise, echoed the liberal democratic sentiments that were heard throughout the country in the midcentury constitutional debates. Their basic argument was that the fundamental principle of democratic government was majority rule. Society had been formed to protect not only property but also life and liberty.

The spokesmen of conservatism put forward the timeworn arguments of Old Virginia. They began with the proposition that government was designed basically to protect property; consequently, representation should reflect a "majority of interest" rather than "the new doctrine that mere numbers are to possess the power of this government." In practical terms the planters feared for slavery. Two-thirds of the state's revenues came from taxes on the eastern gentry's land and slaves. Any additional taxation by a western-dominated antislavery legislature might lead to the death of the peculiar institution.

Richard L. T. Beale, a Westmoreland County Democrat, ably represented the old Junto ideals. Attacking the concept of the natural equality of men, he urged the protection of the minority from the "plundering propensities" of the masses, associated those who favored a "majority of mere numbers" with those who would "plunder" the state treasury for internal improvements, pronounced railroads as "unnatural" when compared to the "rivers God has placed upon this earth," criticized party politics, and defended slavery against the threat from the west. He ascribed Virginia's problems to the federal government, which he portrayed as a "vampire" sucking out the lifeblood of the Old Dominion. The debates became so heated that the son of one of the delegates and a newspaper editor who had been critical of the father killed each other in a brawl in Lynchburg.

The questions of reform that related directly to matters of suffrage and representation did not divide the convention along party lines but into sectional factions. Amid talk of secession, the western reformers carried the day. Representation was made more equitable through a compromise that gave the west a majority in the House of Delegates based on white population and the east a majority in the Senate, with a promise of equal representation within fifteen years. Suffrage was granted to all white adult males, but oral voting was retained instead of a written ballot. The governor was now to be popularly elected, with a term of four years. Perhaps the most radical revision allowed the people to choose the justices in the county courts. Overwhelmingly, Virginians approved the new constitution. The most immediate effect of the revisions came months later with the election of Joseph Johnson, the first governor from the Trans-Allegheny region.

The convention dealt gingerly with the issue of slavery. It did not debate abolition or colonization. It imposed additional restrictions on manumission, permitted the deportation of free blacks, and limited the taxing of slave property. In fact, the Eastern Shore eccentric Henry Wise "believed that protection of slavery, not the liberalizing of Virginia's constitution, was the most significant business before the convention." Easterners conceded enough to the west to ensure the unity of the state that they felt was necessary to resist Northern hostility and to regain the influence that the commonwealth once had in national politics.

Virginia was one of the last states to accept popular democracy. The constitution of 1851 brought the Old Dominion belatedly and hesitantly into the nineteenth century. Overnight the commonwealth's constitution, except for its acceptance of slavery, became nearly as democratic as any in the nation. This revision along with the socioeconomic changes that were occurring made the new political order seem foreign and potentially dangerous for the Old Dominion's traditional leaders, but their fears were exaggerated. A new emerging bourgeoisie gained some economic authority, and the suffrage had been expanded, but the planter patriarchy continued to dominate the politics of the Old Dominion through patronage, a closed party nominating process, and racism. They now had to share power in a new political culture, but there was a conservative Virginia cast to it all. Old Virginia had adjusted to the democratic changes, and its traditional leadership was nearly as powerful as ever.

SOURCES CONSULTED

Charles Henry Ambler, *Sectionalism in Virginia, 1776–1861* (1910); Ambler, *Thomas Ritchie: A Study in Virginia Politics* (1913); Richard R. Beeman, *The Evolution of the Southern Backcountry: A Case Study of Lunenburg County, Virginia, 1746–1832* (1984); Ira Berlin, *Slaves without Masters: The Free Negro in the Antebellum South* (1974); Dickson D. Bruce Jr., *The Rhetoric of Conservatism: The Virginia Convention of 1829–30 and the Conservative Tradition in the South* (1982); Daniel Crofts, *Old Southampton: Politics and Society in a Virginia County, 1834–1869* (1992); Charles R. Dew, *Bond of Iron: Master and Slave at Buffalo Forge* (1994); Maurice Duke, ed., *Don't Carry Me Back: Virginia Slave Narratives* (1995); Wilma A. Dunaway, *The African-American Family in Slavery and Emancipation* (2003); Douglas R. Egerton, *Gabriel's Rebellion: The Virginia Slave Conspiracies of 1800 and 1802* (1993); Richard E. Ellis, *The Union at Risk: Jacksonian Democracy, States' Rights, and the Nullification Crisis* (1987); Melvin Patrick Ely, *Israel on the Appomattox: A Southern Experiment in Black Freedom from the 1790s through the Civil War* (2004); Alison Goodyear Freehling, *Drift toward Dissolution: The Virginia Slavery Debate of 1831–1832* (1982); Eugene

D. Genovese, *The World the Slaveholders Made* (1969); Kenneth S. Greenberg, ed., *Nat Turner: A Slave Rebellion in History and Memory* (2003); Richard P. McCormack, *The Second American Party System: Party Formation in the Jacksonian Era* (1966); Drew R. McCoy, *The Last of the Founders: James Madison and the Republican Legacy* (1989); J. R. Pole, *Political Representation in England and the Origins of the American Republic* (1966); Joseph C. Robert, *The Road from Monticello: A Study of the Virginia Slavery Debate of 1832* (1941); Robert, *The Tobacco Kingdom* (1938); Philip J. Schwarz, *Twice Condemned: Slaves and the Criminal Laws of Virginia, 1705–1865* (1988); William G. Shade, *Democratizing the Old Dominion: Virginia and the Second Party System, 1824–1861* (1996); James Roger Sharp, *Jacksonians versus the Banks: Politics in the States after 1837* (1970); Henry H. Simms, *The Rise of the Whigs in Virginia, 1824–1840* (1929); Mechal Sobel, *Trablen On: The Afro-Baptist Experience in Virginia* (1989); Brenda E. Stevenson, *Life in Black and White: Family and Community in the Slave South* (1996); Robert P. Sutton, "Nostalgia, Pessimism, and Malaise: The Doomed Aristocrat in Late-Jeffersonian Virginia," *VMHB* (Jan. 1968); Sutton, *Revolution to Secession: Constitution Making in the Old Dominion* (1989); Ralph A. Wooster, *Politicians, Planters, and Plain Folk: Court House and State House in the Upper South, 1850–1860* (1975).

9

VIRGINIA AT MIDCENTURY
1840–1860

At the time of the Revolution, the commonwealth was dominated by a homogeneous planter elite of landowners, slaveholders, and Anglicans descended from English families who had migrated years earlier and were related by bonds of marriage and kinship. Upper-class white Virginians still refer to them as the First Families of Virginia. In the course of the next three-quarters of a century, this traditional order became a more pluralistic society. The politics of republican consensus gave way to a politics of liberal conflict. Slaveholders were a minority and planters a tiny elite; sectarianism dominated a vibrant religious life. The distribution of Virginia's white population shifted dramatically with the development of the Piedmont and the multiplying counties west of the Blue Ridge, while the economy expanded and diversified and small towns proliferated. Nearly all of the state's farmers, however small, raised a portion of their crop to feed the expanding commercial market; and the nonagricultural sector of the economy grew rapidly as a modest industrial and urban revolution occurred.

At the time of Washington's first inauguration, the Old Dominion was the most populous state in the Union with nearly three-quarters of a million people. Over the next seventy years, the state's population grew to well over 1.5 million people, of whom 1 million were white, 490,000 were slaves, and 58,000 were free blacks. By 1860 Virginia had declined in relative position and power, yet it was the fifth largest state in the Union and was still a major factor in American politics with the most slaveholders and the most slaves. The commonwealth continued to have a large congressional delegation and two extremely powerful senators. It had become a diverse, dynamic, and complex society that might have made

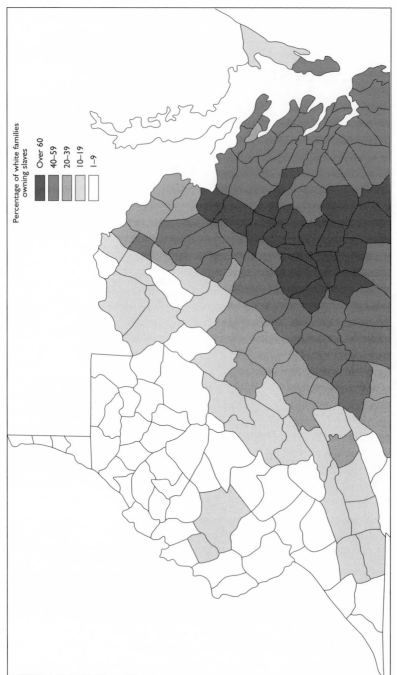

Percentage of white families
owning slaves

Over 60
40–59
20–39
10–19
1–9

SLAVES AND SLAVEHOLDING IN VIRGINIA, 1860.

From *Roots of Secession: Slavery and Politics in Antebellum Virginia* by William A. Link.
Copyright © 2003 by the University of North Carolina Press. Used by permission of the publisher.

the great advocate of change, Thomas Jefferson, feel uneasy. (See map on facing page and table below.)

In a mobile society the influence of the local community where one is living is often as important a determinant of voting behavior as class or economic position. Planters tended to be Democrats; but many small farmers, especially in the Southwest, were as well. Urbanites, including laborers, were more likely to be Whigs, although international merchants tended to be Democrats. But community mattered most; and that often meant ethnicity and religion, especially in the rural areas of the commonwealth, influenced political affiliation and positions on the issues. Episcopalians and Scotch-Irish Presbyterians generally preferred the Whigs, while Methodists and German Lutherans leaned to the Democrats.

Ethnic differences among antebellum white Virginians were far less noticeable than those of race or gender. Virginia was not the destination of a large number of nineteenth-century immigrants. Only 3 percent of the population in 1850 had been born in Europe; about half were Irish and another one-fourth Germans. These immigrants generally settled in the cities and towns. Over one-third of the free workingmen in Richmond on the eve of the Civil War had been born abroad. Frederick Law Olmsted observed "a considerable population of foreign origin, generally of the least valuable class; very dirty German Jews, especially, abound, and their characteristic shops . . . are thickly set in the narrowest and meanest streets, which seem to be otherwise inhabited mainly by negroes."

The census figures on foreign-born inhabitants in 1850, however, fail to reflect the ethnic mosaic in the Old Dominion during these years. The older areas of Tidewater and Southside had the largest proportion of men with English surnames. The small French-descended population clustered in these counties as well. In the northern Piedmont those of English ancestry made up slightly less than half the white population,

SLAVE POPULATION, 1860

Region	Total	White	Free black	Slave	% Free black	% Slave	% Slave and free black
Piedmont	509,747	241,669	17,992	250,086	4	49	53
Tidewater	415,204	205,496	31,597	178,111	8	43	51
Southwest	193,037	172,055	1,536	19,446	1	10	11
Valley	215,601	172,960	5,857	36,784	3	17	20
Northwest	262,612	255,119	1,055	6,438	0.4	3	3

Source: Inter-University Consortium for Political and Social Research, University of Michigan.

while the descendants of Scots, Scotch-Irish, and Welsh contributed about one-third. To the west relatively fewer Englishmen appeared, and there were more Scotch-Irish and Germans, large numbers of whom still spoke their native tongue with an ancient accent. Two-thirds of the Valley whites were the progeny of either German or Scotch-Irish, who also heavily populated the Trans-Allegheny counties. Westerners called those east of the mountains "Tuckahoes," from the Indian name for a swamp root; and themselves they labeled "Cohees," from "quoth he," an expression of pietistic sects.

Ethnic and regional differences were often matched in intensity by religious competition. The Reformation had etched sharp lines of battle across Europe that spawned emigration to the British colonies. Conflicts between Catholics and Protestants, Anglicans and reformers, were transplanted to the New World as dissenters fled persecution. While denominationalism defined the shape of American Protestantism, the Great Revival of the early nineteenth century heightened sectarian tensions.

At the turn of the century, religion no longer seemed relevant to the lives of most Virginians. The disestablished Anglican Church, with its cold formality, weakened even further in the post-Revolution era of the Enlightenment. Congregations met infrequently; ministers were not being replaced; ascetic deism captured the imagination of a few. Commented a visitor to Richmond: "Christianity is here breathing its last. I cannot find a friend with whom I can even converse on religious subjects."

Reacting to such apathy and spurred by a surge of evangelicalism, spiritually deprived Virginians reignited the flame. The camp meeting, which began in Kentucky in 1800 and spread across the South, was the vehicle for the Second Great Awakening. It produced a contagious emotional experience lasting for days, with speakers calling upon their listeners to repent and pledge themselves to Jesus. The result was the reinvigoration of Southern religion, particularly among the evangelical sects, that endures to this day. By emphasizing an individual conversion experience, revivalism cultivated a democratic spirit as well as conformity to a strict moral code. Religious populism encouraged denominational schism by rejecting formal theology and putting a premium on biblical authority.

In the contest for souls, Protestants dominated the Old Dominion scene. Only seventeen Roman Catholic churches were scattered about the state in 1850, mostly in the cities, where small contingents of Jews could also be found. The 1850 census enumerated fourteen Protestant sects and denominations that had churches in Virginia. The two largest were the Methodists and the Baptists, who together accounted for 70 percent of the churches in the state; Presbyterians and Episcopalians followed. There were also over 100 "Free" churches, whose facilities were shared by several sects.

Even before the Revolution, Anglicans were being challenged for dominance by Presbyterians and Baptists, who together claimed a majority of adherents by 1776. Within the fold of the Church of England itself, revivalism spawned Methodism; and the new group split free in 1784. The legislature ended compulsory support of the clergy in 1776, adopted Jefferson's Bill for Establishing Religious Freedom a decade later, and, after a heated debate, took over the old glebe lands from the church in 1799, completing the process of disestablishment. Episcopalians regained some of their strength by 1825 because their conservative ritual and theology appealed to the gentry.

At the time of the first census in 1790, there were reportedly 20,000 Baptists and 18,000 Methodists in the state; by 1830 each group had more than doubled in size. The growth of these two denominations was due, in part, to their pursuit of black congregants. The contemporary human geographer Joseph Martin estimated that one-fifth of the Virginia Methodists in 1835 were "colored" and half of the 54,000 Baptists were "slaves." As a result of revivals in the 1820s and 1830s, Methodists surpassed all of their rivals, making up at least 40 percent of all the churchgoers in the Old Dominion by the mid-nineteenth century. Methodists not only were more numerous than Baptists but also were more evenly spread across the commonwealth, being particularly strong in the Southside and most popular in the Trans-Allegheny region. Although the Methodists retained a rigid structure of church governance, they increasingly turned to itinerant preachers who brought an emotional evangelical appeal and simplified liturgy to their preaching. The circuit rider and the camp meeting characterized the Methodists.

Nearly one-third of Virginia's churchgoers were Baptists, who were concentrated more heavily east of the Blue Ridge, where they competed for souls primarily with the Methodists. The Baptists were a doctrinally simple sect, distrustful of the pretensions of education, the "intrigues of lawyers," the "frauds of priests," and government generally. They were congregational in polity and Antinomian in spirit. But in contrast to their frontier image, the Virginia Baptists had their greatest support among Tidewater planters and their slaves. The leading proponent of the biblical defense of slavery was a Baptist minister, Thornton Stringfellow.

Early historians of western Virginia emphasized the importance of the Scotch-Irish, mostly Presbyterians, who were firmly devoted to religious and political liberty and enthusiastic for education. By 1850 the Scotch-Irish Presbyterians had taken over the role of the "intellectuals of Virginia Protestantism." They founded the Virginia *Religious Herald* in Lexington in 1804 and the *Virginia Evangelical and Literary Magazine* in 1818, edited by John Holt Rice. Insisting upon an educated clergy, they established schools and colleges, including Washington College in Lexington and Hampden-Sydney College in Prince Edward County where, according to the visiting free spirit Anne Royall, they manufactured puritanical "blue-skins wholesale and retail." The Presbyterians had strongholds in the Valley but were prevalent in the southern Piedmont as well.

The Germans, who descended from the Pennsylvania "Dutch" migrants of the eighteenth century, included a handful of "sect people" like Mennonites, Moravians, and Tunkers (German Baptists sometimes called Dunkers), but most were "church people": Lutheran or German Reformed. By 1850 most of these German groups still lived in the Valley, where eight of nine of the German Reformed churches and thirty-two of Virginia's fifty Lutheran churches were located.

The Great Revival also stimulated the conversion of blacks to Christianity. Many of them had attended the camp meetings; others were converted by owners who sought another means of controlling their bondsmen. Most slaves worshipped in white churches, albeit in separate areas; some planters allowed separate services with a white observer present. Free blacks formed their own churches, offering opportunities for powerful preachers to become leaders in the community.

During the 1830s and 1840s, all of the major denominations divided over questions of dogma and polity. Presbyterians split into advocates of the "New School" and followers of the "Old School." In the 1830s the Baptists were in turmoil over the Campbellite reformers and "home missions," which led to the creation of the Disciples of Christ by Virginian Alexander Campbell. In the 1840s the Methodists split over slavery, an issue that would divide all three of these major churches nationally. These schisms in the state's most populous churches reflected the potential for religious conflict in what has often been viewed as a homogeneous Protestant population. The tenor of religious debate in the Old Dominion was described on all sides as a state of "Holy War." Campbell attacked the Baptists as "proscriptive, illiberal and unjust" and insisted that he would sooner send a sinner for salvation to a Muslim than a Methodist circuit rider. At the same time his Presbyterian opponents called Campbell "the curse of the West—more destructive and more injurious . . . than avowed Infidelity itself."

Competition among the churches during this time contributed to advances in higher education. Each denomination had to have a college, primarily for the instruction of its ministers. Following the lead of the Presbyterians, Methodists established Randolph-Macon and Emory and Henry; Baptists founded a seminary that later became Richmond College; Lutherans had Roanoke College; and the Disciples of Christ founded

Bethany College. Churches also established three female institutes for women before 1861, two of which were the predecessors of Hollins and Mary Baldwin colleges.

Yet the preeminent institution of higher learning in the state was the deliberately nonsectarian University of Virginia, chartered by the assembly in 1819 at the behest of its founder, Thomas Jefferson, to whom it owed everything: its setting, architecture, library, curriculum, and professors. Unlike the smaller colleges, Jefferson's university was free of any religious association; it had no ministers on the faculty. The assembly created another public institution in 1839: Virginia Military Institute, the first state military college in the country. Professional schools also emerged, including the medical school at the University of Virginia and Union Theological Seminary and the Medical College of Virginia, both of which began as affiliated schools of Hampden-Sydney College.

Virginia's efforts to create a state public school system foundered at the hands of conservative planters. Several early plans were hampered by inadequate funding mechanisms. In 1839 Governor David Campbell renewed the call for such a system funded by a grant from the Literary Fund, but he was rebuffed. Henry Ruffner, president of Washington College, put forward a plan to establish a common school system funded by a special tax that would finance a state board of education, establish a system of normal schools for training teachers, and provide libraries in each new school. It met a similar fate; Democrats, representing their planter constituents, resisted both the centralization and the cost of such a system.

In 1845 an eclectic State Educational Convention met at Richmond and reached a consensus on the need for "a more enlarged, energetic and liberal system of primary schools." The specific recommendations, however, shied away from the Ruffner plan and simply encouraged the assembly to act. A year later the Democratic legislature passed a modest reform measure, far short of Ruffner's proposal, that allowed any county to establish a free school if two-thirds of the eligible voters supported the idea in a referendum and were willing to tax themselves to pay for the school. By 1860 eleven counties and four towns were running public systems. In the absence of public schools, private academies and "old field" schools were available for those who could pay. Some 85,000 children were attending school, perhaps one-third of those eligible. A comprehensive system of public education would have to await the aftermath of war. Despite the paltry effort, 90 percent of Virginia's white adults were literate.

Another reform effort of the antebellum period in Virginia was the attempt to change the drinking habits of its citizens. Widespread concern about the impact that drunkenness was having on families and elections

led to the formation in 1826 in Charlotte County of the Virginia Society
for the Promotion of Temperance, whose members took a pledge of ab-
stinence. Supported by the churches, notably the Methodists, the society
grew to fifty chapters and joined the American Temperance Society in
1829. Poor organization and the association of temperance with abolition
in the North caused the state society to fold; but it was replaced in 1843 by
a new national organization, the Sons of Temperance. Within the decade
the Sons grew to 15,000 members in the state, most of whom were middle-
class Whigs. Shifting focus from individual conversion to attacking dis-
tilleries and taverns, temperance advocates petitioned the state legislature in 1853–54 to restrict the manufacture and sale of liquor. The assembly failed to act on the law; and although antiliquor people continued to
lobby the public and politicians, the Civil War brought an end to the temperance crusade for the moment.

Unlike the North, where the reform crusades of temperance, abolition, mental health, and women's rights attracted a large female contingent, the limited reform activity in the Old Dominion and the South
was restricted primarily to men. The patriarchal society kept women in
a subordinate position. Although economic developments and the new
democratic order were generating a more bourgeois culture, especially
in the cities, women, who made up over half of the society, were still
expected to be submissive exemplars of "republican motherhood." They
trained their sons in the practice of civic virtue and their daughters to
be ladies. Education was negligible for girls except in a few private academies for the well-to-do. As Ellen Glasgow later wrote, the concept of
educating women was "founded on the simple theory that the less a girl
knew about life, the better prepared she would be to contend with it."

There was not just one "feminine experience" in the Old Dominion because women's lives differed greatly, depending on class and situation, yet most expected to be married when they came of age and to
become mothers. Befitting their position as representatives of virtue in
society, women were more religious than men, or at least more likely to
be church members. The vast majority of married white women were
"plain folk," who endured hard physical labor at endless chores, numerous pregnancies, and years of child care. Divorce was difficult to obtain,
requiring an act of the legislature. For poor women, this often led to desertion. Women had few property rights but could set up separate estates
that exempted property from their husbands' control.

Life for the white "Southern lady," those privileged women who
were part of the planter elite, was certainly easier than it was for women
of lesser station, but hardly a life of leisure. Also bearing many children
and risking death in the process, they supervised the domestic aspects
of their farms. However, in a dramatic challenge to the existing order,

perhaps aroused by the revival movement, Virginia women began to expand their public visibility by involving themselves in benevolence with charities, orphanages, asylums, and temperance groups and promoting piety through Bible and missionary societies, thus fulfilling their moral roles without attracting criticism for their activism. Some, notably Mary Blackford of Fredericksburg, formed female auxiliaries of the American Colonization Society to further the cause of antislavery. In 1832, 200 women of Augusta County petitioned the legislature "for the speedy extirpation of slavery from the Commonwealth," proclaiming, "Although it be unexampled, in our beloved State, that females should interfere in its political concerns . . . yet we hold our right to do so to be unquestionable, and feel ourselves irresistibly impelled to the exercise of that right by the most potent considerations and the perilous circumstances which surround us."

Other elite women founded the Mount Vernon Ladies' Association for the Union to preserve George Washington's home. Some pursued opportunities in higher education with the opening of female academies. Although not joining the nascent woman suffrage movement, Virginia women were politically involved, attending rallies, writing letters, offering legislative petitions, and making public speeches, usually on behalf of Whig candidates, who were more supportive of the reform activities these women had undertaken than were Democrats. In 1840 Daniel Webster spoke to the Womens' Wigwam in Richmond extolling the family values of the Whig Party. It would be another eighty years before women achieved the right to vote, but the road to emancipation had begun.

Perhaps even more significant for the state than the shift toward political democracy was the expansion of Virginia's economy in the antebellum years, bringing prosperity and fostering a variety of personal experiences that encouraged the culture of political liberalism in the Old Dominion. Such good fortune, however, was not constant. The Panic of 1819 had ushered in a period of depression that hit the Old Dominion particularly hard. Madison lamented in 1820, "The remarkable downfall in prices of two of our great staples, breadstuffs and tobacco, brought privations to every man's door." The depression was followed by a modest revival, and during the 1830s prices increased. They fell during the Panic of 1837 that lasted into the 1840s before rising during the boom of the 1850s. The fortunes of Virginia's farmers rose and fell with the nation's economy. In the long run prices of all products of Virginia agriculture were rising, and farmers prospered; in the short run they faced fluctuating prices for their produce from year to year; in fact, from month to month. They were the hostages of the market revolution over which they had no control.

CAPITOL SQUARE, RICHMOND, 1859

Nevertheless, Virginia clearly held its own as the leading agricultural state in the South. At the end of the 1830s, the Old Dominion stood first among the states in tobacco production, third in corn production, and fourth in wheat production. In the southeastern corner of the state, slaves were picking 3 to 4 million pounds of cotton. General farming could be found throughout the state. Wheat, corn, oats, and potatoes grew in every county; and farmers everywhere raised cows, sheep, and pigs as well. Virginia raised over 10 percent of the nation's corn crop, as every farmer produced some corn to feed his family and his livestock. Corn bread, hominy grits, and hoecakes formed the basis of the common man's diet in the Old Dominion.

Regional variation in the relative importance of crops and livestock did exist, however. From its colonial beginnings Virginia was associated with growing tobacco. The culture of tobacco dictated the rhythms of planter life and the growth of slavery in the eighteenth century. By the War of 1812, tobacco growing had fully migrated to the Piedmont, primarily the Southside counties between the James River and the North Carolina border. Following the Panic of 1819, tobacco prices plummeted; they then stabilized for fifteen years. During that time, however, there were calls for agricultural reform to control productivity. Using the pages of his *Farmers' Register,* Edmund Ruffin advocated the generous application of fertilizers and crop rotation to revitalize worn-out soils, and when a state Board of Agriculture was created in 1841, he became its leading propagandist. Following a series of bad years during the depression of the early 1840s, the tobacco business revived. In 1850 Virginia was the nation's leading tobacco producer and stood on the threshold of a decade of exceptional prosperity.

Wheat was primarily a cash crop grown for the market. It could be profitably raised with slave labor on large plantations. In fact, the crop required more land than tobacco to be profitable, and production increased with the size of the slaveholdings. Nearly all planters and two-thirds of nonslaveholding farmers raised at least a few bushels for the market. The greatest concentration of wheat production in the state was in the counties stretching north from Augusta in the Valley and the northernmost counties in the Piedmont.

The production of wheat received a major boost when Cyrus McCormick, a farm boy mechanic from Rockbridge County, invented the "Virginia reaper" in 1831. His mechanical reaper increased a farmer's capacity to harvest wheat or oats from three acres a day to fifteen, revolutionizing American agriculture. McCormick perfected his invention and then moved to Chicago where he mass-produced his reaper, becoming one of the country's wealthiest industrialists.

Industrialization was coming to antebellum Virginia as well. While the federal census of 1840—the first that provided information on the society's occupational structure—confirms traditional wisdom that eight of ten Virginians worked on farms, it also shows that a large number of individuals were involved in other pursuits. The nonagricultural sector grew by 50 percent between 1820 and 1840. "Manufactures and Trades" employed 54,000 people, while "Commerce," the "Learned Professions and Engineering," "Navigation," and "Mining" together occupied an additional 15,000 Virginians.

The census of 1850 listed the occupations of 226,875 free men, providing an occupational profile of nearly all Virginia's white adult males. They were employed in 280 different job classifications, from "Agents" to "Woolen manufacturers." Nonagricultural employment played a much larger role than is sometimes realized. Those who described themselves as "Farmers" or "Planters" made up only 48 percent of the total. Over one-fifth of those listed described themselves as "Laborers," exclusive of the significant number of artisans—carpenters, smiths, wheelwrights, and millers—listed separately and specifically designated "non-agricultural."

Virginia's antebellum industrial movement began with the growing bituminous coal trade. America's first coal mines were located just west of Richmond, and until 1828 Virginia led Pennsylvania in coal exports; in the 1840s the state was still the nation's third leading producer. In the two decades preceding 1842, the mines in the Richmond coal basin exported 2 million tons of coal and employed three out of every five Virginians in the coal industry. Eventually coal emerged as the economic backbone of the Alleghenies, and by 1840 western mines far outstripped eastern production.

In 1850 the Old Dominion ranked third among the states in the production of pig iron, fourth in iron castings, and fifth in wrought iron. Eighty-eight furnaces were smelting iron. Both iron and coal were important to the economy west of the Blue Ridge, which employed 70 percent of the state's ironworkers, with Wheeling the leading producer. Brunswick County in the southern Piedmont produced the largest tonnage of cast iron in the state, and sizable furnaces operated in Buckingham and Nelson counties in the western Piedmont and Spotsylvania County in the east. Richmond contained the most important iron producer in the South, the Tredegar Iron Works owned by Joseph R. Anderson.

Two of Virginia's leading antebellum industries, flour milling and tobacco manufacturing, involved the processing of the commonwealth's major commercial crops. Flour mills, like sawmills and gristmills which served local needs, could be found in practically every county of the Old Dominion; there were 1,381 in 1861. Flour was one of the state's major exports, and Richmond became a major antebellum milling and distribution center. Joseph Gallego's Richmond mills were the largest in the world, producing 1,000 barrels of flour daily. Mills that produced for the markets of the northeastern cities and Latin America stretched west from Richmond into the central Piedmont along the James River–Kanawha Canal. Alexandria, Petersburg, Fredericksburg, and Norfolk were also involved in the flour trade.

The Old Dominion led the nation in tobacco manufacturing, with 252 factories in 1860. Virginia's factories, which devoted their efforts primarily to the production of chewing tobacco, underwent their greatest expansion between the 1830s and the Civil War. By 1840 Virginia produced over 40 percent of the national product and purchased two-thirds of the crop of the Old Dominion. Tobacco factories employed more men, women, and children than any other form of manufacturing. Richmond rapidly became the most important tobacco manufacturing center in the world, its city directory listing forty-three tobacco factories in 1850. Lynchburg, Petersburg, and Danville were also major tobacco manufacturing cities. Virginia had become the most industrialized state in the South, and Richmond was being hailed as the future "Manchester or Birmingham of America."

Accompanying the development of industry was the trend toward urbanization. The 1850 census listed thirty-four "cities and towns," but the actual number was probably closer to one hundred. Townspeople constituted over 10 percent of Virginia's population. About half of these "urbanites" lived in the seven largest cities listed. Richmond, the largest, had grown close to 30,000, while the smallest, Lynchburg, had just over

CANAL BOAT ON JAMES RIVER–KANAWHA CANAL, 1870

8,000 people. An even larger number of Virginians lived in the thirty towns that ranged in size from Charleston in Kanawha County with a population of 1,000 to Fredericksburg with 5,000 residents.

These rapidly growing cities and towns were centers of manufacturing, commerce, and politics and served as the nodes of the system of communication. The professional elite also were concentrated in the towns, which established libraries, lyceums, and institutes like the Franklin Society at Lexington where a notable debate over Dr. Henry Ruffner's scheme for gradual emancipation west of the Blue Ridge occurred in 1847. Many of Virginia's towns had newspapers, such as the *Lexington Gazette*, the *Warrenton Jeffersonian*, and the *Charlottesville Advocate*, along with the thriving religious press and the more widely circulated partisan papers from the larger cities; the state had fifty-one newspapers in 1840, whose pages promoted local development and debated issues for an avid readership. Thomas Ritchie's *Richmond Enquirer* and John Pleasants's *Richmond Whig* appeared daily and had national reputations. Despite these developments, urbanization in the Old Dominion could not compare with similar growth in Northern cities that truly reflected the market revolution.

The bourgeois urban context created social and political perspectives at variance with those of the planter aristocracy and yeomen farmers who had adopted Jefferson's prejudices against urbanization and industrialization. By the mid-nineteenth century the pinnacle of Virginia society was shared by the descendants of the eighteenth century's richest "One Hundred" with a new entrepreneurial elite. On the whole the planters were not as wealthy as their ancestors, and they owned fewer slaves. The emerging entrepreneurs were highly mobile new men who accumulated their fortunes as they moved from town to town in the commonwealth seeking the main chance; nearly two-fifths of them were professionals, merchants, and manufacturers. Historian Clement Eaton suggests that "the spirit of feverish money making and of business enterprise that was emerging in the Southern cities brought their inhabitants closer to the sense of values of the Yankees than to the ideal of the agrarian gentry."

Town fathers combined their agricultural and industrial interests with a desire to promote banks and railroads. Money constituted the lifeblood of bourgeois commercialism, and the credit system spread slowly across the Old Dominion during these years as banks appeared in the major cities and towns. President Jackson's veto of a new charter for the Second Bank of the United States in 1832 heightened the pressure on the assembly to create more bank capital. At first it dragged its feet, defeating in 1836 a broad proposal to double bank capital in the state. A year later, however, two months before the onset of the Panic of 1837, a new general banking law liberalized the system by opening up banking to those who would comply with a prescribed set of regulations. The same legislature established the Exchange Bank of Virginia in Norfolk with branches in Richmond, Petersburg, and Clarksville and further increased the capital of the older banks. Before this massive program could go into effect, the panic hit.

During the depression of the late 1830s and early 1840s, circulation, deposits, and discounts all declined as the banks curtailed their operations. No banks failed in Virginia, however, and the revival of business brought a slow increase in discounts and deposits back to the prepanic levels of the mid-1830s. Total capital in the state actually expanded by about 50 percent between 1838 and 1842. To answer the increased demand for more banks as the economy grew, the Virginia legislature authorized a new free banking system in 1851.

The economic development of antebellum Virginia depended upon transportation and communication as much as money and credit. Sectional and local rivalries over state aid to internal improvements were important in every state in the Union, and Virginia was no exception. The assembly had created a Fund for Internal Improvement and a Board of Public Works in 1816, which over the next thirty-five years constructed 3,000 miles of turnpikes, nearly 900 miles of canals, ten plank roads, and twelve bridges. By the Civil War the state and local governments of the Old Dominion had invested $55 million in roads, railroads, and canals.

Although the James River Company had folded during the depression of the 1820s, the dream of a westward passage did not die. In part to placate westerners who were dissatisfied with the results of the 1830 constitutional convention, the assembly chartered a new James River and Kanawha Company in 1832 under the direction of Joseph Carrington Cabell. Thousands of slaves along with German, Scottish, and Irish immigrants worked on the project, but once again, bad economic times, inadequate funding, and other obstacles, notably a series of floods, hampered the effort. By 1851 the canal had been completed beyond the Blue Ridge to Buchanan, but at a cost far greater than the original estimate. By that time the canal was competing with railroads and could never repay its original investment or cover maintenance costs. Nevertheless, hauling thousands of passengers and over 200,000 tons of freight annually— wheat, iron, and hogsheads of tobacco eastward and manufactured goods westward—it proved an economic stimulus for towns along the way. The canal reduced the travel time between Lynchburg and Richmond to one-and-a-half days. Facing bankruptcy, it was sold to the railroads in 1880.

State and local aid also fostered the construction of railroads. The assembly chartered several in the 1830s, two of which never materialized because of the depression. Better economic times in the mid-1840s led to the chartering of several more, one of which, the Virginia and Tennessee Railroad, had a strong impact on the economy of the Southwest after it opened in 1856. A traveler described the scene at Bristol: "There are warehouses full of wheat and corn, great herds of grunting unambitious swine . . . crowds of busy men drinking 'bald-face' and chewing tobacco, speculators in land and pork, insolent stage-drivers, gaping country folks, babbling politicians, careless Negroes." Regrettably, the Virginia and Tennessee was built with a five-foot gauge track instead of the more standard four feet eight inch gauge, complicating its connection with other Virginia railroads and lines to the West.

County and city governments were willing to use local taxes to buy the securities of railroad companies they believed would improve their economies. Norfolk and Petersburg competed for the tobacco traffic of North Carolina until Richmond entered the fray in the 1850s with a line to Danville. The Baltimore and Ohio Railroad captured much of the Valley wheat until the Virginia Central Railroad extended its lines across the Blue Ridge to Staunton in the 1850s.

At that time Virginia was sixth in the country in miles of track laid or under construction, having increased its track by 1,000 miles in the decade, but it lacked trunk lines that connected larger markets. The state had invested heavily in many smaller lines, at a total cost of $21 million, but not in major railroads. Inadequate planning and limited vision were at the root of the problem. Penurious funding, local competition, and an early preference for a central canal over railroads may have prevented Virginia from becoming a leader in exploiting routes to the West. The result, said one critic, was "a canal made at enormous expense half way to the Ohio River, and a rail road as long made in the same direction, and then the makers stand in stupid amazement that the two halves have not reached the wealth of the great Mississippi Valley." Tidewater planter Joseph Segar defined the problem as "sectional jealousies, local feuds, and wrangling among ourselves about this road and that." Segar's neighbors, with access to river networks, had no need for internal improvements that were costly and far away.

Despite all its efforts to modernize, Virginia did not fully commit to the market revolution and thus failed to close the gap with Northern competitors. No system of public education, high illiteracy when slaves were counted, and rural poverty indicated all was not well in the commonwealth. Limited urban growth kept in-state markets small and isolated; the transportation network was localized, without major road and rail connections; and a large supply of skilled labor was not readily available.

Part of the explanation was structural. Slavery absorbed capital and labor that might have been invested elsewhere and discouraged the migration of free labor into the state. Large farms inhibited population concentrations, ensuring fewer markets for manufactured goods; and slaves had little buying power. There was a large out-migration from the state; by 1850 nearly 400,000 Virginians had been attracted to more fertile soils and opportunities in other states.

Part of the explanation was philosophical. Most Virginians still had a traditional Jeffersonian prejudice for the rural life and animosity toward urban commercial development that produced "corruption," a parochial outlook that preferred the known to the unknown, and a conservative attitude that simply said "go slow." They lacked a bourgeois mentality. The *Enquirer* editorialized in 1852, "As other States accumulate the means of material greatness, and glide past us on the road to wealth and empire, we slight the warnings of dull statistics, and drive lazily along the field of ancient customs, or stop the plough, to speed the politician."

This languid attitude was reflected in the effort to perpetuate the idyllic image of a cavalier commonwealth. The elite, in imitation of Sir Walter Scott's medieval knights, participated in jousting tournaments; defended their honor in duels, in violation of legislation outlawing the practice in 1810; visited the "waters" of the hot springs; rode to the hounds; and took honorary titles. Antebellum Virginia writers William Caruthers, John Esten Cooke, and Nathaniel Beverley Tucker wrote novels of colonial Virginia that romanticized this behavior. Native son George William Bagby declared, "There was in our Virginia country life a beauty, a simplicity, . . . a cordial and lavish hospitality, warmth and grace which shine in the lens of memory with a charm that passes all language at my command."

That memory concealed the more realistic world of most Virginians that included hardscrabble farmers who enjoyed the more modest pleasures of hunting, fishing, county days, and camp meetings. There was also the reality of yellow fever, cholera, and smallpox epidemics that killed hundreds of Virginians; high infant mortality rates; slave rebellions; poor roads; and poorly educated citizens. Yet as far apart as rich and poor white Virginians seemed to be, they shared a love of the land, a prejudice against black people, a dislike of "Yankees," and a commitment to preserve a slave society that would unite them in common cause if their world was imperiled.

It is the latter set of attitudes that better explains the Old Dominion's reluctance to enter the modern age. Greater economic diversification, with its immigrants, mechanics, businessmen, and industrialists, threatened to undermine slavery, to challenge the planters' domination of Virginia politics, and to risk the loss of white supremacy. The ruling hierarchy would fight to prevent this from happening. Dollars, power, and race still mattered.

SOURCES CONSULTED

Sean Patrick Adams, *Old Dominion, Industrial Commonwealth: Coal, Politics, and Economy in Antebellum America* (2004); Edward Ayers and John C. Willis, eds., *The Edge of the South: Life in Nineteenth-Century Virginia* (1991); R. Bennett Bean, *The Peopling of Virginia* (1938); Kathleen Bruce, *Virginia Iron Manufacture in the Slave Era* (1931); Richard Beale Davis, *Intellectual Life in Jefferson's Virginia, 1790–1830* (1972); Langhorne Gibson Jr., *Cabell's Canal: The Story of the James River and Kanawha* (2000); Daniel Goldfield, *Urban Growth in the Age of Sectionalism: Virginia, 1847–1861* (1977); Carter Goodrich, *Government Promotion of American Canals and Railroads, 1800–1890* (1960); Suzanne Lebsock, *The Free Women of Petersburg: Status and Culture in a Southern Town, 1784–1860* (1986); Ronald Lewis, *Coal, Iron, and Slaves: Industrial Slavery in Maryland and Virginia* (1979); John Majewski, *A House Dividing: Economic Development in Pennsylvania and Virginia before the Civil War* (2000); Robert D. Mitchell, *Commercialism and Frontier: Perspectives on the Early Shenandoah Valley* (1977); Mitchell, ed., *Appalachian Frontiers: Settlement, Society, and Development in the Preindustrial Era* (1991); Kenneth W. Noe, *Southwest Virginia's Railroad: Modernization and the Sectional Crisis* (1994); C. C. Pearson and J. Edwin Hendricks, *Liquor and Anti-Liquor in Virginia, 1619–1919* (1967); Garnett Ryland, *The Baptists of Virginia, 1699–1926* (1955); John T. Schlotterbeck, "The Social Economy of an Upper South Community: Orange and Greene Counties, Virginia, 1815–1860," in *Class, Conflict, and Consensus: Antebellum Southern Community Studies,* ed. Orville Vernon Burton and Robert C. McMath Jr. (1982); Frederick F. Siegal, *Roots of Southern Distinctiveness: Tobacco and Society in Danville, Virginia, 1780–1865* (1987); William Warren Sweet, *Virginia Methodism: A History* (1955); Sweet, *Religion in the Development of American Culture, 1765–1840* (1952); Elizabeth R. Varon, *We Mean to Be Counted: White Women and Politics in Antebellum Virginia* (1998); Klaus Wust, *The Virginia Germans* (1969).

10

SLAVERY, SECESSION, AND THE CIVIL WAR
1850–1865

From the perspective of economic development, Virginians had every reason to be optimistic about the future in 1860. Their economy was thriving in the fields and in the factories. Transportation links were connecting them to new markets. Diversity challenged the traditional power structure: fewer than half of the state's white men were farmers, and the power of the planters among the social elite had declined dramatically. But the issue of slavery and a decadelong debate about its future cast a shadow over this prospect. At its end, Virginians chose secession over the Union and involved themselves in a great civil war that had devastating consequences for the state.

Virginians debated the slavery issue throughout the antebellum era. The proslavery argument grew increasingly more intense after the debates of 1832 and the defenses advanced by Thomas Roderick Dew. By the 1850s George Fitzhugh of Port Royal had become slavery's most ardent advocate, extolling it as a "positive good." In *Sociology for the South* and *Cannibals All! or, Slaves without Masters,* Fitzhugh proclaimed the advantages of a slave society over a free society, condemning the wage slavery in the North while waxing eloquent about the advantages of plantation slavery. Although likely agreeing with him, most elite Virginians simply demanded security for their property; and the mass of common whites seemed to concur. When Governor Johnson commuted the death sentence of a tobacco factory slave for the murder of a white overseer in May 1852, a mob of white workers surrounded the governor's mansion, threatening to hang him before dispersing. The issue raised concerns related to the control of slaves.

After the great debate in 1832, a few Virginians contemplated the gradual abolition of an institution they believed constituted a drag on the commonwealth's economy. However, the Old Dominion spawned no immediate abolitionists, and the visible antislavery advocates were usually connected to some colonization project or were recent immigrants like John Underwood from New York, who was forced to leave his farm in Clarke County under threats to his life. The most widely discussed antislavery tract produced in Virginia during the 1840s, Henry Ruffner's *Address to the People,* proposed the abolition of slavery west of the Blue Ridge, but it was labeled an incendiary tract and forgotten. Other voices were silenced by fines or threatened jail terms. When John Hampden Pleasants, longtime editor of the *Richmond Whig,* revived the colonization arguments of Jefferson, he was attacked as an "abolitionist" and killed in a duel by one of Thomas Ritchie's sons in 1846.

Although both political parties played the politics of slavery, attacking their opponents for being soft on slavery, the Democrats were more vociferous in their defense of the peculiar institution. On related issues, Virginia Democrats encouraged the annexation of Texas in 1845 and defended the Mexican War, while Whigs in the commonwealth were critical of both. Northern Whigs saw annexation and war as mechanisms

CHALLENGED TO A DUEL BY JOHN HAMPDEN PLEASANTS, THOMAS
RITCHIE JR. KILLED PLEASANTS IN RICHMOND IN 1846

for extending slavery. The Wilmot Proviso, introduced into Congress in 1846, attempted to prohibit the expansion of slavery into any territory acquired from Mexico, raising the issue that eventually divided the country and led to civil war. To combat this possibility, John C. Calhoun offered a set of resolutions outlining a doctrine of "equality of rights" in the territories that denied congressional power to restrict slavery.

Most Virginians were alarmed by the sectional appeal of the Proviso. The *Enquirer* despaired, "The madmen of the north have, we fear, cast the die and numbered the days of the glorious Union." Agreeing with Calhoun, the 1847 assembly unanimously denounced the Proviso and affirmed that "all territory belongs to the several states of the Union as their joint and common property in which each and all have equal rights." These new "Virginia Resolutions" asserted that the Constitution gave Congress "no control, directly or indirectly . . . over the institution of slavery." As the editor of the *Enquirer* put it, "Whatever may be the fate of slavery, our own destiny is united with it and no hands but ours must touch it." In the debates over the Wilmot Proviso within the Old Dominion, no Virginia politician defended the measure, Whigs finding it inexpedient and insulting, Democrats condemning restriction as unconstitutional. The assembly elected to the U.S. Senate two strong supporters of Calhoun and Southern rights, James Mason and Robert Hunter. Although it never passed Congress, the Proviso generated further sectional hostility.

A monthlong debate over slavery and states' rights in the 1849 assembly highlighted party differences. Democrats continued to insist on full access to the territories for slaveholders, while Whigs believed that the debate over the extension of slavery into the distant and desolate territories was dangerous and unnecessary. In the congressional elections of 1849, Virginia Democrats relied on the appeal of Southern rights to rout the Whigs. Throughout the state Democrats charged their opponents with temporizing and linked Northern Whigs to the Wilmot Proviso and attempts to eliminate slavery from the District of Columbia. None of the six Whigs who had served in the Thirtieth Congress was returned.

The 1850 congressional session faced issues with serious national implications: slavery in the territories and the admission of California as a state. The discovery of gold in that territory in 1848 had drawn thousands of "49ers" in search of fortune, producing a chaotic "Wild West" society that required governmental authority. Statehood seemed imminent, but should it be admitted as a slave or a free state? President Zachary Taylor pressed for the rapid admission of California and New Mexico, presumably as free states since very few slaves lived in the region. The impression that Taylor, perhaps influenced by Northern Whigs, was indifferent

Zachary Taylor, by F. D'Avignon from a
daguerreotype by Mathew Brady

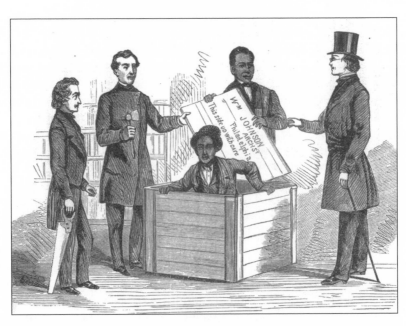

The escape of Henry "Box" Brown

to the interests of the South angered Southerners, who feared losing parity with the free states in the Senate.

The aging Henry Clay stepped forward one last time to propose a compromise. California would enter as a free state; but the rest of the Mexican cession area—the Utah and New Mexico territories—would be open to slavery, with the citizens of each territory making a final determination on its status at a later date, a popular sovereignty solution. Furthermore, a stronger fugitive slave law would be enacted to appease the South, and the slave trade in the District of Columbia would be abolished to satisfy antislavery voices. Almost the entire congressional session was consumed by the debate over these proposals.

The fugitive slave law was of particular concern to Southern slaveholders, especially Virginians, whose slaves had ready access to free states. Slaves were being smuggled to the North on ships sailing out of Norfolk and Richmond. The most celebrated case was that of Henry "Box" Brown, who had himself boxed up in Richmond and transported to Philadelphia and freedom in 1849. Slaves crossing the Mason-Dixon Line or the Ohio River received assistance from the Underground Railroad, and their recapture was often obstructed by "personal liberty laws" that prohibited state officials from assisting owners who were searching for the runaways. The attempt by Boston abolitionists to prevent the return to Virginia of Anthony Burns, who escaped from Richmond in 1854, required the efforts of the Massachusetts militia to fend off a crowd of 20,000 people intent on saving Burns. Although the number fleeing was not large compared to the overall slave population, Southerners worried about the example of resistance set by runaway slaves not returned and were outraged at the violation of their constitutional right to recapture slaves. As Virginia's Senator James Mason explained, "The loss of property is felt; the loss of honor is felt even more."

The votes cast by Virginia's representatives in Congress revealed the Democrats' hostility to the Compromise of 1850. Led by Senators Mason and Hunter, most accepted Utah and New Mexico without restrictions on slavery and the stronger fugitive slave law that Mason had written; but they opposed a free California and the restrictions on the slave trade in the District. The only Virginian who voted for all measures was Thomas Haymond, a Whig from Morgantown. Different majorities were created to pass the compromise, but Mason predicted that it would be "fatal . . . either to the Union . . . or to the institution of slavery." Although few were satisfied with the result, the Compromise of 1850 did have the immediate effect of temporarily removing slavery from national debate. The *Enquirer* reported "a calm . . . in the political universe."

That calm was broken by the introduction of the Kansas-Nebraska bill in 1854. Senator Stephen Douglas of Illinois, who had engineered passage of the Compromise of 1850, wanted to organize the portion of the Louisiana Purchase territory west of Missouri to facilitate building a transcontinental railroad through the region. Douglas's bill was controversial because it included the language of popular sovereignty that would give the people of the new territory, which lay north of 36°30′, the power to legislate on slavery, a clear violation of the Missouri Compromise of 1820. Southerners, led by Senators Hunter and Mason, saw an opportunity to eliminate this stigma of dishonor—this line that had long denied them the right to take slaves into the territory—and pressed Douglas to alter his bill to declare the crucial portion of the Missouri Compromise that restricted slavery "inoperative and void." Passage of the revised statute after four months of heated debate undermined the political stability achieved by the Compromise of 1850. It destroyed the Whigs, split the Democrats, and led to the organization of the new Republican Party founded on opposition to slavery in the territories. In Virginia, Whigs did not disappear at once, but they were fighting for their political lives in subsequent elections. Some of them defected to the Know-Nothings, a nativist, anti-Catholic party that built up strength primarily in urban areas and almost won the governor's race in 1855 against Democrat Henry Wise, who accused his opponents of being abolitionists.

On 16 October 1859 the abolitionist John Brown led a small band of sixteen whites and five blacks across the Potomac River to attack the federal arsenal at Harpers Ferry. He hoped to seize arms and encourage slaves in the area to rebel. Brown's occupation of the town lasted thirty-six hours before he was surrounded and captured by U.S. Marines led by Colonel Robert E. Lee. Brown was tried, convicted of treason against the commonwealth, and hanged in December. His raid was a chilling reminder of Gabriel, Nat Turner, and general slave resistance and stimulated further consideration of how Virginians could best protect themselves from the specter of abolition. Richmonder Elizabeth Van Lew concluded, "There is no denying the fact that our people were in a palpable state of war from the time of the John Brown raid." Governor Wise, who had interviewed Brown and recommended his hanging rather than a judgment of insanity, spent $250,000 to expand the militia to defend against invasion, encouraged postmasters to ban subversive publications, censored the telegraph, searched trains, and established de facto martial law in the area.

Virginians were also incensed by the sympathetic Northern response to Brown, who was recognized by many as a martyr who had given his life in a just cause. Outraged as well by further Northern obstruction of the fugitive slave law, they questioned the wisdom of staying in a union with "such people." Editorialized the Richmond Whig, "There are thousands of men in our midst who, a month ago scoffed at the idea of a dissolution of the Union . . . who now hold the opinion that its days are numbered." Similarly, Northerners saw in the Kansas-Nebraska Act, the subsequent struggle to bring slavery to the Kansas territory, and the Supreme Court's Dred Scott decision in 1857 that overturned the Missouri Compromise evidence of a Southern conspiracy to make the country into a slave nation. The creation of enemies made the steps toward war easier to take.

Surprisingly, given the general alarm among Virginians and Governor Wise's openly secessionist stance, Unionism retained its hold on the Old Dominion. In the election of 1860, a former Whig, John Bell of Tennessee, running as a Constitutional Unionist, gained the electoral vote of Virginia with 44 percent of the popular vote. Democrats divided between the Southern Democrat, Vice President John C. Breckinridge, and the regular party nominee, Stephen Douglas, who ran as a staunch Unionist. The Republican Abraham Lincoln won less than 2,000 votes, most of them in western Virginia; but it was his election nationally that precipitated the secession of South Carolina in December. Within two months seven lower South cotton states had seceded and formed the Confederate States of America. Amid much talk about Virginia joining this confederacy, a special session of the assembly called elections for a state convention to consider the issue.

Virginia's course of action remained unclear. Its economic associations with the South through the slave trade and tobacco manufacturing were strong. Slaveholders continued to sell slaves to the Cotton South at a tidy profit as slave prices rose. The heritage of Jeffersonian republicanism and the "Doctrines of '98" made the Old Dominion the natural leader of the South, a factor reinforced by its being the largest slave state. During all the major controversies of the past forty years, Virginia's politicians had stood alongside those of the other Southern states in protecting their interests.

And yet Virginia was also different from its sisters. In economic terms the commonwealth was more like the states to the north and west than Southern states. From the mid-1840s to the Civil War, its economy was flourishing. Every indicator of economic activity was considerably higher in 1860 than ten years earlier. Virginia's cities were growing, and most of the rural areas were thriving as well. The practice of renting or hiring out slaves was spreading, and slaves were being used increasingly in the state's prospering industrial sector, developments that lessened the planters' control. The total number of people employed in manufacturing jumped from 29,000 to 36,000. Wages were up, and the value of the product of manufactured articles in Virginia nearly doubled. Indeed, one of the arguments used by the statesmen of the lower South to lure Virginia into the Confederacy was that the Old Dominion could become the New England of the new nation.

Politically, the Old Dominion was also unlike the Deep South because of the continuing stability of the electorate. Although the national
Whig Party had disappeared, its fraternity of voters, the anti-Democratic
cadre who had manned the grassroots party machinery, and the old leadership continued to sustain Virginia Unionism. During the 1850s only
a small number of Virginians actually switched party allegiance. The
changes in the percentage of the vote going to the dominant Democrats
in presidential and gubernatorial races were minimal. Turnout mounted
in each presidential election, and in 1860, 71.5 percent of Virginia's white
adult males went to the polls. Early in the decade the Democrats held a
slight edge among new voters; but toward the end of the 1850s, this group
favored Unionist candidates. Indeed, Democrat John Letcher of Lexington, whose support of slavery was ambiguous at best, barely defeated
Whig William Goggin for the governorship in 1859.

Demographic trends within the Old Dominion were also disturbing to the planter elite. The number of planters grew slightly, but the
proportion of nonslaveholders increased as the western half of the state
outstripped the east in population growth. With each census a declining
proportion of families were intimately entwined with the peculiar institution. The number of slaveholders in the commonwealth fell from 55,000
in 1850 to 52,000 in 1860. Even east of the Blue Ridge, the proportion of
nonslaveholders increased significantly. These men had the vote, and the
constitution of 1851 provided for future reapportionment that would provide more power to the growing majority of the commonwealth's whites
who lived beyond the Blue Ridge. Part of Virginia's population increase
was due to an influx of outsiders. The state's cities drew a considerable
immigrant population from Europe; by 1860 there were 35,058 foreign-
born immigrants in Virginia. Even more dangerous in the minds of the
scions of the First Families was the influx of "Yankee" businessmen.

Trends that historians have not usually associated with the Old
Dominion—immigration, urbanization, and industrialization—were all
proceeding at a pace disconcerting to those trained to rule. Perhaps most
startling to the traditional leaders of Old Virginia was the emergence of
new families among the commonwealth's social and economic elite. The
remnants of a paternalistic planter aristocracy were under siege from an
emerging bourgeois coalition of businessmen and lawyers—many of
whom held slaves but did not depend upon them for their income—who
were talking about becoming more like the North, at least in attitude.
This was the view of a group of younger Virginians, who, in their quest
to return the state to its original greatness, were dissatisfied with "old
fogy" professional politicians. In Peter Carmichael's words, they wanted
"mental, moral, and material improvement in the Old Dominion." In the

short run the greatest threat posed to planter power was not the abolition of slavery but the taxation of their slave property, which had been
sheltered by the provisions of the state's constitution. In the long run
planters worried about the future of Virginia and slavery if the "new
men" and recently enfranchised nonslaveholders assumed command.

The 1861 Virginia convention that met in February and ended with
a declaration of secession on 17 April was a product of the new democracy of the 1850s that set nonslaveholding Unionists against slaveholding
secessionists. Although the election for delegates drew a slightly smaller
turnout than the presidential election, over three-fifths of Virginia's voters went to the polls and chose a generally conservative body committed,
at least in February, to the preservation of the Union. Their Unionism,
however, was not unconditional; many preferred to remain in the Union,
but only if Lincoln forswore any coercion of the seceded states. Former
Whigs made up a majority of the Unionist delegates, the most loyal from
the Northwest, while most of the secessionists, who constituted less than
one-third of the delegates, were younger Democrats who had not been
associated with the party battles of the 1840s. Significantly, there were
more slaveholders in the convention than in the assembly, although the
proportion of planters was about the same. The most striking characteristic of these men was the large number of lawyers, who constituted over
half of the convention. Both ex-governor Wise and John Tyler, Virginia's
only living former president, attended. Wise, who was contemplating a
coup to install a secession government in Virginia, attempted to prod the
delegates into calling a "Spontaneous Southern Rights Convention," but
they refused to be stampeded. In February, Tyler presided over a national
peace convention in Washington that had been called by the Virginia assembly to attempt another sectional compromise, but the failure of the
seceded states to attend doomed this "Old Gentlemen's Convention" to
failure.

After carefully hearing the entreaties of commissioners from the seceded states and discussing the issues, the Virginia convention on 4 April
voted almost two to one against secession and sent a three-man delegation to talk with President Lincoln. But the Confederate attack on Fort
Sumter on 12 April and Lincoln's call for troops to suppress the rebellion
three days later caused an immediate reversal and a vote to secede on
17 April. News of the surrender of Sumter brought on a wild celebration
in Richmond with a 100-gun salute and the firing of rockets. The size
and organization of the demonstration suggest that the public was more
inclined toward secession than the delegates had been. Indeed, students
at many of the state's colleges had been demanding secession for several
months. Further jubilant public celebrations across the state followed

HENRY WISE, ENGRAVING BY A. B. WALTER

the vote for secession. Notable for their presence at Fort Sumter were Virginia's most rabid Southern nationalists, Roger Pryor and Edmund Ruffin, who, as legend has it, fired the first shot of the Civil War.

Clearly the vote of 88 to 55 to remove Virginia from the Union of their fathers was far more difficult for the former Whig delegates, a majority of whom voted against secession, than it was for Democrats, all of whom favored it. These die-hard Unionists included longtime western Whig leaders Alexander H. H. Stuart, Samuel McDowell Moore, George W. Summers, and John Janney, who presided over the convention. William Ballard Preston, who had served as assemblyman, congressman, and member of Zachary Taylor's cabinet, had been with them. After voting against secession on 4 April, Preston visited his old Whig colleague, President Lincoln, to obtain assurances that the administration would not coerce the Confederate states. After Lincoln's call for troops, Preston was forced to shift his position; and on 16 April, in secret session, he introduced the ordinance of secession that was passed the following day. Three decades earlier he had proposed in the assembly that the commonwealth consider some way to end slavery.

Although the wealth of the members of the convention had little to do with the way they voted on secession, slaveholding certainly did. The

secessionists of 17 April included 85 percent of the planters in the convention, while two-thirds of the nonslaveholders opposed Preston's ordinance. The Piedmont contained the highest proportion of secessionists,
and four-fifths of the men from the Tidewater joined them. In contrast,
63 percent of the Valley delegates and 83 percent of those from the Northwest voted against secession. The anomaly in the vote was the strong
support of secession in the Southwest, whose representatives were more
radical than those from the Tidewater. John Apperson of Smyth County
enthused: "Every house in Marion nearly has a secession flag floating
over it. Men are excited to the highest pitch of their animal power, and
well they may."

Shortly before the delegates voted on Preston's secession resolution,
former governor Wise, brandishing a pistol, told the convention that he
had already set in motion the wheels of revolution. The armory at Harpers Ferry and the Gosport Navy Yard were or soon would be in the
hands of "loyal" Virginians. During the 1850s Wise had led the moderate wing of the Virginia Democracy opposed to Robert Hunter and his

EDMUND RUFFIN

followers, but in the 1861 convention he seized the reins of the secession movement. When Governor Letcher refused to act against the federal installations, Wise forced his hand by consulting with militia officials to implement these seizures.

Although the secession of Virginia was accompanied by conspiracies, bravado tactics, paramilitary activity, and the use of money by special interests like the Richmond slave traders, the process was essentially a democratic one. Convention delegates had been elected by free and open elections in which there was widespread participation. The proceedings were published daily in the *Enquirer*. These conservative lawyers rebelled against the administration in Washington because it was, in their view, subverting constitutional authority and practicing tyranny. Even Virginia's religious leaders, who had cautioned against defiance of duly constituted authority, now joined the secessionist throng that condemned Lincoln's policy of coercion. On 9 April the *Enquirer,* urging secession, called upon the convention to be true to the "Virginia platform" expressed in the resolutions of '98 and '99 and the Report of 1800 to oppose "the doctrine of consolidated, *coercive* government." Thus the Old Dominion publicly seceded from the Union in the name of Thomas Jefferson and the "Doctrines of '98," citing dangerous tendencies toward centralized power that subverted states' rights and strict construction of the Constitution.

But what rights were being violated? What was the nature of the coercion? Virginia was not being threatened by Lincoln's action. The conflict over secession pitted a party dominated by slaveholders against one representing men with no direct stake in the peculiar institution; it divided the electorate in a sectional fashion that had previously been associated with questions of constitutional reform. Those portions of the state that had opposed the democratic reforms of representation and the suffrage now advocated secession. External events over which Virginians had little control—Brown's raid and the election of a Republican committed to restricting slavery in the territories—heightened fears for the continued existence of the peculiar institution in the Old Dominion. And internal events, the acts of resistance by slaves themselves—runaways, physical assaults, insurrections—over which planters were supposed to have some control, were a direct threat to their authority. As Wise lectured the delegates, "You talk about slavery in the territories; you talk about slavery in the District of Columbia—when its tenure in Virginia is doubtful. Are we to be submissive to these wrongs? . . . Virginia is brave enough and strong enough distinctly to say to all that rather than be deprived of self-government—rather than be deprived of social safety . . . she will stand erect, sovereign and independent by herself." Very simply, slaveholding Virginians came to believe that their property, their social and political status, and their honor could best be preserved in a proslavery Confederacy rather than in a modernizing American nation that appeared to be drawing Virginia into its vortex. Staying in the Union threatened their authority in the Old Dominion and eventually would cost them their slaves. As John Randolph said years before, "Slavery is to us a question of life and death." The appeal to states' rights was merely the rhetorical device concealing these fears. Nonslaveholders, who benefited from slavery's system of race control, followed their lead, driven more by a desire to defend the homeland against an invading foe than their support for slavery.

Henry Wise's precipitous action had actually brought the Civil War to Virginia weeks before the voters ratified the ordinance of secession on 23 May by a four-to-one margin. One thousand state militiamen had seized the arsenal at Harpers Ferry and transferred most of the machinery for manufacturing arms and several thousand rifles to Richmond. A larger force seized the Gosport Navy Yard at Norfolk and carried off most of the 1,200 cannon and 2,800 barrels of gunpowder there despite the efforts of the defending garrison to scuttle the ships and burn the yard.

Politically, the state government was ahead of the voters as well. On 20 April the convention created an advisory council to assist Governor Letcher in preparing for the state's defense and authorized him to mobilize as many troops as necessary to repel the expected invasion. At the council's recommendation Letcher, who had rejected Lincoln's request for troops, offered command of the Virginia forces to Robert E. Lee on 22 April. Although not an advocate of slavery or secession, Lee, out of loyalty to Virginia, which he identified with home, family, honor, and the gentleman ideal, accepted the commission after turning down a similar offer to command Union armies.

Letcher's government also had begun negotiations with the Confederate vice president, Alexander Stephens; and on 25 April, Virginia joined the Confederate States of America. Lobbied hard by Robert Hunter, who had resigned his U.S. Senate seat and gone to Montgomery, Alabama, as Virginia's representative to the Confederate Congress, the new nation shifted its capital from Montgomery to Richmond, and President Jefferson Davis arrived there in late May. The choice of Richmond rewarded Virginia for its decision to join the Confederacy, but more significantly it recognized the strategic and economic importance of the city to the Southern war effort. Overnight the city was transformed into a melting pot of government officials, job seekers, and an odd and colorful assortment of volunteers that included New Orleans Zouaves, Tennessee frontiersmen, and Baltimore gang members. Assisted by cadets from the Virginia Military Institute and a few regular army officers who had joined the cause, Lee whipped together a 40,000-man Virginia contingent; and on 8 June, Governor Letcher turned it over to the Confederate government.

Clearly, without Virginia the Confederate cause would have been doomed. The state and its resources were essential to the success of the rebellion. In 1860 the Old Dominion was the most populous of the slave states. It was also the most economically diverse and industrially developed Southern state, a fact that had concerned slaveholders, who feared this orientation might eventually tilt Virginia toward abolition. Virginia would produce nearly all of the Confederacy's iron, coal, lead, and salt. Richmond was one of the largest cities in the South and a manufacturing center with its eight flour mills, fourteen foundries, six rolling mills, six ironworks, and fifty iron and metal shops. Joseph Anderson, president of the huge Tredegar Iron Works, which turned out 1,100 cannon during the war, has been called the "iron maker to the Confederacy."

But Virginia was also important to the Confederacy because of the human capital it offered. The commonwealth had the largest white population in the South and provided more soldiers and generals than any other Southern state. One cannot imagine the South surviving for long without Lee, Jackson, Joseph Johnston, Jeb Stuart, and A. P. Hill. Yet Virginians also fought for the North as well, notably Commander of the Armies Winfield Scott; the "Rock of Chickamauga," George Thomas; and 30,000 soldiers, mostly from western Virginia.

Virginia became the primary battleground of the war because of the proximity of the two national capitals. The Union high command devised an "Anaconda" plan that sought to squeeze the Confederacy by establishing a blockade of the entire Southern coast and controlling the Mississippi River. Concurrently, Union forces would attack Virginia from various points with the aim of capturing Richmond, a strategy which forced President Davis to emphasize that city's defense. The pattern was clear in the first months of the war. In northwestern Virginia Federal forces under the leadership of George McClellan achieved early successes at Philippi and Rich Mountain. On the peninsula between the James and the York rivers, Northern troops moved up from Fort Monroe under the command of Benjamin Butler, but they were repulsed at Big Bethel. A more serious invasion of the Valley was turned aside by Joe Johnston.

The Federal successes across the mountains reinforced an already strong preference in these counties to remain in the Union. With few slaves and stronger economic ties to the North, these westerners had long felt themselves ignored and discriminated against by slaveholding planters in the east. Having opposed the secession votes in convention and referendum, western Virginians from thirty-five counties assembled in Wheeling on 11 June and created a new government for Virginia with Francis Pierpont as governor. They did not have the support of most of the counties south of Charleston, which instead sided with the Confederacy. The Unionists later convened a general assembly, elected representatives to the commonwealth's vacated congressional seats, and recruited troops for Northern armies. President Lincoln immediately recognized the new government as the legitimate government of Virginia. Then in a very irregular procedure, these Unionists, emboldened by Union success in the region, seceded from Virginia and proceeded to create a new state of West Virginia. They gained the necessary approval of the Pierpont government and Congress and entered the Union on 20 June 1863 with a constitution providing for gradual emancipation. Pierpont moved to Alexandria, from where he governed "Virginia"—the areas around Washington, Norfolk, and the Eastern Shore that were under Union control—until the end of the war. The "restored" legislature abolished slavery and disfranchised Confederates through passage of a new state constitution.

The most important battle of 1861 took place on 21 July near Manassas Junction, thirty miles from Washington along Bull Run Creek. The gravity of the war had not yet struck either Union or Confederate leaders, and members of Congress with their lady friends and cases of champagne came out to see the spectacle. With bystanders and ill-prepared armies in place, the battle became a scene of chaos in which the advantage shifted from one side to the other throughout the day. The smoke and dust were so thick that neither the observers nor the participants could see what was going on. At the most dramatic point in the fray, as Federal troops seemed ready to turn the rebel flank, a retreating South Carolina officer saw General Thomas Jackson and his brigade at the crest of the hill. "Look, men," he shouted. "There stands Jackson like a stone wall! Rally around the Virginians!" Both man and brigade were thereafter called "Stonewall." The stand by Jackson and the fortuitous arrival of Southern reserves late in the day overwhelmed tired Northern soldiers, who, along with the private citizens, clogged the roads back to Washington that night. Nearly 5,000 men were killed, wounded, or captured. Most Virginians believed this victory would bring the war to a quick conclusion, but Manassas was only the beginning.

Lincoln now called General McClellan from the West to become commander in chief of Union forces. Over the next six months, the general assembled and trained an army of over 100,000 men; but then he seemed hesitant to move. Finally, under Lincoln's orders, he transported his Army of the Potomac by water to the James-York peninsula for a march northwestward to attack and seize Richmond. For the Confederates,

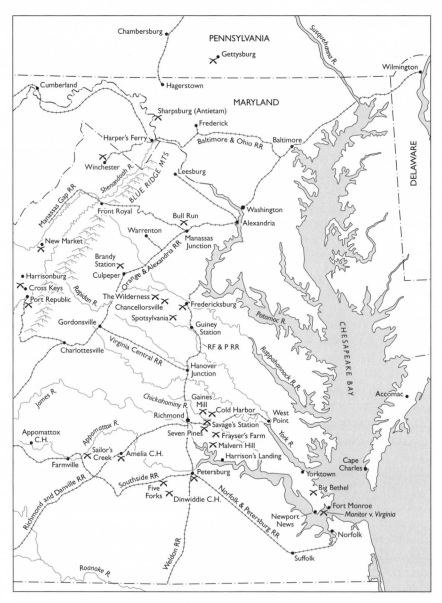

CIVIL WAR BATTLES AND EXISTING RAILROADS

General Joseph Johnston had taken command of the Manassas defenses; but he was now forced to shift his 60,000 troops southward to counter McClellan's advance.

In early March 1862, as the preparations for the march on the Confederate capital were being finalized, the first battle of ironclad ships in naval history took place at Hampton Roads. The Confederates, having seized the Union navy yard at Norfolk, had reconstructed the USS *Merrimack* into a floating iron-plated houseboat and rechristened it the CSS *Virginia*. On its first foray on 8 March, it sank two blockading Union warships. Returning to finish off the rest of the fleet the next day, it encountered the USS *Monitor*, a Northern ironclad of entirely different design: low and sleek with a single revolving turret in the center of the ship. Although the *Monitor* was faster and more maneuverable than the *Virginia*, their six-hour battle ended in a draw; but the *Monitor's* presence neutralized Confederate control of Hampton Roads and permitted McClellan's campaign to continue.

McClellan moved slowly up the peninsula until his forward units reached Seven Pines just outside Richmond, the closest large Union forces would come to the capital until late in the war. However, his disposition of the army on both sides of the Chickahominy River left it vulnerable to attack, and Johnston seized the opportunity on 31 May. Although the fighting at Seven Pines was heavy, there was little change in the situation but for the wounding of Johnston. President Davis selected Robert E. Lee, in whom he had developed great confidence, to command the Confederate army defending Richmond, now renamed the Army of Northern Virginia. Meanwhile, during the spring of 1862, Stonewall Jackson had been running circles around three Union generals from one end of the Shenandoah Valley to the other, keeping Federal forces from assisting the attack on Richmond until he could join Lee, who was busy planning a counteroffensive.

These two Virginians would form a unique partnership and achieve lasting fame for their wartime exploits. Although both had gone to West Point and were career military officers, by background and character they were quite different. Lee, who was seventeen years Jackson's senior, came from a family with impeccable Virginia credentials. His father was Light-Horse Harry Lee of Revolutionary fame, and his mother was a Carter. Graduated second in his class, he became a proficient military engineer and compiled an admirable record in the Mexican War. During the Civil War he developed into a superb tactician, known for his offensive audacity as well as his defensive abilities. A gentleman of unblemished character—modest, honest, self-controlled, and duty bound—the handsome Lee married Mary Custis, daughter of George Washington's adopted son, which gained him ownership of Arlington Mansion across the Potomac from Washington.

Jackson, on the other hand, had been orphaned at a young age, was not a particularly good student at the Point, and was totally lacking in the social graces that Lee had in abundance. He was, however, an outstanding soldier, who had proved his courage and toughness in the Mexican

ROBERT E. LEE, COPY OF MATHEW BRADY PHOTOGRAPH
BY MICHAEL MILEY

War. A professor of mathematics at VMI and a teacher of a black Sunday school in the decade before the war, "Old Tom Fool," as his soldiers called him, was a true eccentric, known for sucking lemons to relieve stomach distress and refusing pepper because he believed it made his left leg weak. A strict Presbyterian who refused to send mail on Sundays, Jackson was an aggressive terror on the battlefield, "mystifying, misleading, and surprising," being where he was not supposed to be and then relentlessly hammering the enemy in battle.

The first joint venture of these two military giants did not go well. Over the course of the Seven Days—the name describing a series of five battles from 25 June to 1 July 1862 to defend Richmond—Jackson, worn out from his Valley campaign, was usually late into battle, preventing Lee from applying maximum force against McClellan's divided army. Yet Lee's daring and aggressive tactics forced the timid McClellan to give up his plan to take Richmond and to retreat to the safe confines of his base on the lower James River. In the final engagement on 1 July at Malvern Hill, Lee's charging rebels were decimated by Union artillery; and he chose to return to Richmond, but not without having achieved his objective of driving the enemy away from the capital. Although Mc-Clellan had conducted a brilliant retreat and his army had won most of the individual engagements, he had failed his president. The Peninsula Campaign changed the course of the war. The South would now go on the offensive; but more importantly, the casualties—Lee lost one-fourth of his army—informed both sides that the war would be long and costly, requiring revolutionary methods if victory was to be won. The early rush of post-Sumter enthusiasm had died on the fields of Shiloh and Malvern Hill.

Now a year into the war, the contest was producing some unexpected and undesirable consequences. Both state and Confederate governments had instituted conscription for all white males between the ages of eighteen and forty-five. Exemptions were permitted, but the practice produced animosity against the government and those who avoided service. The wealthy could buy substitutes; and the "twenty-slave" rule allowed an owner or overseer of twenty or more slaves to remain at home, a policy which suggested to some that this had become a "rich man's war and

STONEWALL JACKSON, PHOTOGRAPHED IN WINCHESTER IN 1862

a poor man's fight." Valley Mennonites and Dunkers sought exemptions for their nonviolent beliefs, which were eventually granted for a price of $500, a "tax on faith." In time, over 90 percent of Virginia's eligible males would serve or be exempted. For folks raised on a diet of states' rights, the emergence of centralized authority was difficult to accept; but shortages of salt, leather, and dollars, the necessity of raising large armies, and the need for martial law in the presence of the enemy required extraordinary measures. Lee's success in defending Richmond and the incursions of Yankee raiders balanced this irritation and kept support for the Confederacy high.

After the Peninsula Campaign, Lee could not allow Union armies to unite and regain the initiative; and so he moved his army northward, willingly dividing his forces in order to achieve surprise. On 29 August, General John Pope attacked Jackson's wing just two miles from the site of First Manassas. On the following day Pope resumed his assaults; but the remainder of Lee's army under General James Longstreet had arrived and hit Pope's flank, driving him from the field and forcing him back toward Washington. Second Manassas confirmed Lee's brilliance as a commander.

To retain the offensive and take the war out of Virginia, Lee crossed into Maryland, hoping to win that state's allegiance, gain European recognition of the Confederacy, and bring an end to the war. At that moment the British government was considering the possibility of intervening in the struggle. Although morale was good, the army was not sufficiently supplied for such an advance, and many soldiers chose not to go north. McClellan, back in full command of the Army of the Potomac, moved to repel the rebel invasion. At Frederick he obtained an incredibly valuable piece of information—a copy of Lee's marching orders had been found that revealed the divided status of Lee's army—but McClellan failed to move fast enough to take advantage of his good fortune. Lee pulled his army together at Sharpsburg and dug in along Antietam Creek, where McClellan attacked with a force twice his size, pressing Lee rearward but failing to break his line. This day, 17 September, was the bloodiest in American military history, with over 23,000 men killed, wounded, or captured. The battle ended in a draw; but Antietam proved to be a strategic victory for the North, perhaps the most important of the war. Lee was forced to retreat back to Virginia, unsuccessful in achieving his major objective of winning foreign intervention, now delayed, perhaps permanently. More importantly, Lincoln seized this partial success to issue the preliminary Emancipation Proclamation, a document that would transform the Civil War into a revolutionary event. As of 1 January 1863, all slaves in territory still held by the Confederacy—which did not include the slave border states and Southern lands then controlled by

Northern armies—would be "henceforth and forever free." Ending slavery now became a goal of the war second only to preserving the Union.

Months before the proclamation, thousands of Virginia slaves had already registered their desire for freedom by fleeing their owners to areas controlled by Union forces around Norfolk and Washington. Living in refugee camps, they worked for Federal forces or cultivated land abandoned by white planters. The proclamation also led to their enlistment in Northern armies; over 5,000 black Virginians signed up and served with distinction in many battles in spite of the threat of retribution. After the battle of Saltville in October 1864, victorious rebel troops murdered 150 black prisoners.

Blacks also served the Confederacy. Just as before the war, they constituted half the labor force at Richmond's Tredegar Iron Works, which made the iron plates for the *Virginia,* rails for Confederate railroads, and most of the South's cannon. They also worked the mines and railroads of the Confederacy. Most slaves remained on the plantations raising food for the armies, while thousands of slaves and free blacks were temporarily impressed into military service, usually to prepare defensive fortifications, but not as armed soldiers. There were seven requisitions for slave labor during the war by both the state and national governments, a policy not always approved by planters, who worried they might not see their slaves again. The Confederacy authorized their official use in the armies as teamsters, cooks, musicians, and laborers; others volunteered or accompanied their masters as they went off to serve. Although a few undoubtedly fought for the South, it was only in the final weeks of the war that Lee and Davis won legislative approval to arm slaves. The Virginia legislature had already authorized this step, and two companies were drilling in Richmond at war's end.

Virginia women, many of whom "wished they were a man," also assisted the cause of rebellion. Manpower shortages forced them to take over plantations and assume jobs as nurses, government clerks, and factory workers, forty of whom died in an explosion in a Richmond ammunition factory. Several women in Harrisonburg offered to serve in local defense forces because the government was not providing enough security for the area. They also served as spies: Belle Boyd for the South and Elizabeth Van Lew for the North, who received information from former slave Mary Bowser who worked in the Confederate White House. Women knit socks and sewed clothing for soldiers, made soap, and sacrificed for the war effort by limiting entertainment and creating food substitutes for coffee, sugar, and flour. Richmond's Constance Cary Harrison recalled, "Every crumb of food better than ordinary, every orange, apple or banana, every drop of wine or cordial procurable went straightaway to the hospitals . . . many of the residents had set aside at least one room of their stately old houses as hospitals, maintaining at their own expense as many sick or wounded soldiers as they could accommodate." Years afterward, John Goode wrote: "The women of the Confederacy, although its greatest sufferers, were the truest of the true. . . . it was their unfailing constancy that nerved the arms and strengthened the hearts of their fathers, husbands, sons and brothers. . . . the women of the Confederacy made the men of the Confederacy what they were." Not surprisingly, their bitter memories of the suffering and defeat endured long after the war was over.

During the winter of 1862–63, after Lee had repulsed a mindless Federal attack at Fredericksburg in December, the two armies camped on their respective sides of the Rappahannock River, which now represented the northern border of Virginia. Although the Army of Northern Virginia had turned back Yankee invasions, Lee's victorious troops were beginning to experience shortages in shoes, food, and horses that limited his offensive capability. Toward the end of April, the new Union commander, Joseph "Fighting Joe" Hooker, moved his army upriver and crossed the Rapidan near Chancellorsville to strike at the rear of Lee's position. But the subsequent battle of Chancellorsville was to be Lee's finest hour. Splitting his forces, he sent Jackson on a wide flanking movement to attack Hooker from the west. Stonewall achieved complete surprise and crushed the Union right. On the following day the Confederates resumed their attack all along the line, and Hooker decided to withdraw his battered army back across the river. The victory led Lee to believe that his army was invincible: "There were never such men in an army before. They will go anywhere and do anything if properly led." But the battle also proved costly. There were nearly 13,000 Confederate casualties, the most important of which was Stonewall Jackson, mistakenly shot by his own troops when he had gone out after dark to reconnoiter the area. He died days later of pneumonia.

Lee once again decided to invade the North, hoping a victory would win European recognition of the Confederacy, increase Northern dissent, and force a negotiated peace. Furthermore, he needed to relieve pressure on a ravaged central Virginia which could no longer supply his army. In preparation for the invasion, Lee built up his army to 75,000 men divided into three corps under James Longstreet, A. P. Hill, and Richard "Baldy" Ewell, who replaced Jackson, and Jeb Stuart's cavalry division, which had repulsed the Union cavalry at Brandy Station on 9 June in the largest cavalry battle of the war. As Lee moved north into southern Pennsylvania in late June, his army was shadowed by the Army of the Potomac, now under the command of George Meade.

The two armies met at Gettysburg in a battle that took place over the first three days of July 1863 and produced 50,000 casualties. The fighting began as a chance encounter between a division of A. P. Hill's corps and John Buford's Federal cavalry. On the first day the Confederates drove the Yankees back to a defensive position south of the town but failed to capitalize on this success. On the second day Longstreet's divisions nearly pierced the southern end of Meade's line at the Round Tops and Wheatfield but fell short of victory. On the third day Lee unwisely ordered a direct assault on Meade's center, ignoring the strength of the position. Led by George Pickett and his Virginia division and accompanied by units from two other divisions, the charge failed, wiping out half the attacking force. It was Lee's worst blunder of the war. On 4 July he retreated back to Virginia, having lost one-third of his men. He would never again be on the offensive.

That same Independence Day, General Ulysses S. Grant won the surrender of the Confederate stronghold at Vicksburg with its 30,000 defenders, opening up the Mississippi River from St. Louis to New Orleans and dividing the Confederacy. Vicksburg revealed a truth that many Southerners, including Jefferson Davis, never fully comprehended: the significance of the Western theater to the outcome of the war. Grant's successes at Fort Henry, Fort Donelson, and Shiloh in the spring of 1862, the fall of New Orleans in April, the repulses of Braxton Bragg's army at Perryville and Stones River, and Grant's masterful Mississippi campaign predicted Confederate defeat. His victory at Chattanooga in November 1863 checked Bragg's success at Chickamauga and opened the door for William Tecumseh Sherman's campaign into Georgia. It was in the West that the North won the Civil War.

By the winter of 1863–64, both the Confederacy and the commonwealth were in political and economic crisis. Throughout the war adherence to states' rights plagued the government of Jefferson Davis and hampered the Confederate military effort. The most notable obstructionists were Vice President Alexander Stephens, Governor Joe Brown of Georgia, and Governor Zebulon Vance of North Carolina. On the other hand, Virginia's John Letcher cooperated so closely with the Confederate government that many in the assembly, which shared the Capitol in Richmond with the Confederate Congress, thought he too easily surrendered the state's traditional rights and privileges. Letcher had favored remaining in the Union, but once Virginia seceded, his loyalty to the new nation knew no bounds. He even organized an auxiliary military unit known as the Virginia State Line composed of men ineligible for the draft. Predictably it proved ineffective and was disbanded in 1863. Letcher's successor, William "Extra Billy" Smith, raised a similar "home guard" that did contribute to the defense of Richmond late in the war. He also involved the state in a modest blockade-running venture that ran at cross-purposes with the needs of the central government. And both governors could find no solution to the state's rising debt in a time of scarcity. To offer some relief to citizens, tax collections were suspended in March 1864.

Letcher and Smith had to govern a state whose problems were compounded by its being the central theater of the war. One-third of the state had seceded, while large areas were controlled by plundering Union forces and ruled over by the rump Pierpont government. Federal raiding parties seemed everywhere, tearing up railroad track and canal locks and burning barns. Letcher formed local committees of safety to scrutinize the suspicious and arrest the disloyal, and patrols were ever more watchful of the activities of the slaves.

Virginia's entire economy was devoted to the Confederate war effort. Farms provided food for the armies, while arsenals and factories in Lynchburg and Danville, iron furnaces in the Valley, lead mines around Wytheville, and salt from Saltville in Smyth County kept the military supplied. At the heart of this effort was Richmond, whose factories produced the bread, tobacco, and armaments to sustain the armies in the field. It is no wonder that Richmonders could not forget the war for years thereafter, for no city of the South was so transformed by its total commitment to the Confederacy. Overcrowded with soldiers, refugees, government workers, and industrial laborers, it became a gambling den, a brothel, and a black market for all kinds of commodities. It was the home of two major prisons for Union soldiers and was the primary care center for Confederate wounded. Chimborazo Hospital became the largest hospital in the world, caring for 76,000 patients in its 150 buildings.

The commonwealth like the Confederacy had to deal with shortages of practically everything, which produced skyrocketing inflation. A Lexington woman wrote in early 1862: "How I loathe the word *war*! Our schools are closed, stores shut up. Goods not to be bought, or so exorbitant we must do without." The Confederate government made the situation worse by issuing $100 million in paper currency. By the midpoint of the war, prices of flour, cornmeal, butter, sugar, and coffee all doubled and then tripled. Flour in Richmond was $300 a barrel and butter $15 a pound; near the end of the war, with Grant tightening the siege at Petersburg, flour was $1,200 a barrel and butter $25 a pound. Commonplace items such as soap and salt were scarce, and medicines went to the military. The mounting price of salt turned Letcher into the "Salt Czar" to ensure its proper distribution. The rising price of flour led to the Richmond bread riot on 2 April 1863 in which a mob of 1,000 women and children looted stores on Main Street. Eventually the mayor, governor, and even President Davis, with the aid of Richmond's home guard, dispersed the crowd.

Further dissent was fueled by opposition to conscription and the impressment of food for Southern armies. Even the usually pliant Governor

Letcher labeled the draft "the most alarming stride toward consolidation that has ever occurred." The Richmond press was particularly critical of Davis's direction of the war. As the war progressed and conditions worsened, apathy and disillusion descended on the state, particularly among poorer whites, who had long believed they had been abused by the planter class. Desertion rates were going up; deserters were being hanged. Cornelia McDonald wrote in December 1864, "Groups of murmuring men were all around, and I first began to realize that the patience of the people was worn out; that their long suffering and endurance was to be depended upon no longer; that they were beginning to see that it was of no avail to deliver the country from her enemies." To combat such despair, city leaders in Richmond, Lynchburg, and Staunton in the final weeks of the war were still exhorting their listeners to remain loyal and donate their last resources to the cause.

Although the great majority of white Virginians remained loyal to the cause throughout the war, there were sizable pockets of Union sentiment in the state. Areas with little slaveholding saw no reason to support a government committed to preserving slavery. Considerable partisan rivalry existed in northern Virginia, where the rangers of Colonel John Mosby wreaked havoc with Union military forces and their supporters. He was so effective that the region he operated in became known as "Mosby's Confederacy." Much guerrilla activity—"bushwhacking"—took place in the Southwest as well. People suffered for their misplaced loyalties. Unionists were often forced to "conform," depart, or endure harassment. John Minor Botts, a prominent Whig politician before the war, served jail time for his pro-Union sentiments, while Confederate loyalists in Yankee-controlled regions also suffered for their allegiance, often being banished from their homes or arrested. A peninsula planter wrote in 1864 of Union violations: "They have murdered my first born, burned my houses, . . . carried off my stock, indeed robbed me of all I had. . . . I can but think they desire possession of our lands . . . and to reduce us to want and beggary."

Another change in the Northern command occurred in 1864 as Lincoln called Grant from the West to become general in chief of all Union forces. He and Sherman, with Lincoln's blessing, now applied concepts of modern warfare: a strategy of exhaustion characterized by the constant engagement of armies on all fronts accompanied by a direct assault on the enemy's economic resources. Grant would confront Lee in Virginia, while Sherman was to cut through Georgia; additional pressure would be applied in the Valley and Alabama; and the blockade would be tightened.

In early May, Grant crossed the Rapidan and began his relentless Overland Campaign. The best hope for the Confederacy was that Lee's army could hold off the better-equipped Army of the Potomac long enough to cause European opinion to shift and Northern voters to defeat Lincoln in the 1864 presidential election. In battle after battle Lee seemed to win, brilliantly countering Grant's offensive thrusts, but Grant, unlike his predecessors, would not retreat and continued southward, trying to turn Lee's flank and moving ever closer to Richmond. Three of the bloodiest battles of the war took place in the span of one month from 5 May to 3 June—Wilderness, Spotsylvania, and Cold Harbor—in which Grant absorbed enormous casualties, perhaps as many as 50,000 troops. A Confederate soldier wrote of the carnage at the "Bloody Angle" at Spotsylvania, "The battle of Thursday was one of the bloodiest that ever dyed God's foot table with human gore." At Cold Harbor, Grant lost 7,000 men in thirty minutes, a mistake he acknowledged as his worst of the war. Although Lee's losses were smaller, proportionately he suffered greater attrition; and in the cavalry battle at Yellow Tavern on 11 May, he lost his "eyes and ears" with the death of Jeb Stuart.

Grant then decided to shift his focus to Petersburg and its rail lines that supplied Richmond and Lee's army. However, failure to take the city forced him to initiate a siege that would last for nine months. Citizens of Petersburg endured constant bombardment and dwindling supplies as Grant extended his siege lines westward. The most intriguing event of the siege was the Union effort to create a break in the Confederate defenses by tunneling under the line and setting off an explosion that could be exploited. The ensuing Battle of the Crater proved disastrous for the ill-prepared attacking forces as Confederates under the command of William Mahone quickly recovered from the blast and massacred the attackers who got mired in the crater.

During these engagements between Grant and Lee, Confederate forces under General John Breckinridge, with the aid of teenaged cadets from VMI, routed Federals at New Market. This success was followed by Jubal Early's drive down the Valley into Maryland all the way to the outskirts of Washington, compelling Grant to use troops from the Petersburg trenches to force Early back into Virginia. Angry with these distractions, Grant ordered Phil Sheridan to rid the Valley of Confederate forces once and for all. In September and October, Sheridan routed Early's forces in several battles and introduced a scorched-earth policy known as "the burning." The diminutive general informed the War Department that "the Valley, from Winchester [which had changed hands over seventy times during the war] up to Staunton . . . will have little in it for man or beast." The wholesale destruction of crops, thousands of livestock, 2,000 barns, and seventy flour mills meant that not only Lee's army but the people of Richmond would be threatened with starvation.

As 1865 dawned, the fate of the Confederacy seemed ordained. Grant was extending the siege around Petersburg; and Sherman had knocked Georgia out of the war and was preparing to march through the Carolinas, laying waste to that area as well. Lincoln's reelection in November doomed any effort at a negotiated peace because he insisted upon the return of the seceded states to the Union and an end to slavery. As had happened after previous defeats, another wave of evangelical revivals hit the Army of Northern Virginia as it endured the winter of 1864–65 in the Petersburg siege lines. Outnumbered by more than two to one, Lee made one last effort to break the siege line at Fort Stedman in March, but he was repulsed. Days later Sheridan quashed Pickett at Five Forks, cutting the last rail line into Petersburg. The next day, 2 April, Grant attacked all along the line, overwhelming Southern defenders and forcing Lee's withdrawal.

When word of this disaster reached the capital, both Confederate and state governments prepared to leave. Departing soldiers blew up the arsenal and several ships in the James River and set fire to tobacco warehouses to prevent any stores from falling into the hands of the Yankees. With drunken mobs in the streets, the fires quickly spread, soon consuming twenty blocks of the downtown. Only a bucket brigade saved

RICHMOND BURNING, 2 APRIL 1865, LITHOGRAPH BY CURRIER AND IVES

the governor's mansion from the flames. The next day Federal troops entered the city, accepted the surrender offered by its mayor, and helped extinguish the fires. On 4 April, President Lincoln visited, sitting in the chair of the departed President Davis, who had set up a temporary capital in Danville before continuing his flight southward.

The fleeing Lee united the Petersburg and Richmond defenders at Amelia Court House, hoping to replenish them before moving south to join Joe Johnston's army in North Carolina. The two armies would then attempt to defeat the two Union forces separately. Through a masterful pursuit, Grant would not permit such a juncture, blocking Lee at every turn. The failure to receive food at Amelia forced Lee to continue westward with his hungry, demoralized soldiers. At Sailor's Creek outside Farmville on 6 April, Federal cavalry and infantry caught Lee's two trailing corps and wagon trains, forcing the surrender of General Ewell and 6,000 men.

Three days later at Appomattox Court House, after a failed attempt at a last breakout, Lee reluctantly notified Grant of his willingness to concede. They met that Sunday afternoon in the McLean house where Grant offered Lee very generous surrender terms. Four years earlier Wilmer McLean had left his farmhouse near Manassas after that first battle and moved south "to get away from the war." It now ended in his front parlor. Although the capitulation of other Southern armies would follow in the next month, it was the surrender on 9 April 1865 at Appomattox of Robert E. Lee and the Army of Northern Virginia, the force that had come to represent the ferocity and nobility of the Southern resistance, that symbolically ended America's Civil War.

SOURCES CONSULTED

Edward L. Ayers, *In the Presence of Mine Enemies: War in the Heart of America, 1859–1863* (2003); William Blair, *Virginia's Private War* (1998); F. N. Boney, *John Letcher of Virginia: The Story of Virginia's Civil War Governor* (1966); Daniel W. Crofts, *The Reluctant Confederates: Upper South Unionists in the Secession Crisis* (1989); Richard Orr Curry, *A House Divided: Statehood Politics and the Copperhead Movement in West Virginia* (1953); Charles B. Dew, *Ironmaker to the Confederacy: Joseph R. Anderson and the Tredegar Iron Works* (1966); Ernest B. Furgurson, *Ashes of Glory: Richmond at War* (1996); Gary W. Gallagher, *The Confederate War* (1997); Patricia Hickin, "Gentle Agitator: Samuel M. Janney and the Antislavery Movement in Virginia, 1842–1852," *JSH* (May 1971); Ervin L. Jordan Jr., *Black Confederates and Afro-Yankees in Civil War Virginia* (1995); Gregg D. Kimball, *American City, Southern Place: A Cultural History of Antebellum Richmond* (2000); Nelson K. Lankford, *Richmond Burning* (2002); William A. Link, *Roots of Secession: Slavery and Politics in Antebellum Virginia* (2003); Richard G. Lowe, *Republicans and Reconstruction in Virginia, 1865–1870* (1991); James M. McPherson, *Battle Cry of*

Freedom: The Era of the Civil War (1988); Lynda J. Morgan, *Emancipation in Virginia's Tobacco Belt, 1850–1870* (1992); Merrill D. Peterson, *The Legend Revisited: John Brown* (2002); James I. Robertson Jr., *Civil War Virginia: Battleground for a Nation* (1991); Robertson, *Stonewall Jackson: The Man and the Legend* (1997); Henry T. Shanks, *The Secession Movement in Virginia, 1847–1861* (1934); Craig Simpson, *A Good Southerner: The Life of Henry A. Wise of Virginia* (1985); Emory M. Thomas, *The Confederate Nation, 1861–1865* (1979); Thomas, *The Confederate State of Richmond* (1971); William G. Thomas III and Edward L. Ayers, "An Overview: The Differences Slavery Made: A Close Analysis of Two American Communities," *AHR* (Dec. 2003); Elizabeth R. Varon, *Southern Lady, Yankee Spy: The True Story of Elizabeth Van Lew, a Union Agent in the Heart of the Confederacy* (2003); Peter Wallenstein and Bertram Wyatt-Brown, eds., *Virginia's Civil War* (2005); Russell F. Weigley, *A Great Civil War: A Military and Political History, 1861–1865* (2000); Ralph A. Wooster, *The Southern Secession Conventions* (1962); James W. Young, *Senator James Murray Mason: Defender of the Old South* (1998); Edward Younger and James Tice Moore, eds., *The Governors of Virginia, 1860–1978* (1982).

11

THE RECONSTRUCTION ERA
1865–1885

In the closing days of the war, Judith McGuire, who was tending the wounded in a Richmond hospital, made several entries in her diary: "They say General Lee has surrendered. We cannot believe it, but my heart became dull and heavy. . . . An order came out in this morning's papers that prayers for the President of the United States must be used. How could we do it? . . . General Johnston surrendered on the 26th of April. My native land good-night."

The mood of freed slave Fannie Berry of Pamplin was less melancholy: "Never was no time like 'em befo' or since. Niggers shoutin' an' clappin' hands an' singin'! Chillun runnin' all over de place beatin' tins an' yellin'. Ev'ybody happy. Sho' did some celebratin'."

Winners and losers experience the results of war differently, and their memories of the event often magnify those differences, influencing the way subsequent generations use history. In the case of the American Civil War, the memories lingered longer than normal, particularly in the South, where for more than a century the Confederate battle flag was still flying, "Dixie" was being sung, and states' rights survived as a rallying cry for opponents of civil rights and federal intrusion. The sectional hostilities produced by the war, the horrific casualties, and the enormous physical destruction of the South were not easily forgotten, but the factor that likely had the greatest bearing on the memory of the Civil War and the region's postwar reconstruction was the emancipation of the slaves. That was certainly true for African Americans, but it was so for white Southerners as well, who would fabricate sinister images of what black freedom did to the South: a "Black Reconstruction."

Reconstruction was not the "torture chamber" that journalist Claude

Bowers described in his 1926 history *The Tragic Era*. The retribution imposed on the South by the North was relatively mild compared to other end-of-war reprisals. Jail time for Confederate leaders was negligible, except for Jefferson Davis, who spent two years in a Fort Monroe cell; loss of political rights—voting and office holding—was brief; the military occupation was likewise limited; and blacks did not control any Southern state. Understandably the restrictions on personal liberty were uncomfortable and insulting to a proud people who had endured great loss and faced a difficult recovery, but some penalties for rebellion against the government should have been anticipated. What disturbed former Confederates the most, however, was the activity of African Americans as they embarked upon the journey of freedom: casting votes when many whites could not, sitting beside them in legislative bodies, strolling the streets without stepping out of the way, bringing their own crops to market. The changes were exhilarating and threatening; not exactly "black rule," but for whites it might as well have been. Having lost the war and slavery, they sought to reestablish conservative white control and create a history that would justify their performance, a history not always consistent with the facts.

The end of the war confronted the country with two related issues: the political restoration of the seceded states to the Union and the place of the newly freed slaves in that society. In Virginia, over the next twenty years, former Confederates, Republicans and Conservatives, Readjusters and Funders, Democrats, blacks and whites, Washington and Richmond politicians, and businessmen of every stripe vied for control of the state's political, economic and racial future. Self-interest and racism dominated the struggle, leaving the Old Dominion bitterly divided and less disposed to address the mental and physical legacies of the war.

No other Southern state suffered the devastation that Virginia experienced during the war. It had been the chief battleground in the conflict. More than 40,000 citizens had perished, most of them in military service to the Confederacy. Thousands more were crippled. Railroads had been demolished, bridges torn up, towns burned down, factories damaged, farmlands trampled by troops and horses, and livestock killed. Fredericksburg and Petersburg were gutted by fire and cannon shell, a large section of downtown Richmond had been consumed by the inferno set by departing Confederates, and the barns and crops of the Shenandoah Valley likewise lay smoldering. A vast campground for two great armies for four years, the area from Washington to Richmond and west to the Blue Ridge had been ransacked for provisions and fodder and wood, its inhabitants left homeless and hungry. Six months after Appomattox thousands of black and white Virginians were surviving on rations provided by the Union army. Disease was rampant. With Confederate currency worthless and personal savings wiped out, a barter economy developed. *Nation* correspondent John Richard Dennett commented: "Trade is dead, the people have no money, nor is there a prospect of their soon getting any. . . . The shelves of the shops are scantily supplied with poor goods." Nearly a half million slaves in the state had been freed, an enormous loss of capital that also left the plantations bereft of labor. One-third of its people and territory had been wrenched from it in the creation of West Virginia. A postwar assessment of Virginia's wartime financial losses, including the value of the freed slaves, put the figure at nearly half a billion dollars. For the moment, the war shattered the patriarchal political culture that had dominated life in the Old Dominion for two centuries. As one slave proclaimed, "Bottom rail on top now, massa!"

Not surprisingly, after four years of sacrifice, defeat, and desolation, white Virginians despaired for their future. A few left for Brazil or Mexico, such as the renowned oceanographer Matthew Fontaine Maury; rabid secessionist Edmund Ruffin, who had been present at Fort Sumter and the first battle of Manassas, went home and put a bullet through his head; the rest awaited the verdict of the conquering foe. Many ex-Confederates were unrepentant, continuing to malign the Yankees and Northern capitalism, seeking no amnesty, and opposing any political rights for blacks. General Jubal Early wrote from Canada in 1867, "If I were made governor, I would have the whole state in another war in less than a week." Most, however, weary of warfare, accepted the outcome of the conflict and sought pardons. In the view of one Union officer, "The secessionists here have apparently given up all idea of a Confederacy and appear to be inclined to commence anew." A voice of moderation until his death in 1870 was Robert E. Lee, who, having assumed the presidency of Washington College, urged his fellow Virginians to look forward, not backward, to renew their loyalty to the Union, and to accept the freedom of the former slaves.

For the first two years after the war, the course of Reconstruction was in doubt, as the parties maneuvered for advantage. For black Virginians like Fanny Berry, war's end brought much promise and not a little apprehension. What was possible? Their former masters would be of little assistance. Reluctantly conceding the end of slavery, whites did not believe freedom meant independence and equality. Indeed, most did not think the freedpeople would be able to survive on their own but would need supervision. Nor was the liberating army always supportive, imposing curfews, requiring passes, and arresting blacks for insolence. Newly arrived missionaries and teachers from the North frequently could not understand why the freedpeople did not fully embrace their stern Calvinist theology and white middle-class values and behavior, wanting blacks to be something they were not. Nevertheless, with a little help from their emancipators, the former slaves struck out on their own to test the waters of freedom. Leaving their old plantations, they went in search of families and jobs, experiencing the emotional release of being free. They legalized their marriages, seized control of their churches, and avidly pursued education through missionary and Freedmen's Bureau schools. One such school in Lexington enrolled over 300 students, who pooled their resources to rent space and provide books.

Despite white charges of idleness, freedpeople sought any kind of employment, many going to towns and cities for higher-paying jobs, army protection, and the assistance of Freedmen's Bureau agents and free blacks. An assembly of Fredericksburg blacks "scorned" the charge of indolence, declaring, "We do understand Freedom to mean industry and the legitimate fruits thereof." They used skills learned on the plantation to become independent blacksmiths, shoemakers, and draymen. Blacks continued to be employed in tobacco factories and flour mills, but the postwar depression would draw many whites into the factory system that in time would change the composition of the industrial workforce to the detriment of African American workers.

Most former slaves, without land or resources, became hired agricultural laborers, frequently on their old plantations, being paid a little more than $9 a month in 1866. On the James-York peninsula they supplemented farmwork with jobs in the lumber and fishing industries. Some freedmen formed cooperatives to buy land or occupied farms that had been abandoned during the war, but as many as 20,000 blacks were evicted from land in southeastern Virginia after President Andrew Johnson, who had succeeded the assassinated Lincoln in April, ordered seized rebel property returned. One such evicted farmer from Yorktown lamented: "We has a right to the land where we are located. For why? I tell you. Our wives, our children, our husbands, has been sold over and over again to purchase the lands we now located upon; for that reason we have a divine right to the land. . . . And den didn't we cleare the land, and raise de crops ob corn, ob cotton, ob tobacco, ob rice, ob sugar, ob everything. And den didn't dem large cities in de North grow up on de cotton and de sugars and de rice dat we made? . . . I say dey has grown rich, and my people is poor." Freedpeople believed the promise of "forty acres" was not a gift but theirs by right for uncompensated past labor, but such hopes went unfulfilled.

In March 1865 the Bureau of Refugees, Freedmen, and Abandoned Lands, known as the Freedmen's Bureau, had been created to assist blacks in the transition from slavery to freedom. Supervising and enforcing labor contracts, providing medical care, subsistence, and schooling, and adjudicating disputes between the races, the bureau faced a daunting task given white opposition. For four years its agents and military courts

FREEDMEN'S VILLAGE AT HAMPTON, 1865

provided the freedpeople with protection and support, but adhering to the free labor ideology of Northern capitalism—"labor is wealth and money is power"—agents often sided with landowners in ensuring that black labor was available. In fact, the bureau's vagrancy policy—"work or be hired out"—was similar to Virginia's new vagrancy law. Landowners, relying on legislation, intimidation, and subterfuge, sought to maintain control of their labor force. They opposed education for blacks and apprenticed parentless children to work for their former masters. Resignedly, a freedman concluded: "What kin we do? . . . Dey kin give us jes what dey choose. Man couldn't starve, nohow; got no place to go; we 'bleege to take what dey give us." Nonetheless, their labor gave them leverage. Accepting wage labor, they negotiated agreements that granted them more control over their lives—time off, an end to the gang system of labor, removal of family labor from the fields, and the right to keep garden crops—but this arrangement quickly evolved into a system of sharecropping and tenancy because of a lack of cash.

Perhaps more than education and employment, blacks valued the right to vote as evidence of real freedom and their ability to protect their interests. Men and women formed political clubs, joined the Republican-inspired Union Leagues, and met in public assemblies in Norfolk, Richmond, and Alexandria to demand protection from police brutality, repeal of discriminatory laws, and equal suffrage. One group in Norfolk, which had become a refuge for fleeing slaves during the war, managed to vote in May 1865 without being registered. As time went on, freedpeople became bolder, taking seats on Richmond streetcars and striking for higher wages. Understandably, they affiliated with their Republican liberators rather than the defenders of slavery and the Confederacy. Their leaders often were literate free blacks who owned farms or were in the professions. By the end of the decade, freedpeople had made remarkable progress, independently working the land, casting ballots, sitting in legislative seats, freely moving about, their children going to school. They were hardly the "bewildered, shiftless, lazy lot" they were accused of being. Indeed, their lack of deference toward their former owners frightened and angered whites.

Shortly after Appomattox, Governor Francis Pierpont, who for four years had led the "restored" government of Virginia that had governed Union-occupied areas of the state, first from Wheeling and then from Alexandria, arrived in Richmond to supervise the Reconstruction process set in motion by President Johnson's amnesty and pardon proclamations. Although the field armies had been disbanded, a small military force remained to assist the governor in preserving order. Pierpont naively believed that leniency toward former Confederates would facilitate the creation of a new Virginia, so at his behest the sixteen-member "restored" General Assembly granted voting privileges to most rebels who took a loyalty oath to the United States. The governor even intervened to stop the confiscation of rebel property by federal judge John Underwood, the New York abolitionist who had helped found the Republican Party in Virginia. Unionists, Republicans, and African Americans were shocked by this appeasement of their recent enemies and began demanding black suffrage to counter the return of the ex-Confederates. Said one Fauquier County Unionist, "We are even now suffering outrages and if there is not some protection given us we will be compelled to leave our homes again."

Elections in October 1865 produced a new legislature, composed mostly of former Whigs and Confederates and a few Republicans. They rejected Governor Pierpont's conciliatory advice and repealed Virginia's permission for the formation of West Virginia; removed Unionists from office; repealed the old slave code but denied black testimony against whites in court, black service on juries, and black voting; and enacted a harsh vagrancy law that allowed the state to hire out idlers and those who had no "visible means of subsistence." General Alfred Terry labeled the law as "slavery in all but its name" and annulled its enforcement, although it was similar to military and Freedmen's Bureau labor regulations. The assembly also removed the office-holding disqualification for former Confederates, ratified the Thirteenth Amendment abolishing slavery, legalized slave marriages, and guaranteed payment of the state's prewar debt, but it refused to allocate funds for public schools.

Virginia's actions were less confrontational than those of other Confederate states where unpardoned Confederates were elected to office and the infamous "black codes" were passed that seriously compromised the freedom of the former slaves. Predictably, congressional Republicans would not tolerate such acts of defiance that appeared to deny them the fruits of victory. Lobbied by Virginia Unionists, they refused to seat any of the newly elected Southern representatives and initiated an investigation to determine if the seceded states were ready for readmission. Although their political and economic interests and a desire for revenge would dictate a harsher reconstruction, many of them also felt some obligation to secure a meaningful emancipation. When President Johnson vetoed legislation that provided greater protection and rights for the freedpeople, moderate Republicans joined forces with party radicals to adopt a more extreme position. In June 1866 Congress approved the Fourteenth Amendment, which, when ratified, would guarantee citizenship to the freedmen, compel the states to provide "equal protection of the laws" to their citizens, and deny office holding to those who had violated an oath of allegiance to the U.S. Constitution and engaged in rebellion. Although the amendment did not confer the ballot on blacks, Congress could reduce the representation of states that did not. Any lingering hopes for a quick readmission seemed dependent on ratification by the former Confederate states.

Racial and political tensions in Virginia heated up in 1866. Black celebrations of freedom reminded whites of their defeat; several people of both races were killed following one such celebration in Norfolk. Whites felt some unease with the drilling of black militia companies, although their own private units were similarly parading. Presiding over the grand jury hearing for Jefferson Davis, Judge Underwood antagonized Confederates and impartial observers alike with his bitter attack on slaveholders, secessionists, and Virginia newspapers.

In such an atmosphere, the legislature met in December to consider ratification. Governor Pierpont, who by now had lost influence with all factions, exhorted the legislators to endorse the Fourteenth Amendment so as to forestall additional penalties, but they rejected his advice. Moderates in the assembly understood the necessity of accepting some change, but they could not overcome their fears of black equality, their sense of being betrayed by the radicals, or their hope that President Johnson might save white rule. Their wartime sacrifices had forged a bond of loyalty to a "lost cause" that precluded the foresight necessary for a self-directed reconstruction. It was their intransigence as well as radical Republican desires for a more dramatic overhaul of Southern society that dictated the final result.

Consequently, harsher terms were forthcoming in March 1867 when Congress passed the first Reconstruction Act. The new law established five military districts in the old Confederacy, of which Virginia was District Number One. It also enfranchised blacks, disqualified many former Confederates from voting, required new state constitutions, and stipulated ratification of the Fourteenth Amendment before a state could be readmitted to the Union. General John Schofield was appointed commander in Virginia to oversee the registration of voters and the election of delegates to a constitutional convention. Although he was sensitive to conservative sentiments on black voting and Confederate disfranchisement, he could not prevent newly empowered Republicans from controlling the process.

Virginia Republicans were generally united in their desire for an open society of free men and free labor that would permit black suffrage and initiate a new social order, but they could not agree on the means to attain those objectives. Blacks wanted equal rights and opportunity and access to education and jobs, perhaps even some confiscation of land from the defeated rebels. While a few whites supported such a social transformation, others were more forgiving of the ex-Confederates and less interested in advancing black rights and property redistribution. The conflict came to a head in two organizational meetings in Richmond in April and August 1867 in which the blacks, clearly in the majority, and their white allies practically read the moderates out of the party. One of their most outspoken leaders was Thomas Bayne, a former slave who had escaped to Norfolk from North Carolina and then, using the Underground Railroad, to Bedford, Massachusetts, where he practiced dentistry before returning to Norfolk in 1865. Fearing that moderation would lead to a restoration of conservative white rule, Bayne had no tolerance for the centrist views of Governor Pierpont and John Minor Botts, both former Whigs and wartime Unionists. Bayne's uncompromising position was supported by the firebrand Baptist minister James W. Hunnicutt, a white South Carolina native who had attended college in Virginia, owned a few slaves, and edited a Fredericksburg newspaper before being forced to leave the state in 1861 because of his Unionism. The banishment radicalized him, and he became an outspoken advocate for black rights; it was said he resembled John Brown. The division between radicals and moderates hampered Republican efforts to create a majority party in Virginia throughout Reconstruction and eventually led to their defeat.

The registration of voters in September revealed the dramatic political change wrought by Confederate defeat. Almost 106,000 blacks registered to vote, just 14,000 fewer than the number of white registrants.

Perhaps 20,000 former Confederates were denied the ballot; others simply refused to participate. In October these voters approved a constitutional convention and elected delegates. The *Richmond Enquirer* deplored the "horrible and loathsome" elevation of black men over white men: "We unfurl the standard of resistance to the wretched creatures who are soon to meet to complete the work of Africanizing Virginia."

Dominated by their radical wing, Republicans controlled the gathering that convened in Richmond in December 1867 to write the new basic law of the commonwealth. Although more blacks than whites voted for convention delegates, a black majority did not result. Of the 104 delegates, 68 were Republicans, only 24 of whom were African Americans; 23 were from the North or of foreign birth, and 21 were native white Virginians, called "scalawags" for their new Republican loyalties. Of the 36 conservatives, most were Confederate veterans. Conservatives contemptuously labeled the Northerners "carpetbaggers"—opportunistic recent arrivals—although several of them had lived in Virginia for years. They were an important element in the Republican Party, and one of them, Judge Underwood, was elected president of the gathering that was derisively called the "Mongrel Convention" and the "Bones and Banjo Convention" by the Richmond press.

Although many critics questioned the competence of the delegates, the document they wrote over a four-month period, to be known as the Underwood Constitution, was a model of democracy. It established manhood suffrage for blacks and most whites, required a written secret ballot, created Virginia's first public school system, reduced the residency requirement for voting, granted the governor veto and pardoning power, established a homestead exemption from debt collection, and limited the state's power to contract debts. It did not provide for confiscation of rebel property as desired by Hunnicutt and many blacks, nor did it mandate the integration of the schools. It did include controversial clauses that required an oath of officeholders that they had never supported the Confederacy and disfranchised those who had held civilian or military office under the Confederacy. Although these provisions were in keeping with the disqualification provision of the Fourteenth Amendment, they were clearly designed to institute the rule of radical Republicans and blacks.

Such a prospect frightened conservative whites into pursuing alternative strategies. Traditionalists like General Early abstained from participation throughout Reconstruction, hoping that sympathetic heads in the North eventually would prevail. Most, however, decided to defeat the Republicans at the polls with a new Conservative Party, whose core was not old planters but businessmen and attorneys who, although Confederate in their loyalties and values, were constructing a new order of railroads and factories and high finance.

Conservatives had the ear of General Schofield, who disliked several provisions of the Underwood Constitution, notably the test oath and disfranchisement clauses. Realizing that Governor Pierpont had lost all influence among the competing parties, Schofield replaced him with an old Michigan friend, Henry H. Wells, who, he hoped, could unite the bickering Republicans. However, Wells, seeking to win the governorship in the next election, shifted allegiance to the radical position and unconditionally endorsed the new constitution. The disillusioned Schofield retreated to Washington to become secretary of war, but not before postponing both the election and the constitutional referendum, delaying the expected Republican victory. At the same time, in the spring of 1868, the newly formed Ku Klux Klan entered Virginia with posters, costumes, and reports of assaults, but its impact was negligible, and it quickly disappeared.

Seeking to avoid extremist rule and to end military government, which although not oppressive was still "foreign," Conservatives modified their position against black suffrage and the Underwood Constitution. Now they advocated Virginia's readmission to the Union on the basis of universal suffrage and acceptance of the new constitution without its two anti-Confederate clauses. To this end, a "Committee of Nine," whose most prominent member was Alexander H. H. Stuart of Staunton, the respected antebellum Whig leader, negotiated with federal officials in early 1869. With the help of moderate Virginia Republicans, the committee won the approval of newly elected President Ulysses S. Grant for a gubernatorial election and a referendum on the constitution with separate votes to be taken on the controversial clauses.

What followed was one of the most crucial elections in Virginia history as radicals battled conservatives for control of the Old Dominion's future. The "kingmaker" was ex-Confederate general William "Billy" Mahone, who desired political stability and friendly faces to support his emerging railroad empire. Governor Wells was unacceptable to Mahone because of his conversion to radicalism and his alignment with out-of-state railroad interests. To undermine Wells's appeal among white voters, Mahone orchestrated the nomination by Republicans of black physician J. D. Harris for lieutenant governor. Again, with Mahone's involvement, moderate Republicans, alienated by the radicals, formed a new party, the True Republicans, and selected one of Mahone's business associates, Gilbert C. Walker, to be their nominee. The thirty-seven-year-old Walker, a carpetbagger from New York, had settled in Norfolk in 1864 where he became a leading businessman. He had assisted the "Committee of Nine" in their Washington negotiations.

Hoping to benefit from the Republican split, the Conservative Party nominated Colonel Robert Withers, but his candidacy threatened to divide the conservative vote in the state between Withers and Walker, giving the prize to Wells. Conservative leaders, perhaps influenced by the ubiquitous Mahone, withdrew their ticket and coalesced with the True Republicans, agreed as they were on the Underwood Constitution without its disagreeable clauses. Thus the pragmatic conservatives, not the radicals, formed the coalition necessary for victory.

On election day, 6 July 1869, voters overwhelmingly approved the Underwood Constitution and, by margins of 40,000 votes, rejected the "obnoxious clauses." Walker won a comfortable victory over Wells, but the racial dividing line could not have been more obvious: 125,000 whites voted, and Walker received 119,535 votes; 97,000 blacks voted, and Wells received 101,204 votes. Further signifying the end of Republican authority, Conservatives, who would soon absorb the True Republicans and some of the traditionalists, won more than a two-thirds majority in the legislature; but twenty-seven of the new representatives were black, the first of their race to make laws for the Old Dominion.

The joy throughout the Commonwealth at the end of military rule was palpable, with parades, bonfires, and music marking the celebrations in Norfolk and Richmond. Virginia, the only Confederate state to avoid an elected radical Republican government, had been redeemed; conservative white rule had been restored. Proclaimed the *Lynchburg Virginian,* "Shout the glad tidings, Virginia is free! The carpetbag and scalawag power has been broken, and Virginians will rule Virginia." Fulfilling the requirements for readmission, the General Assembly ratified the Fourteenth and Fifteenth Amendments, the latter prohibiting the denial of the right to vote because of "race, color, or previous condition of servitude." On 26 January 1870, President Grant signed the legislation returning Virginia to the Union.

Reconstruction was over, a period uncomfortable for many, comic for others, one of opportunities lost but also of significant advances for black Virginians. What happened in the Old Dominion was of relatively brief duration and far less oppressive and violent than what was happening elsewhere in the South, yet an amicable restoration was not achieved. White Virginians would blame carpetbaggers, bayonets, and federal tyranny for the failure, but in reality it was racism and the memory of the war that denied success. The central issue of Reconstruction was the struggle for interracial democracy, and although briefly experimented with, it was ultimately defeated by white Virginians who made every effort to abort it and white Northerners who, after some half-hearted attempts, lost interest in imposing it. The losers would be African Americans.

❖

The primary issue confronting the victorious Conservatives over the next decade was Virginia's public debt, which had reached $45 million, with wartime interest added to prewar investments in railroad and canal building. The departure of West Virginia, declining land values, and the loss of capital in slaves aggravated the Old Dominion's financial situation. Nevertheless, Governor Walker and the Conservative legislators committed the state to repaying the full debt with interest; it was a question of "the essential credit and unsullied honor of the Commonwealth." The Funding Act of 1871 generously funded the debt with new coupon bonds paying 6 percent guaranteed interest and allowed the coupons to be used to pay state taxes in lieu of cash; West Virginia was expected to pay one-third of the debt, but that had not been negotiated. Virginians owned only one-fourth of the debt. The bill had the support of brokers, speculators, and Northern and British bondholders, for whom honor was secondary to the money made from the financing and payment of the debt; their victory was likely assured with well-placed bribes. James Tice Moore has concluded that the funding bill was "the most disastrous piece of economic legislation in Virginia history. Instead of putting the government on a sound financial basis, . . . it shackled the state into a grinding cycle of deficit spending."

Reaction by the public was swift. Rumors of graft, concerns for unfunded schools, and anger against wealthy bondholders who would be sharing none of the costs of war generated a popular outcry that turned many legislators out of office. Reflecting this discontent, the 1872 assembly voted to suspend the Funding Act, but it was overruled by Governor Walker's veto. An effort to repeal the coupons-for-taxes provision that was robbing the treasury of revenue passed over another veto, but the state Supreme Court of Appeals voided the legislation. Additional attempts over the next few years to modify the act by postponing payment or lowering the interest rate were rejected by the "Funder" Conservatives committed to preserving property rights and Virginia's honor; in their view the debt was a contract that could not be voided without bondholders' consent. Opponents, largely from rural areas, foreseeing higher taxes to pay the debt and declining revenues that would leave state services unfunded, urged a readjustment of the debt downward. Honor, they claimed, could not "buy breakfast or set a leg." Their opposition congealed into a "Readjuster" movement that would challenge Funder authority.

Readjusters found a friendly audience among small farmers, who, since the end of the war, had been in depression-like conditions now worsened by drought and high property taxes that in 1870 constituted 61 percent of state revenue. To the distress of the farmers, railroads were paying practically no taxes at all. Furthermore, producers of fire-cured dark tobacco were facing new competition with the cheaper air-cured white burley of Kentucky.

The breakup of the antebellum plantation system had produced a totally new land and labor situation in Virginia. Without slave labor, Tidewater and Southside tobacco plantations had been divided into smaller parcels, the number of farms doubling but their size reduced by half. Many of the farmers on these lands were marginalized poor whites and the overwhelming number of blacks, who, without the resources to purchase even small landholdings, had entered into sharecropping or tenancy arrangements. In sharecropping, the landowner, often a former slaveholder, paid the laborer a share of the crop, usually about a fourth, and supplied a cabin and the materials and tools necessary for farming. Former slaves preferred sharecropping over the postwar wage labor system for its autonomy and privacy, hoping that it might lead to ownership. To them sharecropping meant shared management with some control over their lives; they would make the decisions about when to work and who would work. In tenancy, the laborer rented the land from the landowner, paying him a portion of the crop or money. Renters usually owned some property of their own such as a mule and tools. In an era of declining crop yields and prices, the small landowners, croppers, and tenants, who were frequently beholden to local merchants for loans on food, seed, and fertilizer, found themselves in an ever-downward cycle of debt. By 1900 nearly a third of Virginia's farmers did not own the land they tilled.

Elsewhere in the Old Dominion, the picture was less bleak, and this is where Conservatives drew most of their support. Upper Piedmont and northern Virginia farmers, whose crops were more diversified, enjoyed greater prosperity and less tenancy. The larger towns and cities that served as agricultural marketplaces and railroad centers were bustling, as were the tobacco factories of Richmond, all to be the heart of a "New South" movement in the following decade. Competition for control of rail lines and markets was fierce, with lobbyists plying lawmakers with passes, money, and liquor in return for charters; several unsavory scandals within the Conservative regime were uncovered, reflective of the corruption nationwide during the Grant years. With many former planters or their sons moving to the cities but often remaining absentee landlords, Virginia's new aristocracy became a mix of new and old breeds who were reconciled to a reconstructed Union but committed to preserving a laissez-faire economic order and the rule of gentlemen.

The end of the war also had a significant impact on the lives of Virginia women. Black women were no longer compelled to work the fields, and planters' wives were doing chores. Although still limited by traditional attitudes against doing work outside the home, women were tolerated in domains deemed appropriate for them: education, benevolence work in orphanages, and temperance; by 1900 they constituted more than half the teachers in public schools, and others started private schools for girls. There was an outpouring of literary work by female Virginia authors such as Mary Virginia Terhune; Amélie Rives; Elizabeth Keckley, a former slave who became Mary Todd Lincoln's confidante; and journalist Orra Langhorne. Although traditional politics remained a man's world, black women were in the forefront of claiming postslavery rights, and a few white women such as Langhorne and Anna Whitehead Bodeker unsuccessfully attempted to gain the suffrage. In 1877 Virginia granted married women the right to own property in their own names, the last state to do so. Upper-class white women also found a new niche that won broad applause across the state: the memorialization of the war. They established cemeteries for Confederate dead and monuments to rebel soldiers through their Ladies Memorial Associations, participated in veterans' reunions, and formed the United Daughters of the Confederacy in 1894 to pay homage to the "Lost Cause."

Virginia's debt dilemma worsened when a financial panic caused by excessive railroad building financed with speculative credit hit the country in 1873. It lasted the rest of the decade, bringing severe unemployment and industrial strife to the North. Richmond's Freedman's Savings Bank closed its doors, wiping out $166,000 in accounts, including those of black mutual-aid associations and churches. The city's streets were filled with "able-bodied paupers, vagrants, and tramps," and the numbers on outdoor relief doubled in two years. William Mahone's consolidated Virginia railroad system went into receivership. Old Dominion farmers experienced sharp price declines that threw them deeper into debt and made it harder for them to pay taxes. The depression further crimped Virginia's ability to finance its debt. By mid-decade the state's surplus had become a deficit; it could not pay the interest on the bonds; two-fifths of its revenue was in worthless coupons that could only be retired, not spent; and it was borrowing to pay its bills.

The election of a new governor in 1873 brought no relief. James Lawson Kemper was the first of seven consecutive former Confederates to serve as governor: "Virginians ruling Virginia." A brigadier general wounded in Pickett's charge at Gettysburg, he had served as Speaker of the House of Delegates before the war. His victory confirmed the dominance of the Conservative Party, but Kemper was no Confederate reactionary, being reasonably impartial in addressing issues of race, national reconciliation, and finances. On the debt question he called the Funding Act a "disastrous mistake" and invited bondholders to accept a reduction in the interest on bonds; but failing to get assembly approval or bondholders' consent, he embarked upon a modest economy program to cut

WILLIAM HENRY RUFFNER

administrative expenses. However, he could do nothing to alleviate the shortage of funds that was adversely affecting schools, asylums, and prisons. Virginia could not even afford to participate in the nation's centennial celebration. Desperate for revenue, the state expanded a convict lease system instituted in 1870 whereby prisoners from the crowded penitentiary were hired out at twenty-five to forty cents a day to private contractors who worked and maintained them in quarries and on railroads and the Kanawha Canal. The result was a horrible living environment that in some cases produced a death rate three times that of prisoners left in the penitentiary.

The primary victim of Virginia's debt problem and the depression was the state's new educational system. The Underwood Constitution had mandated public schools, and over the objections of the traditionalists, one of whom labeled universal education a "Yankee error," the new system was created in 1870 with enthusiastic support from freedpeople, poor whites, and middle-class groups, the very people for whom there had been few schools in the antebellum period. William Henry Ruffner was appointed superintendent of public instruction. A man of wide-ranging interests in scientific and social questions who had opposed slavery, Ruffner became an advocate of public free schools for both races, believing education produced more productive workers who contributed to economic growth and less criminal behavior. He designed a statewide system of racially segregated schools as mandated by the assembly. In the first year (1870–71), 130,000 students were taught in 2,900 schools; within five years enrollment reached 185,000. To advance higher education, Virginia used federal land grant funds in 1872 to create the Virginia Agricultural and Mechanical College (later Virginia Tech) and to promote agricultural and technical education at Hampton Normal and Agricultural Institute. Hampton had been founded as a teacher-training school for African Americans in 1868 by the American Missionary Association and the paternalistic Samuel Chapman Armstrong; 84 percent of its first twenty classes became teachers.

However, Virginia's efforts to operate a system of public education foundered on inadequate funding. Most rural schools were one-room, single-teacher schools; terms were approximately five months; and teachers' pay averaged $30 a month. Even before the depression hit, the assembly was cutting school appropriations because tax payments with the worthless bond coupons were reducing revenue. By 1876 schools were receiving half a million dollars less than what they were entitled to from the capitation and property taxes; two years later, many schools closed. In a contest with bondholders, education lost, as Governor Kemper had the state auditor divert funds from the schools to pay debt interest. By publicly blaming the loss of revenue for schools on debt payments, Ruffner inadvertently embarrassed the Funders—often called "Bourbons" for their defense of the aristocratic old order—and lent support to the Readjusters.

A revolution was on the horizon, and the leading insurgent was William Mahone. At five feet, five inches tall, weighing not much more than 100 pounds, squeaky-voiced Billy Mahone did not cut an imposing figure, but no one had a greater impact on Virginia in the two decades after the Civil War than he. A native of Southampton County and a graduate of the Virginia Military Institute, he embarked upon a railroad career, demonstrating both engineering and administrative talents that enabled him to become president and chief engineer of the Norfolk and Petersburg Railroad in 1861. During the war his leadership skills elevated him to a generalship in the Confederate army, and he achieved fame as the "hero of the Crater" and the "savior of Petersburg," now his hometown. One of his soldiers called him "the biggest little man God Almighty ever made."

After the war Mahone returned to the railroad business with the dream of merging three lines across southern Virginia that would permit him to control all the traffic between Norfolk and Bristol. Needing legislative approval for such a consolidation, Mahone entered the political arena, where he influenced the selection of Governor Walker and won assembly approval for the creation of the Atlantic, Mississippi and Ohio Railroad, a name which suggested an even more grandiose Mahone idea. His plans hit a snag, however, when the assembly, at Governor Walker's request, also agreed to sell railroad stock owned by the state. This opened the door for the Pennsylvania Central Railroad and the Baltimore

and Ohio Railroad and its affiliate, the Orange and Alexandria, to challenge Mahone's domination, much to the delight of Lynchburg and Richmond businessmen who preferred competition, not monopoly. Next to
the debt question, the battle over railroad issues—routes, taxes, regulation, and ownership—consumed more attention than any other subject
in the 1870s.

Competition with the Northern companies and the Panic of 1873
thwarted Mahone's plans for a railroad empire. Perhaps piqued at the
Funders, on whom he blamed his downfall, he turned his enormous en-
ergies and talents to politics, joining the Readjuster movement in a bid
for the governorship in 1877. He demanded "a complete readjustment of
the debt" and attacked the diversion of funds from public schools as "sub-
versive of popular rights," but his reputation as a railroad tycoon and
political manipulator denied him the Conservative nomination, which
went to Frederick Holliday of Winchester.

Readjuster advocates, however, supported by public dissatisfaction
with debt payments to wealthy bondholders while schools were closing,
won enough seats in the 1878 assembly to pass legislation to restrict the
use of coupons and to guarantee funds for state government and schools;
the bills would render debt payment at the present levels problematic.
Governor Holliday, who during the campaign had promised to leave the
issue in the hands of the legislature, vetoed the bills, calling free schools
"not a necessity" but "a luxury . . . to be paid for, like any other luxury,
by the people who wish their benefits." Reacting to such insensitivity,

WILLIAM MAHONE

Mahone called for the creation of a new political party to contest Funder-Conservative control on a platform of readjustment, lower taxes, and public education. In February 1879 farmers from the Valley and Southwest, blacks, independents, Republicans, and a few Conservatives, led by Mahone, James Barbour, "Parson" John Massey, and Harrison H. Riddleberger, enthusiastically launched the Readjuster Party. "Our cause . . . is the cause of the people," proclaimed Massey.

African Americans, whose political influence had been diminishing since the end of Reconstruction, constituted the largest bloc in the new party. Their voting had declined under Conservative legislation that gerrymandered heavily populated black districts, made poll tax payments a requirement for voting, and denied the vote to those convicted for petty larceny. They chafed at codification of earlier antimiscegenation statutes that they argued were emblematic of political inequality. The *Washington National Republican* editorialized, "What need of a Ku Klux in a State where the Legislative Assembly does so well the work attempted by the Klan in other states?" Betrayed by the Conservatives and ignored by a weakened Republican Party, many blacks turned to the Readjusters.

In a campaign eerily reminiscent of the bitterly fought governor's race in 1869 between radicals and conservatives, the Readjusters, benefiting from Mahone's organizational brilliance, defeated the Funders in the 1879 elections. With the help of thirteen black Republicans in the assembly, they began dismantling the Conservative edifice. The Riddleberger bill totally restructured Virginia's debt, repudiating two-fifths of it and repaying it over fifty years with new bonds that paid only 3 percent interest and carried no tax-receivable coupons. Use of the old coupons was severely restricted. Readjusters did not have the votes to override Governor Holliday's predictable veto, but they confidently awaited the next gubernatorial election. In the interim they elected Mahone to the U.S. Senate and filled other state positions with their supporters.

To ensure victory in the 1881 gubernatorial race, Mahone entered into a coalition with Republicans. The party of Lincoln had not done well in Virginia since its defeat in 1869. Fragmented by the debt issue, the minority Republicans lost ground, offering no gubernatorial candidate in 1877, its seats in the legislature dwindling to fourteen in 1878, and many of its black members departing for the Readjusters. But they still held the trump card of federal patronage, which Mahone pursued by helping Republicans organize the U.S. Senate, for which he was rewarded with federal jobs for Readjusters. In 1881 both Readjusters and Republicans pragmatically rallied behind the gubernatorial candidacy of William Cameron, who had compiled an enviable reform record as mayor of Petersburg; he won a decisive victory over state Senator John W. Daniel of Lynchburg, the Conservatives' most eloquent defender.

Political success expanded the Readjusters' vision of the possible, and what ensued was one of the most remarkable chapters in the commonwealth's history. Readjusters attacked the elitist old order with a biracial coalition that reformed Virginia society along more liberal lines: in James Moore's words, "a Virginia with opportunity for the able, democracy for the masses, and public education for all." The first order of business was passage of the Riddleberger bill that restructured payment of the state debt downward. In addition to settling the debt question, which saved Virginia millions of dollars, Readjusters cut property taxes, increased assessments on railroads, imposed regulations on corporations, and improved tax-collecting machinery to turn the state's deficit into a surplus.

Significant funds were channeled to the schools: 90 percent of all school taxes would be retained by localities; annual payments of $100,000 would be made until all previously diverted funds were restored; and $500,000 from the reorganization of the Norfolk and Western Railroad would be distributed: $400,000 to schools and $100,000 for the establishment of the Normal and Collegiate Institute for Negroes (later Virginia State University). The result was a spectacular increase in the number of white and black schools and in enrollments. Appropriations for colleges, prisons, and mental hospitals increased, and an asylum for blacks was constructed. Readjusters repealed the poll tax as a prerequisite for voting and abolished the whipping post, a punishment long condemned by black Virginians because persons punished by whippings lost their vote. Insurgency opened the door to a more democratic community that Reconstruction had not realized.

However, the Readjuster coalition soon collapsed of its own missteps and the challenge of a reinvigorated Conservative Party relying on the race issue. Bound by common commitment to debt reduction, the unstable coalition broke down once the major goal had been achieved. Mahone's heavy-handed leadership generated dissent over patronage and power-sharing arrangements that sidetracked Readjuster efforts to solidify control of the legislature. His affiliation with the Republican Party led to accusations of selling out to the enemy. Several party leaders revolted; "Parson" Massey even went over to the Conservatives. "Mahoneism" came to stigmatize everything the reformers had done.

But it was the exploitation of racial fears that was central to the demise of the Readjusters. Labeled the radical work of "niggers and poor white men," their record was criticized for endangering white supremacy and returning Virginia to dreaded radical Reconstruction. And the Conservatives were partially correct. The freedmen did play an essential role in the success of the Readjusters, although they were nowhere close to controlling state politics. They had regained some of the political power lost since Reconstruction, now holding sixteen seats in the assembly, and they had benefited from the legislation that struck down old symbols of subservience and improved their opportunities for advancement with jobs and education. Patronage had made them teachers, prison guards, postmasters, and state office clerks. In Danville, Hampton, and Petersburg, they had assumed positions on town councils, school boards, police forces, and as justices of the peace. Such advances were viewed as a threat to white rule, although, as Jane Dailey has postulated, they were a greater threat to white identity. Matters of honor, masculinity, sex, and the protection of white women were at stake. Readjusters were accused of "mongrelizing" Virginia, "making white men into niggers."

Mahone and the Readjusters were not racial liberals of the twentieth-century variety; their political motives for using black votes are obvious. They, too, remained defenders of white supremacy, but they drew a distinction between political equality and social equality, deciding that the former did not require the latter, whereas most whites thought the two were inseparable. And in the face of Conservative charges of "Africanization," they did not back away from their commitment to interracial democracy. They were ahead of their time, and it would cost them dearly.

Conservatives prepared to take advantage of the race issue and Readjuster defections. In the 1883 legislative elections, they cast aside the Conservative label for that of the Democracy, contrasting themselves with Mahone's Republicanism and "boss rule." Handed control of the party apparatus, Congressman John S. Barbour, an old railroad foe of Mahone's, reorganized the party and attracted railroad money to finance their effort. With a U.S. Supreme Court decision upholding a portion of the debt settlement, the new Democrats reluctantly accepted the Riddleberger solution to the debt problem, hoping to eliminate that unpopular and emotional issue from political debate. In the final days of the campaign, they shamelessly played the race card. Proclaimed John W. Daniel, "I am a Democrat because I am a white man and a Virginian." Charges of promoting social equality, miscegenation, and mixed schools were leveled against the Readjusters. Propaganda about the "black rule" of Danville irritated tensions there, producing a riot only days before the election in which one white and four blacks were killed. The issue was apparently one of controlling sidewalk space, but Democrats publicized the incident as the forerunner of a race war. In such a climate, they handily defeated the Readjusters, winning two-thirds of the legislative seats.

Over the next few years, through purges, patronage, gerrymandering, and new election laws, Democrats ended the insurgency and Virginia's brief fling with two-party competition and racial equality. Despite national Republican support, Mahone's effectiveness as a Virginia leader also came to an end. In future elections white solidarity would be trumpeted to obstruct black participation. A new patriarchal order would prevail, and the promise of full freedom was deferred.

SOURCES CONSULTED

James D. Anderson, *The Education of Blacks in the South, 1860–1935* (1988); Jane Turner Censer, *The Reconstruction of White Southern Womenhood, 1865–1895* (2003); Jane Dailey, *Before Jim Crow: The Politics of Race in Postemancipation Virginia* (2000); Robert Francis Engs, *Freedom's First Generation: Black Hampton, Virginia, 1861–1890* (1979); Michael Hucles, "Many Voices, Similar Concerns: Traditional Methods of African-American Political Activity in Norfolk, Virginia, 1865–1875," *VMHB* (Oct. 1992); Richard Hume, "The Membership of the Virginia Constitutional Convention of 1867–1868," *VMHB* (Oct. 1978); Richard G. Lowe, "Local Black Leaders during Reconstruction in Virginia," *VMHB* (April 1995); Lowe, *Republicans and Reconstruction in Virginia, 1856–1870* (1991); Jack P. Maddex Jr., *The Virginia Conservatives, 1867–1879* (1970); Edna Greene Medford, "Land and Labor: The Quest for Black Economic Independence on Virginia's Lower Peninsula, 1865–1880," *VMHB* (Oct. 1992); Allen W. Moger, *Virginia: Bourbonism to Byrd, 1870–1925* (1968); James Tice Moore, *Two Paths to the New South: The Virginia Debt Controversy, 1870–1883* (1974); Louis Moore, "The Elusive Center: Virginia Politics and the General Assembly, 1869–1871," *VMHB* (April 1995); Lynda J. Morgan, *Emancipation in Virginia's Tobacco Belt, 1850–1870* (1992); Crandall A. Shifflett, *Patronage and Poverty in the Tobacco South: Louisa County, 1860–1900* (1982).

12

PROGRESS AND PRESERVATION

1885–1915

The defeat of the Readjusters coincided with the emergence in the late nineteenth century of a Confederate cult or "Lost Cause" myth that denied that slavery was the cause of the Civil War and blamed the defeat solely on Northern numbers. The myth allowed Southerners to escape responsibility for the war and defeat while basking in the glow of heroic behavior and smug superiority. They raised wartime defenders to the level of stainless perfection and turned Richmond into a shrine with its Confederate White House and a Monument Avenue lined with the statues of the great Confederates. In a more practical way, the cult was used by Democratic politicians to recapture and retain power by vilifying Republicans and African Americans for their disloyalty to the "Cause." The message was sounded at the dedication of every Confederate monument in courthouse squares and cemeteries across the Old Dominion; and for the last quarter of the century, Virginians elected Confederate veterans to be their governor. The memory of the "Lost Cause" would be an impediment inhibiting an emancipation offered by New South and Progressive reform movements.

Their reverence for the past did not make Virginians totally insensitive to the embarrassment of poverty and the lure of new opportunities. They enthusiastically embarked upon an economic revival in the 1880s known as the New South movement that envisioned a new day for the region if it could overcome its nostalgia for the past and stimulate new ways of implementing capitalistic thinking. In Thomas Rosser's words, "Precedents are valueless, circumstances are constantly changing, and to succeed you must discover and apply new ways and means of progress and development." Given voice by *Atlanta Constitution* editor Henry Grady, the

New South Gospel aimed at promoting regional economic development by diversifying agriculture and expanding industry. Emerging from the depression of the 1870s, Virginia's boosters included Confederate heroes Rosser, Jedediah Hotchkiss, and John Imboden, whose links to the past provided legitimacy for this future-oriented endeavor. They extolled the plentiful resources of coal and iron and the economic opportunities available in Virginia with the hope of restoring the commonwealth to "a foremost rank amongst the States of the Union." Self-promotion and the pursuit of wealth gripped the Old Dominion as Northern capital seemingly invaded every town and hamlet.

The heart of this activity was railroad building, which over the last three decades of the century increased track in Virginia by 2,380 miles. The railroad had become the transforming agent in American life: a stimulant for economic growth, a vehicle for travel and opportunity, the arbiter of success in the competitive world of business, and the regulator of new lifestyles driven by the minutes and hours of time schedules and the recently created national time zones. Fueled by the mining of coal deposits in Southwest Virginia—the Pocahontas field was among the largest bituminous deposits in the country—new rail lines stretched from the mountains and the Ohio River to the expanding ports of Norfolk and Newport News. There railway magnate Collis Huntington, owner of the Chesapeake and Ohio Railroad, established a new shipbuilding facility, the Newport News Shipbuilding and Dry Dock Company, which became the largest manufacturing plant in Virginia, employing 6,000 men and constructing ships for the U.S. Navy. From 1883 to 1890 the Norfolk and Western Railroad, reorganized in 1881 from the remains of Billy Mahone's rail lines, increased its hauled tonnage of coal and coke from 105,805 tons to 2.7 million tons, making Norfolk the largest coaling station in the world. The city was a leading exporter of lumber, cotton, and peanuts as well. The area's confidence was reflected in the grand hotels constructed at Old Point Comfort.

Villages and towns hustled to be watering stations along the way. Transformed from a sparsely populated agricultural area into a heavily populated industrial region, Southwest Virginia promoted its coalfields, its forests, and its resort possibilities, advertising Wytheville as the "Saratoga of the South." When the Norfolk and Western and Shenandoah Valley Railroads chose the hamlet of Big Lick to be the site of their new machine shops for the construction of locomotives and freight cars, within a decade it reached a population of 25,000 and was renamed Roanoke. Said a New Yorker: "From Roanoke, through Southwest Virginia to Birmingham, Alabama, a wave of speculation is rolling, white-capped with dollars of the rich and poor. . . . Dazzling bewildered excitement is everything. Where cannons boomed in the sixties, dollars are rattling now."

Elsewhere, the mass production of cigarettes, fostered by the cultivation of bright leaf tobacco that was replacing Turkish imports, revolutionized the tobacco industry. This new product helped turn a war-devastated Richmond into a banking center and home of the South's first central telephone exchange and the nation's first extensive electric street railway system (1888). In 1880 the city was the second largest manufacturing center in the South, a leader in flour milling, ironmaking, and tobacco production. Its ninety-five tobacco companies employed half the city's workers, a majority of whom were African Americans. During the next decade its investments in manufacturing increased 250 percent.

To capitalize on changing consumer tastes, John Allen and Lewis Ginter, a New York carpetbagger who had served in the Confederate army, entered into a partnership in 1872 to manufacture cigarettes in Richmond. Relying on innovative marketing techniques and cheap female and child labor, they made Richmond into the cigarette capital of the world. Seeking to expand their operations and lower costs, Allen and Ginter sponsored Virginian James Bonsack's invention of a new cigarette-making machine, one of which could replace forty-eight workers rolling cigarettes by hand. However, they failed to utilize it adequately and

TOBACCO FACTORY, RICHMOND

were forced to merge with James Buchanan Duke of Durham, North Carolina. Duke had gained a near monopoly on the use of the Bonsack machine and established the American Tobacco Company trust, which eventually controlled 95 percent of the cigarette market. In 1888 Richmond, now the state's largest city with over 80,000 residents, many of whom were enjoying electric streetlights and telephones, held a grand exposition to highlight recent improvements in agriculture and industry in the Old Dominion that demonstrated a "true spirit of enterprise and progress."

Under the banner of the New South, Danville prospered as a center of tobacco marketing and textile manufacturing, while real estate booms hit Norfolk, Lynchburg, Petersburg, and Portsmouth. Flour mills, tobacco factories, iron furnaces and foundries, and fertilizer and furniture plants were mushrooming everywhere. Towns changed their names to Basic City, Clifton Forge, and Bessemer to suggest an urban, industrial development that they hoped would lure investors. Boosters claimed Iron Gate was "destined to be one of the largest cities in the state." When Lynchburg was ridiculed for enticing a chewing gum factory to town, the local paper replied, "Money's money whether it is made in iron or soap, pig's feet or pickles, chewing tobacco or chewing gum; and just so a man or community makes enough of it the world will not be fastidious about the manner of making it." By 1900 Virginia was first in the South in the value of manufactured products, with tobacco, flour milling, lumber, iron and steel, and general shop repairing leading the way.

Yet the New South prosperity did not run deep. Much of the capital for this expansion, estimated to be $100 million, had come from the North, and the profits generated were returned to those investors. Most Virginia railroads were controlled by Northern corporations. Coal mining and coke manufacturing around Big Stone Gap attracted, in the words of one speculator, "shrewd investors, . . . land sharks, . . . real estate agents, curbstone brokers, saloon-keepers, gamblers, card sharks—all the flotsam and jetsam of the terrible boom"—people looking for the quick buck who added little to the community and demonstrated less concern for the environment. Although some of this development was financed by local citizens, particularly in the coal and textile businesses, little of the money trickled down to the working classes. Much of the industrial growth was in the extractive industries of lumbering and mining, whose unsafe and low-paying jobs attracted poor whites fleeing rural poverty and blacks and European immigrant groups seeking new opportunities. According to Crandall Shifflett, "Miners worked . . . in the dark, sometimes in pools of water, at difficult tasks for long hours in constant danger and uncertainty. Falls of rock and coal from the roof and explosions of methane gas and coal dust placed the miners at tremendous risk." The worst mining disaster in Virginia history occurred at the Pocahontas mine in 1884 when explosions caused by unvented methane gas killed up to 150 miners.

Furthermore, 80 percent of Virginia's 1.7 million citizens in 1890 remained rural residents, for whom there was no boom. They were already in the grip of an agricultural depression complicated by overproduction and the new labor system of sharecropping when the panic of 1893 caused a major contraction that plunged farmers deeper into debt. At the same time it wiped out many of the newest industrial enterprises that had been financed with little more than boosterism. The experience of the small town of Buena Vista was typical. Trying to build on its iron furnaces and "mountain of iron," its citizens excitedly ventured into hotel building, electrification of the town, and real estate development, only to see the rampant speculation collapse with the onrush of depression. Even the prosperous railroads went into bankruptcy and reorganization that often led to more outside control. The gains of the New South were substantial, but they did not enable the region to close the economic gap with the North; indeed, Virginia's national ranking was declining. Although the richest Southern state in per capita wealth, Virginia placed below the poorest non-Southern state. Ranking as the fifth most populous state in 1860, the Old Dominion dropped to seventeenth by 1900.

Nor was there much interest among business and political leaders in improving the lives of the working class. This indifference was most noticeable in the growing textile mill and mining communities, which often became little more than feudal villages where workers relied upon the generosity of paternalistic owners for their existence. Coming from rural poverty, they developed few skills other than those demanded by the mill or the mine and so found themselves trapped in low-wage jobs in an environment that made them even more dependent: stores, homes, schools, and churches all provided by management. Some workers were paid in scrip, redeemable only at the company store. The New Jersey–owned Stonega Coal and Coke Company pursued a policy of "contentment sociology": "Contentment is necessary for the stability of labor and prevention of unions and lockouts. Playgrounds, amusement halls, night schools, and domestic science classes have been carefully worked out for the benefit and contentment of the employee and his family." Accommodating to the system, workers developed a strong sense of community in the towns through the shared hardships of ever-present hazards and low pay balanced by the joys of baseball teams and quilting parties that relieved the monotony of the place.

Perhaps the worst feature of this paternalistic system was the utilization of child labor. Ten- and twelve-year-olds were a common sight in the cotton mills, coal mines, and tobacco factories of Virginia, their

STONEGA COAL CAMP, 1920

development stunted by limited educational opportunities and employment in unsafe conditions at low wages. Southern mill owners were not
inclined to dispense with child labor because it provided a competitive
edge over Northern textile mills that had to abide by child labor laws.
Parents, who needed all the income they could get, did not strenuously
object to the practice.

Indeed, workers rarely protested their working and living conditions
or attempted to unionize. Cheap labor could easily be replaced. Furthermore, whites feared that unrest would lead to racial competition. At the
time, cotton mill labor was practically all white, and tobacco factories
gave the better-paying skilled jobs to whites, reserving rehandling and
stemming for blacks. Workers traditionally deferred to owners, while,
paradoxically, a virulent individualism balked at "outside agitators."

Management's concern for profits and control, combined with a
public fear of collective worker action, further inhibited the union movement in Virginia. Nonetheless, the Knights of Labor achieved some organizing victories in the 1880s among tobacco workers and urban tradesmen, winning strikes for wage increases, attacking the use of convict
labor, and helping elect black councilmen in Richmond and Lynchburg.
Defying local sentiment, the union organized assemblies for women and
blacks as well as white male workers and held its 1886 national convention in Richmond, whose local Knight assemblies totaled 10,000 workers
of both races, including two-thirds of the tobacco workers. However,
subsequent strike defeats, inadequate financial resources, and association

with the Chicago Haymarket bombing in 1886 destroyed the Knights, who despite their liberal orientation were not able to overcome the racial tensions that inhibited white and black workers from uniting in common cause. A handful of conservative American Federation of Labor trade unions, including metalworkers, machinists, and railroad workers, replaced the Knights, but they represented only 10 percent of the Richmond workforce and did not contest traditional patterns of racial segregation.

The failure to achieve a broader-based and longer-lasting economic transformation is attributable in part to prejudice and paternalism and the power of the "Lost Cause" mindset that consumed even the new industrial entrepreneurs of the New South. They desired economic growth but not at the expense of their elitist political and social order or a continuing glorification of the Confederacy. As Richmond merchant Lewis Harvie Blair said in 1896, "We look to the past, and not to the risen sun; we live in the past, and not in the present." Ellen Glasgow's most perceptive novels about Virginia life emphasized this stifling sentimentality about the old order that forever seemed to obstruct the road to progress. Richmond, which was already losing the race for tobacco manufacturing dominance to North Carolina, lacked, in Michael Chesson's view, the necessary entrepreneurial spirit to overcome tradition, sentiment, racism, and its "passion for the Lost Cause."

The erection of the Monument Avenue statue of Robert E. Lee in 1890, taller by a few inches than that of George Washington in Capitol Square, confirmed the real affections of Richmonders, as did the 200,000 observers who turned out for the unveiling of Jefferson Davis's monument in 1907. In 1888 Virginia established a modest pension program for its Confederate veterans that by 1912 consumed 11 percent of the state's budget. Commenting on the 1896 Confederate reunion that attracted thousands of veterans, the *Richmond Times* stated, "We have no apology to offer the world for the love we bear the fallen Confederacy." One of the more extreme representatives of this backward orientation was Robert Lewis Dabney, a Presbyterian minister who had served on Stonewall Jackson's staff. Dabney rejected the New South ideology and the evils of modern society: corporations, factories, public schools, and free blacks, all of which violated biblical authority and the principles of the Old South.

Confronting such attitudes, Lewis Blair remonstrated that prosperity "depended on the elevation of the Negroes," yet Virginia's African Americans, now one-third of the population, were being excluded from equal opportunity by a resurgence of antebellum racial attitudes and practices that were exacerbated by deteriorating economic conditions. The defeat of the Readjusters and return to power of the Democrats had quickened the political emasculation of black Virginians, undermining the gains made during Reconstruction. The Anderson-McCormick election law in

1884 put appointment of election boards in the hands of a now Democrat-controlled legislature determined that there be no future biracial coalitions to disturb its mastery of the state. The *Richmond Dispatch* called the bill "a white man's law. It operates to perpetuate the rule of the white man in Virginia."

Billy Mahone made one last effort to revive the Readjuster-Republican coalition in his 1889 gubernatorial race, but despite significant black support, he was soundly trounced by Philip Watkins McKinney, who unashamedly made the specter of black rule the key issue of the campaign. Eighty-seven blacks had served in the General Assembly between 1869 and 1890; by 1891, with black voting in a free fall, there were none. When Joseph Holmes attempted to run for the legislature the following year, he was murdered during a campaign speech. The Walton Act of 1894, which provided for a secret ballot, increased the likelihood of voting irregularities and further restricted black voting by placing a premium on literacy. There was a growing movement to eliminate the black vote altogether through constitutional revision, ostensibly to eliminate election fraud but more likely to advance white supremacy.

In the social realm no legal form of discrimination had been imposed, and African Americans continued to have access to public accommodations, but the practice of racial separation on railway cars and in hotels was growing. Black Virginians searched for friends in radical labor unions and in the Farmers' Alliance movement, but at every turn they confronted discrimination in housing and jobs as well as at the ballot box that prevented development of a biracial class consciousness. Editorialized the *Richmond Times,* "The black man must build his own society, for race prejudice . . . is sufficient to keep him from entering the inner circle of the white man." Not surprisingly, the out-migration of blacks from Virginia proceeded apace.

Virginia had the fewest lynchings among Southern states due to a traditional commitment to law and order and greater economic diversification that required, and thus tolerated, more varied black employment. Because white Virginians believed they could maintain racial control without resorting to violence, Ku Klux Klan activity had been insignificant in the state. Nevertheless, in the volatile period of New South industrialization that followed the racially charged years of the Readjusters, white anxiety over job and sexual competition led to a spate of lynchings, with black victims outnumbering whites five to one. Four black miners were murdered in Clifton Forge in 1891, and four black railroad workers were hanged in Richlands in 1893, all for fighting with whites, not for raping white women, which was the usual justification for lynching. John Mitchell, the fearless black editor of the *Richmond Planet,* crusaded against this mob violence, encouraging blacks to fight back:

"A Winchester rifle is a mighty convenient thing when two-legged animals are prowling around your house in the dead of night." Local officials and governors seemingly turned a blind eye to the murders, but an incredibly brutal atrocity in Roanoke in 1893, in which the victim was hanged and his body mutilated and cremated, finally caused an ashamed state leadership and public to question the lawlessness and institute measures to prevent a reoccurrence. Thereafter, Virginia's governors were less reluctant to use the militia to protect the accused, and lynchings declined. Governor Charles O'Ferrall, in particular, vehemently condemned mob activity, dispatching troops to suppress possible violence and urging passage of antilynching laws. On the other hand, imprisoned blacks who escaped lynch law faced the possibility of being leased out to private companies to serve their sentences or pay their fines. Convict leasing was not as widely used in Virginia as in the rest of the South, but it was highly discriminatory; in 1877, 561 blacks but not a single white were serving as leased labor.

In spite of these obstacles, African American Virginians were making remarkable contributions to state and nation. The first black-owned bank in America was chartered in Richmond in 1888, and although its life was brief, the Savings Bank of the Grand Fountain United Order of True Reformers, most of whose owners were former slaves, had a positive impact on the formation of other black businesses and associations. Booker T. Washington, a native of Franklin County and a product of Hampton Institute, was now the president of Tuskegee Institute in Alabama and the acknowledged leader of black Americans; his successor at Tuskegee would be educator Robert Russa Moton, born in Amelia County. Carter G. Woodson of Buckingham County would become known as the father of black history, promoting its study while producing a dozen books on the subject. Richmond's Maggie Walker, founder of a department store, a newspaper, and St. Luke Penny Savings Bank, became the first woman bank president in the country. Virginia's first black congressman was John Mercer Langston. Born in Louisa County to a white planter and his freed slave, Langston was educated at Oberlin College and went on to become dean of the law school at Howard University, minister to Haiti, and the first president of Virginia Normal and Collegiate Institute. He ran for Congress in 1888 and was declared to have lost in a three-man race, but he contested the results and won the seat only months before the term expired; he was defeated for reelection in 1890.

By the mideighties, the Democratic Party in Virginia, through its careful utilization of the race card and its alliances with big business, had finally secured political control of the state. Republicans and Readjusters could not survive their affiliation with emancipation and "Black Reconstruction." Many of these Democratic leaders, including Senators John W.

JOHN MERCER LANGSTON   BOOKER T. WASHINGTON

MAGGIE WALKER

Daniel, who took Mahone's Senate seat, and John S. Barbour, were owners, directors, or legal counsels of railroads. Having reorganized the party, Barbour led it to victory in the 1885 governor's race by exploiting the "Lost Cause" with candidate Fitzhugh Lee, Jeb Stuart's cavalry lieutenant and nephew of Robert E. Lee. Having redeemed the state from Mahoneism, Democrats would not lose another gubernatorial election for eighty-four years. The portly Lee was little more than a figurehead for the emerging Democratic machine, presiding over the exhilaration of New South activity and promoting national reconciliation. In the words of Harry Readnour, his "greatest success was his increasing personification of the 'Confederate cult,' which flowered during his tenure amid monument dedications, memorial services, and reunions."

Ironically, Northerners, too, adopted an attitude of reconciliation, delighting in the novels of Virginian Thomas Nelson Page that sentimentally worshipped antebellum plantation life and accepting the Supreme Court's 1896 decision in *Plessy v. Ferguson* that opened the door for Southern states to enact racial segregation laws. Further efforts to enforce black voting rights were defeated in Congress. The inclusion of Robert E. Lee on the first list of distinguished Americans to be inducted into the Hall of Fame reflected this spirit of reunion.

The Spanish-American War in 1898 became another vehicle for national unity. Ex-Confederate general Fitzhugh Lee was appointed a major general in the United States Volunteer Army and sent to Cuba to subdue the Spanish. Moreover, 15,000 Virginians enthusiastically renewed their national loyalty by volunteering for service in Cuba, where one of their own, Dr. Walter Reed, an army physician from Gloucester County, conducted experiments that confirmed the mosquito as the carrier of yellow fever, a discovery that led to the eradication of this deadly disease.

For black soldiers, the war was a less salutary experience. Having successfully lobbied to get black officers for their militia units, black militiamen protested the subsequent decision to replace blacks with white officers, for which they were charged with mutiny and labeled the "mutinous Sixth Virginia." Black newspapers called them the "immortal Sixth Virginia" for confronting the discrimination. At Camp Haskell, Georgia, several of the black soldiers chopped down a local tree known as "the hanging tree." Demanding equal treatment in Macon, Georgia facilities, they were arrested and jailed for twenty days. After the war Virginia prevented blacks from continuing to serve in the state militia.

During Governor McKinney's term, Virginia moved closer to a settlement of its troublesome prewar debt problem. The Riddleberger solution, although accepted by the Democrats, had proved unworkable and had been overturned by a Supreme Court ruling in 1885. After another lengthy and acrimonious debate with bondholders, the Olcott Settlement of 1892 extended the interest payment plan to 100 years and increased the size of the debt to be paid off by several million dollars, but kept it well under the original debt. Virginia's honor was secured but at the cost of neglecting necessary public services. The battle to determine West Virginia's share of the debt continued until 1918 when, under court order, that state agreed to pay one-third.

Senator Barbour's death in 1892 left open the party's leadership position, which was filled by Thomas Staples Martin, a modest, dignified lawyer from Scottsville who had an amazing facility for organization. More comfortable in boardrooms than on the stump, he was so unimposing a political figure that his enemies frequently misjudged him. After building a successful legal practice in central Virginia, he became counsel for the Chesapeake and Ohio Railroad, whose money he dispensed to candidates who promised to support legislation beneficial to his client. At the same time, he cozied up to Democratic leaders in the state and moved into the inner circle of power. When Barbour's Senate seat became available, Martin called upon his considerable resources, including railroad money, to curry favor among state legislators and to defeat popular former governor Lee for the position, thus establishing himself as the leader of the Democratic Party in the Old Dominion.

A key Martin operative in the Senate contest was Hal Flood. A young lawyer from Appomattox who had won a House of Delegates seat in 1887 and moved to the state Senate in 1891, Flood was attracted to Martin by his pro-business positions and his pragmatic politics. Relying on railroad money, the support of well-to-do farmers and businessmen, and the race issue, they constructed a political organization that would endure well into the twentieth century. But it was not easily accomplished. Over the next ten years, they confronted Populists and progressives intent on destroying the machine by democratizing the election process and regulating the railroads. Leaders of the "Organization," as the machine was known, were not always victorious; but their ability to unite and to compromise when their survival depended upon it ensured their longevity. In their favor was the decline of the Republican Party in the state, which, except in the Valley and the Southwest, could not overcome the legacies of war and Reconstruction and Mahoneism.

Farm unrest, depression, and free silver threatened to overturn the new machine even before it was up and running. Virginia's farmers had not enjoyed even the whiff of prosperity that the New South was producing. A national depression in farm commodity prices over the last quarter of the nineteenth century caused the price of wheat in Virginia to drop from $1 a bushel in 1883 to 51 cents in 1894; corn declined from 82 cents a bushel in 1882 to 29 cents in 1896; farm income was down by one-third to one-half. From 1860 to 1900 the number of farms tripled while their average size was reduced by a third. Tenancy and sharecropping had risen to 31 percent of the total number of farmers, being particularly high in the Southside tobacco counties, now competing with North Carolina farms for the growing of bright leaf tobacco, the staple of the cigarette industry. Having a smaller area of the sandy soil appropriate for bright leaf production, Virginia lost its position as the leading tobacco producer to North Carolina and Kentucky, a great irony since it had been Colonel Robert Ragland of Halifax County who was responsible for the seed production and curing formula for the "yellow leaf." Truck farming on the Eastern Shore was enjoying a modest expansion because of improved rail connections to the North, but elsewhere low crop prices, declining land values, inefficient farming practices, and competition with world supplies threatened the stability of rural regions.

With the establishment of the Virginia Agricultural and Mechanical College in 1872, a state Department of Agriculture in 1877, and an agricultural experiment station in 1886, Virginia attempted to address the farmers' problems, but these efforts could not cope with unfair railroad rates, high tariffs, and monopolistic trusts that farmers were blaming for their plight. They felt victimized by the new industrial order that seemed to discriminate against their unmechanized, poorly educated rural world. Everyone seemed to be against them. In 1877 they lost out to warehousemen and merchants who won repeal of the state inspection law for the sale of tobacco that had been in effect since 1730. Sharecroppers were delivered a severe blow in 1884 when the Virginia Supreme Court of Appeals upheld the landowner's legal right to the crop until time of settlement; this effectively ended the distinction between cropper and wage laborer, producing, in the words of one scholar, "an agricultural proletariat."

In their search for fairer competition, reduced railroad rates, and higher prices for their crops, Virginia farmers, like farmers elsewhere, created their own organizations. In the 1870s, through the Patrons of Husbandry or Grange, they lobbied for and won appointment of a state railroad commissioner to fight arbitrary railroad rates, but the office proved ineffectual because it lacked rate-setting authority. In the 1880s, first through a Farmers' Assembly and then through the more aggressive Southern Farmers' Alliance, they pressed for a more powerful railroad commission with authority to set rates. By 1890, 30,000 Virginia farmers had joined the alliance, with additional thousands in the Colored Farmers' Alliance. To offer members lower prices on commodities and services and to eliminate monopolistic practices, the alliance, like the Grange before it, established cooperative stores and warehouses, but these usually failed for lack of capital and too few participating farmers. These organizations also offered educational and social support with their picnics, rallies, and dances that ameliorated the isolation many farm families were experiencing. Virginia's alliance leaders included many well-to-do farmers and few of the radicals that populated the organizations of the Midwest and Deep South, yet Virginia alliance president Mann Page sounded like a future populist when he declared: "We belong to that particular class of people who do not think we have got our share of the profits of the world. . . . We are asking nothing but simply justice under a government that is supposed to be a government of the people by the people."

When the legislature ignored its request for a railroad commission, the alliance turned to political action to achieve its goals, unsuccessfully running candidates for office in 1891. Passage of a watered-down commission bill a year later that created a one-man commission whose salary would be paid by the railroads angered farmers. With their alliance collapsing, many rushed to join the national People's Party or Populists, who were demanding more forceful federal action to deal with farm problems. However, despite the presence on the ballot of vice-presidential candidate James Field, a former Confederate general from Gordonsville, the Populists won only a small percentage of the presidential vote in Virginia in 1892.

As a national depression hit the following year, Virginia Populists intensified their efforts to overthrow the conservative Democrats who seemed so insensitive to their problems. Their platform expressed their alarm: "Our products are selling below the cost of production; our lands are valueless, except to support the state by taxation; the labor in our cities is ground down, and goes unemployed; we are compelled to make bricks without straw, to pay taxes without money, to support useless officers in unaccustomed luxury, and to foot the bills for governmental extravagances we can ill afford." They demanded new election laws, state and national income taxes and corporation taxes, and the coinage of more silver. Some effort was made to bring together poor white and black farmers under the Populist banner, but white Populists worried that such a coalition would doom their cause just as it had killed the Readjusters, while blacks feared their defection from the Republicans would leave them at the mercy of another white-dominated party, and so no formal union was arranged.

Faced with the liability of being a third party and Democratic charges that they were "cranks" and "radicals" whose victory would restore "Black Reconstruction" or Readjuster rule, Virginia Populists suffered a devastating defeat in the 1893 governor's race. Their candidate, Edmund Randolph Cocke, an aristocratic Cumberland County farmer, was overwhelmed by Democrat Charles T. O'Ferrall; their political demise was symbolically confirmed weeks later with the selection of railroad lawyer Tom Martin for the U.S. Senate. Strongest in the tobacco counties, Populism had a modest impact in the Old Dominion, where crop diversity and better farm conditions minimized its appeal. Furthermore, the national Populists' demand for a government-operated crop warehouse system, the sub-treasury, had limited attraction in a state whose fruit and vegetable growers and livestockmen needed no long-term storage facilities. Finally, Populism's potential for restoring a black-white political coalition, more imagined than real, frightened small farmers into remaining with the Democracy and encouraged a drive for electoral reform. Conservative Virginia farmers wanted no association with radical activities that might undermine white supremacy.

The dying gasp of the Populists came in the hotly contested presidential election of 1896 when the issue of free silver threatened the Martin machine. The Populist demand for the coining of more silver by the government in the hope of raising commodity prices had been a controversial national issue for two decades, pitting farmers and the silver interests against the "gold bug" business community that favored repeal of the Sherman Silver Purchase Act and the maintenance of the gold standard. The onset of a severe depression in 1893 aggravated this issue as railroads defaulted, factories closed, and urban unemployment skyrocketed. Coxey's Army, a contingent of angry unemployed workers from across the country, descended on Washington to demand congressional action, but Governor O'Ferrall and the Virginia state militia summarily dispersed them from their Alexandria encampment. A year later O'Ferrall, preferring "war to anarchy," used the troops to break a strike at the Pocahontas coal mine in Tazewell. Such political conservatism buttressed a stable banking environment and agricultural diversity that allowed Virginia to fare better than most Southern states during the depression.

Virginians divided on the free silver issue, which was fast taking on the tones of a moral crusade that arrayed the people against privilege. In describing the election of 1896, Carter Glass's *Lynchburg News* saw it as a contest between "the common people, who industriously observe the laws and love their country" and "the great money-combinations, the grinding trusts, the tariff-robbers, and the election purchasers." Defecting from President Grover Cleveland's defense of the gold standard, most Virginia Democrats, led by Senator Daniel and a reluctant Tom Martin, who was always testing the political wind, supported the candidacy of Nebraska's William Jennings Bryan, who had stunned the party's convention with his "Cross of Gold" speech that favored more coinage of silver. Dispirited Populists, who had hoped to capitalize on bad economic times and the growing popularity of free silver, had little choice but to throw their support to Bryan as well. Some Gold or Cleveland Democrats, with Republican financial assistance, formed their own party, but most of them, including Governor O'Ferrall, backed Republican William McKinley, who won a smashing victory in a bitterly contested race noted for its fist fights, high oratory, and voting irregularities. Bryan won Virginia and most of the rural South and West, but his national defeat, the return of prosperity, and the animosity of the campaign killed the Populist Party and left Old Dominion Democrats uneasily divided.

As a new century dawned, farm problems paled alongside the trend toward urbanization in Virginia that would increase dramatically over the next two decades. The number of city folk rose from 18 to 30 percent of the population. Urban standards of living compared favorably to the poverty of rural areas with their poor roads and schools and absence of electricity. Norfolk and Richmond were experiencing building booms with new banks, hotels, and downtown shopping centers. Facilitated by trolley lines, the cities expanded their boundaries outward. Virginians were beginning to experiment with automobiles and movie arcades, while enjoying the growing popularity of professional baseball and college football, which was nearly terminated by the General Assembly when two players died in University of Virginia games. The racial makeup of the state also changed as new segregation laws encouraged the migration of black Virginians out of the state.

Problems generated by urbanization contributed to the progressive current sweeping the country in the early twentieth century. Progressivism was a broad-based reform movement directed at the industrial-urban revolution that had devastated the landscape, changed the nature of work and human relationships, and made the United States into a world power. Progressive reformers were upset with corrupt politicians, urban decay, social disarray, and powerful corporate monopolies that were destroying the competitive economic order and undermining a stable community system controlled by the "better sort of people." Across the land at every level of government, reforms were instituted to deal with these problems: railroad regulation, prohibition, meat inspection laws, conservation of natural resources, child labor laws, tariff and banking revisions, and direct primaries and direct election of senators, which were designed to put political power into the hands of the people. In the South more modest changes were introduced that regulated business, improved education, attacked the region's health problems, and reinvigorated politics. Similar advances occurred in Virginia where insurgents confronted the political order dominated by the emerging machine of Senator Martin.

Aided by the growing reform impulse, repeated charges of election fraud, and concern about apathy among the "better sort" of white voters, progressive-minded Virginians elected independent Andrew Jackson Montague to the governorship in 1901. They also won popular support for a constitutional convention to replace the detested Underwood Constitution of 1868, which the *Richmond Dispatch* called "that miserable apology to organic law which was forced upon Virginians by carpetbaggers, scalawags, and Negroes supported by Federal bayonets." Reformers wanted to revamp state government and eliminate what remained of the black vote, whose manipulation, they claimed, corrupted politics and sustained the machine. Carter Glass shamelessly asserted that the purpose of the convention was "the elimination of every Negro who can be gotten rid of, legally, without materially impairing the strength of the white electorate."

The convention, consisting of twelve Republicans and eighty-eight Democrats, a majority of whom were independents, met in Richmond from June 1901 to June 1902. After considering a number of franchise options, the delegates settled on provisions that eventually would disfranchise most black Virginians and about half of the white electorate as well through the imposition of a poll tax and other constitutional restrictions, including literacy and understanding clauses. Recent U.S. Supreme Court decisions had encouraged Southern states to use such subterfuges to circumvent the Fifteenth Amendment that prevented discrimination by race in voting. The suffrage article established two voting lists. The "permanent roll," prepared before 1 January 1904, enrolled Union and Confederate veterans and their sons, citizens who paid property taxes, and those able to read or offer reasonable explanations of sections of the constitution. A second roll of those registering after that date required prospective voters to pay the poll tax, which was $1.50 per year for up to three years and had to be paid six months before the general election, to apply in their own handwriting, and to answer questions concerning their qualifications. Local registration boards, controlled by the Democratic machine, were given wide discretion in interpreting and implementing the new voting provisions.

The convention also restructured state and local government, increased the number of elected state officials, and created a State Corporation Commission to deal with the monopolistic power of the railroads and other corporations. The commission, primarily the work of A. Caperton Braxton, a Staunton lawyer and a staunch advocate of regulation, was empowered to fix rates and make rules and regulations for corporations, even to declare acts of the legislature unconstitutional; but its independence was compromised by gubernatorial appointment of the three commissioners, whose rulings could be appealed to the state Supreme Court of Appeals. At the end of the session, delegates, who were largely lawyers, businessmen, and local officeholders, fearing rejection by the voters, arrogantly proclaimed their handiwork in effect rather than submit it to the electorate as had been promised. State and federal courts rejected later challenges to this high-handed action.

Designed to liberalize politics and to overthrow the machine, the new constitution, ironically, strengthened the Martin Organization, which had been reluctant to support the convention. It eliminated voters who were more likely to vote against the machine, it undermined weaker parties and independent candidates by creating a smaller electorate that was more easily controlled by the group with the best organization and the most money, and it placed a premium on control of patronage and election machinery. The effort to reduce apathy only produced more apathy and less democracy: from 1900 to 1904 the percentage of Virginians voting in the presidential election declined by over half and would not get back to 1904 levels until 1952. Although fraud would be reduced, it would not be eliminated, especially in the ninth district, where Republicans led by the Slemp family remained competitive.

Organization authority was further enhanced through the creation of a circuit court system, which replaced the venerable county courts and their convivial monthly court days. Appointed by the General Assembly, the new judges had the power to select county electoral boards and other lesser local officials. They complemented the preexisting "ring" of county or "courthouse" officials—commonwealth's attorney, treasurer, commissioner of revenue, clerk of the circuit court, and sheriff—who, along with their prescribed duties, were responsible for getting out the vote and dispensing patronage. An infamous fee system rewarded many of these local officials by allowing them to keep a portion of the fees they charged for their services. The interlocking network of General Assembly members, circuit judges, "courthouse ring," and machine leaders, dependent upon one another for job security, salaries, and election support—and now undergirded by a constitution that kept the electorate small—became the key to the Organization's power for the next sixty years.

Despite the obstacles of racial prejudice and machine self-interest, the progressive temper did generate some modest gains in a state not known for promoting progress. Indeed, as the reformers had hoped, a sense of security produced by settlement of the race question encouraged a reform spirit. Fueled by new prosperity, the leadership of Montague, and the progressive penchant for pursuing moral restoration through new lobbying organizations, Virginia reformers, many of whom were women, led movements for better schools and roads, stronger child labor laws, primary elections, and farm demonstration programs. Montague, "the Red Fox of Middlesex," had been a railroad attorney and Organization stalwart early in his career, winning the race for attorney general in 1897, but he broke with Martin on the issues of a direct primary and the constitutional convention, both of which he favored. This established him as an independent, supposedly free of the corrupt practices of the machine, and he handily defeated Martin's candidate, Claude

Swanson, for the party's nomination for governor in 1901. Montague remained an outspoken advocate for improvements in education and roads, but he lacked the constitutional authority and the political will to do battle with the machine in the General Assembly, which defeated his plans for a state highway commission and a primary bill. There was enough public support for the latter, however, that Martin allowed the party convention to enact it in 1904.

A similar public murmur was advancing the cause of better schools. Despite the early efforts of Superintendent William Henry Ruffner, the schools remained woefully underfunded. Rural poverty and isolation, localism, and hostility to government militated against state spending for education. In 1900 little more than half the school-age population was enrolled, most schoolhouses had only one room, the state had only one four-year public high school, terms were abbreviated, and teacher salaries were abysmally low. The illiteracy rate in the Old Dominion was 23 percent: 11 percent for whites and 45 percent for blacks. Similar conditions across the South had prompted Northern philanthropists to direct funds to the newly created Southern Education Board and the General Education Board, and Governor Montague used these efforts as well as the embarrassment of the statistics to arouse Virginians to participate in this reform movement.

But a group of Richmond women, including Lila Meade Valentine and Mary Cooke Branch Munford, were ahead of him. They had formed the Richmond Education Association in 1900 to promote an interest in education in Richmond and Virginia. Increasing economic and educational opportunities for women and declining family size made the Progressive Era noteworthy for the emergence of more women into the public arena, even in the South with its antifeminist tradition. In 1900, 125,000 Virginia women were employed outside the home, a majority in domestic work, but also as teachers, social workers, secretaries, factory hands, seamstresses, and farmers. Many became involved in numerous reform activities, often through the Federation of Women's Clubs, to protect their new positions and to broaden opportunities in education and social welfare where the problems of Virginia's growing cities were most obvious. The Richmond Nurses' Settlement, similar to the settlement houses of Northern cities, provided nursing care to the poor, classes in cooking and hygiene, and recreation opportunities. Valentine, an excellent public speaker, pursued interests in public health and woman's suffrage as well as education, while Munford was involved in advancing higher education for women and child labor laws.

In March 1904 all of these educational reformers created the Cooperative Education Association of Virginia to publicize the need for nine-month school terms, more high schools, improved teacher training,

LILA MEADE VALENTINE

and agricultural and industrial training. The following spring, at the behest of Munford and others, the association undertook a statewide campaign, the "May Campaign of 1905," that reached into ninety-four counties with 100 speakers making over 300 addresses. It appeared that a new
day for education in Virginia was on the horizon. Even the cynical Tom
Martin, then in a U.S. Senate race with Governor Montague, was jolted
into giving lukewarm support to the crusade.

The election of Claude Swanson to the governorship and Martin's
defeat of Montague in the first Democratic senatorial primary in 1905
appeared to threaten this success, but Swanson demonstrated his own
brand of independence by expanding upon Montague's reform efforts in
education and road building. Passage of the Mann High School Act in
1906 appropriating state funds to match local contributions had a revolutionary effect; by 1909 the state had 345 high schools. Under the aggressive
administration of Joseph D. Eggleston Jr., the first elected superintendent

of public instruction, significant increases in teachers' salaries, length of school terms, and per pupil expenditures occurred; the state took control of the College of William and Mary and established three new normal or teacher education schools for women. With their fondness for professionalism, bureaucracy, and improved sanitation, the reformers instituted teacher certification, school consolidation, and school privy requirements. From 1900 to 1920 education revenues rose 900 percent. Nevertheless, Virginia was spending only half the national average for education, and much of the new money did not trickle down to the black schools, which endured gross inequities in teacher salaries and school appropriations. Four years of education were now compulsory, but a local option provision, granted out of fears about educating blacks, rendered the bill ineffective. And once the ardor for reform faded, Organization support for more spending declined as well.

Swanson proved to be an exceptionally able governor, balancing the interests of the Organization with the demands for progressive change. That pragmatism had always been his political mode of operation,

Thomas Martin

necessitated by the loyalty demanded by the Martin forces and the services he owed his rural constituents over a thirteen-year career as a congressman from the fifth district. Like so many progressives, Swanson came to believe that government had an obligation to ensure individual opportunity in a society where the ordinary citizen seemed stymied by the growing power and wealth of corporate America. His governorship reflected that reform temper. Approvingly, the *Richmond News Leader* claimed Virginia had "turned its face to the morning with a hopefulness and faith in herself and the future she has not shown in long over a generation."

Next to schools, roads were the primary focus of the reformers. Virginia's roads were labeled "the worst known to civilization" by the *News Leader* in 1903. Tourists were warned to avoid the direct route from Washington to Richmond through Fredericksburg, for it was "practically impassable." Supported by the new automobile industry, good roads advocates and farmers pressed for "farm to market" roads and formed the Virginia Good Roads Association to lobby for improvements. With a surplus in the state treasury, Swanson convinced legislators, who were now meeting in the recently expanded state Capitol, to create a State Highway Commission in 1906 and appropriate $250,000 for road building in 1908. Costs were to be kept low by the use of convict labor. The assembly fixed speed limits at twenty miles per hour in 1910, at which time 2,705 vehicles were registered in the state.

Additional government expansion followed. The General Assembly created a new Department of Public Health to deal with the infirm and high rates of disease and a Board of Charities and Corrections to attend to the welfare of inmates in penal and correctional institutions. Flogging was abolished in 1910. Child labor under the age of fourteen was prohibited in most cases, although its application was compromised by inadequate enforcement and the opposition of working-class parents. Swanson also put more teeth into the regulatory power of the State Corporation Commission. Over the objections of the railroads and Senator Martin, he pressured the SCC into establishing lower rail rates and higher property assessments. Although still subject to political influence—for years many of its commissioners were loyal members of the Organization— the SCC became a more independent regulatory body, promoting business interests in an ethical manner with rulings usually upheld by the state and federal courts. At the local level, Staunton became the first city in the country to adopt the city manager form of government in 1908.

Virginia's rural residents, three-fourths of the state's population, were not ignored by the tide of progressivism. Agricultural reformers, most of them well-to-do farmers who formed the Virginia State Farmers Institute in 1904, lobbied for improvements in education and for scientific farming methods. Many of the new high schools were authorized for rural areas in order to emphasize agricultural education for boys and domestic science for girls. Demonstration farms were established in Virginia in 1907, and under the Smith-Lever Act of 1914, the U.S. Department of Agriculture began funding county home demonstration and agricultural agents. In 1912 farmers won assembly support for the creation of state lime-grinding plants to reduce the cost of fertilizers. In the first two decades of the twentieth century, Virginia farmers, with the assistance of new tractors and trucks, experienced increases in farm productivity and prices, a doubling of acreage values, and a reduction in tenancy. Greater crop diversification into potatoes, peanuts, apples, and livestock production was lessening the dependence on tobacco, still the largest cash crop; there was even a Peking duck ranch in Riverton.

In the midst of this reform activity, Virginia celebrated the three-hundredth anniversary of the English landing in Jamestown. The Tercentennial Exposition opened in Norfolk on 26 April 1907 to much fanfare, with a rousing address by President Theodore Roosevelt and a parade of ships from the world's navies. Backed by national, state, and local resources, the fair promised to mark the Old Dominion's entry into a new century of progress. Behind the bright bunting, however, was a facility inadequately financed and months behind schedule and a city without enough rooms and transportation for the visitors. In six months of operation, attendance was less than half the anticipated six million, and the exposition closed over $2 million in debt. It was a familiar story for a state struggling to free itself from post–Civil War poverty while saddled with a conservative social and political order.

An incident that dramatized the tensions generated by the transition from a rural to a progressive order occurred at Hillsville on 14 March 1912: the great Carroll County shootout. Floyd Allen, head of a clannish mountain family, had been charged with aiding his nephews escape from the sheriff's deputies after a fistfight. Found guilty and sentenced to jail, Allen, surrounded by his kinsmen, proclaimed that he would not go to jail. At that moment shots rang out in the courtroom, killing the judge, the commonwealth's attorney, a juror, and a spectator and wounding Allen. Apprehended after a brief flight, Allen and his son Claude were convicted of murder and sentenced to die in the electric chair; three other family members received prison sentences. Despite an outpouring of pleas to commute the sentences, Governor William Hodges Mann refused, and the Allens were executed on 28 March 1913, a result confirming a progressive commitment to state authority and law and order over old-style individualism.

The most controversial issue of the Progressive Era in Virginia, one that also reflected the struggle between individual rights and public order, was prohibition. Temperance had emerged once again as an issue in

the 1880s out of fear for the social chaos and moral decay attributed to industrialization and urbanization: alcoholism, prostitution, family abuse,
and desertion. Much of this antisocial behavior emanated from the sa-
loon. Rallying women to this threat to the family, the Woman's Christian Temperance Union established a Virginia chapter in 1883, and three
years later the General Assembly permitted localities to ban saloons. In
Norfolk a grassroots Prohibition Party, backed by the local WCTU chapter, won citywide elections in 1894 but quickly faded from the scene. Further successes awaited a climate more conducive to change than that provided by the troublesome 1890s with its economic and racial problems.

Combining the twentieth-century reform spirit to clean up society
with a rural animosity toward the growing power of urban elements, the
revived temperance movement was strongest in the South, where Baptist and Methodist preachers, primarily through the Anti-Saloon League,
fought to restrict the sale of liquor. Organized in Virginia in 1901, the
league won its first significant success in 1903 with the passage of the
Mann law that prohibited the sale of liquor in the state without a license.
By 1905 seventy of Virginia's one hundred counties and three independent cities were dry, but the antiliquor crusaders were not content with
local option. Under the leadership of Methodist minister James Cannon,
president of the Virginia Anti-Saloon League, who vigorously lobbied
legislators and the public through temperance publications, they pursued
statewide prohibition with letter and petition campaigns. Senator Martin, who had enjoyed the financial backing of the liquor interests, was
loath to risk the Organization's power over such a volatile issue; but correctly reading the public temper, he began acceding to Cannon's wishes.
The tacit alliance between the two men was revealed in 1908 when the
Speaker of the House, Richard Byrd, no teetotaler himself, sponsored
legislation that restricted the sale of liquor in areas where there was no
police protection and provided for further regulation of the traffic. A year
later Martin endorsed a noted temperance advocate, William Hodges
Mann, for governor rather than risk a divisive primary fight on that issue.
In return he and Hal Flood convinced Cannon to moderate his campaign
for statewide prohibition.

The liquor question returned to haunt the Organization in 1912, as
the national movement for total prohibition gathered momentum. Once
again pressing Senator Martin to support a statewide referendum on prohibition, Cannon suggested that defeat of the enabling act setting up the
referendum could have political repercussions. When the Virginia Senate rejected the bill, Cannon indicated that his future endorsement of the
machine was in question. By now Organization leaders were aware that
another defeat of the act would have disastrous consequences for their
political futures. Accordingly, the 1914 General Assembly passed a bill

authorizing a public referendum on the question. The final Senate tally was 20–19, with Lieutenant Governor J. Taylor Ellyson casting the key vote. What followed was a six-month battle in the newspapers and on public podiums between the well-organized moral reformers of the Anti-Saloon League and antiprohibition forces—the makers of beer, wine, and spirits—who argued the loss of self-government and economic calamity if the people were denied their libations. On 22 September 1914 Virginians, by a three-to-two margin, converted the Old Dominion into a dry state, effective 1 November 1916. But the vote did not settle the issue, as prohibition remained a political hot potato for almost two decades.

Although badgered by Cannon into a position it had preferred to side-step, the Martin machine was in no difficulty, having secured its control over Virginia politics through two earlier elections. With the death of Senator Daniel in 1910, Governor Mann appointed Claude Swanson to fill the seat. A year later Martin and Swanson easily dispatched challenges to their Senate seats from independents William A. Jones and Carter Glass, despite the resurrection of the vote-buying charges against Martin in the 1893 Senate race. In 1912 the nomination and election of progressive New Jersey governor Woodrow Wilson to the presidency, the eighth native Virginian to serve in that office, forecast rewards for Old Dominion independents. However, Martin once again proved his political agility by belatedly backing Wilson at the Democratic convention and then mending fences with the president by supporting his legislative agenda. In return, Organization personnel received the greater portion of federal jobs, further frustrating the independents.

Virginians proudly identified with the new chief executive, even though he had come to the White House from the North. Born in Staunton in 1856, Wilson had spent his boyhood in Georgia, where his father took a pastorate in Augusta shortly after his birth. After undergraduate days at Princeton, he attended the University of Virginia law school before going to Johns Hopkins University for his graduate degree in history, his preparation for an academic career that eventually led to the presidency of Princeton and thence to the New Jersey governorship. But he always proclaimed himself a Virginian, stating that "a man's rootage is more important than his leafage." In an ironic twist of fate, Wilson would be remembered more for his leadership of the nation through World War I and his quest for a League of Nations than for his contributions as a progressive president in creating the Federal Reserve banking system and the Federal Trade Commission and supporting federal aid to education and roads.

The war would bring an end to the Progressive movement, but it had achieved some successes in Virginia in education, public health, agriculture, and regulation of big business, perhaps even an enlarged social con-

WOODROW WILSON, BY FRANK GRAHAM COOTES

science, thanks to the efforts of new lobbying organizations and people like Lila Valentine, child labor leader Alexander McKelway, Kate Waller Barrett and her missions for unwed mothers, and Governors Montague and Swanson. However, compared to what was necessary and what was happening elsewhere, its achievements were compromised by racism, localism, and individualism. Racism eliminated voters, produced costly dual school systems, and precluded cooperation between lower-class whites and blacks who most needed the assistance. Rural folk remained hostile to threatening changes foisted upon them by outsiders. The reformers themselves, paternalistic in their distrust of the masses and often a part of the prevailing power structure, chose not to press for more fundamental change. And one-party politics—for the machine remained dominant despite the efforts of the independents—prevented the political competition that might have produced better services. In Raymond Pulley's view, progressivism in Virginia did more "to conserve and strengthen the Old Virginia order than to rid the state of political bosses and broaden the base of popular government." Virginia would change, but slowly, and certainly not at the expense of the ruling class.

Representative of this ambivalence between a desire for progress and the wish to preserve the old order was the work of the Association for the Preservation of Virginia Antiquities, the first statewide preservation agency. Created in 1888 to protect Virginia's historical sites and buildings for future generations, the APVA, according to James Lindgren, seemed more concerned about sustaining a traditional culture founded on conservative leadership, state rights, and racial separation. In its early years the organization did very little restoration work or archaeological investigation and paid little attention to the artistry or craftsmanship in buildings, preferring instead to memorialize places with tablets that identified the heroic characters who had inhabited these spaces, like John Smith or Mary Washington, people who symbolized Virginia's past greatness and values. Much like other organizations founded in this period, such as the Daughters of the American Revolution and the United Daughters of the Confederacy, members of the APVA, whose founding and early operation were also led by women, were reacting to the materialism of the New South, the emancipation of blacks, labor and farmer radicalism, and a wave of new immigrants that threatened the social and political power of the "better sort" of people. They preferred a history that would reinforce their cultural supremacy, a history that had no place for blacks or slavery or Spanish explorers. In the words of James Branch Cabell, these "custodians of culture" excelled in "the superb and philanthropic romanticizing of Virginia history and in a free-spirited invention of priorities and relics. . . . How very differently do we shape our history in Virginia, where we accept such facts as we find desirable and dismiss those which are not to our purpose." This was the kind of history that Virginians were being offered at the turn of the century in their history books, a history that concealed economic and social shortcomings with myths of cavaliers, the "Lost Cause," and "Black Reconstruction."

SOURCES CONSULTED

Anne Field Alexander, " 'Like an Evil Wind': The Roanoke Riot of 1893 and the Lynching of Thomas Smith," *VMHB* (April 1992); Edward L. Ayers, *The Promise of the New South* (1992); Edward L. Ayers and John C. Willis, eds., *The Edge of the South: Life in Nineteenth-Century Virginia* (1991); W. Fitzhugh Brundage, *Lynching in the New South: Georgia and Virginia, 1880–1930* (1993); Michael B. Chesson, *Richmond after the War* (1981); Virginius Dabney, *Virginia: The New Dominion* (1971); Henry C. Ferrell, *Claude A. Swanson of Virginia* (1985); Joseph Gerteis, "Populism, Race, and Political Interest in Virginia," *Social Science History* (Summer 2003); Randal L. Hall, "A Courtroom Massacre: Politics and Public Sentiment in

Progressive-Era Virginia," *JSH* (May 2004); Robert A. Hohner, *Prohibition and Politics: The Life of Bishop James Cannon, Jr.* (1999); Jeffrey R. Kerr-Ritchie, *Freedpeople in the Tobacco South: Virginia, 1860–1900* (1999); William Larsen, *Montague of Virginia: The Making of a Southern Progressive* (1965); James M. Lindgren, *Preserving the Old Dominion: Historic Preservation and Virginia Traditionalism* (1993); William A. Link, *A Hard Country and a Lonely Place: Schooling, Society, and Reform in Rural Virginia, 1870–1920* (1986); Link, *The Paradox of Southern Progressivism* (1992); Richard Love, "The Cigarette Capital of the World: Labor, Race, and Tobacco in Richmond, Virginia, 1880–1980," Ph.D. diss., Univ. of Virginia, 1998; Allen W. Moger, *Virginia: Bourbonism to Byrd, 1870–1925* (1968); C. C. Pearson and J. Edwin Hendricks, *Liquor and Anti-Liquor in Virginia, 1619–1919* (1967); Raymond H. Pulley, *Old Virginia Restored: An Interpretation of the Progressive Impulse, 1870–1930* (1968); Howard N. Rabinowitz, *Race Relations in the Urban South, 1865–1890* (1978); Peter J. Rachleff, *Black Labor in the South: Richmond, Virginia, 1865–1890* (1984); Lex Renda, "The Advent of Agricultural Progressivism in Virginia," *VMHB* (Jan. 1988); Emily J. Salmon and Edward D. C. Campbell Jr., eds., *The Hornbook of Virginia History*, 4th ed. (1994); G. Terry Sharrer, *A Kind of Fate: Agricultural Change in Virginia, 1861–1920* (2000); Crandall A. Shifflett, *Coal Towns: Life, Work, and Culture in Company Towns of Southern Appalachia, 1880–1960* (1991); Shifflett, *Patronage and Poverty in the Tobacco South: Louisa County, 1860–1900* (1982); Stuart Seeley Sprague, "Investing in Appalachia: The Virginia Valley Boom of 1889–1893," *Virginia Cavalcade* (Winter 1975); Lloyd C. Taylor Jr., "Lila Meade Valentine: The FFV as Reformer," *VMHB* (Oct. 1962); Robert Taylor, "The Jamestown Tercentennial Exposition of 1907," *VMHB* (April 1957); William G. Thomas, "'Under Indictment': Thomas Lafayette Rosser and the New South," *VMHB* (April 1992); Charles E. Wynes, *Race Relations in Virginia, 1870–1902* (1961); Edward Younger and James Tice Moore, eds., *The Governors of Virginia, 1860–1978* (1982).

13

THE RISE OF THE BYRD ORGANIZATION

1915–1930

While the issues of progressive reform and prohibition were redefining political loyalties in state and nation from 1914 to 1916, abroad the European powers were slaughtering men and sinking ships in a way that threatened to drag America into the conflict. In Virginia the Martin machine had come to an accommodation with the Reverend James Cannon and his prohibition forces, but the subsequent debates over enforcement legislation, woman suffrage, better roads, and more efficient government splintered Organization unity. Wartime diversions furthered weakened Senator Martin's leadership, and with his death in 1919, a struggle ensued for control of the Old Dominion's future. Out of this conflict, Harry F. Byrd emerged to create a more powerful political machine that would dominate the state for forty years.

The General Assembly session of 1916 was better known as the "Great Moral Reform Session." It passed a prohibition bill that outlawed the manufacture and sale of liquors but allowed residents to acquire modest amounts outside the state. Named for Eastern Shore senator G. Walter Mapp, the Mapp Act was in reality the handiwork of James Cannon, who, though unelected, sat on the floor of each house as the bill worked its way through the assembly. Listening to the voices of progressive antivice crusaders, the legislature also approved antigambling and anti–white slave laws and attacked houses of ill repute.

Prohibition resurfaced in 1917 to undermine the carefully laid plans of the Organization to promote Lieutenant Governor J. Taylor Ellyson to the governorship. The predicted contest with the independents, who were supporting Attorney General John Garland Pollard, was disrupted by the entry of Westmoreland Davis, a gentleman farmer from Loudoun County who had made his fortune through marriage and a lucrative New York legal practice. With both Ellyson and Pollard endorsing prohibition, Davis, who preferred local option, won the primary by a narrow plurality when his opponents split the "dry" vote. His victory over the Republicans in November proved a formality.

But in November 1917 Virginians had little time to reflect on state politics. The previous April, following Germany's decision to use unrestricted submarine warfare against all merchant vessels on the oceans, President Wilson had asked for and received from Congress a declaration of war against Germany. America, which for almost three years had refrained from participation in Europe's folly, immediately began preparing for a crusade to "save the world for democracy."

The war was a mixed blessing for the Old Dominion. Governor Henry Carter Stuart, who had been elected without opposition in 1913, exhorted Virginians to fill conscription quotas and increase food production in their gardens and window boxes. Almost half a million Virginians registered for service, and the state was the first to fill its quota of men for military camp. Stuart, a nephew of General Jeb Stuart, also appointed a state Council of Defense to oversee Virginia's preparations. The council established a Women's Committee to utilize women's organizations for patriotic work in conserving food, improving labor conditions, and preserving the moral fiber of the commonwealth. Mary Munford served as chairman, assisted by home demonstration agent Ella Agnew and social activist Lucy Randolph Mason. A similar organization for black women was also created. In the mold of morality-minded progressives, the council formed a Commission of Religious Forces to recruit ministers to preach sermons on the moral and spiritual welfare of the troops, diligence in food production, investment in Liberty Bonds, and the "protection of camps from intoxication and the social evil." As at the national level, state leaders worried that America's traditional policy of nonentanglement would inhibit support for the war, and so they intensified their efforts to foster patriotism, even encouraging community singing and the closing of poolrooms to reduce loitering.

In February 1918 newly elected Governor Davis, with legislative authorization, reconstituted the Council of Defense to improve efficiency and reduce costs. Local councils were also established to parallel the work at the state level. By war's end 22,000 Virginians were involved in the council's efforts to improve transportation and housing, food production and conservation, and fire prevention in the state. Strains on manpower, transportation, and food and fuel supplies were ever present, leading the governor to proclaim the need for "thrift" to "save the world from the slavery of Prussianism."

The desire to serve and sacrifice permeated all aspects of Virginia life. Quotas of the Liberty Bond drives were invariably exceeded. Colonial Dames and DAR and UDC ladies enlisted in the charitable organizations of the War Orphans' League, Mothers of the Regiment, and the Fatherless Children of France. Women sold Liberty Bonds, took factory jobs, sponsored dances, and knit garments for the troops. A state "gas mask day" was organized to collect fruit pits and nutshells, sources of carbon for the masks, but the war blessedly ended before the collection could begin. Schools and colleges offered military training classes and established Student Army Training Corps and Reserve Officer Training Corps programs. Cooperation between labor and management resulted in few strikes and greater union membership.

The winter of 1917–18 was colder than usual—Hampton Roads froze over—prompting Virginia's fuel administrator, Harry Byrd, to urge Virginians to replace coal with wood in their furnaces and stoves, reduce the consumption of electricity, and meet in joint church services on Sundays. Electric signs for advertising purposes were turned off; convict labor was used to cut wood to be sold to private citizens at $2 a cord; and the Gayton Coal mines in Henrico County ten miles outside Richmond were readied for reopening. Daylight savings time was instituted. Accustomed to the countrywide "meatless" and "wheatless" days that had already been prescribed to conserve food supplies, Virginians cooperated fully with the "heatless" days of that winter.

The heightened community spirit and patriotism reduced sectionalism and improved cooperation with Washington, where Senator Martin, as majority leader and chairman of the Appropriations Committee, Congressman Flood, chairman of the Foreign Affairs Committee, and Senator Swanson, chairman of the Naval Affairs Committee, guided key wartime legislation through Congress. The navy base in Norfolk was created in 1917, and with the expansion of existing facilities, the Hampton Roads area was soon awash in shipbuilding contracts and increased trade; exports, primary of which was coal, jumped exponentially. Thanks to greater foreign demand and reduced world supplies, farmers enjoyed high prices for their crops, especially the tobacco planters, who were "seen hugging each other over the amazing prices they are getting and pinch[ing] themselves quite frequently to see if they have been dreaming." Cigarette production soared as cigarettes became part of the soldier's ration. Richmond's Lucky Strikes and Chesterfields emerged to challenge Winston-Salem's Camels as America's most popular brand.

Creation of defense plants, a new marine base at Quantico, and several army camps (the largest of which was Camp Lee near Petersburg) and the expansion of chemical, tobacco, and textile production brought new prosperity to the state, but not without costs. Shortages in housing,

coal, and farm labor occurred. As in the nation, there was some persecution in Virginia of German Americans and the "slackers" who were
accused of less than 100 percent enthusiasm for the war. Virginians were
angry with the Pamunkey and Mattaponi Indians who registered for the
draft but then filed for exemptions as noncitizens (their legal status in
the commonwealth) before eventually volunteering, and the University
of Virginia dismissed Professor of Journalism Leon Whipple for his "disloyal" pacifism. Governor Stuart declared martial law and called out the
militia in Hopewell in 1915 to combat the rise of gin mills, brothels, and
gambling created by the arrival of a DuPont munitions plant that had
turned that crossroads into a "western" boomtown. Three years later
troops again invaded the city to quell a race riot.

Racial hostility during the war was minimized by the patriotic fervor
and the existence of separate wartime units and organizations for each
race; but at Camp Lee 1,700 white carpenters refused to work alongside
37 recently hired black carpenters, and the latter were discharged with a
day's pay for their troubles. An investigation acknowledged the discrimination but concluded that the urgent need of housing for recruits war-
ranted the release of the black workers, who received no support from
the segregated labor unions.

Thousands of "doughboys" departed for Europe through Old Dominion ports, many of them in units of the Virginia National Guard,
which had been federalized in July 1917 after its service against Pancho
Villa on the Mexican border. Twenty-one state units went to France, including two black engineer service battalions that were responsible for
digging trenches and building roads. Over 1,000 Virginia women, called
"goblettes" or "yeowomen," served in the navy as clerks, draftsmen, and
recruiting agents; many others served as nurses in hospitals in France.
Richmond physicians under the direction of Dr. Stuart Maguire, dean of
the Medical College of Virginia, cared for the sick and wounded in Red
Cross Base Hospital No. 45 near Toul, France; they also raised money
from the folks at home to purchase medical supplies and equipment.
During the war 100,000 Virginians saw military duty; over 3,600 of them
died. To perform the duties of the absent guard, Governor Stuart organized the Virginia State Volunteers and the Virginia Home Guard. The
Volunteers consisted of 3,000 members in twenty-two community units;
but without adequate weapons, they did little more than bolster citizen
morale. The Home Guards aided local police forces, providing their own
equipment and serving without pay. Most veterans remembered the war
as a positive experience that provided them with new skills and perspectives, but combat left a more sobering memory. Said one Virginia Yank,
"The war made such an impression that it would be pretty hard to get
me in another such war."

WORLD WAR I "DOUGHBOYS," VIRGINIANS IN THE EIGHTIETH DIVISION,
IN FRANCE, 1918

Virginians greeted the news of an armistice and the war's end on 11
November 1918 with unprecedented celebration. Mass parades—"home-
coming jubilees"—were held months later to welcome the troops home.
The war had stimulated economic expansion, preparing the state for further growth in the Roaring Twenties; and indirectly it was a major force
behind the growth of unions, improvements to the road system, and
passage of woman suffrage and national prohibition. It also ushered in
changes that were less desirable, such as urban congestion, strikes, racial
violence, violations of civil rights, and a postwar Red Scare. And at its
end a worldwide influenza epidemic killed millions, including 700,000 in
the United States and over 11,000 in Virginia, where schools, churches,
dance halls, and theaters were closed to limit contagion.

Although disruptive, the war did not deter all efforts to sustain a reform temper in the state. The demand for better road networks to facilitate the war effort and the availability of federal funds for highway development encouraged the 1918 assembly to improve the commonwealth's
roads. The first State Highway Commission had been established in 1906,
but it controlled no roads and had few funds to disburse. Most of the
road building was done by counties and cities, which produced a trun-
cated system of "miry, rock-strewn, tortuous highways" that were poorly
constructed and maintained except in places such as the Valley, which
had invested in a private turnpike. Tourists were still bypassing the Old

Dominion to avoid the muddy roads, which in some areas were worsened by local residents who created mudholes so their towing services would be used. Highway advocates visualized a $20 million, 3,500-mile road network to advance trade and tourism. Faced with the question of whether Virginia should finance this construction with taxes or with bonds, the assembly decided to use both sources, raising the property tax by four cents and voting to amend the constitution to permit the issuance of bonds that provided Virginia with its first fully funded state road system.

In his initial message to the General Assembly, Governor Davis challenged the lawmakers to modernize Virginia's government. Adhering to his campaign promises and the recommendations of the latest commission on economy and efficiency in government, Davis proposed enactment of the executive budget, centralization of state finances, a workmen's compensation law, and improvements in the school system. The budget bill, which transferred budget-making responsibility from the legislature to the executive, passed easily, as did the other legislation and ratification of the Eighteenth Amendment that culminated the decades-long struggle to achieve national prohibition.

Advocates for equalizing educational facilities for women were less successful. For years Mary Munford had been fighting to establish a co-ordinate college for women at the University of Virginia. The newly created normal schools were below standard and would not be accredited until 1930. Explaining her motivation, she wrote to a friend, "Education

AUTOMOBILE STUCK IN MUD NEAR DUMFRIES, 1917

has been my deepest interest from my girlhood, beginning with an al-most passionate desire for the best education for myself, which was de-nied because it was not the custom for girls in my class to receive a col-lege education at that time." But the assembly rejected her proposal three times, along with a bill to admit women to the graduate programs at the University of Virginia. However, the statute authorizing coeducation at the College of William and Mary was approved, and two years later women were permitted to attend the university's graduate and profes-sional schools as well as practice law in the state. Because women had essentially been denied access to the legal profession before 1920, this was a major breakthrough in gender equalization.

Governor Davis's further success with a special assembly session in 1919 to deal with highway construction, combined with Senator Mar-tin's death in November, increased the anxiety of Organization leaders over the governor's future ambitions and ensured an acrimonious regu-lar session in 1920 that opened with a heated debate over the newly en-acted Nineteenth Amendment providing for woman suffrage. In 1909 a few Virginia women, including the celebrated writers Ellen Glasgow and Mary Johnston and progressive reformers Lila Valentine and Lucy Randolph Mason, had organized the Equal Suffrage League of Virginia to educate Old Dominion citizens on the issue. They were following the path blazed by two unsuccessful late nineteenth-century efforts to obtain the vote for women in Virginia. Rejecting radicalism for a more moder-ate approach, the suffragists capitalized on the evolving view of women's new roles in the society to argue that women taxpayers and citizens de-served the vote and that the quality of politics and government would improve significantly through their participation. They also believed that the vote would translate into more reform legislation to protect the interests of women and children. Woman suffrage, said Adele Clark of Richmond, was "a working force for the betterment of society." By 1919 the league, now affiliated with the National American Woman Suffrage Association, had grown to over 100 local chapters and 32,000 members, but on three different occasions it had failed to win assembly approval for a voting rights amendment to the state constitution. In the face of these disappointments, many Virginia women had joined the militant National Woman's Party that was more aggressive in pressing for a federal amend-ment, which finally passed Congress in 1919 primarily as a result of the democratic enthusiasm and women's contributions in the recent war.

Opposition to woman suffrage in the Old Dominion rested upon tra-dition and politics. Earlier votes against equal education for women and equal access to the professions clearly indicated a male bias in the legisla-ture against upsetting time-honored gender distinctions that risked men's control of the political order. Conservatives also believed that women

WOMAN'S SUFFRAGE RALLY ON CAPITOL SQUARE, 1915

were more likely to support costly social welfare programs such as child labor laws. In the 1919 special session, the House of Delegates had condemned the Nineteenth Amendment as an "unwarranted, unnecessary, undemocratic, and dangerous interference with the rights reserved to the states." As if these hurdles were not substantial enough, opponents of woman suffrage, including many female antisuffragists who had formed their own organization in 1912, played upon racist fears by claiming that the amendment would open the doors to voting by black women. A pamphlet was circulated in Virginia that pictured national suffragist Carrie Chapman Catt alongside Frederick Douglass and accused her of favoring free love and racial equality. To counter such charges, moderate white suffragists, who had chosen not to affiliate with black suffragists, played a similar race card by claiming that present restrictions against voting by black men could also be applied to black women. Nevertheless, like most other Southern state legislatures, the 1920 assembly once again rejected the amendment. In fact, Virginia's legislators did not approve the amendment until 1952, but ratification at the national level allowed Virginia women to vote for the first time in 1920.

Immediately, women gained access to political and professional domains long off-limits to them. In 1921 Maggie Walker ran for statewide office on a "lily-black" Republican ticket, and in 1924 Sarah Lee Fain of Norfolk and Helen T. Henderson of Buchanan County became the first women to serve in the General Assembly. However, women did not assume important public roles in the life of the commonwealth for another four decades. Forecasting greater equality in the workplace and in marriage, Mary Johnston had proclaimed the twentieth century as the "Woman's Century," but such dreams would require another feminist revolution in the 1960s. Exhausted by the long struggle for the vote and then restricted economically by the Great Depression, Virginia women, with few exceptions, remained in the traditional roles men were willing to grant them, their voices of advocacy confined largely to their business and professional organizations.

With the legislative session over, the Davis and Organization forces began jockeying for position in the governor's race in 1921 and the contest for Senator Swanson's seat in 1922. Westmoreland Davis initially appeared to hold a commanding lead. His wartime leadership had been applauded, and his personal intervention in a coal mine strike in St. Charles in October 1919 had reduced tensions and avoided the use of troops. Defiantly, he had maneuvered much of his legislative program through an obstinate assembly, winning public praise for his executive budget process and securing a central purchasing agency, prison reforms, and an end to the convict lease system. And he had filled Senator Martin's vacated seat with Carter Glass, a longtime opponent of the machine, whom Davis believed would now become his ally in the battle with the Organization.

Glass had been a thorn in the Organization's side for two decades. The diminutive Lynchburg newspaperman possessed a strong individualistic ethic that condemned any interference with a free political and economic order, whether by government or political machine. A leader in the fight at the constitutional convention to disfranchise African Americans, he became the most prominent opponent of the Organization over the next fifteen years, serving in Congress, running an unsuccessful Senate campaign against Swanson in 1911, and supporting Wilson for the presidency in 1912. For his efforts in helping to create the new federal banking system—for which he was known as the "Father of the Federal Reserve System"—he was appointed secretary of the treasury in 1918. One of the most popular men in the commonwealth, the acerbic Glass could make Davis into a formidable opponent, but he had begun to tire of his constant struggles against Martin and Swanson and was susceptible to their overtures to join the Organization.

With Glass effectively neutralized, machine leaders rallied behind the candidacy of E. Lee Trinkle, a little-known state senator from Wytheville, to defeat Henry St. George Tucker of Lexington, another longtime independent, in the 1921 gubernatorial primary. In the fall contest against

Republicans, Democrats used the race card, deriding their opponents' efforts to repeal the poll tax as an invitation to black power. To counter such demagoguery, the Virginia GOP declared itself "an exclusively white political party," which forced African Americans to run their own candidate, *Richmond Planet* editor John Mitchell, on a "lily-black" Republican ticket. Predictably, Trinkle's victory was never in doubt. Days after directing this successful campaign, Hal Flood, who had gained the party chairmanship to solidify his position as party leader, died. With near-unanimous support, state committeemen elevated Flood's nephew, Harry Byrd, to party leadership on 31 January 1922.

By virtue of service and power, Harry Flood Byrd Sr. was the most prominent Virginian of the twentieth century. Indeed, he had more influence over events in the Old Dominion for a longer period of time than any other Virginian since the settlement at Jamestown. As a state senator, governor, and U.S. senator, Byrd made notable contributions to his state and nation, but it was through his leadership of the Democratic political organization—the "Byrd machine"—that he wielded the authority that shaped the history of the commonwealth for the next forty years.

A direct descendant of the colonial William Byrds, Harry Byrd was born 10 June 1887 in Martinsburg, West Virginia. His father, Richard Evelyn Byrd, was commonwealth's attorney for Frederick County and later Speaker of the House of Delegates and an influential member of the political organization led by Senator Martin. The Byrd name would be further illuminated by the exploits of Harry's brother Richard Evelyn Byrd Jr., the famed polar explorer.

At age fifteen Harry took over the failing family newspaper, and through the old-fashioned values of hard work and thrift, he turned the *Winchester Evening Star* into a profitable business. Seeking additional income opportunities, he purchased two other newspapers, leased apple orchards, and managed the Valley Turnpike Company, which operated the toll road between Winchester and Staunton. These produced the resources that permitted Byrd to expand into orchard purchases and ownership of apple cold-storage facilities, which he built into a multimillion-dollar business that brought him financial security and a national reputation as an orchardist.

Tutored by his father in the intricacies of Virginia politics, Byrd served an appointed term on the Winchester City Council and was elected to the state Senate in 1915, where he served for ten years. More a behind-the-scenes manipulator than a visibly active legislator, Byrd pursued interests in highways and finance that earmarked his political career. As the new party chairman, he won immediate acclaim by achieving victories in the crucial 1922 congressional races in the seventh and ninth districts and in Swanson's U.S. Senate contest with former governor Davis. Even more importantly, in the 1923 special session of the General Assembly, he emerged as the leading opponent of using bonds for the construction of Virginia's roads, preferring instead a pay-as-you-go approach that relied on gasoline taxes.

Byrd's deliberations on road building revealed the competing forces that were typical of the Virginia mind-set: a conservative preference for traditional practices, especially when it came to spending money, versus a zest for progress, growth, and the utilization of resources in the most efficient and productive manner possible. Roads were necessary for development, but one had to be careful not to overextend in financing them. This personal dichotomy reflected the current mood of cautious optimism in Virginia. The war had been a boon to segments of the state's economy, but the postwar recession increased unemployment and anxiety as the state retreated to "normalcy." Hopewell almost disappeared when the DuPont plant closed at war's end. Farming entered a deep trough that would last for two decades. Between 1919 and 1921 Virginia gross farm income declined by 55 percent and prices of produce by 65 percent; farmers' enthusiasm for more progress waned, and retrenchment became the order of the day. While urban residents and manufacturers, whose businesses revived in the twenties, supported bond plans to underwrite good roads, rural residents, who made up two-thirds of the population and whose income did not rebound, cautioned against debt that they feared would lead to higher property taxes.

After heated debate the assembly passed a Byrd-inspired three-cent gasoline tax but also approved a public referendum on a $50 million bond issue. Having staked so much of his reputation on his pay-as-you-go solution to road building, Byrd worked tirelessly to defeat the bond issue, relying on the rural voters of the Valley and Southside for his victory. The only consolation for the bond people was the fulfillment of their prediction that the roads would not be built on time. Seven years later the gasoline tax was up to five cents per gallon, and the system was still not complete. However, the 1923 bond referendum had a significance far beyond that of how roads would be built in Virginia. It confirmed Byrd's leadership of the Organization, launched his campaign for the governorship in 1925, and solidified a pay-as-you-go mentality in the Old Dominion that would be the ideological basis for the state's fiscal policy for several decades.

The major difference between the Martin machine and the new Byrd machine was the close personal supervision that Byrd exercised over his forces. The Organization remained a group of like-minded men who agreed upon a conservative economic policy and paternalistic politics, but Byrd broadened its circle of supporters and established himself as first among equals. What Byrd brought to a revived Organization was an intimate approach. Whereas Martin had left much of the routine operation to Hal Flood and Claude Swanson, preferring to hobnob with railroad executives rather than clerks of the court, Byrd comfortably mingled with the local officeholders, relishing their Brunswick stew and talk of weather and farm prices. In addition to the officeholders and farmers, Byrd cultivated friends in the business and banking communities and among journalists, whom he catered to with his news releases. His way of leading was not to coerce but to reward with praise, jobs, roads, and legislation. His hands-on leadership generated a firm bond of loyalty that permitted Byrd great freedom to select his candidates for state office and to implement the policies he desired. What he created was a political organization that ran smoothly, efficiently, and powerfully and was beholden to one man for its direction for forty years, an oligarchy far more dominant than the one Martin had ruled over. Its power was first apparent in his easy victory for the governorship.

Quickly seizing command, Governor Byrd pursued tax and administrative reform. His model for success was the corporation, whose survival was predicated on cutting costs, maximizing profits, satisfying customers, and cultivating decisive executive leadership. He was a businessman who wanted a businesslike government. The primary feature of his tax plan was tax segregation: the separation of tax sources between state and localities, allocating real estate and tangible personal property to the local governments and leaving most of the remaining sources, such as personal income, to the state. On governmental reorganization he recommended the consolidation of nearly a hundred bureaus into eight departments; abolition of seven boards, commissions, and departments; and reduction of elected state officials from ten to three—the governor, lieutenant governor, and attorney general—the "short ballot." The 1926 assembly expeditiously endorsed Byrd's fiscal proposals, the short ballot, and his request for an independent study of government reorganization.

Less laudable was its passage of the Public Assemblage Act that required separate seating of the races at public gatherings. Disturbed by recent assemblies at Hampton Institute where people had been seated without regard to race, a small but influential group of Virginians, including pianist-composer John Powell and newspaper publisher Walter Copeland, demanded racial separation. Despite opposition from racial moderates and leaders of Hampton Institute, the public assembly segregation law easily passed. Governor Byrd, who had been urged privately to veto the bill, allowed it to become law without his signature, making Virginia the first state to require racial segregation in all places of public entertainment or assemblage.

HARRY F. BYRD SR.

It was not a new experience for black Virginians. In the post-Reconstruction period, urban crowding, job competition, and changing residential boundaries aggravated longtime racist attitudes to precipitate a white demand for racial segregation that received legal support from the U.S. Supreme Court's *Plessy* decree of "separate but equal." From the late 1890s on, Virginia, following the pattern in other Southern states, instituted a system of Jim Crow laws that separated the races on all public conveyances—railroads in 1900, streetcars in 1906—strengthened antimiscegenation laws, and further refined racial identification. Segregation, abetted by fears of race mixing and progressive desires for racial control, quickly spread throughout the commonwealth, rarely producing the equality stipulated by the Court.

Separate educational facilities for the two races, instituted by law in 1870 and now stipulated by the 1902 constitution that also restricted black voting, resulted in gross inequities in school funding. In the twenties Virginia's per pupil spending was four times as much for white students as it was for black students. The state had 8 four-year black high schools and 400 white high schools; on one occasion a bill was proposed calling for appropriations for white schools only. African Americans were no longer sitting on juries, and the state Democratic Party excluded them from voting in its primaries in 1912. Blacks in need were denied access to some white-only hospitals. Restrictive covenants in the sale of urban property and mandated residential segregation were becoming more common, exemplified by Norfolk's passage of a segregated residential ordinance in 1914 that was frequently enforced by white citizens who threatened blacks trying to locate in border areas. Furthermore, that city provided no parks for black residents. Richmond's white leaders gerrymandered the vibrant black Jackson Ward out of existence, costing its residents any influence on city council. Advertising the attractiveness of Richmond, a Virginia real estate journal proclaimed, "Separate schools for whites and blacks, separate churches, hotels, railroad coaches, and in fact, no intermingling of the races socially, though relations otherwise are amicable and friendly."

In 1922 an organization called the Anglo-Saxon Clubs of America was founded in Richmond to preserve "the supremacy of the white race in the United States" and to find "final solutions of our racial problems." Members included John Powell and Dr. Walter Plecker, first registrar of Virginia's Bureau of Vital Statistics. They lobbied for passage of the 1924 Racial Integrity Act that defined white persons as having no trace of black blood—the one-drop rule—and made it illegal for whites to marry nonwhites, including Asians. It left one loophole for the descendants of Pocahontas: that a person with one-sixteenth or less American Indian blood would be classified as white. Thereafter, Plecker aggressively interpreted the law to allow no race mixing in marriage, in schools, or in cemeteries. He stipulated the race of people regardless of how they identified themselves; in his view Indians were "colored" or "negro" because the roots of both groups were ineradicably intermixed. Old Dominion tribes, who wanted to be neither white nor black, unsuccessfully fought the registrar's designations, which influenced their census classification in 1930 and their draft classification in 1941. Years later, Plecker's racial integrity efforts were labeled "documentary genocide."

Also in 1924 the assembly, influenced by a eugenics movement that was similarly motivated by the obsession with racial and genetic purity, passed a statute permitting involuntary sterilization of those considered mentally defective. In the celebrated case of *Carrie Buck v. J. H. Bell* (head of the state institution for epileptics and the feebleminded), Virginia courts and the U.S. Supreme Court upheld Virginia's sterilization law, with Justice Oliver Wendell Holmes Jr. pithily proclaiming that "three generations of imbeciles were enough." Carrie Buck was sterilized on 19 October 1927, the first of over 8,000 Virginians similarly treated by the commonwealth down to 1974; the state ranked second in the country in the use of this procedure. Virginia's law became a model for thirty other states and was mirrored by a racial hygiene program adopted in Nazi Germany in 1933 that later included a ban against interracial marriage between Germans and Jews.

For the most part race relations in the Old Dominion had reached an uneasy accommodation. Neither blacks nor whites were comfortable with the situation. Many African Americans, who constituted one-third of the state's population, continued to demand justice by boycotting segregated Richmond streetcars, running their own candidate for governor in 1921, successfully challenging a Richmond segregated housing ordinance, and regaining access to the Democratic Party primary in 1929 through court action. The National Association for the Advancement of Colored People established branches in Falls Church and Richmond in 1915, and several other chapters were formed after the war. In the pages of his *Richmond Planet,* John Mitchell fulminated against lynching, segregation, and lily-white Republicanism.

Other black leaders, however, like P. B. Young, editor of the *Norfolk Journal and Guide,* the largest black-owned weekly in the South, feared greater protest would result in the racial terrorism so recently visited on the Deep South by a revived Ku Klux Klan. In the tradition of Booker T. Washington, they chose to work within the structure of segregation, challenging its more obvious inequities and excesses but not pressing for real change. They formed their own religious and fraternal organizations and relied on the traditional network of mutual-aid associations. Predictably, there was a significant out-migration of blacks from Virginia during the war that carried over into the twenties, contributing to the smallest population increase in the state since the 1830s.

White Virginians agreed upon maintaining the system of "separate but equal" but differed over the appropriate methods to achieve this. The bigoted extremists like Powell and Plecker wanted harsher discriminatory legislation, while moderates like Governor Byrd and Richmond newspaperman Douglas Southall Freeman tolerated a degree of black autonomy within the confines of a white supremacist order: a "Virginia way" of genteel racism that avoided both violence and amalgamation. Their paternalistic scheme of managed race relations, part white supremacy and part white responsibility, attempted to balance extremist demands with fairness toward African Americans, but it proved unsustainable in the face of black challenges over the next two decades.

While personally favoring racial separation, Governor Byrd would have preferred not to have the issue injected into debate because, like the liquor question, it threatened political stability and economic progress. Political self-interest was never far from his mind, always influencing the extent of his progressivism. Almost as important as the "courthouse crowd" to the perpetuation of his program and power was the creation of a loyal state bureaucracy, now to be made more responsive to the governor by the reorganization. Key administrative positions in state government were staffed by friends and political allies, whose appointive power created a costly, ponderous patronage system in which jobs were exchanged for votes and contributions. Virginia would soon have one of the largest state workforces per capita in the country.

Although the reorganization effort was Byrd's highest priority, other matters distracted him in the spring of 1926. Brother Richard had succeeded in his heroic flight over the North Pole (although some question remains about whether he ever got there). The event produced a popular delirium that was repeated many times in this zany decade, notably over Charles Lindbergh's transatlantic flight a year later. Technological innovation, the political emancipation of women, greater sexual freedom, and postwar disillusionment forced Americans into an escapist mode during the 1920s. While the darker side of this behavior produced a Red Scare and the revival of the Klan, Americans in their frothier moments turned to sports, movies, and alcohol for their entertainment. Out of their anxiety and the materialistic pleasures of the day, they created bogus heroes and heroines to satisfy their inner needs.

Virginians did not abstain from the activities of the Roaring Twenties. In downtown Richmond they listened to radio accounts of the World Series and the Jack Dempsey–Gene Tunney prize fights that were broadcast over outdoor loudspeakers. And thousands of film fans frequented the dozens of spectacular new movie palaces such as Loew's and the Byrd in the capital to watch Rudolph Valentino and Clara Bow.

Prohibition was observed more in the breach than in the law. Although it had high hopes of burying "demon rum," the Prohibition Commission, established in 1916 under the direction of J. Sidney Peters, a Methodist minister and friend of the Reverend James Cannon, found the enforcement task overwhelming. Smuggling networks infiltrated from the Midwest into the Shenandoah Valley, from Maryland down the Eastern Shore, and at any convenient Chesapeake Bay landing site. Furthermore, local moonshining became a popular and lucrative enterprise, notably in the southern Virginia Blue Ridge where mountain stills satisfied the thirsts of mill towns and urban centers of the mid-Atlantic region. Typical was Mrs. Texanna Chappell of Norfolk, who, with a recipe from a relative, copper kettles and piping, pint jars, and a small stove, operated a wholesale business over her apartment. Despite the zealous efforts of the insufficiently funded commission, whose gun battles with bootleggers, invasions of privacy, and political meddling forced Peters's dismissal, citizens of the commonwealth continued to enjoy their bootleg whiskey or bathtub gin. Although 3,183 of them were arrested in 1928 for violating the drinking laws and 35,655 gallons of liquor were confiscated, juries often would not convict offenders; and local officials, sometimes the recipients of bribes, gave little support to the prohibition agents.

While prohibition put a crimp in the liquor traffic, the prosperity of the Jazz Age did not escape the Old Dominion. Along with an influx of new and diverse industries into the state, notably in rayon textiles, substantial increases in wages and salaries and in per capita wealth and income occurred between 1925 and 1929. Women constituted sizable portions of the workforce in the tobacco, textile, paper, and peanut industries. Tobacco production continued to thrive with the advent of more women smokers. Philip Morris came to Richmond in 1926, and the city's factories produced 36 billion cigarettes and 350 million cigars and cheroots in that year. In the number of automobiles, almost 400,000 in 1930, in wholesale and retail trade volumes, and in the percentage of banks avoiding suspension, Virginia ranked in the upper half of the forty-eight states. Agriculture, too, was diversifying with growth in dairy farming and orcharding, yet the commonwealth was clearly becoming more urban, with one-third of its citizens now residing in cities.

Set apart from the jazz that came to characterize the decade was a more traditional yet equally creative music from the mountains of Southern Appalachia. From the earliest settlers, people from this region had combined a variety of songs and instruments to produce "hillbilly" music. In 1927 the Carter Family and Jimmie Rodgers began recording their music in Bristol, the "Bristol Sessions" that evolved into the commercial country music business and led to its fiddle and banjo offshoot, bluegrass. Over the course of the century, this mountain music with its heart in Southwest Virginia became a multimillion-dollar industry with audiences in the thousands and recordings in the millions.

Virginia also experienced a modest literary flowering in the twenties similar to that occurring elsewhere in the nation and region. In the tradition of the *Southern Literary Messenger* of 1834–64, Richmond's Emily Clark started the *Reviewer* as an outlet for Southern poets and writers. It lasted only four years but was succeeded by the *Virginia Quarterly Review* in 1925. Novelists Ellen Glasgow and James Branch Cabell won plaudits for their rebellion against the romantic plantation novels of Thomas Nelson Page and Mary Johnston, Glasgow with her stoical fiction about ordinary Virginians confronting an unromantic world and Cabell with his satirical representations of the Richmond society in his eighteen-volume biography of Manuel.

Good times and the governor's early success with the General Assembly hit an unpleasant bump in the road during the summer of 1926. Moonshiners killed a state prohibition agent, a black prisoner accused of criminal assault was taken from the Wytheville jail by a masked mob and killed, and Ku Klux Klan activity in the state increased. Thanks to antiforeign hysteria generated by the war, the "Invisible Empire" was making a comeback across America in the 1920s. It had little influence in

Virginia—one historian estimates it had 20,000 members in the state—
but in the "Fighting Ninth," where party competition forced politicians
to latch on to any advantage, the Klan found fertile ground. It seemed to
favor the Republicans, but politicians of both parties, including Byrd's
close aide E. R. "Ebbie" Combs, joined the organization out of political
necessity, if only to keep tabs on the opposition. Byrd had no use for the
Klan, but even he conceded its political power when he voted against
an anti-Klan plank at the 1924 Democratic national convention. In the
summer of 1926, a Catholic priest was abducted in Norfolk, and a masked
mob flogged two women in Bristol. In a more public ceremony attended
by 5,000 Klansmen, Hiram Evans, Imperial Wizard of the national Klan,
presented an American flag and flagpole to the College of William
and Mary.

Faced with such embarrassments, Byrd looked forward to the beginning of a new year and submission of the reorganization report by
the highly regarded New York Bureau of Municipal Research, whose
purpose was the promotion of efficient management of state and local
government. Most of the bureau's recommendations were approved by a
citizens' panel of thirty-eight prominent Virginians chaired by William
Reed, Byrd's closest adviser. The Reed committee recommended consolidation of the state bureaucracy into eleven major departments, a uniform accounting system, and the short ballot. Another commission on
constitutional changes endorsed the pending amendments on the short
ballot and tax segregation and proposed eighty lesser changes. Among its
more significant proposals was a limitation on future bond issues by the
state of 1 percent of the assessed value of all land in the state (an estimated
limit at that time of $12 million), with any bond issue to be approved by
the people. In a remarkable demonstration of unanimity, the 1927 special
assembly session passed the reorganization bill without dissent, while
the constitutional revisions were approved by the House of Delegates
76–6 and by the Senate 35–1.

What remained to complete Byrd's program was another session
of the General Assembly and a public referendum on the constitutional
changes, both set for 1928. In the interim the governor continued to be
Virginia's number one booster. Industrial development, highways, and
tourism were his primary pursuits. The first national advertisement extolling Virginia as a location for business appeared in the *New York Times*
in September, part of a $50,000 appropriation by the assembly to publi-
cize the state. Coincidentally, several large companies announced plans
to construct plants in Virginia. At the suggestion of the APVA, the governor instituted the highway signs that mark places of historical importance in the state and advocated building roads to state shrines such as
Jamestown and Monticello; he also encouraged the restoration of Colo-

nial Williamsburg, the idea of the Reverend Dr. W. A. R. Goodwin, rector of Bruton Parish Church, who had interested John D. Rockefeller Jr. in the project in 1926. Dedicated in 1934 by President Franklin Roosevelt, Williamsburg became the preeminent example of historic preservation in the country and a major tourist attraction.

One problem whose solution eluded Byrd was the ongoing conflict with independent Virginia watermen, who were raiding private oyster beds in the York River in violation of state lease arrangements. Byrd intervened in the dispute on several occasions, even sending in a National Guard contingent to repress armed violence, but the "oyster wars" continued to confound him to the end of his term.

In 1928 Byrd presented his "Program of Progress" to the legislature, requesting increased revenues for highways and education, the latter now ranked forty-third in the nation by the federal Bureau of Education. He also requested a state antilynching law that would make such a crime a state offense and require localities where the lynchings occurred to pay $2,500 to the estates of the victims. Angry at the recent mob actions in the state and influenced by the courageous editorials of Louis Jaffe of the *Norfolk Virginian-Pilot*, Byrd sought legislation that would prevent their recurrence. The final bill was stripped of its penalty provision, but what remained was one of the strongest antilynching laws in the country. The assembly and the electorate also approved the constitutional amendments, the capstone to the governor's reorganization efforts.

Byrd's last eighteen months in office were dominated by the presidential election in 1928 and the gubernatorial election in 1929, both of which challenged his leadership and threatened his "Program of Progress." The injection of religion and prohibition into these campaigns made the elections uncontrollable and unpredictable, the very things that Byrd dreaded. The culprits were the competing spirits of nativism and modernism that afflicted the 1920s. Made insecure by the fast-paced cultural and technological changes of the day, many Americans took out their frustrations on the powerless, the different, and the new—blacks, Catholics, Jews, and immigrants—relying on the Klan and prohibition as means of controlling undesirable behavior by these "outsiders." Although not restricted to the South, these anxieties made that rural, Protestant region particularly vulnerable to political demagoguery.

The nomination by Democrats of New York governor Al Smith for the presidency caused Organization leaders to worry about their political future. Smith, a Catholic who opposed prohibition, urged a review of the national experiment to permit some sort of local option. Virginia Democrats knew they were in for a fight when James Cannon, now a Methodist bishop, immediately called for a party revolt and the election of a "dry" candidate. No longer as influential in state politics since the election of Harry Byrd, Cannon was searching for issues and candidates that would restore his prominence. His prayers seemed answered when Republicans endorsed prohibition and nominated Secretary of Commerce Herbert Hoover, a Quaker who was personally "dry."

The fall campaign was marked by demagoguery, acrimony, and vituperation not witnessed in a presidential contest in Virginia in years. Republican ranks were swelled by Klansmen, Anti-Saloon League advocates, and rabble-rousing preachers, all condemning the "rum and Romanism" of the Democrats. The Patriotic Sons of America distributed a pamphlet in the state claiming a Smith victory would result in the teaching of the Catholic religion in the public schools. Additional propaganda predicted papal rule, a return of the Spanish Inquisition, and wars against Protestants. Democrats retaliated by employing race. In warning against the prospects of a Republican victory, Byrd revived the memory of "Black Reconstruction" and appealed to racial prejudice in order to combat religious bigotry. "Virginia owes white supremacy to the Democratic Party," he reminded voters. Because Byrd so rarely used the race issue in his long political career, his several references to it in 1928 indicate the desperation of the cause.

The impact of emotional issues like prohibition and religion and the booming prosperity of the 1920s that many attributed to Republican policies made Hoover's nationwide landslide predictable, but the results in the Old Dominion could not have been more astonishing. In the biggest turnout for a presidential election since 1888, Republicans carried Virginia for the first time since Reconstruction. Receiving the votes of many Democrats, called "Hoovercrats," Hoover won all but one congressional district in the Old Dominion and carried the urban vote in his majority of nearly 25,000 votes. Republicans also gained three congressional seats. Smith's defeat was ample testimony to the power of prejudice and fear in politics.

As 1929 progressed, attention turned to the race for governor. Byrd decided that the surest way to retrieve the Hoover defectors was to give them a candidate they could like but one who was committed to his reorganization. Several names surfaced, but no one matched the desired profile better than John Garland Pollard, dean of the School of Government and Citizenship at the College of William and Mary. Pollard was an unusual choice, for he had spent most of his adult life fighting the Organization, but his prominence as a Baptist layman would put the religious issue to rest, and he was "dry." Pledging his personal allegiance, Pollard won Byrd's endorsement and easily dispatched Walter Mapp in the primary.

During the Democratic primary race, the "Hoovercrats" entered into the anticipated coalition with the Republicans and nominated Dr. William Moseley Brown, professor of psychology and education at

Washington and Lee University. They adopted a platform that denounced the short ballot and current election laws and praised the sanctity of the Eighteenth Amendment. Over the summer coalition forces were staggered by the revelations that their acknowledged leader, Bishop Cannon, had been involved in the shady practices of stock market gambling, flour hoarding during the war, and misappropriation of church funds. The embarrassed cleric withdrew from the campaign and in mid-October sailed for Brazil to oversee his episcopal conferences. Not only was the bishop discredited as a moral leader, but his departure signaled the defeat of Brown. Pollard's landslide triumph in November put to rest hopes of a competitive two-party system in Virginia for another twenty-four years. Cannonism was repudiated, and the Organization reigned supreme.

In his final days as governor, Byrd concerned himself with budget preparations and appointments. The recent stock market crash raised nary an eyebrow. He heartily concurred with President Hoover's request to maintain prosperity by increasing road building and other construction. In his last address to the General Assembly, Governor Byrd reviewed the past record one more time: the industrial progress, a $4 million treasury surplus, tax segregation, the reorganization of the executive branch, over 2,000 miles of new roads, and creation of the Shenandoah National Park.

Byrd's efforts have been labeled "business progressivism," a progressivism of the twenties that emphasized expanded and efficient governmental services for purposes of economic development, as opposed to the older, more moralistic brand of progressivism that accentuated democracy, corporate regulation, and social justice. Virginia was not alone in experiencing this reincarnation of a New South in the 1920s, as North Carolina, Alabama, and Tennessee pursued similar programs. State government expenditures for highway construction and schools rose significantly in the twenties. In Virginia this was accompanied by sizable increases in the number of businesses, amount of capital invested, value of production, and employment in manufacturing. However, "business progressivism," like its earlier reform cousin, did not run very deep. Little attention was paid to the problems of agriculture, poverty, labor relations, or child labor, not to mention race relations.

Within the narrow parameters of "business progressivism," Harry Byrd was a successful governor. But despite all the bright lights—and unquestionably the excitement of the times contributed to a sense of forward motion—Virginia changed very little in the twenties. Its industrial growth was impressive, but the commonwealth continued to languish at the bottom of the states in appropriations for schools, public welfare, state hospitals, and correctional facilities. Most of the recommendations of an education commission were ignored. Even in highway construction, despite all the hoopla, the Old Dominion was lagging behind North Carolina, and it was costing more than predicted. The reforms that were adopted had a superficial quality to them, a musical chairs arrangement that shifted agencies around but left them without central direction. Always concerned about his leadership of the Organization, Byrd left the corrupt fee system intact and the grossly incompetent and inefficient county governments untouched. As Raymond Pulley has written, "During the late 1920's the traditionalist ruling class of the Old Dominion simply lost interest in creating better social services for the people."

SOURCES CONSULTED

"Advertising Virginia: Tourism in the Old Dominion in the Twenties and the Great Depression," *Virginia Cavalcade* (Summer 1994); Andrew Buni, *The Negro in Virginia Politics, 1902–1965* (1967); Nancy Carter Crump, "Hopewell during World War I: 'The Toughest Town North of Hell,'" *Virginia Cavalcade* (Summer 1981); Virginius Dabney, *Dry Messiah: The Life of Bishop Cannon* (1949); Arthur Kyle Davis, ed., *Publications of the Virginia War History Commission,* 7 vols. (1923–27); Anne Hobson Freeman, "Mary Munford's Fight for a College for Women Coordinate with the University of Virginia," *VMHB* (Oct. 1970); Sara Hunter Graham, "Woman Suffrage in Virginia: The Equal Suffrage League and Pressure Group Politics, 1909–1920," *VMHB* (April 1993); Elna C. Green, *Southern Strategies: Southern Women and the Woman Suffrage Question* (1997); Grace Elizabeth Hale, *Making Whiteness: The Culture of Segregation in the South, 1890–1940* (1998); Alvin L. Hall, "Virginia Back in the Fold: The Gubernatorial Campaign and Election of 1929," *VMHB* (July 1965); Ronald L. Heinemann, *Harry Byrd of Virginia* (1996); Jack Temple Kirby, *Westmoreland Davis: Virginia Planter-Politician, 1859–1942* (1968); Suzanne Lebsock, *"A Share of Honour": Virginia Women, 1600–1945* (1984); Earl Lewis, *In Their Own Interest: Race, Class, and Power in Twentieth-Century Norfolk, Virginia* (1991); Thomas C. Parramore, Peter C. Stewart, and Tommy L. Bogger, *Norfolk: The First Four Centuries* (1994); Richard B. Sherman, "'The Last Stand': The Fight for Racial Integrity in Virginia in the 1920's," *JSH* (Feb. 1988); Dennis E. Simmons, "Conservation, Cooperation, and Controversy: The Establishment of Shenandoah National Park," *VMHB* (Jan. 1994); J. David Smith and K. Ray Nelson, *The Sterilization of Carrie Buck* (1989); J. Douglas Smith, *Managing White Supremacy: Race, Politics, and Citizenship in Jim Crow Virginia* (2002); James R. Sweeney, "Rum, Romanism, and Virginia Democrats: The Party Leaders and the Campaign of 1928," *VMHB* (Oct. 1982); George B. Tindall, "Business Progressivism: Southern Politics in the Twenties," *South Atlantic Quarterly* (Winter 1963); *Virginia Cavalcade,* Summer 2001 issue on World War I; Marjorie Spruill Wheeler, "Mary Johnston, Suffragist," *VMHB* (Jan. 1992).

14

DEPRESSION AND WAR

1930–1945

From 1930 to 1945 the Old Dominion was shaken by two events over which it had no control, but which had a greater impact on the state than any other sequence of events in the twentieth century. The Great Depression brought the American economy to a standstill and produced untold misery for Virginians, reminding them of the dark days of the Civil War. World War II, on the other hand, revitalized the national and state economies, and although it demanded great sacrifices of the people, it restored public confidence in America's future and prepared the way for new opportunities.

The Great Depression of the thirties was brought on by a combination of negative economic factors including overproduction, inequitable distribution of income that affected consumption, and the stock market crash of 1929. It was one of the watershed events of twentieth-century America, shattering the people's optimistic faith in a utopian future, challenging their belief in rugged individualism, and leading to a revolution in the role of government in their lives.

Virginia had a delayed reaction to the financial calamity. The nature of its economy—the balance between agriculture, industry, and commerce, subsistence-level farming, and the support of federal money in the Washington and Norfolk areas—immunized the state from the immediate effects of the crash. Agriculture was diversified and not enslaved to one crop. Old Dominion manufacturing, absent the heavy industries of steel and automobiles that sustained huge national losses, was more consumer oriented, producing those necessities that even a poverty-stricken people could not do without: food, clothing, and cigarettes. By 1933 the value of manufactured products in Virginia had fallen by 30 percent from 1929 levels, but the nation's production had declined by more than 50 percent. In 1934, 40 billion cigarettes were made in Richmond, which yielded only a modest decline in the production value of tobacco.

These buffers eventually broke down, but they did minimize the total effect of the depression in Virginia and contributed to its more rapid recovery by 1935. The conservative nature of the Old Dominion and the strength of traditionalism also helped to insulate the state from the worst shocks of the depression. Ledger books in the black, a reluctance to borrow, a stoical outlook, and a strong self-help ethic had a very stabilizing effect when times turned bad. During the 1930 drought that seriously crippled the state's farmers, a Red Cross official remarked, "Virginians are prouder and less willing to seek outside help than citizens of the other states in the drought areas."

Nevertheless, Virginia was not "depression-proof." Although the crisis was late arriving, its impact was strongly felt by early 1931. Unemployed Danville textile workers, who had been unsuccessful in their four-month strike to restore wage cuts at Dan River Mills, were on the verge of starvation; soup kitchens were feeding hungry schoolchildren in the mountain regions, and school terms were ending early in several counties; cities were making major budget cuts; farm prices, notably for tobacco, continued downward; and the unthinkable occurred: Governor Pollard announced a possible budget deficit. C. D. Bryant, director of a Danville tobacco warehouse, wrote his congressman: "The farmers are wrought up at a high pitch, a great many declaring vengeance due to the deplorable condition of their families suffering for want of clothing, medicine and other absolute necessities. . . . We find men on our warehouse floor actually weeping after they have had to sell their tobacco at prices that will mean nothing less than complete disaster."

Over the next two years, the economy hit rock bottom. Despite their self-sufficiency, it became a time for rigid economizing on Virginia's farms. Many farmers stopped growing tobacco because it did not pay the fertilizer and marketing costs and turned to a "cow, sow, and hen" extension program that generated some income through the sale of chickens, pulpwood, and cream. Practically no agricultural machinery was purchased, and deterioration in buildings and equipment was widespread. Albemarle farmer Clarence Holt recalled, "Money for necessities was scarce—for luxuries, non-existent . . . work clothes bore many patches and did not always match. Dresses were made from chicken feed bags; more undergarments carried the trademark of 4X flour than of any department store." Gasoline became a luxury, and money was not available to repair cars, so some farmers stripped down the chassis, hitched up the team to it, and went to town in a "Hoover cart." Rural businesses were ruined by the loss of farm income, and farm foreclosures did occur, although not with great frequency. Agricultural agent John Freeman recollected: "People were in a daze—shock actually. There was not much unrest, per se, but had steps not been taken, as were taken in 1933–34, the situation could have become chaotic."

Urban centers, experiencing wholesale industrial layoffs and attracting large numbers of unemployed drifters, did not survive as easily as the rural areas. Soup kitchens and breadlines became common features on city streets. A Portsmouth church was feeding 100 people a day with leftovers collected from the naval base. Although the presence of the military mitigated the worst of the storm, Norfolk released many firemen, policemen, garbage collectors, and teachers from employment, closed city kindergartens, and turned off streetlights. A Richmond lawyer recalled: "It was bad here. Everybody was bewildered at the change. Money was scarce and almost everybody suffered a reduction in standard of living. Economically everything slowed down about half. Nobody wanted anything done." People did their own laundry, garaged the car, allowed automobile licenses to lapse, and did without vacations. Smokers turned to "roll your own" cigarettes, while factories in the capital converted production from their major brands to ten-cent varieties that gained 23 percent of the market. Studies of Richmond unemployed showed a high rate of illness, debt, and emotional problems among their families, many of whose members had turned to begging, excessive drinking, and criminal activity, even prostitution. Private relief agencies like the Family Service Society and the Salvation Army exhausted their resources, forcing greater reliance on public relief.

Black Virginians, usually the "last hired and first fired," were among the hardest hit. Already experiencing inferior health, housing, and education conditions, they now confronted economic devastation compounded by heightened discrimination. For Hattie McNamara, whose husband and father were both unemployed, life was precarious; at times, she said, the family was "just about to give up." They did without food and clothing and frequently were behind in their rent. There were reports of nearly starving black children around Suffolk who were not going to school because they had no clothes and who were without medical services. African American businesses, reliant almost solely on black buying power, were severely squeezed, and many closed, including some of the few black banks in the state. Unemployed whites took jobs normally reserved for blacks, and some organizations were calling on employers to fire blacks and hire whites. Scarce relief funds invariably were unfairly distributed, sometimes denied altogether. Continuing a trend begun in the twenties, black farm holding declined. The only consolation in all this was that decades-old discrimination and poverty made greater deprivation somewhat easier to bear; in fact, some blacks noted very little change, being "used to hard times anyway."

Demonstrating an attitude prominent at the national level, Virginia's leaders were reluctant to institute expensive relief measures, believing that budget balancing would have a more vital impact on business confidence. Assuming the chairmanship of a new Committee on Unemployment in 1931, William Reed optimistically concluded, "I believe Virginia is in better shape in this respect than any state in the Union, ... even better than she was a year ago." Grossly underestimating the number out of work at less than 20,000, probably only a third of the real figure, the committee recommended no state relief effort, preferring, instead, reliance on the Community Chest and Red Cross, whose funds were drying up. A compassionate, generous man, Reed did not want to acknowledge suffering on a large scale, fearing that public efforts to deal with it would undermine individual character and the "Virginia Way." He advised Harry Byrd, "We must keep Virginia like she is without any changes."

The depression also complicated Byrd's efforts to maintain a balanced state budget. Although no longer governor, he remained actively involved in Virginia affairs. Worried that deficits would lead to attacks on his tax segregation system, Byrd counseled Governor Pollard to oppose higher taxes and relief plans and to cut appropriations. Almost without exception his proposals were enacted into law by the 1932 General Assembly. To placate those demanding tax relief, Byrd proposed a road plan under which the state would take over the county road system, saving the counties $3.4 million in road expenditures and adding 36,000 miles to the state system. In spite of urban opposition, the Byrd Road Act passed the rural-dominated assembly overwhelmingly, leaving no doubt about Byrd's continued influence in state politics.

The winter of 1932–33 was the nadir of the depression. For millions of Americans the necessities of life had become luxuries; itinerants, soup kitchens, and shantytowns, derisively named "Hoovervilles" for the outgoing president, were common features on the urban landscape. Steel production had fallen to 12 percent of capacity, and industrial construction was less than 8 percent of what it had been in 1929; more than a quarter of the workforce was unemployed. In the countryside farmers struggled to prevent foreclosures on their farms, declared farm holidays, and destroyed farm produce rather than sell it at ridiculously low prices. At the moment of Franklin Roosevelt's inauguration, the nation's banking system was on the verge of collapse.

In Virginia the situation was only slightly better. Unemployment averaged 100,000 workers during 1932, peaking in July at 145,000. Industrial wages and manufacturing output had fallen by over a third; farm income had been cut in half. Faced with falling revenues, city, county, and state governments reduced salaries, staffs, and services, leaving a depleted private relief sector to cope with growing relief rolls. Hunger marches occurred in the capital of the Confederacy, and 3,000 schoolchildren in Lee County were reported "undernourished and underclothed." Virginia avoided the worst aspects of the crash, but suffering in the commonwealth differed from hardships elsewhere only by a matter of degree.

Confronting such a crisis, President Franklin Roosevelt, in an inspiring but candid inaugural address, called on Americans for new resolve and asked for "broad executive power to wage a war against the emergency, as great as the power that would be given to me if we were in fact invaded by a foreign foe." Sworn in only moments before on that cold, blustery March morning, Harry Byrd, recently named to the U.S. Senate seat vacated by Claude Swanson's appointment as navy secretary, responded enthusiastically to the president's call, supporting limited debate on Roosevelt's program in order not to impede its progress. The ensuing congressional session of 1933—the Hundred Days—produced more significant legislation than that of any previous American Congress. It would be known as Roosevelt's "New Deal." Within a week the president closed the banks, stampeded Congress into passing emergency banking legislation, delivered the first of his comforting fireside chats, and reopened the banks, all leading to a restoration of public confidence in the government and its new leader.

In the midst of the Hundred Days, Virginia began the process of electing a new governor. George Campbell Peery was Harry Byrd's choice to maintain his control of state politics. A tall, distinguished-looking lawyer from Tazewell County, Peery had impeccable Organization credentials, having redeemed the Fighting Ninth from the Republicans in 1922 and served three terms in Congress. However, the inflammable issue of prohibition threatened to disrupt his ascendance. Public rejection, enforcement difficulties, and an economy starved for new sources of revenue in liquor taxes generated widespread support for repealing prohibition. With Richmond restaurants openly selling beer and Peery's opponents pressing for state repeal, Senator Byrd coerced Governor Pollard into calling a special session of the General Assembly that legalized beer, taxed it, and set up an October referendum on the Twenty-first Amendment that overwhelmingly ended the "noble experiment" in Virginia. With the controversy diffused, Peery rolled to easy victories in the primary and general elections.

Although Peery proved slightly more independent of Byrd than Pollard, he paid homage to economy in government and did not overturn any of Byrd's reforms. On the liquor issue Peery insisted on tight state control rather than liquor-by-the-drink and private licensing. The result was the creation of a three-man Alcoholic Beverage Control Board to supervise operation of state liquor stores. Over time, with careful appointments, the ABC Board remained free of political scandals and funneled millions of dollars in liquor taxes into state coffers. Ironically, state control and local option laws did not end the illegal whiskey trade but may even have perpetuated it; Franklin County became the self-proclaimed "Moonshine Capital of the World." To replace the fee-paid justices of the peace, the 1934 General Assembly also created a system of salaried local trial justices that eventually evolved into Virginia's district courts.

With the ink hardly dry on the handiwork of the assembly, Senator Byrd made his first major attack on the New Deal over agricultural policy. He had endorsed the creation in 1933 of the Agricultural Adjustment Administration that offered farmers money in return for reducing acreage planted—the domestic allotment plan designed to combat crop overproduction that had kept prices low. But he did not like the coercive and bureaucratic features of the legislation, and when a new farm bill was introduced in 1934 that extended the power of the government over agriculture, Byrd rebelled, referring to Secretary of Agriculture Henry Wallace as a potential "Hitler of American agriculture." Many Virginians did not agree with the senator on the farm legislation, including farmers, who year after year gave it their overwhelming endorsement. Farm prices and income were going up.

Another point of contention with Roosevelt was emerging over Virginia's response to the New Deal relief programs. Persistent high unemployment levels had exhausted the capacities of private charities and local and state relief agencies to deal with the problem, leading to the creation of a federal program operated by the Federal Emergency Relief Administration. FERA funded food, clothing, and shelter for the destitute and provided work relief for employables where possible. By mid-1935, 40,000 to 50,000 Virginians were at work on over 2,500 projects, constructing schools, roads, parks, and sewers, while thousands of others received aid from special programs for transients, college students, and impoverished rural residents. A Women's Work Division under the direction of Ella Agnew created jobs for women in libraries, clerical and recreational positions, and sewing rooms, 100 of which were producing thousands of garments for the needy. Despite the large number of aid recipients, the percentage of Virginia's population on relief always was among the lowest in the nation—8.6 percent compared to the national average of 15.6 percent—reflecting the state's lesser need and more parsimonious nature.

Virginia was one of the few states that never authorized the required matching funds for direct relief during FERA's existence. From the inception of the program, state leaders claimed that money spent providing work for the unemployed on the highways, begun during the severe 1930 drought, was the equivalent of direct relief appropriations. Federal relief director Harry Hopkins retorted that Virginia was sacrificing not at all because other states were spending for both roads and relief. The argument lasted for the life of FERA, and although Hopkins threatened to end allotments to Virginia, he never carried out his ultimatum, a decision that allowed the Old Dominion to follow a more independent course of action. Faced with such obstruction, the federal government wound up paying 92 percent of Virginia's relief bill ($26 million), with the localities putting up about 8 percent and the state contributing a paltry $34,000.

Down in Abingdon, Robert Porterfield designed a local solution to the unemployment problem: a theater to employ out-of-work actors from around the country. The Barter Theater opened in 1933 and charged canned goods or other commodities—jams, eggs, ham, cakes—as the price of admission. It made $4.30 its first year, but the actors gained 305 pounds. Barter survived the depression, becoming the first state theater in the country.

The advent of a new relief program in 1935, the Works Progress Administration, which emphasized work rather than the dole, did not convert Byrd, who unsuccessfully lobbied to reduce the size of this $4 billion relief bill, the largest peacetime appropriation in U.S. history to that point. With words that would echo through the halls of Congress for another thirty years, he called for an end to the "spending orgy at Washington," declaring that he was "opposed to mortgaging the future welfare of our children, grandchildren, and even generations to come." In his view crisis legislation must now yield to sound principles.

Since the WPA was a federally directed program that required no matching state funds, Organization leaders could do little to obstruct its work other than to admonish Washington for its extravagances. Although it was susceptible to charges of "leaf-raking," the WPA performed splendidly in the state during its eight-year life, employing an estimated 95,000 Virginians who earned $66 million. Mirroring FERA but on a much larger scale, it built schools, roads, and airports, provided school lunches, produced clothes in its sewing rooms, employed jobless white-collar workers in art, library, writing, and music projects, and improved public health through its clinics and construction of privies. It also supervised the National Youth Administration, which provided modest employment for young people in order to keep them in school. The WPA complemented the role of the Public Works Administration, which for two years had been alleviating unemployment by funding major construction projects, such as the state library in Richmond, Alderman Library at the University of Virginia, and the Roanoke Veterans Administration hospital.

The WPA was part of a new legislative program put forth in 1935 (called by some historians a second New Deal) to address the more deeply rooted social and economic ills affecting American life. Other major components included social security legislation, the Wagner Labor Relations Act, and long-term farm legislation. The introduction of a national social security program was dictated by inadequate private and state support for the aged, the disabled, and the unemployed. None of these groups received assistance from Virginia, whose welfare commitment in 1935 was judged among the worst in the country, the product of a shortsighted devotion to fiscal conservatism and a faith in the power of self-help. Over the objections of Virginia's two senators, the security program, which incorporated pension programs for current and future elderly, unemployment insurance, aid for dependent children and the disabled, and public health services, was approved by Congress.

Characteristically, Virginia became the last state to join the security program. Fearing federal control and future costs, Byrd and Governor Peery delayed participation until 1938 when the assembly consented to have Virginia join the other forty-seven states in the basic pension program but on a more limited basis than that recommended by the Virginia Commission on Old Age Assistance. Virginians began receiving benefits three years after Congress had enacted the plan into law. Nevertheless, with federal encouragement and pressure, Virginia's public welfare programs were significantly upgraded.

Byrd's record on labor had also taken a decidedly negative cast, culminating with his vote against the Wagner Labor Relations Act, which placed the power of government behind the rights of workers to organize and bargain collectively. Organized labor had never been a powerful force in the Old Dominion, whose low-value-added industries of tobacco, coal mining, textiles, and food processing depended upon inexpensive, easily replaced unskilled or semiskilled labor with limited bargaining power. Strikes were infrequent and unsuccessful. In the textile strike at Dan River Mills in 1930, 4,000 workers left their jobs demanding restoration of wages and a reduced workweek, but they confronted an obstinate mill president, H. R. Fitzgerald, who refused to mediate. When violence broke out, Governor Pollard sent in National Guard troops to preserve the peace and continue the operation of the mill with nonstriking workers, effectively breaking the strike. Similarly, the United Mine Workers' efforts to unionize the Virginia coalfields in 1933 were vigorously opposed by management, scabs, and armed state troopers, resulting in strikes, evictions from company housing, discharges, and violence. In the nationwide textile strike in 1934, the United Textile Workers Union was so weak in Virginia that state union officials declined to participate.

Nevertheless, the authority of the Wagner Act and the competition between the American Federation of Labor and the newly formed Congress of Industrial Organizations for new members resulted in increased union activity in the state. Strikes became more numerous, and membership rose. Even the shocking sit-down strikes instituted by Detroit auto workers came to Virginia in 1937 when employees struck the Industrial Rayon Corporation in Covington. Much like his predecessor, Governor Peery, at the first sign of violence, used state police to escort some workers back to their jobs, thus breaking the strike. However, in a bandwagon effect, rayon plants in Waynesboro and Ampthill, cotton mills in Martinsville and Danville, and tobacco plants in Richmond raised wages before strikes could begin. In the Richmond tobacco stemmeries, black women, who made up 60 percent of the workforce in the preparation of the leaf for manufacturing, walked off the job at the Carrington and Michaux tobacco plant protesting low wages, which for some of them was five cents an hour. Rejected by the largely segregated AFL Tobacco Workers International Union, they formed their own independent union with the support of the Southern Negro Youth Congress and the CIO and won a wage increase, a forty-hour week, and recognition of their union. Several other Richmond tobacco plants were similarly organized. By the end of the decade, most of Virginia's coal mines were unionized as well. Nevertheless, despite the benefits Virginia's workers gained through federal legislation and their own courageous efforts, unions did not become a major voice in the state's political life. Indeed, unionization and minimum wage laws forced many plants to mechanize, costing many tobacco stemmers their jobs.

Despite Senator Byrd's reservations, the New Deal was very much in evidence in the Old Dominion. Its ubiquitous programs aided almost every segment of Virginia society, easing them through the calamity of depression. Because the commonwealth provided practically no money for relief and the localities appropriated only meager amounts, the federal programs deserve the credit for feeding and clothing Virginia's needy. The roads and bridges, schools and post offices, hospitals and libraries they constructed were more than concrete monuments to federal generosity; they were the means by which thousands of Virginians began to live better lives. The farm programs of the New Deal alleviated the immediate problem of overproduction, raising prices and restoring farmers to a position of respectability. A state park system, compliments of the Civilian Conservation Corps, which put unemployed young Virginians to work in the state's forests, an improved welfare system, a minimum wage, electrified farms through the auspices of the Rural Electrification Administration, homes saved through the Home Owners' Loan Corporation, and farms saved with the help of the Farm Credit Administration extended opportunity and security to all groups.

Yet for all its good intentions and money, the New Deal did not convert Virginia into a modern progressive state. Neither did it end the depression. The peculiar nature of Old Dominion agriculture with its crop diversity and large number of subsistence farms made it less well suited for the crop control programs of the AAA that assisted farmers in Iowa and Nebraska. Initiatives for small farmers and tenants, always underfunded, did not address the issues of mechanization and agribusiness that were threatening the future of the family farm. Improvements in welfare assistance avoided embarrassment but did not bring social transformation to an impoverished population, and most New Deal programs remained racially segregated. They were not radical enough in design to overcome the political opposition, local interests, and allegiance to an older ethic of rugged individualism that they confronted. In Virginia this meant Harry Byrd.

There was some validity to Byrd's actions. Balanced budgets and reduced expenditures had preserved the financial integrity of the Old Dominion, contributing to a faster recovery. By 1937 all manufacturing indexes exceeded those of 1929: salaries, wages, number of workers, and value of products. For those depression years Virginia ranked first in the country in the increase in the value of its industrial products. Over 500 new manufacturing firms settled in the Old Dominion in the last half of the decade. New parks and roads and the development of Colonial Williamsburg were turning the state into a tourist mecca. However, Byrd's measures had not prevented adversity from gripping the state, nor had they alleviated the more deep-seated problems affecting the state. The depression had brought undue misery to thousands of Virginians, impoverishing, disrupting, and scarring their lives, in some cases permanently. Yet Byrd and his lieutenants became captives of their own propaganda about how well-off Virginia was and refused to recognize and correct existing conditions. Hardened into dogma, pay-as-you-go became a barrier obstructing the road to progress.

Byrd's independent political course in the face of Roosevelt's popularity in the Old Dominion defied all logic, yet Virginians, in a surprising display of impartiality, divided their loyalties between the New Deal and the Organization in the mid-1930s. Other than the political leadership and the business community, few groups in the state were openly hostile to the national program; most Virginians endorsed the energetic actions of an administration that had pulled the nation out of the despair of 1932. Roosevelt won 70 percent of the state vote in his landslide reelection in 1936. Yet these same people also returned to office Organization men whose philosophies were diametrically opposed to those of the New Dealers. Senator Byrd and his pay-as-you-go program were equally well liked.

The structure of Old Dominion politics permitted the coexistence of the New Deal and the Organization. The state's off-year election arrangement kept state elections from being influenced by the heat of a national contest. The "courthouse crowd," provided with jobs in a period of great scarcity, remained intensely loyal to the leadership. The electorate remained small and controllable; the people who received most of the New Deal money and who might have opposed the Organization had no political voice. Urban interests, which tended to favor increased spending for educational and welfare facilities, were grossly underrepresented in the legislature and thus powerless. Finally, there was rarely an alternative to vote for. Virginia was a Democratic stronghold, and party loyalty demanded that both state and national leaders be endorsed.

Coexistence, however, did have its limitations. FDR's popularity waned in the late thirties as Senator Byrd's economy drive received greater support. Most Virginians still liked Roosevelt, but his spending policies and political maneuverings, notably his abortive court-packing scheme, made it unlikely that they would depose their favorite sons, who were trying to protect them from the high taxes and federal interference that had always been anathema to them. They would not turn their backs on federal money, but neither would they reject the time-honored bromides of states' rights, rugged individualism, and economy and efficiency. Such an attitude permitted Byrd to follow his independent course of attacking the New Deal while maintaining his personal hegemony over the Old Dominion.

Byrd's plate was full in the late thirties. Not only was he waging critical battles with the New Dealers, but he also confronted a serious challenge to his leadership of Virginia: Jim Price's election to the governorship. The emergence of a political opposition jolted Byrd, who may have been lulled into a false sense of security by Peery's easy victory in 1933 and his own electoral successes. There had always been differences of opinion between moderate reformers and conservatives within the machine dating back to the Martin years, but Byrd's rise to power and the progressive nature of his governorship had unified the two wings of the party, leaving only a few renegades and discontented office seekers on the outside. However, the scarcity of top political jobs at the state level and disagreement over ways to combat the depression produced a growing number of dissatisfied followers who were soon to be labeled anti-Organization or "antis": enemies of the machine.

The "antis" included former governors Westmoreland Davis and E. Lee Trinkle, Lieutenant Governor James Price, Congressman John Flannagan, party secretary Martin Hutchinson, and editors Norman Hamilton and Charles Harkrader. Although they remained loyal Democrats, their political ambitions and personal philosophies were incompatible with Organization objectives. A few of them had liberal backgrounds, but most were fiscal conservatives who simply believed that more money should be made available for services other than highways. The allegiance Byrd demanded precluded their kind of independence, and although many of them remained on the fringes of the Organization because there was no alternative, they chafed at their forced subservience. Worth Smith, who had lost to Peery in 1933, characterized their frustration: "Personally, I tried to be loyal to Senator Byrd, but after a few years I found out that in order to be loyal to him I'd have to become a bullfrog and jump every time he said jump, regardless of my personal views on any subject." For the "antis," the New Deal offered hope of political emancipation.

The specter of Jim Price had been in the minds of Organization leaders for years. Handsome, gregarious, and active in several fraternal organizations, he had represented Richmond in the House of Delegates for seven terms before the machine selected him to be Pollard's running mate in the crucial 1929 race against the Cannonites. While his popularity had made him acceptable to the leadership, he did not move into the inner circle primarily because he had taken positions at variance with those of the Organization. Desiring to be governor more for the honor than the power but aware that Byrd's disfavor might deny him that reward, Price disrupted the normal selection procedure by announcing in July 1935 that he would be a candidate for governor in 1937. Cognizant of Price's ambition, the senator floated a few trial candidates of his own, none of which found a favorable wind. For the only time in his forty-year reign as head of the Organization, Byrd would not personally influence the selection of the governor.

Price's first session with the General Assembly in 1938 proved to be the pinnacle of his success against the machine. Much of his legislative program passed in the face of minimal opposition: social security, a forty-eight-hour workweek for women, and increased aid to schools. The major controversy came when he fired Ebbie Combs from his two positions as comptroller and chairman of the new Compensation Board that had been created to fix the salaries and expenses of local officials. Although the governor also removed the heads of several other departments, his action against Combs, Harry Byrd's longtime friend, was deemed most offensive and threatening, especially because of the crucial patronage power held by the Compensation Board. Price overcame an attempt to restrict his appointive power, but the controversy intensified the struggle between the "antis" and the Organization, whose leaders were concerned about renewed reports from Washington that the administration was out to challenge Byrd's rule in Virginia.

The confrontation broke publicly in July 1938 with President Roosevelt's recess appointment of Judge Floyd Roberts of Bristol to a newly created federal judgeship in the Western District of Virginia. Claiming the president had disregarded the two recommendations that he and Byrd had submitted, Senator Glass termed Roberts's nomination "personally offensive." This slap at two revered solons undermined public support in the Old Dominion for both Roosevelt and Jim Price, who had backed Roberts, and the nomination went down to ignominious defeat when a majority of senators sided with their Virginia colleagues.

Midway through the 1940 assembly session, Price gave the leadership a reason for acting on their suspicions about his future ambitions. He put forward a reorganization plan that would have consolidated several departments at a savings of $350,000. It was a masterful proposal, but the threat to patronage in the lucrative conservation agencies and the Division of Motor Vehicles was obvious. Led by allies of the senator, the House of Delegates killed the governor's plan. A bitter Price blamed his loss on "thinly disguised political activity." The Organization once again reigned supreme in Virginia, and Harry Byrd was reelected to the U.S. Senate in 1940 without any opposition.

On 1 September 1939 Adolf Hitler marched into Poland and changed the world forever. More than the depression and New Deal, World War II transformed the country into a modern welfare state with new international responsibilities. No region experienced greater change than the South, with its one-party politics, sleepy rural existence, one-crop agriculture, and racial segregation pushed to the point of extinction. And although the changes were not quite so dramatic in Virginia, it, too, would undergo a metamorphosis.

Hitler's invasion of France in the spring of 1940 hastened American preparations for a possible engagement with the Nazis. Already government contracts had accelerated shipbuilding activities in Hampton Roads, creating crowding and shortages and exacerbating relations between the military and the locals. To advance military and industrial preparedness, Governor Price created the first state Defense Council in May with Douglas Southall Freeman, editor of the *Richmond News Leader* and biographer of Robert E. Lee and George Washington, as chairman. Price required that African Americans serve on draft boards, and he appointed J. Alvin Russell, president of St. Paul's College, an all-black school, to his Defense Council. Eight regional councils were also organized to coordinate local efforts to deal with housing shortages, scrap drives, health concerns, and recruiting facilities. To replace the soon-to-be federalized Virginia National Guard, the governor established the Virginia Protective Force, consisting of eleven battalions of 3,500 men in thirty-three communities. In March 1941, facing growing labor shortages, the Defense Council began recruiting women for duty in aircraft surveillance, recreation programs, and secretarial work. Daylight savings time was once again instituted.

In the early afternoon of 7 December 1941, Virginians were enjoying their Sunday midday meal, taking a drive in the country, or listening to the Washington Redskins football game when their radios informed them that the Japanese had attacked military facilities at Pearl Harbor, Hawaii. Like many Americans, Virginians were not well informed about events and places in the Pacific and so were shocked to learn that war had begun there rather than in Europe. Relations with the Japanese had been deteriorating for most of the previous decade and had worsened considerably in the last year, but negotiations were still going on, and few expected an outright attack on the United States. The following day, Americans applauded the president's request for Congress to recognize a state of war with Japan. Three days later Hitler declared war on the United States, an action that was quickly reciprocated by Congress.

Word of the surprise attack ended isolationist sentiment and threw the country and Virginia into a frenzy. As men rushed to the recruiting stations, the Virginia Protective Force went on alert, and the aircraft warning service began operations. Police in Norfolk and Suffolk arrested all local Japanese, guards at the shipyards were doubled, and antiaircraft batteries were set up around Norfolk. People were warned not to throw water on bombs that fell into their homes lest they "explode and kill" them. The first blackout in the state was held in the port city on 13 December, and a month later the sale of new cars was banned, tire sales were restricted, and local defense councils were organized. A young Richmond boy remembered his father picking out "all our Christmas tree ornaments that had been made in Japan, taking them outside and smashing them to pieces. Our Christmas tree in 1941 was pretty bare." Anti-German sentiment also surfaced as rumors of poisoned bread caused the Nolde Baking Company in Richmond to take out full-page newspaper ads proclaiming its loyalty to America.

Governor Colgate Darden, inaugurated just weeks after Pearl Harbor, set an example of sacrifice by reducing the costs of the ceremony and garaging the governor's automobile and walking or taking the streetcar whenever possible. To strengthen the state's preparedness effort, Darden terminated the state and regional defense councils and created an Office of Civilian Defense, placing it directly under his supervision and transferring responsibility for the tasks of aircraft spotting, fire watches, and blackouts to city and county officials. The first statewide blackout was held in June 1942, followed by periodic "dark nights" thereafter. Darden also created the Virginia Reserve Militia to assist localities with security problems. Similar to the home guard of WWI, the militia became known as the "minute men"; although it and the Protective Force had little to do during the next three years, their existence allayed public fears about an enemy attack. Under the OCD, an office of Civilian Mobilization, relying primarily on women, operated fifty-four service projects that included rationing, salvage, victory gardens, child-care facilities, carpooling, nursing, and recreation programs for servicemen. By war's end 400,000 Virginians had volunteered for civilian defense service, their only compensation being a service ribbon.

World War II would have a profound effect on the United States. It ended the depression, restored economic vitality to the nation, and left a vastly altered world that demanded greater American involvement at a cost to the country of $320 billion and over 400,000 lives. It uprooted Americans, forcing them into new occupations and places, accelerated urbanization and suburbanization, precipitated a rising birthrate, and empowered blacks and women with ideas and experiences that would lead to subsequent upheavals. Continuing a trend begun during the New Deal, power shifted to Washington—particularly through the strengthened presidency—to deal with the domestic and foreign problems produced by the war. Although many New Deal relief programs were terminated, the foreign conflict increased the role of government in American life through a greatly enlarged defense establishment; a wide array of programs for veterans; greater aid for education, health care, and public housing; and a new commitment to national economic planning. An older America of small farms and towns, stable family life, white over black, men over women, and worldly isolation was vanishing.

In many respects the national story repeated itself in the Old Dominion. It was an economic boom time that ended the depression. Farm prices were up markedly, tobacco from fifteen to forty-three cents per pound. Farmers prospered, but the number of farms declined, indicative of new migratory patterns and greater use of machinery. Sharecroppers and tenants were fleeing the farms for the cities. Tobacco production skyrocketed, yet the demands for "smokes" by the military caused domestic rationing of popular brands. Richmond bank savings more than doubled, and bankruptcies were down by 90 percent. Unemployment disappeared; in fact, labor shortages created by the departure of men for military service forced greater mechanization on the farms and required the use of women in factories and German POWs in some occupations. Industrial production rose most rapidly in shipbuilding, chemicals, clothing, furniture, and tobacco.

Most of this expansion was due to government expenditures for the war. Federal money payments in Virginia rose from $122 million, one-ninth of the state's income, to $902 million, 30 percent of the state's total income. Employment at the Newport News Shipbuilding and Drydock Company quadrupled, and thousands more were employed at the

Norfolk Navy Yard building new ships and repairing hundreds more at a cost of $1 billion; the new Radford army ammunition plant employed 22,000. WWI sites at Langley Field and Camp Lee were reincarnated, and new bases such as Camp A. P. Hill and Camp Pickett sprouted up all over the commonwealth. College campuses were converted into government research laboratories and officer-training units, notably the navy's V-12 program. And Washington, D.C., was transformed from a sleepy Southern city into a world capital, complete with Pentagon and suburbs.

The military rolled into the state, practically taking it over, as 1.7 million soldiers embarked for Europe from the Norfolk area. These outsiders challenged traditional Virginia ways, creating traffic jams, producing overcrowding and housing shortages, and overtaxing schools, hospitals, and public transportation. Despite a lowered speed limit of 35 mph, the highway death rate was the highest ever, as was the more predictable prevalence of social diseases. At Radford they were using everything from trailers to chicken coops to house the overflow of workers, while in Norfolk, which gained an unsavory national reputation as the "worst war town," they were renting beds in shifts. With bars, gambling dens, and brothels proliferating, near lawlessness ruled Norfolk County, requiring state and federal intervention. In the first six years of the decade, Virginia's population rose by 15 percent, double the increase in the depression decade. By 1950 the commonwealth's urban population nearly equaled its rural population, growth that was most noticeable in the Hampton Roads and Northern Virginia areas, the latter increasing by 130 percent. To meet the demand, huge federal housing projects were constructed.

The war presented black Americans with new opportunities for advancement, but their gains produced increased tensions as segregated facilities and job discrimination remained the law in Southern states, even in federal facilities and projects. Proposing a march on Washington in 1941 to protest segregation, labor leader A. Philip Randolph pressured President Roosevelt into creating a Fair Employment Practices Commission to eliminate discrimination in the defense plants of the country, but it had minimal impact in the South. In the capital of the Confederacy, Virginius Dabney, editor of the *Times-Dispatch,* called for an end to segregation on the city's buses and trolleys and asked for improvements in education, health, and employment for Richmond's black citizens. His requests, however, went unheeded as crowded conditions on public conveyances increased racial intolerance. African Americans confronted unfounded rumors that they were planning to "ice-pick" whites on buses or were forming "Eleanor Clubs" to learn how to duplicate the first lady's attacks against discrimination; maids supposedly would insist on entering by the front door. Undeterred by such falsehoods, black Virginians, in their efforts to achieve a "Double V"—victory over racism at home as well as abroad—sought repeal of the poll tax, created new NAACP branches, and began voting in increasing numbers. Spurring them was Virginia State professor Luther Porter Jackson, who organized the Virginia Voters League in 1941 to persuade blacks to pay their poll taxes and register to vote. Dr. Gordon B. Hancock of Virginia Union University led an effort to promote better race relations in the South by helping to create the Southern Regional Council.

Like Americans elsewhere, Virginians faced the home front turmoil with stoic resignation, knowing that the boys abroad needed their courageous resolve. They followed the exploits of family members and friends across the battlefields of Africa and Europe and the islands of the South Pacific through their local newspapers. A total of 300,000 Virginians, including women, served in the armed forces; over 11,000 died, none more heroically than soldiers of the 116th infantry regiment, many of them from Bedford, who landed at Omaha Beach on D-Day. Several Virginians were awarded the Medal of Honor; native sons Generals Alexander Vandegrift, Lemuel Shepherd, and Lewis Puller were among the most highly decorated marines. Transplanted Virginian George Marshall, who had graduated from VMI, was army chief of staff and Roosevelt's primary military adviser. With the call-up of National Guard units, the Virginia Protective Force and the Virginia Reserve Militia took up the defense of the commonwealth, augmented by air-raid wardens and plane spotters, who manned 1,000 observation stations. Air-raid drills and blackouts, of particular importance at Virginia Beach where Nazi submarines could use the city lights to silhouette merchant vessels, brought the excitement of war to the state despite the protests of Norfolkians who temporarily lost their night baseball. Bodies from sunken ships floated ashore at Virginia Beach.

Virginians volunteered for everything: the Red Cross, USO, Travelers Aid, the Gray Ladies. There was a marvelous air of togetherness and sacrifice with scrap drives for every commodity possible—iron, rubber, tin cans, newspapers—and war bond campaigns to pay for the war effort. Over 75,000 tons of scrap were collected in the state with Lynchburg leading the way with over 300 pounds per capita. In Richmond, Margaret Walin remembered these efforts: "Somewhere in the family files there are probably clippings and leaflets with instructions on how to save fuel, metals, rubber, and fats. Bobby pins, curlers, girdles, tea, stockings, sugar and household appliances were the first to go." She also remembered the rationing programs imposed on the people: "Applicants lined up at local schools with identification for themselves and their families. Ration books contained coupons that provided about eight ounces of sugar a week for each family member. Richmond clerical workers who issued the books said that a surprising number of women did not know the color of

CELEBRATING THE END OF WORLD WAR II, NORFOLK, AUGUST 1945

their husband's eyes, and almost no husbands knew their wives' weights. Later coffee was rationed, allowing an average of a cup a day for adults."

By mid-1943 enthusiasm for maintaining a high level of readiness on the home front was lessening. The frequent loss of vessels to German submarines off Virginia Beach had been reduced by an active antisubmarine warfare program. As the threat of foreign attack diminished, the tasks of guarding bridges and spotting planes seemed less essential, although the rumors of German buzz bombs in 1944 sparked renewed scrutiny. Brownouts replaced blackouts as more night lighting was permitted. By the spring of 1945, with victory clearly on the horizon, shipbuilding contracts were being canceled, and workers were being laid off. News of the German surrender in May touched off massive celebrations across the state that were repeated three months later when the Japanese capitulated following the dropping of atomic weapons on Hiroshima and Nagasaki. It had been a stupendous effort that left no community in the country untouched. Now less rural, more congested, and wealthier—per capita income rose from $402 in 1939 to $972 in 1945—the Old Dominion would have to adjust to these changes.

SOURCES CONSULTED

George Gilliam, *The Ground beneath Our Feet: Virginia Fights WWII*, PBS Documentary, 2001; Elna C. Green, *This Business of Relief: Confronting Poverty in a*

Southern City, 1740–1940 (2003); Phyllis A. Hall, "Crisis at Hampton Roads: The Problems of Wartime Congestion, 1942–1944," *VMHB* (July 1993); Ronald L. Heinemann, *Depression and New Deal in Virginia* (1983); Charles W. Johnson, "V for Virginia: The Commonwealth Goes to War," *VMHB* (July 1992); Louis E. Keefer, "Students, Soldiers, Sailors: Trainees on Virginia College Campuses during World War II," *Virginia Cavalcade* (Summer 1989); A. Cash Koeniger, "The New Deal and the States: Roosevelt versus the Byrd Organization in Virginia," *JAH* (March 1982); Nancy J. Martin-Perdue and Charles L. Perdue Jr., *Talk about Trouble: A New Deal Portrait of Virginians in the Great Depression* (1996); Marvin W. Schlegel, *Conscripted City: Norfolk in World War II* (1951); Schlegel, *Virginia on Guard: Civilian Defense and the State Militia in the Second World War* (1949); Richard B. Sherman, *The Case of Odell Waller and Virginia Justice, 1940–1942* (1992); John Syrett, "The Politics of Preservation: The Organization Destroys Governor James H. Price's Administration," *VMHB* (Oct. 1989); Jonathan J. Wolfe, "Virginia in World War II," Ph.D. diss., Univ. of Virginia, 1971.

15

THE POLITICS OF RACE

1945–1960

As transforming events in the nation's history, the Great Depression and World War II had no equals in the twentieth century, but in the Old Dominion social and political conservatism mitigated their effects. Nonetheless, they stimulated challenges to the status quo that precipitated the Organization's last effort to preserve the "Virginia Way" through a policy of massive resistance to the racial desegregation of schools.

Politically the war years were quiet in Virginia. As in the nation, a call for bipartisanship and unity precluded much political infighting. Having neutralized Governor Price, the Organization had secured ascendancy once again, but the selection of a new governor in 1941 was important in maintaining that control and minimizing factional squabbles. The process by which Harry Byrd selected governors—"giving the nod," as it was called—was complex but orderly. Prospects with recognized records of service to the commonwealth often visited the senator in Washington; their names, along with those of other possibilities, were floated before the "courthouse crowd," whose sentiments carried great weight because their enthusiasm for the nominee would be crucial in the primary. Considerable attention was also given to the opinions of influential state legislators and close advisers such as Combs. Demanding integrity, loyalty, and electability in his candidates, Byrd gave consideration to longevity of service and place of residence. Within the bounds of fiscal conservatism, he accepted persons who had demonstrated streaks of independence but were the men most likely to unite the party and win elections. "Success in politics," he reportedly said, "is the candidate—don't ever try to carry a dead horse." Usually through this weeding-out process, one candidate emerged as the obvious choice. Though the final decision was likely made by consensus, Byrd's opinion counted more than all the others combined, despite his consistent denial that he exercised such power. Benjamin Muse was close to the truth when he declared, with only slight exaggeration, that "governors of Virginia are appointed by Harry Byrd, subject to confirmation by the electorate. . . . He ruled not with a command but with a nod." It was not without justification that the Organization was frequently identified as the Byrd machine.

In 1941 Byrd gave the "nod" to Colgate Darden, the tall, handsome congressman from the second district. Darden's wealth—he had married into the DuPont family—his heroic World War I record, and his current service on a naval affairs subcommittee were attractive attributes for the times, and he easily won the primary and general elections. The wartime crisis enabled Darden to push through the General Assembly many of the things Jim Price had requested, as well as his own projects: a Board of Corrections and a Pardon and Parole Board to upgrade Virginia's penal system and end the state's abysmal treatment of prisoners, abolition of the fee system for sheriffs, redistricting of the state, increased teachers' salaries, creation of a teachers' retirement system, and expansion of workmen's compensation. Furthermore, wartime prosperity enabled Virginia to retire its state debt that dated back to before the Civil War. Aided by the weakness of the "antis," who lacked money, candidates, and issues, Byrd's control of Virginia politics, despite the upheavals of depression and war, would never be more secure than it was during Darden's governorship.

Even as it reached the pinnacle of its success, however, the Organization was growing complacent in its authority at a time when Virginia was undergoing significant economic and demographic changes. Continued federal expenditures and employment were sustaining wartime growth and payrolls, spurring expansion in the textile, chemical, and furniture industries. The war had had a huge migratory effect on the population as Virginians left for military training and factory jobs elsewhere before returning. Making contact with the outside world was a transforming experience that caused many to reevaluate perpetuation of the status quo. Furthermore, thousands of "Yankees" had come south for soldiering and jobs, many of whom stayed after the war, marrying and settling down. These modern "carpetbaggers" were not used to an unresponsive government. Indicative of the democratic spirit ignited by the war was the criticism of the state government for its failure to deliver on schools and eliminate voting restrictions, pressure that increased with revelations of voting fraud and Virginia's record of low voter participation.

In the 1945 gubernatorial election, Bill Tuck, a "country boy" from Halifax County with a reputation for blunt talking and hard drinking, won an easy victory, but the race for the lieutenant governorship

produced a scandal that marred the Organization's self-proclaimed record of providing honest government. That record had never been as
clean as the Organization wanted voters to believe. Dating all the way
back to Tom Martin's payments to legislators, there had been numerous
violations of electoral laws—notably the block payments of poll taxes and
misuse of absentee ballots—along with many examples of minor malfeasance. "Qualifying" voters meant ensuring that the poll taxes of "depend-
able" voters were paid six months before the general election in the fall,
often with money collected from Democratic officeholders across the
state. Intense competition between Democrats and Republicans made
the ninth district particularly vulnerable to scandal.

In the primary contest for lieutenant governor, Charles Fenwick
bested L. Preston Collins in a close race marred by some unusual voting patterns. Collins challenged the vote in Wise County, and when the
county clerk announced that the polling books had been stolen, Richmond judge Julien Gunn threw out the Wise figures and declared Collins the victor. Virginians were aghast at such chicanery, and all officials,
including an indignant Harry Byrd, publicly clamored for a full-scale investigation of the fraud, but it was never carried out.

A significant impact of the scandal was the renewed interest in changing the election laws, specifically in repealing the poll tax. Virginia was
one of only eight states still using the poll tax as a weapon to restrict black
voting and keep the electorate small. Highlighting Virginia's abysmal
voting record, journalist Jonathan Daniels, in an article entitled "Carry
Me Back to Dear Ole Bulgaria," scathingly indicted political bossism and
the block payment of poll taxes. Virginia might be getting efficient government, he said, "but trains have run on time where democracy has
died." Virginia ranked forty-third in the nation in the percentage of its
adult population voting in the 1940 election: 22 percent. From 1920 to 1946
an average of 12 percent of the eligible voters participated in Democratic
gubernatorial primaries, the lowest percentage in the nation.

Such criticism struck a raw nerve in the Organization, which now
sought a replacement for the poll tax that would not surrender a limited
suffrage. The leadership was delighted with a study commission plan
that recommended abolition of the tax as a requirement for voting but
replaced it with an annual registration procedure and a literacy test. The
changes passed the General Assembly with strong backing from machine
leaders, but the Campbell amendments were so complicated and so pat-
ently undemocratic that voters overwhelmingly rejected them in a 1949
referendum. The poll tax survived.

Growing dissatisfaction with machine politics produced a challenge
to Byrd's Senate seat in 1946. The major issue in the campaign was organized labor. Although its influence in the state was minimal, the public

image of unions, worsened by the wartime strikes of John L. Lewis and his coal miners, was so negative that they made a convenient target for Organization politicians, who exploited voters' fears of a union takeover of Virginia for their own political advantage. The portent of a labor victory had a certain plausibility in the early months of 1946. Union membership in the Old Dominion had increased during the war, and both the AFL and the CIO now undertook membership drives in the unorganized South, called Operation Dixie, while steel, coal, and rail strikes imperiled the nation's economy. Antiunion sentiment energized the General Assembly to pass legislation that limited strike activity and the efforts of state employees to unionize.

Hostility to labor became an issue in March when a proposed walkout by workers of the Virginia Electric and Power Company raised the specter of power blackouts. Governor Tuck attempted to mediate the local crisis, but when union officials refused to participate, he warned of a possible seizure of VEPCO plants. "I'll be damned if they're going to cut the lights out in Virginia," he exclaimed. Two days before the strike deadline, Tuck declared a state emergency and used an obscure statute of questionable authority to draft the VEPCO employees into the service of the commonwealth. The ploy worked: union officials called off the strike, resumed contract negotiations, and agreed to a settlement two weeks later. Despite some criticism, most Virginians believed Tuck had courageously protected the public interest against greedy, irresponsible union officials. Undoubtedly, the event spurred assembly passage a year later of a bill to prevent strikes in public utilities and a "right-to-work" law that allowed workers to reject mandatory union membership as a condition of employment. On other occasions throughout his term, Tuck, who claimed that "ruthless racketeering labor czars [were] cut in the image of the recently dethroned dictators," used his antilabor "big stick" to thwart strikes. This approach delighted Senator Byrd, who ensured that the right-to-work provision became national law through passage of the Taft-Hartley Act in 1947. Such antilabor sentiment in Virginia muted discontent with the machine and propelled Byrd to an easy primary victory over "anti" Martin Hutchinson.

Election victories, however, did not resolve the problems confronting Virginia. In January 1947 Governor Tuck asked a special session of the legislature for more money to meet an "acute emergency" in the state's school system that had been documented by the 1944 Denny Commission on education. It found the schools poorly financed, overcrowded, and inadequately staffed; it recommended increases in teachers' salaries, free textbooks, and consolidation of rural schools. In spite of modest advances made during the Darden administration, Virginia still languished near the bottom of the states in its commitment to education and public health and welfare services. It ranked forty-fourth in percentage of income spent on education and in percentage of persons receiving welfare assistance and was last in old age assistance. The state had almost 1,500 one-room schools; more than 1,000 schools were deemed fire or health hazards and were labeled "unsuitable" for students. Necessary school construction was estimated at $396 million over the next ten years. Conditions in black schools were particularly shameful; many had no indoor plumbing, central heating, electricity, or bus service; African Americans in Pulaski County had to travel to neighboring Montgomery County to go to high school. Facilities were so unequal that some judges were now ruling that the state would have to "equalize" black schools at considerable cost or risk integration. Although committed to the Organization doctrine of balanced budgets and low taxes, Governor Tuck felt compelled to take some action and asked the assembly for funds to increase teacher salaries. A year later he requested additional expenditures for schools and welfare services and took the revolutionary step of proposing increases in corporate and personal income taxes to pay for them, which a reluctant legislature approved.

In 1948 Virginia faced another crisis that threatened to erode Organization control. A spate of racial violence in the South had caused President Harry Truman to create a Committee on Civil Rights in December 1946 to investigate ways of protecting the civil rights of American citizens. A year later, in a stunning recommendation, the committee urged an immediate end to segregation in American life. Its report, *To Secure These Rights,* called for passage of a federal antilynching law, abolition of the poll tax, creation of a permanent fair employment practices commission, and stronger enforcement of civil rights. The president applauded the report and endorsed its recommendations in a special message to Congress on 2 February 1948. He also initiated the desegregation of the armed forces, while his Commission on Higher Education proposed an end to segregated schools.

Pressure to eliminate racial segregation was not limited to federal intervention. Black Virginians had been contesting such discrimination for much of the century. In the twenties they had successfully challenged residential segregation and their exclusion from Democratic primaries. In the following decade, casting aside an accommodationist position, much to the chagrin of white elites, they protested discrimination in New Deal relief programs, attempted admission to the University of Virginia's graduate school, sat in at Alexandria's segregated public library, and won a salary equalization suit for black teachers in Norfolk. In the post–World War II years, awakening from years of voter apathy, they doubled their number of registered voters, electing William Lawrence to the Nansemond County Board of Supervisors in 1947, the first black elected to political office in twentieth-century Virginia, and Oliver Hill to the Richmond City Council in 1948. Black students gained access to the University of Virginia law and medical schools in 1950. There were now almost 100 state NAACP branches with nearly 25,000 members and a talented corps of lawyers, notably Hill, Spottswood Robinson, and Samuel Tucker, who were vigorously pressing for equal schools.

Precipitating a court case that overcame segregated interstate bus transportation, Irene Morgan refused to move to the rear on a bus traveling from Gloucester County to Baltimore in July 1944. Arrested and fined for violating Virginia's law that required segregated seating, she appealed her case with the aid of attorney Robinson of the state NAACP. They lost in the Virginia Supreme Court of Appeals, but that decision was overturned by the U.S. Supreme Court in *Morgan v. Virginia* (1946), which ruled that only Congress could regulate interstate commerce. Irene Morgan's victory preceded Rosa Parks's challenge to bus segregation in Montgomery, Alabama, by almost a decade.

Fearful that President Truman's civil rights proposals would encourage further black activity in the state to the detriment of the Organization's hegemony, Byrd and Tuck retaliated against the president with legislation that attempted to keep his name off the next presidential ballot and permit the state party to instruct presidential electors to vote for a candidate other than the national party candidate. The law became known as the "anti-Truman" bill. Opposition was immediate and vociferous, especially from newspapers across the state. Douglas Southall Freeman in the *News Leader* concluded, "No more undemocratic proposal ever was advanced responsibly in the General Assembly of Virginia." Surprised by the intensity of the reception, the leadership offered modifications that tolerated a wide array of candidates but left open the possibility that Virginia voters might still be denied a full expression of their choice by party leaders. Such high-handed tactics, duplicated at the Democratic state convention, reinforced the public perception of a machine running roughshod over its members and invigorated the efforts of the "antis" to challenge the Organization.

At the 1948 Democratic national convention in Philadelphia, a bitter struggle ensued over the civil rights plank that concluded with a narrow endorsement of Truman's program and a decidedly unenthusiastic renomination of the president. Two days after the convention ended, Southern dissidents met in Birmingham, Alabama, amid a bevy of Confederate flags, to create a National States Rights Party and to nominate Governor Strom Thurmond of South Carolina for president. Angered at the loss of Southern influence in the Democratic Party and upset with federal intrusion into state affairs, the "Dixiecrats" hoped to unite the South behind Thurmond and throw the election into the House of

Representatives. There they might bargain with both parties on the choice of the next president and the elimination of civil rights legislation.

The emergence of a Southern party threw Organization leaders, who had chosen not to attend the Birmingham gathering, into a quandary. They desperately wanted to defeat Truman because of his pro-labor and civil rights positions, but a public defection from the Democratic Party posed substantial risks. It would threaten the elections of Democrats like Senator A. Willis Robertson, who had replaced a deceased Senator Glass in 1946; but more importantly, it risked the race for governor the following year. Although Governor Tuck was inclined to join the Dixiecrats, Senator Byrd opted for a middle course that he hoped would defeat Truman and still leave the Organization forces intact: a "golden silence." By not committing to a candidate, he would leave his followers free to support either Truman or Thurmond, but his silence would imply a rejection of the president and encourage those so inclined to vote for the Dixiecrats.

But Byrd had not counted on the "antis." Angered by the capricious and dictatorial methods of party leaders throughout the year and hopeful that their loyalty might be rewarded with national support in the future, they organized a Straight Democratic Ticket Committee to back the president. Despite all the polls predicting a victory for Republican Thomas Dewey—even in Virginia—Truman won a smashing upset. Peace, prosperity, and interest group politics won the day. Thurmond and Progressive Party candidate Henry Wallace ran far behind, although the Dixiecrat did win four Deep South states with thirty-nine electoral votes, a result far short of his goal of a united South. Surprisingly, Truman's margin of victory in Virginia was substantial: 48 percent to 41 percent for Dewey and 10 percent for Thurmond. Senator Robertson and the other Democratic congressmen also won handily.

The election of 1948 in state and region and nation was highly significant. It further broadened the Democratic Party, opening doors long closed to African Americans; it began the realignment of politics in the South that would end the long run of one-party rule and restore the region's importance in presidential elections; and it forecast the era of "massive resistance" in which race came to dominate Southern elections. In Virginia, Truman's success in the face of machine opposition did not mortally wound the Organization, but it was a major blow to Byrd's prestige and accelerated his shift away from the national party; more "golden silences" were in the offing.

The postwar changes in Virginia combined with the schism within the national Democratic Party caused Byrd to be unduly concerned about the election of the next governor. The man chosen to lead the Organization into the fray was John S. Battle, state senator from Charlottesville.

The tall, handsome, dignified, and mild-mannered fifty-nine-year-old Battle had impeccable credentials as a loyal supporter of the machine, but he also had a moderate legislative record that would attract independents. Undeterred by the "nod," Francis Pickens Miller, longtime opponent of the machine, businessman Remmie Arnold, and Horace Edwards, the forty-six-year-old state party chairman, who represented younger Organization members who had grown impatient with a selection process that seemed to reward only seniority, also entered the field. Thus, despite all his efforts Byrd confronted a difficult four-man contest for the governorship in 1949 that raised the possibility of an Organization defeat because there was no runoff provision.

Byrd threw himself into the campaign with an intensity not witnessed since John Garland Pollard's election in 1929. The election, he warned, "was one of the most momentous we have ever had in Virginia." Correctly gauging the antiunion sentiment in the state after years of strikes and aggressive CIO-PAC lobbying, Byrd injected life into the Battle campaign by utilizing the labor issue that had propelled him to victory over Hutchinson three years earlier. His friends also encouraged Republican voters to participate in the Democratic primary. In the largest primary turnout in Virginia history to that time, Battle won a sizable plurality, gaining 43 percent of the vote to Miller's 35 percent, Edwards's 15 percent, and Arnold's 7 percent. Although the Republican vote for Battle was significant, even more important was the work of Harry Byrd, who quite correctly referred to the victory as "my election success in Virginia."

Byrd's triumphs against challengers who threatened his domination of commonwealth politics may have insulated him from the grumbling in Virginia over the pace of progress and his authoritarian control. He allowed himself the satisfaction of believing that all was well. Much to his pleasure, son Harry Jr., who entered the state Senate in 1948, introduced a tax reduction plan in the 1950 assembly to counter the tax increases pushed through during Governor Tuck's term. The act would reduce individual and corporation income taxes if state surpluses exceeded anticipated revenues by a certain percentage, which they invariably did.

During the same session the legislators also approved a $45 million appropriation for school construction that attempted to deal with inadequate and crowded facilities, notably the unequal black schools, but the gains would not keep pace with the arrival of the baby boom generation and new residents. Although state expenditures for education doubled during Battle's administration, teacher salaries and per pupil expenditures remained below national averages. The state was last in the nation in the percentage of students attending high school and next-to-last in the percentage of college-age children going to college. Faced with rising inflation and growing populations, localities were strapped for funds with which to provide basic services in education, health, and safety. While the state debt remained low, cities and counties had debts of over $200 million by 1952. Furthermore, Virginia ranked fortieth in appropriations for the care of the mentally ill, and its hospitals and sanatoriums were overcrowded. One official termed the state mental hospitals "a snake pit of the first order."

However, a movement was afoot to address these problems. A group of young Organization members, many of them veterans of World War II representing urban areas, realized the need to change Virginia's tax and spending policies. Not content with the standpattism of the machine or the long apprenticeship of being seen and not heard, several of these "Young Turks" opposed the Byrd tax reduction plan and favored repeal of the poll tax, more equitable redistricting, and a more enlightened policy in dealing with racial segregation. But they faced an obstinate leadership; and the General Assembly, still controlled by Byrd loyalists, acceded to none of their requests in the 1950 and 1952 sessions.

Byrd easily turned aside Miller's challenge to his Senate seat in 1952, proving that his record of economy and efficiency and his independence and integrity were still congenial to a majority of the voters. Having voted with Democrats on only 22 percent of the major Senate roll calls, Byrd was not contested by Virginia Republicans on his reelection; as one party official succinctly put it, "He's the best Republican we've got." He returned the favor by indirectly endorsing General Dwight Eisenhower in the 1952 presidential race, in which Republicans captured Virginia for the first time since 1928.

Eisenhower's victory was due in part to the dissatisfaction with President Truman's handling of the Korean War, which had commenced with the invasion of South Korea by the North in June 1950. When China joined the war a few months later, the United States returned to a wartime footing, fully mobilizing the defense industry and imposing wage and price controls, but not consumer rationing. Employment at the Newport News shipyard doubled, forty-one Virginia National Guard and reserve units went on active duty, and Reynolds Metals in Richmond warned its customers that its aluminum foil would be in short supply. Over 1,000 Virginians lost their lives in this "forgotten war."

The end of the war in 1953 gave Senator Byrd no rest as he faced another difficult gubernatorial contest, which, in light of the party defections in the assembly and the 1949 campaign, took on new significance. In the selection process Byrd gave the nod to another faithful retainer, Tom Stanley, an affable, wealthy businessman, who had served nine terms in the House of Delegates and three terms as a congressman from the fifth district, but who was a bland politician, inarticulate and awkward in formal press conferences, and not very imaginative. Virginia Republicans, buoyed by Eisenhower's victory, countered with Ted Dalton of Radford, a state senator and Republican national committeeman known for his candor on the issues. His hard-hitting tactics put Stanley on the defensive, causing disconcerted Democrats to wave the flag of "Black Reconstruction" in an attempt to frighten Old Dominion voters with memories of "carpetbaggers and Republicans."

As the campaign moved into its final stage, Dalton raised one issue too many. Seeking an alternative to raising gasoline taxes to pay for highways, Dalton offered a "pay-as-you-use" program for road building to be financed with special construction revenue bonds totaling $100 million over a five-year period. Senator Byrd, who had played an insignificant role in the campaign to that point, immediately branded the plan unconstitutional and said he would "oppose with all the vigor I possess this plan of Senator Dalton to junk our sound fiscal system based upon freedom from debt." Said one seventh district Democrat, "Dalton couldn't have hurt himself more if he'd come out for licensed prostitution." With Byrd leading the way, Stanley swept to a 43,000-vote victory in the largest turnout for a gubernatorial election since 1889, but his 10 percent margin of success was the smallest ever for an Organization candidate seeking statewide office.

The major issue of the 1954 assembly session was a renewed effort by the Young Turks to abolish the Byrd Automatic Tax Reduction Act. Encouraged by a growing number of black and white parents pressing for educational reform, they introduced legislation to divert to schools and hospitals the estimated $7 million that would be returned to taxpayers. In an arduous final session that lasted thirty-seven hours, involved five conference committees, and required stopping the clocks in the legislative chambers, a compromise was finally arranged that permitted a diversion of $2.2 million of the $7 million for teachers' salaries and other educational expenditures. The assembly then adjourned, leaving the leadership to ponder its future. Losses to the Republicans, internal squabbles, and the emergence of a more independent electorate suggested that the Organization was losing its control over Virginia politics. Only the emergence of the volatile desegregation issue would grant it an extended life.

On 17 May 1954 the U.S. Supreme Court reversed its fifty-eight-year-old *Plessy* decision that had legalized racial discrimination in America. In *Brown v. Board of Education, Topeka, Kansas,* the Court held that racial segregation in public education was "inherently unequal" and therefore in violation of the Fourteenth Amendment to the U.S. Constitution. Kindling a revolution in American life, this landmark ruling set off a firestorm of acrimony and demagoguery not witnessed in Virginia since the

Funder-Readjuster clashes over the state debt in the 1870s. "Massive re-sistance" became the watchword of the Byrd Organization, dominating the political life of the state and diverting attention from more pressing needs. In the final analysis, however, it was the death knell of the ma-chine, the sad last chapter of Harry Byrd's long reign.

One of the five cases making up the *Brown* decision originated in Prince Edward County. On 23 April 1951, led by sixteen-year-old Barbara Johns, students at the all-black Robert Russa Moton High School in Farmville had walked out, protesting their crowded, poorly equipped school. Johns, the niece of the outspoken Baptist preacher Vernon Johns, was troubled by the dilapidated school buses and the tar-paper shacks thrown up to deal with the overcrowded facilities that were clearly infe-rior to those the white children used. And so she conspired with several other students to strike, a courageous act that would get the black chil-dren a new school but also initiated a court case that culminated in the *Brown* decision when the NAACP interceded on their behalf. Virginia's cadre of NAACP lawyers had been challenging the "separate but equal" doctrine for years, focusing at first on unequal facilities and curricula and now going after racial separation itself.

Following the announcement of the *Brown* decision, Governor Stan-ley contemplated no immediate action but indicated that he would meet shortly with state and local leaders of both races to consider plans "in keeping with the edict of the court." Although many politicians, editors, and school officials commended the governor's moderation, that view was not universal in the commonwealth. Within days the governor's office was deluged with hundreds of letters protesting the decision, ex-pressing fears of race mixing, and charging Communist plots. Said one, "The Parent Teachers Association of Crewe prefers, as the lesser of two evils, the end of public education, rather than unsegregated schools." As-semblyman Garland Gray, who was to figure prominently in the massive resistance movement, urged Stanley to make a fight against the decision or face the "destruction of our culture" and "intermarriage between the races." He warned the governor not to counsel with "educators, clergy, and Negroes."

Stanley's moderation did not last. Two weeks after a June meeting of Southern governors in Richmond, where he seemed to side with the hard-line segregationists from the Deep South, Stanley declared that he would use all means at his disposal to continue a system of segregated education in Virginia. If that was not possible, he suggested the repeal of section 129 of the state constitution, which provided for the maintenance of public free schools. Although Organization stalwarts supported the governor, many Virginians, who had labored for a decade to improve ed-ucation, were shocked at the prospect of closed schools, but few whites had the audacity of Sarah Patton Boyle of Charlottesville, who endorsed integrated education.

The governor did not shift to an obstructionist position on his own but was following the lead of Harry Byrd, whose decision to oppose school desegregation—what came to be known as "massive resistance"— was one of the most significant of his career for the Organization and Virginia. On the surface it seemed out of character. For years Virginia's leaders had disdained the race baiting so common in the rest of the South. The Ku Klux Klan had little clout, and racial violence was minimal thanks in large measure to the effective antilynching bill passed during Byrd's governorship. Moderate editorial voices praised the good relations between whites and blacks and supported improvements in the black community, albeit of the separate kind. Poll tax requirements and a white electoral structure proved intimidating and kept participation low, yet blacks were allowed to vote in Democratic primaries. Although most white Virginians preferred segregated schools, the equanimity with which they accepted token integration five years later suggests that a similar course might have worked in 1955 or 1956; but they were not encouraged in that direction. The vacuum was filled by the demagoguery of racism and political expediency.

Traditional racial attitudes were certainly a factor in the creation of massive resistance. Age-old customs and attitudes that had been legalized for half a century were challenged by the *Brown* decision. The loudest voices defending the overturned separate-but-equal policy came from the Southside, where the black percentage of the population was highest and where fears of race mixing were strongest. As the heartland of the Byrd machine, the region and its racism had an influence on policymaking out of proportion to its population in the state. As Lindsay Almond said years later, "There would have been no hard, unyielding core of massive resistance in Virginia if there were no Southside. Virginia as a whole was opposed to racial mixing in the public schools, but outside of the Southside the state evinced more of a willingness to face reality." That influence was evident when a group of Southsiders, including key state legislators, met at a Petersburg firehouse on 19 June to record their "unalterable opposition to the principle of integration of the races in the schools." They pledged "to evolve some legal method whereby political subdivisions of the state may continue to maintain separate facilities for white and Negro students in schools." Within days of the firehouse meeting, citizens of the fourth district descended on the state capital, and Governor Stanley's reversal followed.

It appears that Byrd and other Organization leaders perceived race as an issue with which to maintain their political hegemony that had been so recently threatened by Miller, Dalton, and the Young Turks. Fears were expressed that if the Organization did not take a forceful stand on the school question, it would lose the initiative to these moderates. Massive resistance was designed, in part, to revitalize a dying political machine. This is apparent in the attention given to Southside interests, the use of the issue in political races, and the gradual development of the final strategy. The policy shifts and planning over a two-year period confirm the ulterior purpose. Had race prejudice alone been the primary motive, Virginia's resort to massive resistance would have been much more immediate and emotional, as it was elsewhere in the South. Throughout their time in power, Byrd and the Organization had used race only when they were in political trouble. Now they would turn to it again in the fight over school desegregation.

Race and politics were reinforcing elements in Organization thinking because black emancipation, particularly through increased political participation, would threaten machine hegemony as well as race control. Recent black political activity and court cases portended such a possibility. Opposing a national amendment that would terminate the poll tax, Willis Robertson commented to Byrd, "Every man who knows anything about Virginia politics is bound to realize that if you suddenly give the vote to several hundred thousand who have not had it before, they are going to use it as directed by their group leader—labor or racial." Predictably, then, Organization leaders fought changes in the poll tax or any civil rights legislation that promised to improve black voting opportunities. The Court's school decision was perceived as another step in dismantling the entire Jim Crow system, including electoral control; it would have to be obstructed.

Finally, Byrd also believed the Court's ruling was another dangerous example of federal interference in state affairs that would undermine the political and social status quo in Virginia, an act reminiscent of the Civil War and Reconstruction. For Byrd, who had spent all of his Senate years fighting the federal octopus, the decision overturned legal precedent and time-honored custom and was another blow to states' rights. It was the final humiliation, and he reacted angrily and bitterly, his frustration producing an unreasonable and overwrought defiance. The "Virginia Way" of managed race relations was coming unglued. A resolve to preserve this traditional way of life, along with political profit and racial conviction, dictated Byrd's response to desegregation.

In August 1954 Governor Stanley appointed a thirty-two-man legislative commission on public education to devise a response to the *Brown* dictum. The long-anticipated Gray Plan, named for its chairman, segregationist assemblyman Garland Gray, was presented on 12 November 1955. It recommended a pupil assignment plan that permitted localities to assign students to schools for reasons other than race in order to keep race mixing to a minimum. The compulsory education law would be amended so that no child would be required to attend an integrated school. In the event of school closings or integration, the commission suggested that the legislature appropriate tuition grants to enable children to attend private schools. Viewed within the context of the times, the Gray Plan struck a reasonable chord by allowing localities to integrate if they chose but advancing legislation to help them avoid it if they wished.

The proposal initially seemed to have the blessing of Organization leaders, but within a matter of weeks, Virginia rejected local option and veered down the road of total noncompliance. The voice that may have had the greatest influence in converting Harry Byrd to massive resistance was that of James J. Kilpatrick, editor of the *Richmond News Leader*. Viscerally and intellectually opposed to governmental power that intruded on the rights of individuals, Kilpatrick wrote a series of crusading editorials in late November 1955 that urged adoption of "interposition" as a defense against integration. Resurrecting John C. Calhoun's concept of nullification and Jefferson's and Madison's defenses of states' rights in the Kentucky and Virginia Resolutions of 1798–99, he argued that states could nullify undesirable federal action by interposing themselves between the central government and their citizens to protect their rights. With more zeal than logic, Kilpatrick drafted an interposition resolution for consideration by the General Assembly that would declare the *Brown* decision "null and void."

Kilpatrick gave Byrd the legal and intellectual foundation for state action against the federal government while appeasing the racist preferences of Virginians without the appearance of demagoguery. He made massive resistance respectable, a prerequisite for the senator, who disdained emotional use of the race issue. Although Kilpatrick remained somewhat skeptical about the ultimate success of interposition and eventually would advise its rejection, Senator Byrd never had such reservations. Obsessed with the battle between federal power and state rights, Byrd wholeheartedly committed to interposition as a legal basis for obstructing court-ordered desegregation and began backing away from his endorsement of the Gray Plan. He was encouraged in this move by a powerful new lobbying group that had been formed in October to give political and emotional support to the resisters. Founded in Blackstone but likely conceived in Farmville in Prince Edward County, the Defenders of State Sovereignty and Individual Liberties advocated maintenance of segregated schools through constitutional enforcement of state rights. Its members eschewed violence and association with any Klan-like organization. Although it established chapters across the state, the Defenders were most powerful in the Southside.

On 9 January 1956, by a resounding two-to-one margin, Virginians approved a constitutional convention that would legalize the tuition grants. Although the referendum was on a single provision of the Gray Plan, most observers believed that it was tantamount to a vote on the entire plan. However, only days after the vote, the Organization hierarchy met in Washington to hear Senator Byrd propose an indefinite delay in implementing the plan. Over the objections of Gray Commission counsel David Mays, who called any rejection of the Gray Plan "a betrayal of the people who worked for the Constitutional Convention," Byrd's suggestion was agreed to. Within days, Governor Stanley announced that additional school legislation would await a special assembly session later in the year. Local school boards were encouraged to do nothing. The Organization had deceived the electorate into believing the referendum was for a "sound and moderate" approach to the school question and then used the vote as a mandate to pursue massive resistance. By that time moderates who had endorsed the plan were confronted with a political fait accompli and the devastating charge that local option advocates were little more than integrationists in disguise.

The 1956 General Assembly was dominated by the desegregation issue even though the leadership had chosen not to take legislative action on that question. A resolution of nullification pledging "our firm intention to take all appropriate measures, legally and constitutionally available to us, to resist this illegal encroachment upon our sovereign powers" passed by huge margins in both houses. Legislators were doing little more than sounding an emotional battle cry for continued defiance, a protest rather than a procedure, but if interposition had little legal significance, it created a favorable climate for obstruction. The assembly also stripped Arlington County of its right to elect its school board, which had approved a gradual plan of integration in accordance with the Gray Plan.

While the legislature was in session, Senator Byrd boldly put forward his idea of massive resistance. In Richmond to deliver a speech at the Jefferson-Jackson Day dinner on 14 February, he offhandedly spoke of "passive resistance" to the Court's decision through Southern unity. Eleven days later in Washington, he adopted more aggressive rhetoric: "If we can organize the Southern States for massive resistance to this order, I think that in time the rest of the country will realize that racial integration is not going to be accepted in the South. . . . In interposition the South has a perfectly legal means of appeal from the Supreme Court's order." Kilpatrick's doctrine had been digested. Interpreting the margin of victory in the recent referendum as a signal for total resistance, Byrd gauged the political climate to be favorable for a more forceful policy. Massive resistance would mean uniform resistance; it would mean recourse to all available means to prevent any integration in the commonwealth. Organization leaders from the Southside, joined by vocal Defenders, jubilantly rallied behind his decision.

So, too, did Southern congressmen, who adopted a "Southern Manifesto" that condemned the *Brown* decision as an "abuse of judicial power" and recommended use of all lawful means to resist forced integration and reverse the decision. Written by Senator Strom Thurmond of South Carolina with the assistance of Harry Byrd, it was signed by nineteen senators and eighty-two House members, including all of Virginia's representatives. Much like state declarations of interposition, the manifesto lacked legal standing, but it served as a rallying cry for Southern segregationists in need of moral support. It initiated the counterrevolution against the Court and integration in the South for which Harry Byrd had become a standard-bearer. Years later his Southern colleagues called him a "prominent" and "powerful" opponent of civil rights legislation. They valued his national reputation for integrity and independence because it legitimated their efforts. Historian Frances Wilhoit has concluded that Harry Byrd, "more than any other single individual, determined the shape and style of the movement as it evolved in the decade after 1954."

Organization leaders were active during the spring of 1956, plotting strategies and discussing constitutional interpretations, usually over the objections of counsel David Mays, who was dubious that massive resistance could be legally sustained. According to him, Byrd was motivated by a fear that integration "would wreck the state machine." Mays sadly concluded, "The top political leadership in Virginia is bankrupt." The wishes of the Southside dictated the final strategy. State Senator Mills Godwin wrote to Byrd on 8 June: "I am convinced we should not pass any State law which would permit integration even in those localities where some may desire it." He argued that doing so would be interpreted as compliance with the Court's decision, an action that most Virginians rejected and one which was contrary to the concept of interposition. Calling for a statement of intentions in "unmistakable language," Godwin asked Byrd to convene a conference of interested parties on the subject.

The clandestine gathering of the "Southside Seven" (seven members of the Gray Commission from the Southside) with Senator Byrd, Governor Stanley, and Congressmen Bill Tuck, Watkins Abbitt, and Howard Smith took place in Washington on 2 July in Smith's Rules Committee conference room. Smith had served Virginia's eighth district since 1931 and had become one of Byrd's most valuable advisers, using his authority on the Rules Committee to thwart undesirable legislation, notably on civil rights. The group determined the agenda for the September special session of the assembly and set the course toward closing schools. It was a plan remarkably similar to one advanced by the Defenders a year earlier. Virginia would maintain a completely segregated public school system; no state funds would go to any locality that attempted to integrate schools; the right to sue local school boards would be repealed; and pupil assignment authority would be transferred to the governor. The participants left the Washington conference confident that they had produced a workable plan to avoid integration.

Convened amid unfurled Confederate flags and heightened passions, the monthlong assembly session was an emotional, draining experience, "tense and unhappy days" in the memory of one participant. Over the objections of moderates who pressed for local option, the assembly, with some modifications, endorsed the "Stanley Plan" created by the Washington conclave that authorized the governor to close schools threatened with integration. Massive resisters were willing to destroy public education to preserve white supremacy. Tuition grants, approved by the constitutional convention in March, would be available to those "forced" into attending private schools. By shifting responsibility for school operations to Richmond and by creating new legal barriers to integration, segregationists hoped that they could sidestep the sweeping nature of the Supreme Court decision; at the very least further litigation would delay the process. The legislature also vindictively passed bills to harass and undermine the work of the NAACP, which continued to pursue equal rights litigation across the state. Moderate opposition to massive resistance, never comfortable with the prospect of integration and long conditioned by patronage and loyalty to defer to Organization leadership, now disappeared.

Byrd next turned to the crucial 1957 gubernatorial election that he hoped would confirm his school policies. J. Lindsay Almond was not his first choice for governor, but the attorney general, whom *Time* magazine called "one of segregation's ablest legal advocates," preempted the field by announcing early and gathering pledges from courthouse officials and legislators whom he had served for so long. A fiery orator with a shock of wavy white hair, Almond was a faithful Organization man with a streak of independence that precluded his entry into the inner circle, but he believed the position was fairly his. A committed segregationist, Almond was a good enough lawyer to know that the Stanley Plan would not likely survive the legal test, but political expediency would make massive resistance the central issue of his campaign and his governorship. He easily turned aside another challenge from Ted Dalton, who was crippled by President Eisenhower's use of troops to integrate Central High School in Little Rock, Arkansas, in September. As Dalton said, "Little Rock was not a little rock, it was a big rock." An elated Byrd described the election result as a testimony to "Virginia's determination to resist integration."

Although Byrd easily won reelection in 1958, the future of massive resistance was more problematic. The General Assembly strengthened the massive resistance laws with the "Little Rock" bill that authorized the closing of schools patrolled by the military. Delegates also enacted a new voter registration law aimed, in Governor Almond's words, "to hit the Negro voter harder than the white voter"; and further efforts were made to undermine the work of the NAACP, but little could be done to intimidate federal judges. On 8 September 1958, over four years after the *Brown* decision, federal judge John Paul ordered Warren County, which had no black high school, to desegregate its all-white high school. When the Fourth Circuit Court of Appeals upheld Paul's order, Governor Almond closed the school. He was forced to repeat this action only days later in Charlottesville and Norfolk, leaving nearly 13,000 white students without public education in Virginia. Almond and Attorney General Albertis Harrison then initiated a suit in the state courts to test the validity of the school-closing laws, hoping for a favorable ruling that would buy them more time or an adverse ruling that would prove to the people that the last alternative had been tried.

The school closings jarred a dormant moderate voice into life. Parent and teacher groups across the state were expressing concern over the threat to public education. Several prominent state newspapers that had been staunch defenders of massive resistance now counseled moderation. Most importantly, civic and business leaders in Richmond began to sound out the governor on other possibilities. Months later, when he was justifying his change of course, Almond mentioned the negative impact that the school closings were having on Virginia's economy. Supporting the governor's contention, the Advisory Council on the Virginia Economy announced that not a single dollar for new industry had been spent in Virginia in 1958 while North Carolina, where token integration had occurred, had received a quarter of a billion dollars in new investments.

On 19 January 1959—Robert E. Lee's 152nd birthday—the Virginia Supreme Court of Appeals ruled that Virginia's school-closing laws were unconstitutional because they violated section 129 of the state constitution requiring the state to maintain free schools. On the same day a federal district court concluded that the laws contravened the equal protection clause of the Fourteenth Amendment to the U.S. Constitution. Addressing the General Assembly on 28 January in somber tones and near-funereal garb, Governor Almond, over the objections of Harry Byrd, acknowledged defeat. Virginia, he said, was now powerless to defy federal decrees. He announced formation of a commission, to be headed by Senator Mosby Perrow of Lynchburg, to deal with the specifics of a new plan that would limit the degree of integration. As the legislators sat, the first black children entered formerly all-white schools in Norfolk and Arlington. Massive resistance was dead.

The economic and social changes that had been taking place in the Old Dominion over the past decade had finally produced a political revolution as well, all of it coming to a head with the school crisis. Moderate leadership, which included many business leaders and some of the staunchest members of the Byrd hierarchy such as Almond and Harrison, would begin to face forward and develop the resources of the commonwealth to their fullest. Members of the Old Guard like Bill Tuck, who demanded that they "never surrender," lost their mandate to lead.

The extent of this political transformation was apparent in the subsequent special session of the General Assembly in April 1959. The Perrow Commission recommended a local option desegregation plan that included new pupil placement laws, a new compulsory attendance law, and tuition grants that would keep integration to a minimum. The euphemism "freedom of choice" was applied to a program whose similarities to the old Gray Plan were striking. Despite lobbying by a Capitol Square crowd of 5,000 Southsiders, who on the eve of the session condemned the governor for his betrayal, the legislators adopted the commission report by a narrow margin. The pace of integration over the next few years would be glacial, but the process had begun. Significantly, massive resistance lines began to crumble across the rest of the South as well.

Massive resistance was a sorry spectacle for Harry Byrd and Virginia. Although it may have produced a few more election victories, it contributed to the demise of the Organization by further dividing the Democratic Party, stimulating black political participation, and encouraging more federal interference. It also tarnished the image of the Old Dominion and complicated the end of state-imposed racial discrimination. Lenoir Chambers, the editor of the *Norfolk Virginian-Pilot*, one of the few Virginia newspapers to oppose massive resistance, put it simply: "There is no justification in injustice, no rightness in moral wrong, and no need for extreme measures when simple measures are at hand." The failure of leadership—the absence of flexibility, foresight, and moral sensitivity—is the real lesson of massive resistance.

Despite the concessions by the state, the most tragic episode was still to come: the closing of schools in Prince Edward County. Rather than submit to court orders directing integration of the county's schools, its leaders, emboldened by Byrd and Kilpatrick, refused to appropriate funds for the schools and so terminated public education in 1959, the only locality in the country to take this step. Supported by state tuition grants and other locally designed tax breaks, white citizens of Prince Edward, under prearranged plans, immediately opened a private academy for their children and offered to do the same for black children. Directed by "the fighting preacher" L. Francis Griffin, black parents, who had challenged the segregated public system, were not about to settle for segregated private schools; and with the advice of the NAACP, they took the county board of supervisors to court. It took five years of litigation before the U.S. Supreme Court in *Griffin v. School Board of Prince Edward County* (1964) determined that the closed schools violated the plaintiffs' right to an education. During these years most of the county's black children received no instruction at all: a generation lost. Despite the constitutional requirement to maintain free public schools, the state callously chose not to intervene in the matter. Prince Edward County mocked the claim that no one got hurt by massive resistance in Virginia.

SOURCES CONSULTED

Ben Beagle and Ozzie Osbourne, *J. Lindsay Almond: Virginia's Reluctant Rebel* (1984); Numan V. Bartley, *The Rise of Massive Resistance: Race and Politics in the South during the 1950's* (1969); William B. Crawley Jr., *Bill Tuck: A Political Life in Harry Byrd's Virginia* (1978); Bruce Dierenfield, *Keeper of the Rules: Congressman Howard W. Smith of Virginia* (1987); Kathleen Dierenfield, "One 'Desegregated Heart': Sarah Patton Boyle and the Crusade for Civil Rights in Virginia," *VMHB* (Spring 1996); James W. Ely Jr., *The Crisis of Conservative Virginia: The Byrd Organization and the Politics of Massive Resistance* (1976); Robbins L. Gates, *The Making of Massive Resistance: Virginia's Politics of Public School Desegregation, 1954–1956* (1964); Donald C. Harrison, *Distant Patrol: Virginia and the Korean War* (1989); Peter R. Henriques, "The Organization Challenged: John S. Battle, Francis P. Miller, and Horace Edwards Run for Governor," *VMHB* (July 1974); Matthew D. Lassiter and Andrew B. Lewis, eds., *The Moderates' Dilemma: Massive Resistance to School Desegregation in Virginia* (1998); Peter F. Lau, ed., *From the Grassroots to the Supreme Court:* Brown v. Board of Education *and American Democracy* (2004); Ira Lechner, "Massive Resistance: Virginia's Great Leap Backward," *Virginia Quarterly Review* (Autumn 1998); Alexander S. Leidholdt, *Standing before the Shouting Mob: Lenoir Chambers and Virginia's Massive Resistance to Public-School Integration* (1997); Andrew B. Lewis, "Wandering in Two Worlds: Race, Citizenship, and Education in Virginia since 1945," Ph.D. diss., Univ. of Virginia, 2000; Robert A. Pratt, *The Color of Their Skin: Education and Race in Richmond, Virginia* (1992); Bob Smith, *They Closed Their Schools* (1965); J. Douglas Smith, "When Reason Collides with Prejudice: Armistead Lloyd Boothe and the Politics of Desegregation in Virginia, 1948–1963," *VMHB* (Jan. 1994); James R. Sweeney, "The Golden Silence: The Virginia Democratic Party and the Presidential Election of 1948," *VMHB* (July 1974); Sweeney, ed., *Race, Reason, and Resistance: The Diary of David J. Mays, 1954–1959* (forthcoming); J. Harvie Wilkinson III, *Harry Byrd and the Changing Face of Virginia Politics, 1945–1966* (1968).

16

A NEW COMMONWEALTH

1960–2007

America in the 1960s was in the grip of social revolution. The election of more liberal presidents, who pushed for comprehensive social welfare legislation; the new activism of the civil rights movement, which in turn inspired other minority groups and women to pursue equal treatment; and a youthful cultural rebellion spurred by the complacency of the Eisenhower years combined to produce an environment uncongenial to Virginia conservatives but fertile for new directions that would transform the Old Dominion into a new commonwealth.

❖

Harry Byrd's final years in public service were not happy ones. Not only was he being outflanked by liberals on the national scene, but his control of politics in Virginia was ebbing. The state Democratic Party was in transition. The liberalization of a growing electorate, the acrimony of the massive resistance fight, and the challenge from the Republicans had generated dissension within the Organization, particularly among those dissatisfied with the policies and practices of the Old Guard. His "golden silences" were alienating some Democrats, thereby weakening the bonds of loyalty to party and machine. As state Senator Robert Whitehead commented to Congressman Abbitt, "Telling Democrats it's all right to vote Republican in national elections will backfire; soon they will ask why they can't do that in state elections."

The governorship of Albertis Harrison was a calm transition between the plodding mediocrity of the old regime and the progressivism of Mills Godwin's subsequent governorship. At the time of Harrison's inauguration in 1962, Virginia ranked last in the country in per pupil expenditures for schools in relation to per capita income and last in per capita expenditures for welfare programs. Even its much-acclaimed highway program ranked only thirty-sixth in spending. The state tax burden was the low-est in the nation, an attraction for new industry, but the Old Dominion was in need of additional revenues with which to balance the budget. Governor Almond's request for a sales tax to fund new endeavors had been summarily rejected, in part out of pique for his defection on mas-sive resistance. The new governor did little to improve this sad record, but he did prepare the way for what was to follow. Harrison's congenial demeanor mended the political fences between conservatives and mod-erates that had been demolished by massive resistance, and he worked assiduously to promote industrial development in the commonwealth, encouraged increases in educational expenditures, and maintained racial calm during the turbulent protest years.

Byrd's involvement in policy matters was now increasingly spiteful. Still bruised by the defeat of massive resistance, he never missed an op-portunity to criticize the Warren Court or the "ruthless federal bureau-crats" for their interference in state affairs. He foolishly expended political capital to prevent elimination of the poll tax in Virginia. When Congress passed the Twenty-fourth Amendment repealing the tax for voters in fed-eral elections, a special session of the General Assembly chose to retain the tax for state elections and imposed an annual residency certification for those who desired to vote in federal elections without paying it. The certification requirement was the juvenile act of a dying machine that had lost touch with the political currents running in Virginia, and it was quickly overturned by the federal courts.

The leadership also procrastinated over legislative reapportionment. Only under court order in 1964 did the assembly redistrict the state to reflect the urbanization that was transforming the Old Dominion eco-nomically and politically. The declining importance of the rural areas in state politics was a key element in the demise of the Organization be-cause it diminished the ability of the "courthouse crowd" to control the vote. Legislative districts in urban areas no longer corresponded with county lines, and county officials had become little more than adminis-trative bureaucrats, a far cry from their former roles as political agents. As Governor Harrison aptly remarked some years later, voters no lon-ger knew their local officials—the treasurers and clerks—and if they did know them, they were hardly the persons one would ask about issues and candidates. The internal network of the machine had evaporated.

Almost leaderless and no longer representative of the new Virginia, the Organization slowly disintegrated. Its defenses of massive resistance and the poll tax were major liabilities among a younger, less white, less native, more urban electorate. These political differences came to a head in the 1964 presidential election. Byrd preferred his philosophical soul mate, Arizona Republican senator Barry Goldwater, to President Lyndon

Johnson, but once more he chose to remain silent, and his closest friends followed his lead. However, Governor Harrison, Lieutenant Governor Godwin, and most Virginia congressmen indicated their preference by literally jumping on the president's train, the "Lady Bird Special" that carried the first lady on a whistle-stop tour of the South in early October. Virginians endorsed their choice by giving Johnson a handsome victory that enhanced his landslide nationwide. His strongest support came in urban areas and black precincts where voter registration drives had proved effective. Although Byrd was reelected to his Senate seat for the seventh time, the 1964 election forecast a new era in Virginia politics. A year later he retired from the U.S. Senate after nearly thirty-three years of service. Governor Harrison quickly appointed Harry Jr. to replace his father, who died within the year of an inoperable brain tumor.

The legacy of Byrd's forty-year rule in Virginia was mixed. The senator always liked to say that he was a progressive conservative who favored "sound progress" within the bounds of fiscal restraint. His own solid governorship reflected this philosophy. His greatest gift to the state was a debt-free government that honestly and efficiently provided basic services to its citizens: good roads, law enforcement, and economic development. But as change engulfed the Old Dominion, Byrd did not keep pace. Honest and frugal government, while commendable, could not compensate for poorly funded colleges, inadequate mental hospitals, and neglected social services. And massive resistance was a discredited and dishonorable course that further obstructed advancement. In the words of V. O. Key, "Men with the minds of tradesmen do not become statesmen."

Despite his forty years in power, Byrd's legacy did not endure. He was not yet in his grave, and the structure was coming down, undermined by those economic, demographic, and externally imposed changes that revolutionized Virginia's political culture. African Americans, Republicans, and Yankees, invisible since Reconstruction, were emerging from the shadows to create an opposition to the machine. The foundations of the Organization—a small controllable electorate, the "courthouse crowd," a one-party General Assembly—had eroded. Gone also was the poll tax and one-sided reapportionment that favored rural areas, always the strength of the Organization. Harry Byrd's world was disappearing.

Many factors conspired to produce this result. First and foremost, Virginia was no longer master of its own house. The outside world had invaded the Old Dominion. The agents of change—depression, war, Supreme Court rulings, and the growth of the federal government—created situations that Virginia's political leaders were unable to control, try as they might. Byrd was not unaware of what was happening, which may be why he vigorously fought all forms of federal interference in the affairs of the state, especially integration. Commenting on the 1954 *Brown* decision, Louis Rubin said that it "not only symbolized all the changes that were being forced upon Virginia . . . but it struck at the heart of the social and economic institutions that had seemed to make possible the old order and which reflected the values and attitudes embodied in the old order." Once that order was disturbed, the machine could not perpetuate its authority. Aged and complacent, the old men of the Organization clung to poll taxes, played the race card, tried strong-arm tactics against renegade members of their own family, and refused to include younger, more moderate members in the inner circle. Their obstinacy and myopia hastened their downfall.

The federal presence also meant more outside money and residents. The state now had twice as many federal workers as farmers. External migration fueled urban and suburban growth that created an "urban corridor" linking Northern Virginia and Hampton Roads which would come to dominate state politics by the end of the century. Between 1940 and 1973 Fairfax County grew from 41,000 residents to over half a million. The Washington, D.C., suburbanites were less Virginian by birth, better educated, and more affluent than most Virginians and thus less inclined to accept the parsimonious policies of the Byrd Organization.

Even the Cold War, through the growth of the military machine and the competition with the Soviets for world allegiances, which coincidentally promoted an end to racial discrimination, impacted Virginia. The landing of Americans on the moon in 1969 was assisted by NASA facilities at Langley Research Center, which had been advancing aeronautical technology at Hampton since 1917. The Newport News Shipbuilding and Drydock Company, with its huge government contracts, became the largest private employer in the state; and Norfolk became the home of the largest naval base in the world. Fueled by the military presence, the region enjoyed unprecedented prosperity. Tidewater cities and counties merged to create the municipalities of Virginia Beach and Chesapeake.

The private sector also saw considerable growth. Stimulated by the development of the interstate highway system begun in the 1950s, manufacturing, which accounted for one-fifth of the commonwealth's labor force, was extending beyond the traditional centers of Richmond and Norfolk into the Shenandoah Valley and Roanoke. The Virginia Port Authority supervised the expansion of Hampton Roads into one of the leading centers of container traffic in the nation; by the 1990s, 3,000 ships a year were entering the harbor. Richmond remained a tobacco center, producing a third of the nation's cigarettes. Tourism was becoming a major economic activity as the state took advantage of its colonial, Revolutionary, and Civil War history. Driven by mechanization and depressed agricultural conditions, rural residents were shifting to urban jobs, further diminishing the power base of the Organization. The farm population

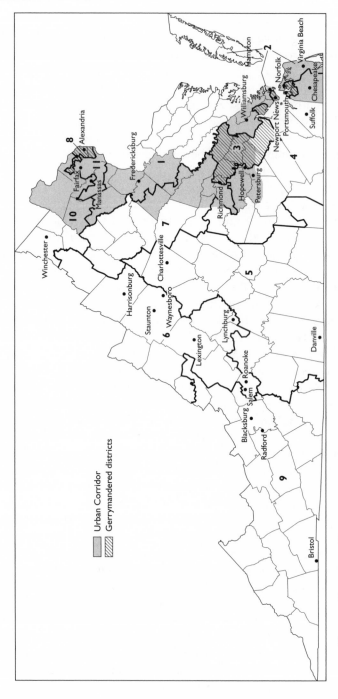

URBAN VIRGINIA: URBAN CORRIDOR, MAJOR CITIES, AND GERRYMANDERED CONGRESSIONAL DISTRICTS, 2001

declined from one-half the state's total in 1920 to one-fourth in 1945 to 5 percent in 1970. New economic vistas, promoted by television and, later, computers, cell phones, and the internet, beckoned Virginians to reject the timeworn advice to "keep Virginia the way it used to be."

Second, race was no longer the touchstone of state politics and society. Citizen protests, congressional legislation, and additional U.S. Supreme Court decisions challenged the policies of the Byrd machine and brought an end to the remaining vestiges of Jim Crow in Virginia. Similar to what was happening across the South, sit-in demonstrations, picketing, and public marches, notably in Richmond in 1960 and Danville and Farmville in 1963, highlighted the emerging civil rights revolution.

Emulating their counterparts in Greensboro, North Carolina, students from Virginia Union University sat in at Woolworth and Thalhimers lunch counters in downtown Richmond on 20 February 1960. Their action resulted in arrests, boycotts, and convictions for the "Thalhimers Thirty-Four" that were later overturned by the U.S. Supreme Court in *Randolph v. Virginia* (1963). Martin Luther King Jr. visited Danville three times in 1963 and at one point considered organizing a Birmingham-like movement there. He deplored the "beastly conduct of Danville law enforcement officers" who had deployed fire hoses and billy clubs against the protesters.

NAACP lawyers continued to press for an end to segregation laws, achieving notable victories in *Johnson v. Virginia* (1963), which ended courtroom segregation; *Loving v. Virginia* (1967), which overturned nearly three centuries of Virginia laws against racial intermarriage; and *Green v. County School Board of New Kent County* (1968), which ended "freedom of choice" plans that had perpetuated school segregation.

At the national level the public accommodations act of 1964, vigorously opposed by Senator Byrd, ended segregation in public facilities and discrimination by sex as well as race. The combined effects of the Twenty-fourth Amendment to the U.S. Constitution, which eliminated the poll tax in federal elections, and the voting rights act of 1965 opened the door to thousands of black Virginians to participate in the electoral process for the first time. The U.S. Supreme Court's 1962 "one person, one vote" dictum increased urban representation in the General Assembly and curtailed the rural authority of the machine. In a 1966 ruling the Court also ended application of the poll tax in state elections, and a year later Dr. William Ferguson Reid of Richmond became the first African American elected to the General Assembly in the twentieth century. Parties could no longer ignore the power of the black vote.

Another rights revolution would also have a major impact on Virginia society and politics. The sixties witnessed the beginning of a new woman's liberation movement. After making a major contribution to the

RUTH TINSLEY BEING CARRIED FROM A CIVIL RIGHTS
PROTEST AND ARRESTED OUTSIDE THALHIMERS DEPARTMENT
STORE, RICHMOND, 1960

WWII effort, women had been barred from many "men's" jobs after the war and forced to retreat to the hearthside. Their political and professional participation in the life of the commonwealth was put on hold; they were even denied jury duty until 1950. For nearly twenty years no women had served in the General Assembly until Kathryn Stone from Arlington was elected in 1953. But the turmoil of the sixties—which offered new experiences and challenges, an expanding job market, and the development of the birth control pill—liberated women from the "feminine mystique" that had insisted they remain in the home. Motivated by studies of widespread gender discrimination and federal legislation banning discrimination by sex, women increased their numbers in the workforce and began organizing to address issues of equal job opportunities and pay (which stood at 59 percent of men's pay in 1970), legal rights and protections, and health care. Their crusade forced the University of Virginia to open its door to women undergraduates in 1970, increased athletic opportunities for women, and encouraged women to apply to professional schools and to run for legislative and executive offices. In notable breakthroughs Governor John Dalton appointed the first black woman, Jean Harris, to a cabinet-level position, and Governor Charles Robb appointed over 600 women to state boards and commissions, including the first woman to serve on the State Corporation Commission, Elizabeth Lacy, who later became the first woman to serve on the state

Supreme Court. Social revolutions, not machine politics, were determining the future face of Virginia.

The final element that undermined the Organization and helped to change Virginia was the development of a competitive two-party system that would bring accountability to Old Dominion politics. After years of being little more than a protest voice in general elections, the Republican Party began to challenge the Democrats in the Eisenhower years. Traditional Republican strength in Southwest Virginia and the Valley was augmented by wealthy newcomers in the suburbs who preferred the fiscal conservatism of the national Republicans. At the same time many Virginia Democrats, alienated by the liberalization of the national Democratic Party, particularly on the issue of race, sought a less contentious political home. Given Byrd's blessing through his "golden silences," they began voting Republican in national elections; and with his death, it became easier to desert the party altogether, especially when it ran liberal candidates like Henry Howell and George McGovern. The creation of modern Republicanism in Virginia—and in the rest of the South—was due in part to this "white flight," a legacy that the GOP in the Old Dominion would have to work hard to overcome.

Clearly Virginia at the time of Harry Byrd's death was a far cry from the state that he had governed in the twenties. However, for all the changes, it did not discard its past entirely. Although now more like a mid-Atlantic state than a Southern state in its economic and social diversity, the Old Dominion could not completely shed its symbolic regional leadership represented by the exploits of Lee and Byrd. Race was no longer the obstacle to progress that it had once been, but lingering individual and institutional prejudices proved more difficult to eradicate. Black farmers and businessmen still faced discrimination in getting loans from federal and state agencies. The state's congenital aversion to taxes and government spending also proved formidable. Many of the newcomers, especially among the military and Republicans, supported balanced budgets and low taxes, the longtime objectives of the machine. And a new group of social conservatives, including women as well as men, moved primarily by religious convictions, joined Republicans to advance their ideas on abortion, parental rights, and school choice. Thus Virginia politics for the remainder of the century—after Byrd—proved a fascinating mixture of the predictable and the unexpected.

The man most representative of this capacity for progress within a traditional framework was Mills E. Godwin Jr. A native of Nansemond County on the eastern edge of the Southside, Godwin was a least likely revolutionary. He won a seat in the House of Delegates in 1947 and moved on to the state Senate in 1952; by this time he had become a dedicated member of the Organization, supportive of its pay-as-you-go fiscal

MILLS E. GODWIN JR.

conservatism and the Byrd Automatic Tax Reduction Act. When the *Brown* decision was handed down, Godwin joined the ranks of hard-core massive resisters who designed the school-closing laws, believing that integration would lead to the destruction of public schools. He later argued that massive resistance was merely a play for time—that Virginia needed time to adjust to a new condition—but his words and actions suggested that he wanted to prevent integration for all time, even at the risk of eliminating public education.

Godwin's great strength, however, was his political pragmatism. Discerning the changing social climate in the Old Dominion, he began to distance himself from his former allies and their policies. During the 1965 gubernatorial campaign, Godwin emphasized his vision for a new Virginia: better public services, improvements in education, urban renewal, and economic development. In a three-party contest against the youthful moderate Republican A. Linwood Holton and William J. Story of the anti-Washington, anticommunist Conservative Party, Godwin won comfortably, albeit with only a plurality of the vote, by piecing together a coalition of old Byrdites and the heirs of the "antis," a testament to the confused state of Virginia politics. But it would be the last success of the

Organization, its demise ensured by a reformed leader, an expanded electorate, vigorous challenges from other parties, and a changed political culture.

The change was abundantly clear when Mills Godwin addressed his first General Assembly as governor and requested a sales tax to fund improvements in education, roads, parks, and prisons. "If there is a watchword for our time," he proclaimed, "it is to move, to strike out boldly, to reach for the heights." The complex sales tax initiative that he had once rejected required the governor's skillful leadership for passage, and Godwin was up to the task. Much of the new money went toward the creation of a system of twenty-two two-year community colleges that increased Virginia's woeful college enrollment level and spurred growth of the existing four-year institutions. The 1966 assembly also increased general expenditures for education by 38 percent, providing funds for kindergartens for the first time, raising teachers' salaries, and establishing a statewide textbook rental system. The governor sounded the new note later in the year: "It is time to shed the comfortable arguments, the warm and familiar excuses, the pleasant encumbrances of the old ways, for we know in our hearts they will not, they cannot serve us now."

Two years later Godwin challenged the most sacred of Byrd's principles, pay-as-you-go, with a request for an $80 million bond issue for higher education and mental health. Gaining assembly approval, the governor then mobilized public opinion to win the popular referendum on the bond issue, forty-five years after Harry Byrd had determined Virginia's fiscal future by defeating bonds for road building. With the new funds in hand, Godwin increased state spending by 42 percent during his term, the money going not only to secondary and higher education but to welfare, corrections, highways, port facilities, and parks. He was particularly active in recruiting new business to Virginia, leading trade missions to Europe and opening a trade office in Belgium. Industrial investment exceeded a billion dollars, tourism increased—"Virginia is for lovers" became the state's alluring slogan—and 60,000 new jobs were created. It was reminiscent of Byrd's activist governorship, but this "Program of Progress" was broader and more inclusive and moved the state into the national mainstream.

Godwin's final contribution to Virginia's future was a major revision of the 1902 constitution. Although there was no fundamental alteration in government structures, the most significant change was discarding the pay-as-you-go straitjacket, replacing it with a flexible debt provision that broadened the state's ability to borrow. Aware that his efforts had been groundbreaking, Godwin later recalled: "I knew Senator Byrd during his career had opposed that type of program. It was not an easy thing to do—to support it as vigorously as I did, to see it successfully concluded—but I thought it was the right thing to do." The new constitution, approved by special assembly sessions and the electorate in 1970, provided for annual legislative sessions and periodic reapportionment, guaranteed every Virginia child the right to a quality public education, guaranteed the civil rights of all Virginians, and ended discrimination based on sex. It liberated Virginia from the dead hand of the past.

Godwin's governorship was the most constructive of the twentieth century, but his accomplishments were not enough to save the Democrats. The excesses of the sixties—Black Power, urban riots, the Vietnam War protests, and the cultural wars of feminism, drugs, and long hair—further fragmented the Democratic Party. More conservatives joined Republican ranks, while liberals, whose efforts to end the poll tax and improve reapportionment had already weakened the machine, now sought to kill it altogether by helping to elect a Republican governor.

The 1966 primary in which "Young Turk" William Spong narrowly defeated Senator Willis Robertson and George Rawlings retired Congressman Howard Smith suggested the deep divisions that existed among Democrats, especially when Rawlings lost to Republican William Scott in the general election because of defections among the Byrd Old Guard. Such fractiousness exploded in the 1969 primary when Lieutenant Governor Fred Pollard, representing the conservative wing of the party; William C. Battle, representing moderates; and liberal Henry Howell contested for the gubernatorial nomination. The owl-eyed, fast-talking Howell had become a political lightening rod. Having worked in Francis Pickens Miller's campaign against Bill Battle's father in the 1949 primary, he was the rightful heir to the "antis," and he needed no encouragement to continue their struggle against the machine and its corporate allies, or the "Big Boys" as he called them. A state senator from Norfolk, Howell was a legitimate populist, successfully challenging state-regulated utility and insurance rates and raging against the sales tax on food and prescription drugs. He intended now to bring the state Democratic Party into line with the national party. Blacks, labor, and Great Society Democrats joined his crusade. The Old Guard, on the other hand, threw its weight to Battle, who defeated Howell in a runoff contest that left the party bitterly divided. An infuriated Howell claimed, "The Big Boys have made their deal."

In the subsequent contest between Battle and Republican Linwood Holton, Howell advised his supporters to vote their consciences; and in their rush to put the final nail in the Organization coffin now represented by the Godwin-backed Battle, they did just that. Said state AFL-CIO head Julian Carper, "The best way to make sure that the Byrd machine is eliminated completely is to elect a Republican." Similarly, many conservative Democrats, who had preferred Pollard and were put off by Battle's association with President John Kennedy, embraced Republicanism, leading to the election of Holton, the first Republican governor in Virginia since Reconstruction. Without a poll tax, 915,000 Virginians voted, a 63 percent increase over four years earlier; cities and suburbs outpolled the rural areas; and money and television became integral campaign ingredients. The 1969 gubernatorial campaign was the defining election in a new political realignment.

However, Republican parity was not yet at hand. Although Richard Nixon had carried the state and the GOP won half of the state's congressional delegation in 1968, neither of Holton's running mates won; the party still had an inconsequential voice in the assembly; and like the Democratic Party, it was infected by internal division. Linwood Holton was a "mountain-Valley" Republican in the tradition of Ted Dalton, who had represented the moderate wing of the party that had been contesting the Organization for years with a platform of fiscal conservatism and social progressivism less affected by race. Now joined by Byrd Democrats who had deserted their party for reasons of race and social engineering, Republicans faced a struggle for party leadership.

The division was exacerbated by the issue of busing and Harry Byrd Jr.'s reelection bid. Freedom-of-choice school assignment plans had become a "passive resistance" expedient by which school districts through selected pupil placement and residential segregation slowed the process of integration to a snail's pace. By 1964 only 5 percent of black children in the state were going to school with whites, forcing the NAACP to continue its litigation efforts. The 1968 *Green* decision ended freedom-of-choice plans and dual school systems and ordered faster school desegregation. Implemented in Richmond in 1970 by federal district judge Robert Merhige, *Green* led to the considerable busing of students; but it contributed to a resegregation of urban schools through white flight. Merhige's decision two years later to consolidate the Richmond, Henrico, and Chesterfield school systems to achieve racial balance was overturned by the U.S. Supreme Court, whose 4–4 vote allowed a negative lower court ruling to stand. The evenly divided vote had been produced by the decision of Virginian Lewis F. Powell, appointed to the Court in 1972 by President Nixon, not to vote because of his former service on the Richmond School Board. Merhige paid a terrible price for his decisions: "Federal marshals were assigned to protect me and my family for almost two years. . . . My dog was shot. Our guesthouse . . . was burned to the ground. Every other week or so we received a cryptic letter warning that our son Mark would never live to see age twenty-one. I was burned in effigy [and] spat upon. . . . At times it got awfully depressing. But I did what I did not only because it was the law, but also because I believed it was right."

Governor Holton, who dramatically increased the number of African Americans working for the state government, was opposed to busing, but he disdained the racial prejudice that motivated much of that opposition and so chose not to contest the court orders. Then, in a heroic gesture that was taken by many conservatives as an act of compliance with busing, he personally escorted his daughter to the mostly black high school to which she had been assigned. Although hailed nationally, Holton's action had dire political consequences for his leadership of the party.

So, too, did his effort against Byrd Jr., who, fearing defeat at the hands of the liberals in a Democratic primary, declared an independent candidacy in the 1970 Senate race. Conservative Republicans did not want to oppose Byrd, hoping to woo him to the GOP. They had the enthusiastic support of President Nixon, who was pursuing his "Southern strategy" of building Republican power in the South preparatory to his reelection bid in 1972. But Holton would not hear of it. Conceding another election to the Byrds, he believed, would undermine the legitimacy that Republicans had only recently achieved: "I can't believe we'll do nothing. Doing nothing would be like having the biggest, shiniest, newest fire engine and not taking it to the fire." Following his lead, Republicans chose to "go to the fire," but their "fireman," Ray Garland, was steamrollered by Byrd, who declined Republican overtures and remained an independent Virginia senator until his retirement in 1983, carrying on in the tradition of his father by sponsoring little legislation and calling for fiscal restraint. Garland's debacle (he received only 15 percent of the vote) further eroded Holton's chances of retaining control of the party.

National events continued to polarize the political realignment taking place in the Old Dominion. The Vietnam War was finally winding down, but not before bitterly dividing the country, disrupting American foreign policy, and costing the lives of 58,000 Americans, nearly 1,500 of whom were Virginians. Bloated military budgets benefited the state's economy, and the unrest that visited cities and college campuses elsewhere was generally unknown to Virginia but for a few significant antiwar protests around the Pentagon and some college closings after the shooting of Kent State University students by Ohio national guardsmen in the spring of 1970. Yet the battles across the nation between working-class "hard hats" and long-haired college kids were replicated in Virginia where the abrasive tactics of the Democratic Party liberals antagonized moderates and conservatives alike. President Nixon's landslide victory over George McGovern in 1972, supported by many conservative Democrats including Mills Godwin, swept moderate Bill Spong out of the Senate and produced a Republican congressional majority for Virginia.

Encouraged by the chaos among Democrats, conservative Republicans under the leadership of Richard Obenshain seized control of the party from Governor Holton, who had alienated them with his patronage decisions and liberal racial positions. A year later they persuaded a reluctant Godwin to join them in combat against Henry Howell for the governorship.

The 1973 gubernatorial race reflected the still fluid state of Virginia politics. Backed by organized labor, blacks, and blue-collar whites who were attracted by his populist rhetoric to "keep the Big Boys honest," Howell chose to run for governor as an independent. Godwin, who entered the race primarily because he feared a Howell victory, belatedly joined the Republican Party, which had no candidate with comparable popularity. In a campaign marked more by personal animus than a discussion of the issues, he eked out a win, 50.7 percent to 49.3 percent, over the reckless Howell, who likely cost himself the governorship with an ill-advised tax program and a prophecy of victory that energized Republicans to get out the vote. Godwin's triumph as a Republican clearly indicated how much party allegiances had changed.

Godwin's second term, however, was less spectacular than his first. Hampered by Nixon's resignation following the Watergate revelations, a worsening national economy caused by a foreign oil embargo, and Democratic control of the General Assembly, Godwin struggled to duplicate his earlier successes. The economic recession forced him to retrench, reducing revenues for the very items he had championed in the sixties. A major crisis was the polluting of the James River in 1975 with the highly toxic chemical Kepone, an event that revealed the inadequacy of Virginia's readiness to prevent and deal with an environmental problem. Fishing in the James and lower Chesapeake Bay was curtailed for years. Further pollution from fertilizer and manure runoff, other toxic chemicals, and inadequately treated sewage threatened the life of the entire bay.

Natural disasters also impacted the state's environment. On 19 August 1969 Hurricane Camille, downgraded to a tropical depression after devastating the Gulf Coast, moved up the Mississippi River, turned east, and crossed the Appalachian Mountains. Without warning, it dumped twenty-eight inches of rain in an eight-hour period on Nelson and Rockbridge counties, flooding streams and creeks along the mountain valleys, sweeping away homes, cars, businesses, and trees and leaving over 150 dead. Some bodies were never found. Three years later Hurricane Agnes caused extensive flooding throughout the state, and in September 2003 Hurricane Isabel took down thousands of trees and power lines in the eastern half of the state, leaving hundreds of thousands of Virginians without power for days.

Godwin's difficulties did not prevent another Republican victory in

HURRICANE CAMILLE, ROSELAND, NELSON COUNTY, AUGUST 1969

the 1977 gubernatorial election, the third in a row. John Dalton's success over Henry Howell suggested that the GOP was on the verge of replacing the Organization as the ruler of Virginia politics, a view confirmed by the election of Republicans in nine of the ten congressional districts along with Ronald Reagan's landslide presidential victory in 1980. Winning big in the wealthy, growing suburbs, Republicans were besting the Democrats in the use of new campaign techniques: phone banks, direct mail, television advertising, and the development of enthusiastic youth groups. The mastermind of this resurgence was Dick Obenshain, a conservative ideologue who was primed to win a U.S. Senate seat in 1978 and become Virginia's next Harry Byrd. But Obenshain was killed in a plane crash shortly after winning the nomination; and although his stand-in, John Warner, won a close election over Andrew Miller, the party lost its newfound cohesiveness, returning to the divisive internal wars that had marked the Holton years.

Aggravating this division was the materialization of the "religious right," social conservatives who wanted government to legislate morality on school prayer, school curricula, and abortion, which had been legalized by the Supreme Court's *Roe v. Wade* decision in 1973. Much like earlier "awakenings," modern evangelicalism emanated from the dissatisfaction with liberal secularism and social permissiveness that seemed to influence recent Court rulings. Animosity was directed at "welfare queens," judicial activists, and Hollywood liberals. Led by fundamentalist Baptist minister Jerry Falwell of Lynchburg, the evangelicals created the "Moral Majority" political organization in 1979 to advance their social agenda. Popular in the rural areas of the state, "Moral Majority" had little appeal in the cities and suburbs, especially in Northern Virginia and among black voters, but it was powerful enough to contest old-line Republicans for control of the party. The controversial Falwell increased the congregation of his Thomas Road Baptist Church from 35 to 24,000 members and also founded Liberty University to advance a "Christian world view." The Reverend Pat Robertson, son of the former senator and head of the Virginia Beach–based Christian Broadcasting Network, also had a strong following among evangelical Christians in the Old Dominion. Ironically, as Republicans increased their authority at the local level, gradually closing the gap with Democrats in the assembly, they began losing statewide contests, the result of bitter convention and primary struggles between the socially conservative evangelicals and fiscally conservative traditional Republicans that often left the party dispirited or running fringe candidates who were ideologically correct but not electable.

Democrats, on the other hand, eschewing their polarized politics of the 1970s, sought candidates and issues in the political center in the 1980s, a middle ground of fiscal responsibility and social progress. Many of the Byrd Democrats returned to their roots, satisfied with the centrist leadership offered by Governors Charles Robb and Gerald Baliles, who benefited from the prosperity of the Reagan years that enabled them to balance budgets while spending for education, public safety, transportation, and the environment, issues that proved attractive to the new electorate. Virginia's economy in the 1980s, bolstered by military expenditures, was outperforming the nation's, being rated the fifth fastest growing economy in the country. Robb, known as a "technocrat" for favoring managerial efficiency over new public programs, proved a careful steward of state finances while creating the Center for Innovative Technology in Northern Virginia and expanding the cleanup of the Chesapeake Bay. Baliles, who had risen to the governorship from attorney general, was more pro-active and politically partisan than Robb in promoting a larger role for government in Virginia that included a multibillion-dollar transportation program that doubled highway construction and a state lottery whose monies would support education.

Robb's Achilles' heel proved to be corrections. Limited funding, poor management, and overcrowding contributed to the 1984 escape of six death-row inmates from the Mecklenburg Correctional Center; although all were recaptured, the embarrassing incident was followed by a hostage siege and additional escapes that highlighted bureaucratic incompetence. Nonetheless, Robb used his gubernatorial record to win a U.S. Senate seat in 1988.

Virginia voters were now more independent and less influenced by party loyalty and ideology. Half of Virginia's population growth in the eighties was due to in-migration. These outsiders and younger voters were concerned about quality-of-life issues like financial well-being, child care, environmental protection, and education more than the morality issues raised by the religious right. The invasion of high-tech industries (creating the "silicon Dominion"), suburban growth, and more women in the workforce reinforced their interest in efficient state management rather than social philosophy. Indicative of the new politics was the election in 1985 of the first African American and the first woman to win statewide office: L. Douglas Wilder as lieutenant governor and Mary Sue Terry as attorney general.

Four years later Wilder became the first black American to be elected governor of any state. A Korean War veteran and graduate of Virginia Union University and Howard University Law School, Doug Wilder was elected Virginia's first black state senator in 1969. An unabashed, outspoken racial liberal with a bent for the theatrical, he sponsored the legislation that recognized Martin Luther King's birthday as a state holiday and ended the designation of the racist "Carry Me Back to Ole Virginny" as the state song. Running for statewide office, however, necessitated a political makeover. Disguising his past liberalism, Wilder moved to the center in the 1989 gubernatorial campaign, basking in the prosperity of the Robb-Baliles years, using the race card to parry personal attacks against him, and tying Republican Marshall Coleman to an antiabortion position. Although race proved to be an issue in many voters' minds, Wilder won a hairsbreadth decision: a 6,741-vote majority out of 1.8 million votes cast.

Wilder then became a victim of the same external force that had curtailed the programs of Mills Godwin and John Dalton: a national economic recession. Oil embargoes, rising unemployment, and inflation forced these governors to curtail their legislative programs and reduce expenditures to avoid major budget deficits. Wilder won the praise of fiscal conservatives for holding the line on spending, causing one journal to rate Virginia the best fiscally run state in the nation. However, his maverick reputation and an abortive presidential campaign, along with revelations of questionable social activity on the part of Senator Robb, with whom Wilder was always tangling, contributed to dramatic Republican gains in the 1991 assembly. Robb barely won reelection in 1994 because

THE INAUGURATION OF L. DOUGLAS WILDER AS
GOVERNOR OF VIRGINIA, JANUARY 1990

of Republican defections from the candidacy of social conservative Major Oliver North, who had been convicted of obstruction of justice in the Iran-Contra case.

Riding a crest of dissatisfaction with twelve years of Democratic rule and rising crime rates, a young, personable Republican, George Allen, after terms in the House of Delegates and Congress, bested an overconfident Mary Sue Terry in the 1993 gubernatorial election. He proceeded to implement welfare and juvenile justice reforms, abolish parole for violent offenders, and initiate major prison construction. Governor Allen also brought in billions of dollars of high-tech industry attracted by Virginia's location, right-to-work law, and low taxes; he went on to defeat Robb for his Senate seat in 2000.

James Gilmore continued the Republican success with his proposal to eliminate the automobile tax, an issue that in 1997 produced the first Republican sweep of statewide offices. Having forged a powerful rural-suburban coalition bolstered by a reenergized religious right, Republicans finally achieved parity with Democrats in the 1998 General Assembly, controlling the state Senate, 21–19, and sharing power in the house with Democrats, who had a paper-thin majority of one delegate. This slim edge was quickly lost the following year, causing Governor Gilmore to proclaim the Old Dominion "free at last" of Democratic rule. Seizing the moment, Republicans rammed through car tax legislation that would phase out this local property tax over several years, with the state reimbursing localities for the lost revenue. They also passed antiabortion laws that provided for parental notification and prohibited partial birth abortion. The political changes in Virginia reflected a similar upheaval at the national level as Republicans, riding the Reagan revolution, gained control of Congress in 1994 for the first time in nearly half a century.

To protect their new authority, Virginia Republicans, like Democrats before them, gerrymandered Virginia congressional districts. Named for Massachusetts governor Elbridge Gerry (1812) and the elongated salamander lizard, a gerrymander is a peculiarly shaped district designed to give preferential advantage to one party. It has been a standard feature of American politics for nearly two centuries. But in 2001 Republicans outdid themselves with grotesquely drawn districts in the Northern Virginia and Hampton Roads areas that ensured their domination of the state's congressional delegation for at least a decade. (See map on p. 354.)

Yet the GOP could not stand prosperity. The continued divide between social and economic conservatives, aggravated by Gilmore's abrasive style and another recession, brought discord and the election of a Democratic governor. During the 2001 assembly, Gilmore and Speaker of the House Vance Wilkins rejected compromises over how to deal with the worsening budget crisis and stuck to the planned reduction formula for the car tax, the elimination of which was proving more costly than predicted. The governor froze state spending, and for the first time in its history, the legislature adjourned without reaching a budget agreement, choosing to rely on the budget passed the previous session. Capitalizing on this record, Mark Warner, who had made his fortune in the cell phone business, promised to restore fiscal sanity and civility to the governing process and won back the statehouse for Democrats in 2001.

In the midst of the gubernatorial race, the nation and the state were struck by the worst terrorist attack in the country's history. On 11 September 2001 Islamic extremists crashed airliners into the two World Trade Center towers in New York City, killing nearly 3,000 people, and into the Pentagon in Arlington, killing 189 people. On a fourth flight, the passengers challenged the highjackers, causing the plane to crash in Pennsylvania before it could hit another building in Washington; all 44 on board died. Americans and Virginians now confronted a threat to their security and sanity unparalleled in their history that appeared to have no foreseeable end. After 9/11, color-coded alerts, time-delaying security checks at airports, challenges to civil liberties, and wars in Afghanistan and Iraq became part of their daily existence. Contributing to the anxiety were the monthlong sniper attacks along the Washington-Richmond corridor in 2002 that killed several Virginians before the two shooters were captured.

Added expenditures for security measures along with the continuing recession did not bode well for the new governor. That Virginia was now very much a part of a global community was confirmed by the loss of jobs to foreign competition, especially in the textile industry along the Carolina border, and by the increasing number of Hispanic immigrants whose presence raised issues of job competition and welfare and education costs. Forced to defer his progressive plans for improving higher education and transportation, both of which had sadly been neglected by previous administrations, Warner deferred full payment of the car tax and cut the budget. But bickering Republicans could not capitalize on his difficulties. In 2004, after a record 115-day session, Warner forged a coalition of Democrats and moderate Republicans to further delay the car tax and to pass a tax increase that stemmed the decline in state services and employee compensation. His popularity was sufficient to elect his lieutenant governor, Tim Kaine, to the governorship in 2005. Another lengthy and contentious assembly session in 2006 almost led to a government shutdown.

Such political infighting brings to mind the words of an old Organization leader: "It makes you appreciate Harry Byrd. He really knew how to run things." Clearly the Byrd machine has long since passed, and the diverse nature of the state and its more independent electorate make another one unlikely. Party discipline and loyalty are fragile, and the parties struggle to maintain unity. This persisting factionalism along with national issues usually determine election winners, while media and money, of little importance in the past, now dominate political contests and legislative maneuverings. The state remains fiscally conservative, and perhaps Harry Byrd's ghost paces the Capitol to remind legislators of this traditional obligation to past practices, but for one who was so important for so long, it is remarkable how little of his regime is left.

SOURCES CONSULTED

Frank B. Atkinson, *The Dynamic Dominion: Realignment and the Rise of Virginia's Republican Party since 1945* (1992); Andrew Buni, *The Negro in Virginia Politics, 1902–1965* (1967); Ralph Eisenberg, *Virginia Votes, 1924–1968* (1971); Jack Irby Hayes Jr., *Dan Daniel and the Persistence of Conservatism in Virginia* (1997); Emilee Hines, *It Happened in Virginia* (2001); V. O. Key Jr., *Southern Politics in State and Nation* (1949); Robert A. Pratt, *The Color of Their Skin: Education and Race in Richmond,*

Virginia (1992); Mark J. Rozell and Clyde Wilcox, *Second Coming: The New Christian Right in Virginia Politics* (1996); Larry Sabato, *The Democratic Party Primary in Virginia: Tantamount to Election No Longer* (1977); Sabato, *Virginia Votes, 1969–1990* (1976–91); Emily J. Salmon and Edward D. C. Campbell Jr., eds., *The Hornbook of Virginia History*, 4th ed. (1994); Philippa Strum, *Women in the Barracks: The VMI Case and Equal Rights* (2002); James R. Sweeney, "Harry Byrd: Vanished Policies and Enduring Principles," *Virginia Quarterly Review* (Autumn 1976); Sweeney, "A New Day in the Old Dominion: The 1964 Presidential Election," *VMHB* (July 1997); Sweeney, "Southern Strategies: The 1970 Election for the United States Senate in Virginia," *VMHB* (Spring 1998); Sweeney, "Whispers in the Golden Silence: Harry Byrd, Sr., John Kennedy, and Virginia Democrats in the 1960 Presidential Election," *VMHB* (Jan. 1991); Peter Wallenstein, *Blue Laws and Black Codes: Conflict, Courts, and Change in Twentieth-Century Virginia* (2004); J. Harvie Wilkinson III, *Harry Byrd and the Changing Face of Virginia Politics, 1945–1966* (1968); Edward Younger and James Tice Moore, eds., *The Governors of Virginia, 1860–1978* (1982).

EPILOGUE

Virginia's history has been marked by conflict between progress and preservation, between the forces of change and the inertia of continuity—a contest that was frequently sharpened by the issue of race and that invariably was won by white political elites. In the later years of each of Virginia's four centuries events unfolded that challenged the old order: Bacon's Rebellion, the American Revolution, the Readjusters, and the political and social transformations of the post-1960s. On each occasion until the present, the Old Dominion drew back from the opportunities for a more egalitarian experience to preserve the status quo.

This pattern of advance and retreat reflects a panoply of human behaviors, but the most prominent characteristic of Virginians, next to their remarkable affection for the state, has been a robust individualism that the nineteenth-century French observer Alexis de Tocqueville found uniquely American. This desire to be rid of arbitrary restraint, to be one's own boss, was the catalyst for the establishment of a society of free and independent people. It fortified white Virginians through the settlement of Jamestown, motivated them to establish a planter patriarchy, precipitated a separation from the mother country, created a states' rights ideology, and encouraged secession from the Union. But Tocqueville also noted that Americans—and Virginians—were conspicuous in their thirst for possessions, for wealth and success, often at the expense of others. Just as Jefferson spoke of human equality while maintaining a slave workforce, so, too, were his fellow Virginians enmeshed in the conflict between opportunity for all and their own self-interest.

Whether motivated by religious idealism as in Massachusetts or by a quest for adventure and riches as in Virginia, the English invasion of North America, although marked by courage, perseverance, and sacrifice, destroyed a native culture in its "pursuit of happiness." Ignorance, prejudice, and avarice would not permit an accommodation of conflicting cultures. Through a series of wars, driven primarily by English encroachment on Indian lands and marked by intrigue and brutality on both sides, the English defeated the Powhatans and secured their hold on Virginia.

The victors imposed English patterns of land tenure on the landscape and developed a tobacco-based economy. To encourage immigration, the Virginia Company offered planters fifty-acre grants for each laborer imported into the colony. English indentured laborers, lured to the colony with dreams of landownership, suffered great hardships; but many who survived were able to become freeholders and themselves transporters of laborers. The inclusion of more women and children allowed the beginnings of family formation and estate development. The result was the creation of a great planter class that would control offices, land, and labor and direct the destiny of the colony.

The English established in Virginia in 1619 an elective assembly, whose officials, representing planter interests, would contest the crown over Indian policy, expansion, and trade. The colony became more diversified as Africans joined the settlement. Increasingly after 1640 the authorities developed a racial system that enslaved Africans. Blacks tried to protect themselves by bringing legal suits and baptizing their children, but with the decline in the immigration of English servants, planters looked longingly to the slave trade. By the end of the century, ships were bringing thousands of Africans to man the tobacco plantations of Virginia, another racial minority victimized by the white majority.

Turmoil in England through civil war, the Interregnum, and the Restoration would complicate the relationship of the outpost to the metropolis, raising questions at an early date about who should rule at home. Bacon's Rebellion in 1676 challenged royal authority and forced Governor Berkeley out of office, but it also revealed deep-seated conflicts in the colony between whites and Indians and landowners and the landless that invariably were resolved in favor of the large planters. By reason of blood, wealth, education, and social standing, the heirs of these farmers-turned-planters would lead Virginia for the next three centuries, governing paternalistically but always intent on preserving their power, even as the world around them changed. They oversaw a Virginia that remained rural, racially divided, suspicious of outsiders, and fiercely independent.

Virginia's rise to preeminence among British North American colonies and early American states rested solidly on this planter patriarchy that expanded its authority in the first half of the eighteenth century. With tobacco as its principal crop and export commodity, the maturing plantation system came to symbolize a hierarchy of men, women, class, and race. In the shadow of the great planters lived the middling farmers—

small landowners representing the majority of Virginia's population—who obtained credit from their wealthier neighbors and usually voted for them on election day. Below them were the tenant farmers and landless men who eked out an existence on the margins of white society. Although white Virginia was a relatively democratic community like the New England or Pennsylvania colonies, it operated in a paternalistic-deferential way. At the very bottom of this world were black slaves who by the eighteenth century represented a mixture of recently arrived Africans and second- and third-generation native-born Virginians. The misery of their lives cannot be exaggerated; but even within the constrained world of slavery, black men and women found ways to establish families and develop rituals and customs that gave meaning to their lives.

Despite the apparent stability and harmony of this planter patriarchy in 1750, forces within and beyond Virginia challenged this seemingly idyllic world. A desire for speculative profits that would supplement the sagging tobacco economy encouraged the Virginia elite to invest in large tracts of western lands that in turn brought the colony into a world war fought primarily in America. Prosecuting the French and Indian War resulted in an increased public debt and renewed conflict with the Indians but also provided important lessons in wartime management and critical military experience to a handful of Virginians.

Britain's need to pay for this costly war and to tighten the administration of a now larger empire challenged Virginia's desire to maintain an independent sovereign polity within the British realm. When the mother country would not leave the colonies alone to manage their own affairs, Virginia planters stepped to the forefront to confront an increasingly stubborn Parliament and crown. The resulting War of Independence witnessed Virginia leadership at every turn from the writing of the Declaration of Independence to military command to the construction of the Constitution of 1787. In Virginia they instituted a bill of rights, established religious freedom, and outlawed the slave trade. The United States of America as we know it could not have been formed without the contributions of Virginians such as Henry, Mason, Washington, Jefferson, and Madison.

This Virginia Dynasty would lead the new country for another generation or so, but then the state would find itself left behind in an America no longer following its lead. Although Virginia's decline from its position of preeminence resulted in part from the explosive population growth and economic development of the North and the West, the Old Dominion suffered from leadership with parochial vision. Virginians continued to serve as president and hold important positions in Congress, but the voices of state leaders began to take on an increasingly negative, antinationalist tone. The Richmond "Junto," committed to the "Doctrines of '98," sacrificed progress in the name of republican orthodoxy. Efforts to broaden and educate the electorate were rejected by the planter aristocracy, which feared losing power. Similarly easterners blocked westerners' efforts to extend transportation and banking facilities. Furthermore, for all its brilliance, the Revolutionary generation had remained devoted to slavery, a racial labor system that the Northern states were rejecting. Early manumission legislation was rescinded and slavery made more secure. Even after the Nat Turner insurrection of 1831, which led to the great debate about colonization and the possibility of gradual emancipation, the planter elite reinforced the Old Dominion's commitment to the peculiar institution.

During these years a market revolution was recasting the American economy, stimulating immigration, industrialization, urbanization, and democratic reform. Virginians confronted a choice between perpetuating the old order or pursuing new opportunities. Political change proceeded slowly; but expanded voting and more equal representation for the nonslaveholding western areas were realized at last in 1851. Economically, new industries and transportation systems, developed by a new class of entrepreneurs, were transforming the countryside. By midcentury, the Old Dominion seemed poised to leave its tradition-bound "Virginia way" behind.

However, this emerging bourgeois and democratic regime with its rumblings of abolition threatened the slave society that had brought wealth and racial security to the planters. Convinced that their hegemony could best be maintained in a new Confederate government, they seceded from the United States in 1861. Although predictable and conforming to the will of most white Virginians, the choice was the most egregious ever made by Virginia's leaders. Generals Lee and Jackson achieved lasting immortality, but the Civil War devastated the countryside, killed and maimed thousands of Virginians, and lost West Virginia. The slave society that secessionists had sought to preserve was destroyed, to the great joy of the half million slaves, who immediately sought to fulfill their freedom.

During the subsequent Reconstruction and Readjuster movement, efforts were made to integrate Virginia's freed black population into the political and economic life of the state. But the race issue once again proved too compelling, and white Virginians opted for a segregated one-party system that a powerful political machine would sustain for nearly a century. The state modestly benefited from the economic reforms of the New South movement and the social changes instituted through progressivism, notably the achievement of the ballot by Virginia's women. Yet the Old Dominion's devotion to the "Lost Cause" and white supremacy, evidenced in the Constitution of 1901–2 and the creation of Jim Crow laws, curtailed a more significant emancipation until midcentury.

"Virginia," wrote historian Arnold Toynbee in the 1940s, "makes the painful impression of a country living under a spell, in which time has stood still." Such is the distinction of traditional, aristocratic societies in modern times. Virginia's leaders usually were content to wait and see, their outstanding characteristic being, in the words of Jean Gottman, a "resistance to change." As a result, the social hierarchy of the Old Dominion remained firm and unyielding, made more so by neglect of its educational system, voting restrictions, and political apathy. The old order prevailed well into the twentieth century, maintained by the authority of the Byrd Organization, which chose to employ massive resistance rather than integrate the state's schools. Virginia's leaders invariably made choices that looked backward, not forward, that preserved the status quo instead of pursuing opportunities that promised greater freedom for Virginians.

Throughout the century, war and depression, the advances of technology, and minority protest voices challenged the continuity of the regime. More recently, under additional outside pressures—federal court decisions, a civil rights movement, a feminist revolution, the migration of Yankees and new ethnic groups into the state—the Old Dominion has been transformed into a new commonwealth whose past is now more an instructive memory than a liability. Indeed, Virginius Dabney declared, "A Virginia Rip Van Winkle who went to sleep in 1950 and awakened in 1970 might have difficulty realizing that he was in the same state."

Virginia experienced colossal changes in the latter half of the twentieth century. Its population—now over 7 million—has more than doubled, ranking it twelfth in the nation, and is 80 percent urban, most of it concentrated in the metropolitan corridor stretching from Washington to Richmond to Norfolk and Virginia Beach that is marked by urban sprawl, air pollution, and traffic congestion. Today about half of Virginians are native to the state, compared to 90 percent in 1900. Women are in the majority. The percentage of the African American population has declined to 20 percent, but the earlier out-migration has been reversed. There has been a significant increase in the Hispanic and Asian populations, notably in Northern Virginia; 8 percent of Virginians are foreign-born.

Virginia's economy is highly influenced by federal spending and the service sector and no longer dominated by farmers or Richmond's "Tobacco Row," which closed its doors in 1981. In fact, farmers constitute little more than 1 percent of the population, and in 2004 soybeans replaced tobacco as Virginia's largest cash crop. Per capita income is above the national average; although 10 percent of Virginians live in poverty, that percentage is below the national level and well below the rest of the South. Virginia's public universities, enhanced with the additions of James Madison, Virginia Commonwealth, Old Dominion, and George Mason, are among the best in the nation, and the percentage of Virginians with college degrees exceeds the national average. Over two-thirds of the eligible voters are registered, and on average one-half of those eligible vote in presidential races, well under participation rates for the nineteenth century but on par with current national levels. The state remains politically conservative, with Republicans replacing Byrd Democrats as the dominant party; they have not lost a presidential election in Virginia since Lyndon Johnson's victory in 1964. Yet its citizens manifest eclectic attitudes, accepting liquor by the drink in 1968, a state lottery in 1987, and horse racing with pari-mutuel betting in 1988, while turning their backs on a Disney theme park and a stadium for the Washington Redskins. In 1988 Virginia's Supreme Court effectively ended the state's "blue laws" that had kept stores closed on Sundays.

Women and African Americans have been the greatest beneficiaries of these changes, now serving in all areas of public life as mayors, legislators, governor, and Supreme Court justices. Their own courageous efforts through protests, court cases, and quiet example compelled the breakdown of white male domination in the state. Bobby Scott became the first African American elected to Congress from Virginia in the twentieth century, and Leslie Byrne was the first female Virginian ever elected to Congress. Black tennis star Arthur Ashe broke the Confederate monopoly on Richmond's Monument Avenue. The University of Virginia admitted blacks and women to its undergraduate program; and that last bastion of male chauvinism, the Virginia Military Institute, admitted women to its cadet corps in 1997. Although the General Assembly continued to refuse to ratify the Equal Rights Amendment, it terminated laws ending different treatment for women and repealed segregation and racial definition laws. It even apologized for the school closings brought on by massive resistance and established a scholarship fund to provide education for those who had been shut out.

Much of this change was not by choice. Outside forces, notably federal law, dictated recent Virginia history, not Virginians, who, but for a reincarnated Mills Godwin and minority protestors, have remained largely reactive, still smitten by provincialism and conceit. As Dabney once said in commenting about Virginia's approach to investing in itself, "God granted Virginia many advantages in physical location and geography, and Virginia spent many years waiting for God to improve upon them."

Many Virginians are still waiting. Although its physical and human resources are plentiful, gaps between rich and poor, white and black, natives and immigrants, city dwellers and suburbanites stand in the way of achieving a more fruitful commonwealth. For all its recent progress, Virginia remains, as it was for the Jamestown settlers, a land of potential, waiting for leaders who can find the will to invest in significant education, transportation, and environmental initiatives to begin a new era for the Old Dominion. As they embark upon another century, Virginians would do well to listen to Ellen Glasgow: "The glory of men and nations is measured not by the strength with which they cling to the past but by the courage with which they adventure into the future." The study of Virginia's history should be a source of that courage.

APPENDIX

VIRGINIA POPULATION FIGURES

Year	Population	White	Black	Slave	Free black		
1610 est.	350						
1650 est.	18,731	18,326	405				
1680 est.	43,596	40,596	3,000				
1700 est.	58,560	42,170	16,390				
1750 est.	231,033	129,581	101,452				
1770 est.	447,016	259,411	187,605				
			(in 1,000s)				
1790	747,610	442	306	293	13		
1800	886,149	518	367	346	20		
1810	983,152	557	426	393	31		
1820	1,075,069	610	465	425	37		
1830	1,220,978	701	520	470	47		
1840	1,249,764	748	502	449	50		
1850	1,421,661	895	527	473	54		
1860	1,596,318	1,047	549	491	58		
(1863: West Virginia becomes a state)							
1870	1,225,163	712	513				
1880	1,512,565	881	632				
1890	1,655,980	1,020	635				
1900	1,854,184	1,193	661				
1910	2,061,612	1,390	671				
1920	2,309,187	1,618	690				
1930	2,421,851	1,770	650				
1940	2,677,773	2,016	661				
1950	3,318,680	2,582	734				
1960	3,966,949	3,142	816	*Hispanic*	*Asian (in 1,000s)*	*Indian*	
1970	4,648,494	3,762	861				
1980	5,346,818	4,230	1,009	80	64	9.3	
1990	6,187,358	4,792	1,163	160	159	15	
2000	7,078,515	5,120	1,390	330	261	21	
2003 est.	7,386,000	5,462	1,475	395	310	24	

Source: Historical Statistics of the United States; Statistical Abstract of the United States.
Note: The sum of group figures does not always equal total population because of census errors, double counting, and "others."

GENERAL BIBLIOGRAPHY

Billings, Warren, ed. *The Old Dominion in the Seventeenth Century: A Documentary History of Virginia, 1606–1689.* Chapel Hill, N.C., 1975.

Billings, Warren M., Thad Tate, and John E. Selby. *Colonial Virginia: A History.* White Plains, N.Y., 1986.

Brant, Irving. *James Madison.* 6 vols. Indianapolis, 1941–61.

Dabney, Virginius. *Virginia: The New Dominion.* Garden City, N.J., 1971.

Dictionary of Virginia Biography. 3 vols. Richmond, 1998–2006.

Draper, Christina S., ed. *Don't Grieve after Me: The Black Experience in Virginia, 1619–2005.* 2006.

Fishwick, Marshall. *Virginia: A New Look at the Old Dominion.* New York, 1959.

Freeman, Douglas Southall. *George Washington: A Biography.* 7 vols. New York, 1948–57.

———. *R. E. Lee.* 4 vols. New York, 1934–35.

Friddell, Guy. *What Is It about Virginia?* Richmond, 1966.

Gottmann, Jean. *Virginia in Our Century.* Charlottesville, Va., 1969.

Heinemann, Ronald L. *Harry Byrd of Virginia.* Charlottesville, Va., 1996.

Hemphill, William, Marvin Schlegel, and Sadie Engelberg. *Cavalier Commonwealth: History and Government of Virginia.* New York, 1957.

Lebsock, Suzanne. *Virginia Women, 1600–1945: "A Share of Honour."* Richmond, 1987.

Malone, Dumas. *Jefferson and His Time.* 6 vols. New York, 1948–81.

Moger, Allen W. *Virginia: Bourbonism to Byrd, 1870–1925.* Charlottesville, Va., 1968

Morgan, Edmund S. *American Slavery, American Freedom: The Ordeal of Colonial Virginia.* New York, 1975.

Morton, Richard L. *Colonial Virginia.* 2 vols. Chapel Hill, N.C., 1960.

Peterson, Merrill. *Thomas Jefferson and the New Nation: A Biography.* New York, 1970.

Rountree, Helen C. *Pocahontas's People: The Powhatan Indians of Virginia through Four Centuries*. Norman, Okla., 1990.

Rubin, Louis, Jr. *Virginia: A Bicentennial History*. New York, 1977.

Salmon, Emily J., and Edward D. C. Campbell Jr., eds. *The Hornbook of Virginia History: A Ready-Reference Guide to the Old Dominion's People, Places, and Past*. 4th ed. Richmond, 1994.

Sydnor, Charles S. *Gentlemen Freeholders: Political Practices in Washington's Virginia*. Chapel Hill, N.C., 1952.

Virginia Writers' Program, Work Projects Administration. *Virginia: A Guide to the Old Dominion*. New York, 1940.

Younger, Edward, and James Tice Moore, eds., *The Governors of Virginia, 1860–1978*. Charlottesville, Va., 1982.

Articles in the *Virginia Cavalcade* and the *Virginia Magazine of History and Biography*.

Web sites discussing Virginia history are too numerous to list. As a starting point we recommend:

http://www.vahistorical.org (Virginia Historical Society)
http://www.lva.lib.va.us (Library of Virginia)
http://www.nps.gov (National Park Service)
http://www.vcdh.virginia.edu/research.html (Virginia Center for Digital History)
http://www.encyclopediavirginia.org (Virginia Foundation for the Humanities Online Virginia Encyclopedia)
http://www.pastportal.com (Colonial Williamsburg digital library)
and the Web sites of libraries of Virginia universities

INDEX

ILLUSTRATION CREDITS

All illustrations are from the Library of Virginia except: